Congressional Procedures
and the
Policy Process

FOURTH EDITION

Congressional Procedures and the Policy Process

FOURTH EDITION

Walter J. Oleszek

A Division of Congressional Quarterly Inc.
Washington, D.C.

Cover: Tina Chovanec, Corvallis, Oregon.
Cover photograph © Architect of the Capitol.

Printed in the United States of America

Library of Congress Cataloging-in-Publication Data

Oleszek, Walter J.
  Congressional procedures and the policy process/Walter J. Oleszek.--4th ed.
    p.   cm.
  Includes bibliographic references and index.
  ISBN 0-87187-704-X (cloth : alk. paper). -- ISBN 0-87187-703-1 (paper : alk.
paper)
  1. United States.   Congress.   I. Title
JK1096.043 1995
328.73'07--dc20   95-31596
                                                                 CIP

For Janet, Mark, and Eric
and
Lee and Missy Isgur

Contents

Tables, Figures, and Boxes

TABLES

FIGURES

BOXES

Preface

Congress is constantly adapting to change. New procedures, processes, and practices come about in response to developing conditions and circumstances. Some procedural innovations are incorporated formally in the rules of the House or Senate; others evolve informally. For all their variability over time, the rules of the House and Senate are constant in this sense: they establish the procedural context within which individual members and the two chambers raise issues and make (or avoid making) decisions. Members of Congress, in sum, must rely upon rules and procedures to expedite or delay legislation, to secure enactment, or to bring about the defeat of bills.

Congressional Procedures and the Policy Process was first published in 1978, in the aftermath of major changes that affected legislative decision making and the political system. The result of many of these developments on Capitol Hill was to diffuse policy-making influence widely throughout Congress. The term often employed to describe this new environment was "subcommittee government." Six years later, when the second edition appeared, the House and Senate had undergone further procedural transformations. The House, for instance, began gavel-to-gavel television coverage of its floor proceedings. The third edition was published in the late 1980s and discussed important procedural and institutional changes in both chambers. Emulating the House, the Senate in 1986 began gavel-to-gavel television coverage of its floor proceedings. Congress revamped its budgetary practices with the enactment of Gramm-Rudman-Hollings I and II; the House Rules Committee crafted unique new "rules" for regulating floor decision making; and greater use was made of comprehensive bills, or "packages," to process much of Congress's annual workload. One effect of these and other changes has been to recentralize authority in fewer legislative hands.

The fourth edition has been updated during another time of momentous change on Capitol Hill. After forty years as the "permanent minority," Republicans captured control of the House in the November 1994 elections and reclaimed control of the Senate as well. Major procedural changes have occurred in both houses, and Congress is discussing fundamental questions of national governance. Today, the political parties, Congress, and the executive and judicial branches are debating which functions are national responsibilities and which can be returned to the states and localities or handled by the private sector. "Toward a New Federalism" is the overarching theme that orients many significant activities of the 104th Congress (1995-1997) and no doubt legislative sessions to follow. That a great deal of change—the central-ization of significant authority in the House Speaker, innovative rules from the House Rules Committee, or new types of filibustering tactics in the Senate, for example—has occurred in Congress is beyond doubt. Accordingly, I have incorporated in this edition discussion of new rules and practices and new examples and materials that highlight how Congress mod-ifies its decision-making procedures.

The fundamental objective of the fourth edition of *Congressional Procedures and the Policy Process* is to discuss how the contemporary Congress makes laws and how its rules and procedures shape domestic and foreign policy. The theme of the book is that the interplay of rules, procedures, prece-dents, and strategies is vital to understanding how Congress works. I empha-size the rules and procedures most significant to congressional lawmaking; I do not attempt to survey all the rules and procedures used by Congress.

While the format and structure of the new edition closely follow that of the third, every chapter has been revised. Chapter 1 presents an overall view of the congressional process. In Chapter 2, the focus shifts to the organiza-tional setting and political environment of Congress to examine differences between the House and Senate; the leadership structure in Congress; pres-sures exerted on Congress; and recent changes in Congress's operations. Chapter 3 examines Congress's budget process, which shapes much of the legislative decision making.

Chapter 4 turns to the initial steps of the legislative process—the intro-duction and referral of bills to House and Senate committees, and commit-tee action on measures. Chapter 5 explains how legislation that has emerged from committee is scheduled for floor consideration in the House. Chapter 6 then examines the main features of floor decisionmaking in the House. In Chapter 7 the spotlight is put on the Senate, with discussion of how legisla-tion is scheduled in that chamber. Senate floor action is the subject of Chapter 8.

Chapter 9 first describes how House-Senate differences are reconciled when each chamber passes a different version of the same bill and then dis-cusses the president's veto power. Chapter 10 deals with how Congress mon-itors the implementation of the laws it has passed. The final chapter reexam-ines the legislative process, pulling together the major themes of the book.

My intellectual indebtedness extends to numerous scholars and col-leagues, and I welcome the opportunity to acknowledge their generous assis-tance. My editor at CQ Press, John L. Moore, contributed greatly to the book's readability. Kerry Kern skillfully steered (or "floor managed") the book through the production stages; her production and editorial assistance was outstanding. My thanks, too, must go to CQ Books executives David R. Tarr, editor-in-chief; Nancy Lammers, director of book editorial design and pro-duction; and Brenda Carter, acquisitions editor for college texts, for their encouragement and support throughout this project.

Much credit for whatever understanding I have of the congressional process is due in large measure to my colleagues at the Congressional Research Service. Over the years I have learned the intricacies of the House and Senate from scores of CRS associates. Their research endeavors have expanded everyone's understanding of Congress's role and responsibilities. There are too many to acknowledge by name (it would constitute scores of outstanding colleagues in the American Law and Government divisions of the Office of Senior Specialists of CRS), but their ideas and insights permeate virtually every chapter of this book. CRS, I should note, bears no responsibility whatsoever for the views or interpretations expressed within these pages. I must also emphasize that whatever errors remain in this book are mine alone.

I am indebted also to scores of past and present House and Senate members and professional congressional aides who over the years have shared ideas and observations and deepened my understanding of the legislative process. The same can be said of numerous colleagues in academia whose research studies have provided us all with a reservoir of knowledge about congressional activities and operations. My intellectual debt also extends to University of Minnesota Professor Steven S. Smith and to Professor Charles Tiefer, currently at the University of Baltimore Law School and formerly the deputy general counsel and solicitor of the House of Representatives, for making useful suggestions for improvement of the manuscript.

Finally, I dedicate this fourth edition to family members. Above all, I am grateful to Janet, Mark, and Eric. They provided a loving and encouraging home environment, good humor, and family support throughout. This book is also dedicated to Missy and Lee Isgur, whose wit, wisdom, and acumen expanded our horizons in so many worthwhile ways.

Walter J. Oleszek

CHAPTER 1

Congress and Lawmaking

Congress is one of the world's most prominent and durable lawmaking bodies. The framers intended this result. Over half of their time during the humid Philadelphia summer of 1787 was spent defining Congress's role and responsibilities. "In republican government," explained James Madison, "the legislative authority necessarily predominates."[1] Madison, among others, tried to ensure that in the new United States government Congress would emerge as the principal policy-making branch.

Lawmaking is Congress's most basic response to the entire range of national concerns, from agriculture to housing, environment to national defense, health to the economy. The process by which Congress transforms an idea into national policy is the subject of this book. This process is complicated and variable, but it is governed by rules, procedures, precedents, and customs, and it is open to the use of some generally predictable strategies and tactics.

Members of Congress have major responsibilities other than lawmaking—to represent their constituents, to review the implementation of laws, and to inform and educate the citizenry about the issues of the day. All these functions are integral parts of the congressional process. This first chapter examines the constitutional foundation of congressional policy making, the functions of rules and procedures in organizations, the interaction of rules (formal and informal) and policy making in the congressional context, and the important features of congressional decision making.

THE CONSTITUTIONAL CONTEXT

Congress's central role in policy making can be traced to the writers of the Constitution. Madison, Alexander Hamilton, and the others developed a political system that established Congress as the lawmaking body and set out its relationship with the other branches of government and with the people. Several familiar basic principles underlie the specific provisions of the Constitution. These include limited government, separation of powers, checks and balances, and federalism. Each principle continues to shape lawmaking today despite the enormous changes that have transformed and enlarged the role of government in American society.

1

LIMITED GOVERNMENT

The framers of the Constitution wanted a strong and effective national government, but at the same time they wanted to avoid concentrating too much power in the central government lest it threaten personal and property rights. The Constitution is filled with implicit and explicit "auxiliary precautions" (Madison's phrase), such as checks and balances and a bill of rights. Limitation of government, the framers believed, could be achieved by dividing power among three branches of national government and between the nation and the states. The division of power ensured both policy conflicts and cooperation because it made officials in the several branches responsive to different constituencies, responsibilities, and perceptions of the public welfare. The framers believed that the "accumulation of all powers, legislative, executive, and judiciary, in the same hands . . . may justly be pronounced the very definition of tyranny."[2] As men of practical experience, they had witnessed firsthand the abuses of King George III and his royal governors. They also wanted to avoid the possible "elective despotism" of their own state legislatures.[3] Wary of excessive authority in either an executive or a legislative body, the framers also were familiar with the works of influential political theorists, particularly Locke and Montesquieu, who stressed concepts such as the separation of powers, checks and balances, and popular control of government.

SEPARATION OF POWERS

The framers combined their practical experience with a theoretical outlook and established three independent branches of national government, none having a monopoly of governing power. Their objective was twofold. First, the separation of powers was designed to restrain the power of any one branch. Second, it was meant to ensure that cooperation would be necessary for effective government. As Justice Robert Jackson wrote in a 1952 Supreme Court case (*Youngstown Co. v. Sawyer*, 343 U.S. 579, 635): "While the Constitution diffuses power the better to secure liberty, it also contemplates that the practice will integrate the dispersed powers into a workable government." The framers held a strong bias in favor of lawmaking by representative assemblies, and so viewed Congress as the prime national policy maker. The Constitution names Congress the first branch of government, assigns it "all legislative power," and grants it explicit and implied responsibilities through the so-called elastic clause (Section 8 of Article I). This clause empowers Congress to make "all Laws which shall be necessary and proper for carrying into Execution" its enumerated or specific powers.

In sharp contrast, Articles II and III, creating the executive and judicial branches, describe only briefly the framework and duties of these governmental units. Although separation of powers implies that Congress "enacts" the laws, the president "executes" them, and the Supreme Court "interprets" them, the framers did not intend such a rigid division of labor. The Constitution, in short, creates a system not of separate institutions performing separate functions but of separate institutions sharing functions (and even competing for predominate influence in exercising them). The overlap of powers is fundamental to national decision making. The founders did grant certain unique responsibilities to each branch and ensured their separateness by, for example, prohibiting any officer from serving in more than one branch simultaneously. They linked the branches through a system of checks and balances.

CHECKS AND BALANCES

An essential corollary of separation of powers is checks and balances. The framers realized that individuals in each branch might seek to aggrandize power at the expense of the other branches. Inevitably, conflicts would develop. In particular, the Constitution provides an open invitation to struggles for power by Congress and the president.

To restrain each branch, the framers devised a system of checks and balances. Congress's own legislative power was effectively "checked" by the establishment of a bicameral body consisting of the House of Representatives and the Senate. The laws Congress passes may be vetoed by the president. Treaties and high-level presidential appointments require the approval of the Senate. Many decisions and actions of Congress and the president are subject to review by the federal judiciary.

Checks and balances have a dual effect; they encourage cooperation and accommodation among the branches—particularly between the popularly elected Congress and the president—and they introduce the potential for conflict. Since 1789 Congress and the president have indeed cooperated with each other and protected their own powers. Each branch depends in various ways on the other. When conflicts occur, they are resolved most frequently by negotiation, bargaining, and compromise.

FEDERALISM

Just as the three branches check each other, the state and federal governments also are countervailing forces. This division of power is another way to curb and control governing power. While the term *federalism* (like *separation of powers* or *checks and balances*) is not mentioned in the Constitution, the framers understood that federalism was a plan of government acceptable to the thirteen original states. The Constitution's "supremacy clause" makes national laws and treaties the "supreme Law of the Land"; however, powers not granted to the national government remain with the states and the people. The inevitable clashes that occur between levels of government are often arbitrated by the Supreme Court or worked out through practical accommodations or laws.

Federalism has infused "localism" into congressional proceedings. As a representative institution, Congress and its members respond to the needs and interests of states and congressional districts. The nation's diversity is given ample expression in Congress by legislators whose tenure rests on the continued support of their constituents. Federalism is an especially prominent theme of the 1990s as many lawmakers seek to return federal functions to state and local governments.

Thus, the Constitution outlines a complicated system. Power is divided among the branches and between levels of government, and popular opinion is reflected differently in each. Both Congress and the president, each with different constituencies, terms of office, and times of election, can claim to represent majority sentiment on national issues. Given each branch's independence, formidable powers, different perspectives on many issues, and intricate mix of formal and informal relationships, it is apparent that important national policies reflect the judgment of both the legislative and the executive branches and the views of pressure groups and influential persons.

CONGRESS: AN INDEPENDENT POLICY MAKER

Much has been written about the growth of executive power in the twentieth century and the diminished role of Congress, but in fact there has been a dynamic, not static, pattern of activity between the legislative and executive branches. Witness, for example, how Speaker Newt Gingrich, R-Ga. (and not President Bill Clinton) became the national agenda-setter with his "Contract with America" during the first hundred days of the 104th Congress. First one branch and then the other may be perceived as predominant, and various periods are characterized as times of "congressional government" or "presidential government."[4] Such descriptions often underestimate the other branch's strategic importance, however. President John F. Kennedy, who served during a period regarded by some observers as one of presidential resurgence, observed that Congress "looks more powerful sitting here than it did when I was there." From his position in the White House, he looked at the collective power of Congress and found it "substantial."[5]

In short, the American political system is largely congressional *and* presidential government. Or, as British historian Paul Johnson put it, "We refer to the British constitution as a parliamentary democracy . . . [and] I would call yours a presidential and congressional democracy."[6]

The strength and independence of Congress contrast sharply with the position of legislatures in other democratic countries. In most, policy making is concentrated in the hands of a prime minister and cabinet who normally are elected members of the legislature and leaders of the majority party. As a result, the policy of the prime minister and his cabinet typically is approved by the legislature, with voting divided strictly along party lines. Conversely, if a prime minister loses a "vote of confidence" in parliament, he or she is expected to resign, and a general election is held to choose a successor government.

The U.S. Congress, by contrast, is elected separately from the president and has independent policy-making authority. As a result, a study of policy making in the United States requires a separate examination of the congressional process.

FUNCTIONS OF RULES AND PROCEDURES

Any decision-making body, Congress included, needs a set of rules, procedures, and conventions, formal and informal, in order to function. These rules and conventions establish the procedural context for both collective and individual policy-making action and behavior (see Box 1-1, "Major Sources of House and Senate Rules").

In the case of Congress, the Constitution authorizes the House and Senate to formulate their own rules of procedure and also prescribes some basic procedures for both houses, such as overrides of presidential vetoes. Thomas Jefferson, who as vice president compiled the first parliamentary manual for the U.S. Senate, emphasized the importance of rules to any legislative body.

> It is much more material that there be a rule to go by, than what that rule is; that there may be a uniformity of proceeding in business not subject to the caprice of the Speaker or captiousness of the members. It is very material that order, decency, and regularity be preserved in a dignified public body.[7]

Rules and procedures in an organization serve many functions. Among them are to provide stability, legitimize decisions, divide responsibilities, reduce conflict, and distribute power. Each of these functions will be illustrated by examples drawn from a college or university setting and by parallel functions in Congress.

STABILITY

Rules provide stability and predictability in personal and organizational affairs. Individuals and institutions can conduct their day-to-day business without having to debate procedure. Universities, for example, have specific requirements for bachelor's, master's, and doctorate degrees. Students know that if they are to progress from one degree to the next they must comply with rules and requirements. Daily or weekly changes in those requirements would cause chaos on any campus. Similarly, legislators need not decide each day who can speak on the floor, offer amendments, or close

---

MAJOR SOURCES OF HOUSE . . .

U.S. CONSTITUTION. Article I, Section 5, states: "Each House may determine the Rules of Its Proceedings." In addition, other procedures of Congress are addressed, such as quorums, adjournments, and roll calls.

STANDING RULES. The formal rules of the House are contained in the *Constitution, Jefferson's Manual,* and the *Rules of the House of Representatives.* The Senate's rules are in the *Senate Manual Containing the Standing Rules, Orders, Laws, and Resolutions Affecting the Business of the United States Senate.* Each chamber prints its rule book biennially as a separate document.

PRECEDENTS. Each chamber, particular the larger House, has scores of precedents, or "unwritten law," based upon past rulings of the Chair. The modern precedents of the Senate are compiled in one volume prepared by the Senate parliamentarian. It is revised and updated periodically, printed as a Senate document, and entitled *Senate Procedure, Precedents and Practices.* House precedents are contained in several sources. Precedents from 1789 to 1936 are found in eleven volumes: *Hinds' Precedents of the House of Representatives* (from 1789 to 1907) and *Cannon's Precedents of the House of Representatives* (from 1908 to 1936). Precedents from 1936 through 1988 can be found in the multivolume series entitled *Deschler-Brown Precedents of the United States House of Representatives.* Hinds, Cannon, Deschler, and Brown were parliamentarians of the House. Further, the precedents now are updated periodically and published as *Procedure in the U.S. House of Representatives.* It is prepared by the House parliamentarian.

BOX 1-1

debate. Such matters are governed by regularized procedures that continue from one Congress to the next and afford similar rights and privileges to every member.

To be sure, House and Senate rules change in response to new circumstances, needs, and demands. The history of Congress is reflected in the evolution of the House and Senate rules. Increases in the size of the House in the nineteenth century, for instance, produced limitations on debate for individual representatives. As veteran Democratic senator Robert C. Byrd, W. Va., said about Senate proceedings:

. . . *AND SENATE RULES*

STATUTORY RULES. There are many public laws whose provisions have the force of congressional rules. These "rulemaking" statutes include, for example, the Legislative Reorganization Act of 1946 (PL 79-601), the Legislative Reorganization Act of 1970 (PL 91-510), and the Congressional Budget and Impoundment Control Act of 1974 (PL 93-344).

JEFFERSON'S MANUAL. When Thomas Jefferson was vice president (1797-1801) he prepared a manual of parliamentary procedure for the Senate. Ironically, the House in 1837 made it a formal part of its rules, but the Senate did not grant it such status. The provisions of his manual "govern the House in all cases to which they are applicable and in which they are not inconsistent with the standing rules and orders of the House."

PARTY RULES. Each of the two major political parties has its own set of party rules. Some of these party regulations directly affect legislative procedure. The House Republican Conference, for example, has a provision that affects the Speaker's use of the suspension of the rules procedure.

INFORMAL PRACTICES AND CUSTOMS. Each chamber develops its own informal traditions and customs. They can be uncovered by examining sources such as the *Congressional Record* (the substantially verbatim account of House and Senate floor debate), scholarly accounts, and other studies of Congress. Several committees and party groups also prepare manuals of legislative procedure and practice.

The day-to-day functioning of the Senate has given rise to a set of traditions, rules, and practices with a life and history all its own. The body of principles and procedures governing many senatorial obligations and routines . . . is not so much the result of reasoned deliberations as the fruit of jousting and adjusting to circumstances in which the Senate found itself from time to time.[8]

Procedural evolution is a hallmark of Congress. The modern House and Senate differ in important ways from how they operated only a few decades ago. For example, the House today operates with more procedural and political powers centralized in the Speaker than it did in the past. In the contemporary Senate the filibuster (extended debate) is a growth industry. Infrequently employed a few decades ago, use or threatened use of the filibuster is today almost a daily occurrence. These kinds of procedural changes will be discussed in the chapters that follow.

LEGITIMACY

Students typically receive final course grades that are based on their classroom performance, examinations, and term papers. They accept the professors' evaluations if they believe in their fairness and legitimacy. If professors suddenly decided to use students' political opinions as the basis for final grades, there would be a storm of protest against such an arbitrary procedure. In a similar fashion, members of Congress and citizens generally accept legislative decisions when they believe the decisions have been approved according to orderly and fair procedures.

From 1993 to 1995 Congress grappled with the issue of applying to itself the laws it passes for the private sector and executive branch. Issues of legitimacy abound in this area. As Rep. Earl Pomeroy, D-N.D., highlighted in a story he told the House Rules Committee:

> Mr. Chairman, at one town meeting recently a constituent stood up and said, "Congressman, how are we supposed to believe the laws you guys pass are good for America, when you're telling us they're not good for Congress?" He was right. To ensure confidence in our laws we need to apply them to ourselves as well.[9]

Hence, Congress devised a process consistent with constitutional principles to bring itself into compliance with appropriate laws (employment, civil rights, and health and safety laws, for example). The bill, titled the Congressional Accountability Act of 1995, was signed into law by President Clinton.

DIVISION OF LABOR

Any university requires a division of labor if it is to carry out its tasks effectively and responsibly, and rules establish the various jurisdictions. Hence there are history, chemistry, and art departments; admissions officers and bursars; and food service and physical plant managers, all with specialized assignments. For Congress, committees are the heart of the legislative process. They provide the division of labor and specialization that Congress needs to handle about ten thousand measures that are introduced biennially, and to review the administration of scores of federal programs. Like specialized bodies in many organizations, committees do not make final policy decisions but initiate recommendations that are forwarded to their respective chambers.

The jurisdiction, or policy mandate, of Congress's standing (permanent) committees is outlined in the House and Senate rules. Legislation generally is referred to the committee (or committees) having authority over the subject matter. As a result, the rules generally determine which committee, and thus which members and their staffs, will exercise significant influence over a particular issue such as defense, taxes, health, or education.

Rules also prescribe the standards that committees are expected to observe during their policy deliberations. These include quorum requirements, public notice of committee meetings and hearings, and the right to counsel for witnesses. These rules also allocate staff resources to committees and subcommittees.

CONFLICT RESOLUTION

Rules reduce conflicts among members and units of organizations by distinguishing appropriate actions and behavior from the inappropriate. For example, universities have procedures by which students may drop or add classes. There are discussions with faculty advisers, completion of appropriate paperwork, and the approval of a dean. Students who informally try to drop or add classes may encounter conflicts with their professors as well as sanctions from the dean's office. Most of the conflicts can be avoided by observance of established procedures. Similarly, congressional rules reduce conflict by, for example, establishing procedures to fill vacancies on committees when several members are competing for the same position or to settle bicameral disputes on legislation. As Rep. Clarence A. Cannon, D-Mo. (1923-1964), a former House parliamentarian and subsequently the chairman of the Appropriations Committee, explained:

> The time of the House is too valuable, the scope of its enactments too far-reaching, and the constantly increasing pressure of its business too great to justify lengthy and perhaps acrimonious discussion of questions of procedure which have been authoritatively decided in former sessions.[10]

DISTRIBUTION OF POWER

A major consequence of rules is that they generally distribute power in any organization. Rules, therefore, often are a source of conflict themselves. During the 1960s many campuses witnessed struggles among students, faculty, and administrators involving the curriculum. The charge of irrelevance in course work was a frequent criticism of many students. As a result, the "rules of the game" for curriculum development were changed on many cam-puses. Students, junior faculty, and even community groups became involved in reshaping the structure and content of the educational program. The 1990s witnessed comparable concerns as groups on various campuses persuaded university officials to adopt rules, guidelines, or codes regarding speech that is perceived as offensive, for example, to minority groups or women (the so-called political correctness movement).

Like universities, Congress distributes power according to its rules and customs. Informal party rules establish a hierarchy of leadership positions in both chambers. House and Senate rules accord prerogatives to congressional committee chairmen that are unavailable to others.

Rules, therefore, are not neutral devices. They help to shore up the more powerful members and influence the attainment of member goals such as winning reelection, gaining internal influence, or winning congressional passage of legislation. As Speaker Gingrich once said: "The rules of the House are designed for a Speaker with a strong personality and an agenda."[11] Thus, attempts to change the rules almost invariably are efforts to redistribute power.

RULES AND POLICY MAKING IN CONGRESS

Rules play similar roles in most complex organizations. Congress has its own characteristics that affect the functions of the rules. First, members owe their positions to the electorate, not to their congressional peers or to influential congressional leaders. No one in Congress has authority over the other members comparable to that of university presidents and tenured faculty over junior faculty or to that of a corporation president over lower-level executives. Members cannot be fired except by their constituency. (Under the Constitution either chamber may expel a member by a two-thirds vote, but the authority is rarely used.) And each member has equal voting power in committees and on the floor of the House or Senate.

The rules of Congress, unlike those of many organizations, are especially sensitive to the rights of minorities, including the minority party, ideological minorities, and individual members. Senate Republican leader Bob Dole of Kansas told a committee considering rules changes, "One of the main traditions of the Senate is that of being the last repository of minority rights and I do not wish to be the [GOP] Leader who presided over the diminution of those rights."[12] Skillful use of the rules enables the minority to check majority action by delaying, defeating, or reshaping legislation. Intensity often counts as much as numbers—an apathetic majority may find it difficult to prevail over a well-organized minority. Except in the few instances when extraordinary majorities are needed, such as overriding presidential vetoes (a two-thirds vote), Senate ratification of treaties (two-thirds), and ending extended debate (a filibuster) in the Senate (three-fifths), the rules of the House and Senate require a simple majority to decide public policies.

Congress also is different from other organizations in its degree of responsiveness to external groups and pressures. The legislative branch is not so self-contained an institution as a university or a corporation. Congress is involved with every significant national and international issue. Its agenda compels members to respond to changing constituent interests and needs. Congress also is subject to numerous other influences, particularly the president, pressure groups, political parties, and state and local officials.

Finally, Congress is a collegial, not hierarchical, body. Power flows not from the top down, as in a corporation, but in practically every direction. While presidents can say, as did Harry Truman, that "the buck stops here," responsibility in Congress is "circular," with everybody and nobody appearing responsible for action or inaction. There is often little centralized authority at the top; congressional policies are not "announced" but "made" by shifting coalitions that vary from issue to issue. Congress's deliberations are more accessible to the public than those of perhaps any other kind of organization. These are some of the characteristics that set Congress apart from other bodies. Inevitably these differences affect the decision-making process.

PROCEDURE AND POLICY

Legislative procedures and policy making are inextricably linked in at least four ways. First, procedures affect policy outcomes. Congress processes legislation by complex rules and procedures that permeate the institution. Some matters are only gently brushed by the rules, while others become locked in their grip. Major civil rights legislation, for example, failed for decades to win congressional approval because southern senators used their chamber's rules and procedures to kill or modify such measures.

Congressional procedures are employed to define, restrict, or expand the policy options available to members during floor debate. They may prevent consideration of certain issues or presage policy outcomes. Such structured procedures enhance the policy influence of certain members, committees, or party leaders; facilitate expeditious treatment of issues; grant priority to some policy alternatives but not others; and determine, in general, the overall character of policy decisions.

A second point is that very often policy decisions are expressed as procedural moves. As Robert H. Michel of Illinois, then a House Republican leader frustrated with his party's minority status for nearly four decades and the majority party's procedural control of that body, said about the procedure-substance linkage:

> Procedure hasn't simply become more important than substance—it has, through a strange alchemy, *become* the substance of our deliberations. Who rules House procedures rules the House—and to a great degree, rules the kind and scope of political debate in this country.[13]

Or as John D. Dingell, D-Mich., then chairman of the House Energy and Commerce Committee, phrased it, "If you let me write the procedure, and I let you write the substance, I'll [beat] you every time."[14]

Representatives and senators, on various occasions, prefer not to make clear-cut decisions on certain complex and far-reaching public issues. Should a major weapons system be continued or curtailed? Should the nation's energy production needs take precedence over environmental concerns? Should financial assistance for the elderly be reduced and priority given to aiding disadvantaged children? On questions like these, members may be "cross-pressured"—the president may exert influence one way while constituent interests dictate another approach. Legislators sometimes lack adequate information or time to make informed judgments. They may be reluctant to oppose powerful pressure groups. Or they may feel that an issue does not lend itself to a simple "yes" or "no" vote.

As a result, legislators employ various procedural devices to handle knotty problems. A matter may be postponed on the ground of insufficient study in committee. Congress may direct an agency to prepare a detailed report before an issue is considered. An outside commission may be established to study a problem. Or a measure may be "tabled" by the House or Senate, a procedural vote that effectively defeats a proposal without rendering a clear judgment on its substance.

Third, the nature of the policy can determine the use of certain procedures. The House and Senate generally consider noncontroversial measures under expeditious procedures, where controversial proposals normally involve lengthy deliberation. Extraordinary circumstances sometimes prompt Congress to use "fast-track" procedures to pass legislation, such as suspension of the rules procedure (see Chapter 5), which limits debate to forty minutes and prohibits floor amendments. Emergency bills or legislation on which there is overwhelming bipartisan consensus can be passed quickly by way of the suspension route.

Finally, policy outcomes are more likely to be influenced by members with procedural expertise. Members who are skilled parliamentarians are better prepared to gain approval of their proposals than those who are only vaguely familiar with the rules. Just as carpenters and lawyers must learn their trade, members of Congress need to understand the rules if they expect to perform effectively. Congressional procedures are confusing to members. "To table, to refer to committee, to amend—so many things come up," declared a junior senator. "You don't know whether you are coming or going."[15] House Speaker John W. McCormack of Massachusetts (1962-1971) once advised House newcomers:

> Learn the rules and understand the precedents and procedures of the House. The congressman who knows how the House operates will soon be recognized for his parliamentary skills—and his prestige will rise among his colleagues, no matter what his party.[16]

Members who know the rules will always have the potential to shape legislation to their ends and to become key figures in coalitions trying to pass or defeat legislation. Those who do not understand the rules reduce their proficiency and influence as legislators. Some members even become parliamentary "watchdogs" or use "guerrilla warfare" tactics to harass the opposition. During the 1980s and 1990s Rep. Robert S. Walker, R-Pa., often performed the role of floor guardian against majority steamrollers. "So long as a floor watchdog exists," he wrote, "all members of the House are afforded some additional protection from precipitous actions."[17] When their party lost majority control of the House in the mid-1990s, several Democrats assumed the role of watchdog, including Barney Frank, Mass., and Harold L. Volkmer, Mo.

Members also learn the rules so they can better circumvent them for their own political and policy ends. There is, in brief, conventional and unconventional lawmaking. Conventional lawmaking involves the traditional parliamentary pathway of committee hearings, markups, and reports; floor consideration; conference committee deliberations; House and Senate approval of the conference reports; and presidential signature or veto (Figure 1-1).

Unconventional lawmaking follows a different procedural route. Typically, both chambers sometimes skirt traditional lawmaking steps. Committees may be bypassed in considering legislation; party leaders may exercise fundamental policy-making influence by establishing informal drafting task forces; floor debate and amendment opportunities may be restricted; or policies may be rushed through the House or Senate in "must-pass" bills during the hectic last days of a legislative session. Changing conditions or circumstances (such as partisan conflict, legislative-executive disagreements, heavy media and lobbying involvement, or the controversiality of the issue) often give rise to unconventional lawmaking. Several will highlight these points.

Wary of the political fallout of voting to raise the national debt during a period of mushrooming deficits, the Senate in 1985 adopted a floor amendment (which eventually became law) that dramatically revamped Congress's budgetary process (see Chapter 3). Initiated by Senators Phil Gramm, R-Texas, Warren B. Rudman, R-N.H., and Ernest F. Hollings, D-S.C., as a floor amendment to a House-passed bill raising the national debt ceiling, their emergency deficit reduction proposal was never previously reviewed in committee or discussed on the floor. Because the House chose to go directly to conference with the Senate on the Gramm-Rudman-Hollings plan, it bypassed its own committee and floor stages as well. Initial House consideration of Gramm-Rudman-Hollings came at the *end* of the bill-enacting process, when representatives debated the conference report.

Beginning with Thomas P. "Tip" O'Neill, Jr., D-Mass., House Speakers have employed partisan or bipartisan task forces to facilitate passage of leg-

14

FIGURE 1-1 How a Bill Becomes Law

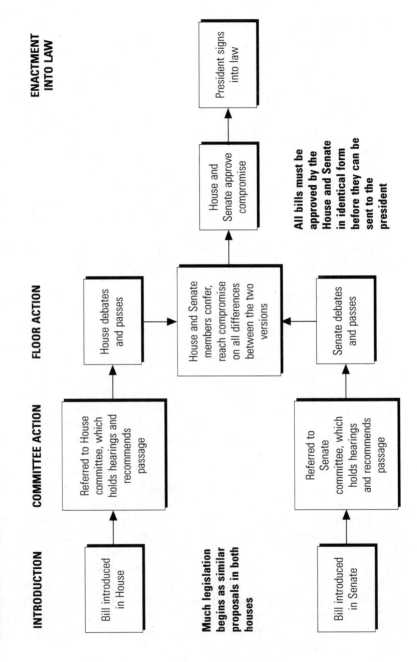

INTRODUCTION

COMMITTEE ACTION

FLOOR ACTION

ENACTMENT INTO LAW

Bill introduced in House

Referred to House committee, which holds hearings and recommends passage

House debates and passes

House and Senate members confer, reach compromise on all differences between the two versions

House and Senate approve compromise

President signs into law

Bill introduced in Senate

Referred to Senate committee, which holds hearings and recommends passage

Senate debates and passes

Much legislation begins as similar proposals in both houses

All bills must be approved by the House and Senate in identical form before they can be sent to the president

islation and to draft legislation or modify committee-reported measures. In 1989, for instance, a pay raise and ethics revision measure was drafted by a bipartisan task force, rather than by the committees with jurisdiction over these matters.[18] Similarly, Senate leaders form task forces or function in other ways to shape legislation. The Senate version of the Clean Air Act of 1990 was drafted "during a month-long series of meetings convened and masterminded by Senate Majority Leader George J. Mitchell, D-Maine. The meetings were held in Mitchell's office, with key Senators and Bush Administration officials attending."[19] In short, activist party leaders superseded the drafting role of the standing committees.

Since the mid-1980s it has been commonplace for party leaders, selected committee leaders, and executive branch leaders to join in "summitry" to devise broad budget agreements. Triggered by the difficulty of dealing with soaring deficits, the decisions of these summits effectively constrain and define committee and floor policy making. Committees, in particular, come under tremendous pressure from their party leaders and the president to comply with the summit's budgetary terms. Many lawmakers have objected to the closed-door summit proceedings. "This process was terrible," said Rep. Henry A. Waxman, D-Calif., about the summit that led to enactment of the Budget Enforcement Act of 1990 (which was extended to 1998 during President Clinton's first year in office). The summit "replaced a thorough airing of views in committees with a closed-door summit."[20] To cite another example of unconventional lawmaking, the House in March 1994 agreed to a measure regulating lobbying activities. The bill was drafted by a bipartisan leadership task force and then endorsed by a House Judiciary subcommittee (bypassing review by the full Judiciary Committee) before passing the House.[21]

In one of Congress's most dramatic departures from conventional lawmaking, the House in early 1995 reviewed, debated, and voted on virtually everything associated with the GOP's Contract with America (see Table 1-1, "Contract Scoreboard," p. 19). The contract had served as a 1994 campaign document for Republicans, who promised to enact it within the first hundred days of the 104th Congress if the electorate gave them majority control, and as a governing document around which GOP House members rallied and focused from January 4 to April 7, 1995. Reflecting the accelerated pace, the House was in session 528 hours during the contract period—more than double the session hours of the first thirteen weeks of the 103d Congress and almost triple those of the 102d. There were about twelve hundred hearings and markups during the hundred days—one-third more than the eight hundred held in the comparable period of the previous Congress.[22] "I'm on the [Judiciary] constitutional subcommittee," said Democratic Rep. Jose E. Serrano, N.Y., "and we're amending the Constitution every week. This should not be happening this way, but [Republicans] have a deadline, and we have no choice."[23]

PRECEDENTS AND FOLKWAYS

Congress is regulated not only by formal rules but also by informal ones that influence legislative procedure and member behavior. Two types of informal rules are precedents and "folkways." Precedents, the accumulated past decisions on matters of procedure, represent a blend of the formal and informal. They are the "common law" of Congress and govern many procedures not explicitly covered in the formal rules. As a noted House parliamentarian wrote, the great majority of the "rules of all parliamentary bodies are unwritten law; they spring up by precedent and custom; these precedents and customs are this day the chief law of both Houses of Congress."[24] For example, formal rules prescribe the order of business in the House and Senate, but precedents permit variations through the unanimous consent of the members. The rulings of the Speaker of the House and presiding officer of the Senate form a large body of precedents. They are given formal status by the parliamentarians in each chamber and then become part of the accepted rules and procedures.

Folkways, on the other hand, are unwritten norms of behavior that members are expected to observe. Like rules and precedents, folkways evolve in response to new times, demands, and lawmakers. During the 1950s, for instance, scholars wrote about norms of "apprenticeship" (junior lawmakers should listen and learn from their more seasoned colleagues before actively getting involved in policy making), "courtesy" (members should be solicitous toward their colleagues and avoid personal attacks on them), or "specialization" (a member should master a few policy areas and not try to impress colleagues as being a "jack-of-all-trades"). Today, these norms no longer apply. In both chambers, lawmakers enter an "entrepreneurial" environment where the incentives—both inside and outside Congress—are to get quickly involved in lawmaking, publicity seeking, and campaign fund raising. "You don't have to wait around to have influence," noted Rep. Charles E. Schumer, D-N.Y., elected in 1981. "Entrepreneurs do very well."[25]

In sum, the "to-get-along, go-along" culture of the 1950s and 1960s Congresses is mainly a thing of the past. Newcomers who quietly sit back and defer to their elders are likely to be viewed as unusual, especially in the Senate where norms of individualism pervade the institution. In today's Senate, wrote a noted scholar, a member "feels minimally constrained by consensual codes of behavior. The relevant distinction in his life is not between the Senate and the rest of the political world but between himself (plus his staff) and everything else. . . . With the help of the Senate's formal rules, he knows he can bring the collective business to a halt. He can be a force to be reckoned with whenever he wants to be."[26] Congressional decision making, then, is shaped by each chamber's formal and informal structure of rules, precedents, traditions, goals, and expectations.

CONGRESSIONAL DECISION MAKING

The congressional decision-making process is constantly evolving, but it has certain enduring features that affect consideration of all legislation. The first is the decentralized power structure of Congress, characterized by numerous specialized committees and a central party leadership that struggles to promote party and policy coherence. A second feature is the existence of multiple decision points for every piece of legislation. The many decision points mean that at each step of a bill's progress a majority coalition must be formed to move the measure along. This leads to the third important feature of the process: the need for bargaining and compromise at every juncture in order to form a winning coalition. Finally, each Congress has only a two-year life cycle in which to pass legislation once it has been introduced. The pressure of time is an ever-present force underlying the process.

DECENTRALIZED POWER STRUCTURE

Congress's decentralized character reflects both political and structural realities. Politically, legislators owe their reelection to voters in widely differing states and localities; structurally, the legislative branch has an elaborate division of labor to help it manage its immense workload. Responsibility for specific subject areas is dispersed among some two hundred committees and subcommittees.

Structural decentralization means that policy making is subject to various disintegrative processes. Broad issues are divided into smaller subissues for consideration by the committees. Overlapping and fragmented committee responsibilities can impede the development of comprehensive and coordinated national policies. Many House and Senate committees, for example, consider some aspect of health, trade, or energy policy.[27] Jurisdictional controversies occur as committees fight to protect or expand their turf. Scores of House and Senate committees and subcommittees, for example, staked out jurisdictional claims for all or parts of President Clinton's health care legislation.[28] Finally, committees develop special relationships with pressure groups, executive agencies, and scores of other interested participants. These alliances, often called *subgovernments, issue networks,* or *sloppy large hexagons,* influence numerous policy areas. Committees, then, become advocates of policies and not simply impartial instruments of the House or Senate.[29]

In theory, political parties are supposed to provide the cohesive force to balance the centrifugal influences of a fragmented committee system. Quite often, the reality is much different. Parties serve to organize their members and elect the formal leaders of Congress. Democrats and Republicans regularly meet in policy committees and caucuses to discuss policy issues. Neither party, however, commands the consistent support of all its members. There is too great a spread of ideological convictions within each party.

Too many countervailing pressures (constituency, region, individual conscience, career considerations, or committee loyalty) also influence the actions of representatives and senators. "I'll fight for my district even though it may be contrary to my national goals," declared a former House majority whip.[30] As a result, public policies usually are enacted because diverse elements of both parties temporarily coalesce to achieve common goals.

The usual lack of disciplined parties, in or out of Congress, underscores the difficult and delicate role of congressional party leaders. They cannot dictate policy because they lack the means to force agreement among competing party factions or autonomous committees and subcommittees. "What influence I have is based upon . . . respect and reasoned persuasion and some sensitivity to the political and other concerns of individual Senators," said Majority Leader Mitchell in an interview following his surprise March 4, 1994, announcement that he would not seek reelection. "I don't have a large bag of goodies to hand out to Senators nor do I have any mechanism for disciplining Senators."[31] A number of legislators, too, are not particularly dependent on their state or local parties for reelection. This means that party leaders cannot count on automatic party support but must rely heavily on their skills as bargainers and negotiators to influence legislative decisions. In addition, the power and style of any party leader depend on several factors, some outside the leader's control. Among them are personality, intellectual and political talent, the leader's view of the job, the size of the majority or minority party in the chamber, whether the White House is controlled by the opposition party, the expectations of colleagues, and the institutional complexion of the House or Senate during a particular historical era.

Many of these factors were clearly evident when the Gingrich-led House completed action on the Contract with America even before the promised hundred-day period ended. The House approved nine of the ten contract items (rejecting only term limits for lawmakers) with most GOP lawmakers, unlike the Democrats, marching in lockstep to enact their plan. "A total of 141 of the 230 Republicans" had party unity scores of 100 percent; the lowest GOP score was by Constance A. Morella, Md., "who voted with the party on 73 percent of the contract items."[32] Moreover, Speaker Gingrich took steps to centralize authority in his own hands and to weaken the power of committee chairs to block action on legislation. He bypassed the seniority custom in naming loyalists to head three standing committees (Appropriations, Commerce, and Judiciary); he also approved a new House rule limiting committee and subcommittee chairmen to three consecutive terms. (The Speaker's own length of service was restricted to four consecutive terms, or eight years, to be consistent with the constitutional amendment limiting presidential service.) The "Newt Deal," then, represented an unusual period when the Speaker exercised "top-down" control over what some commentators previously called the ungovernable and gridlocked House.

TABLE 1-1 Contract with America Scorecard at 100 Days

	Passed by House	Passed by Senate	Signed by President
Congressional reforms	•	•	•
Balanced-budget amendment	•	Defeated	
Line-item veto	•	•	
Anticrime package	•		
Welfare reform	•		
Crime package	•		
Defense package	•		
Unfunded mandates	•	•	•
Regulatory reform	•		
Litigation reform	•		
Tax cuts	•		
Term limits	Defeated		

MULTIPLE DECISION POINTS

Although Congress can on occasion act quickly, normally legislation has to work its way slowly through multiple decision points. One congressional report identified more than a hundred specific steps that might mark a "bill's progress through the Congress from introduction to possible enactment into law."[33]

After a bill is introduced, it usually is referred to committee and then frequently to a subcommittee. The views of executive departments and agencies often are solicited. "Almost every bill that is moving in Congress is sent to my office . . . by the committees for a reaction," remarked the former head of the Justice Department's office of legislative affairs.[34] Hearings are held and reports on the bill are issued by the subcommittee and full committee. The bill then is "reported out" of the full committee and scheduled for consideration by the entire membership. After floor debate and final action in one chamber, the same steps generally are repeated in the other house. At any point in this sequential process, the bill is subject to delay, defeat, or modification. "It is very easy to defeat a bill in Congress," President Kennedy once noted. "It is much more difficult to pass one."[35]

Figure 1-1 outlines the major procedural steps in how a bill becomes law. Congressional procedures require bills to overcome numerous hurdles. At each stage, measures and procedures must receive majority approval. All along the procedural route, therefore, strategically located committees, groups, or individuals can delay, block, or change proposals if they can form majority coalitions. Bargaining may be necessary at each juncture to build the majority coalition that advances the bill to the next step in the legislative process. Thus, advocates of a piece of legislation must attract not just one majority but several successive majorities at each of the critical intersections along the legislative route.

Bargaining and Coalition Building

There are three principal forms of bargaining used to build majority coalitions: logrolling, compromise, and nonlegislative favors.

Logrolling is an exchange of voting support on different bills by different members of Congress. It is an effective means of coalition building because members rarely are equally concerned about all the measures before Congress. For example, representatives A, B, and C strongly support a bill that increases government aid to farmers. A, B, and C are indifferent toward a second bill that increases the minimum wage, which is strongly supported by representatives D, E, and F. Because D, E, and F do not have strong feelings about the farm bill, a bargain is struck: A, B, and C agree to vote for the minimum wage bill, and D, E, and F agree to vote for the farm bill. Thus both bills are helped on their way past the key decision points at which A, B, C, D, E, and F have influence. Logrolling may be either explicit or implicit. A, B, and C may have negotiated directly with D, E, and F. Alternatively, A, B, and C may have voted for the minimum wage bill, letting it be known through the press or in other informal ways that they anticipate similar treatment on the farm bill from D, E, and F. The expectation is that D, E, and F will honor the tacit agreement since at a later date they may again need the support of A, B, and C.

There is even something that can be called *reverse logrolling,* which has arisen during the current era of fiscal austerity and deficit control. Each lawmaker "accepts cuts for his pet programs and then urges colleagues to make commensurate sacrifices."[36] This is a difficult logroll to accomplish, however. Members may rail against profligate federal spending on unnecessary projects—so-called pork—but projects in their own home states or districts are usually viewed as wholesome "bread and butter."

Compromise, unlike logrolling, builds coalitions through negotiation over the *content* of legislation. Each side agrees to modify policy goals on a given bill in a way that generally is acceptable to the other. A middle ground often is found—particularly with bills involving money. A, B, and C, for example, support a $50 million education bill; D, E, and F want to increase the funding to $100 million. The six meet and compromise on a $75 million bill they all can support.

Note the distinction between logrolling and compromise. In the logrolling example, the participants did not modify their objectives on the bills that mattered to them; each side traded voting support on a bill that meant little in return for support on a bill in which they were keenly interested. In a compromise, both sides modify their positions. "Anyone who thinks that compromise is a dirty word," remarked Rep. Charles W. Stenholm, D-Texas, "should go back and read one of the fascinating accounts of all that happened in Philadelphia in 1787" when our Constitution was drafted.[37] As Sen. Alan K. Simpson, R-Wyo., so aptly put it: "In politics there are no right answers, only a continuing flow of compromises between groups resulting in a changing, cloudy, and ambiguous series of public decisions where appetite and ambition compete openly with knowledge and wisdom."[38]

Nonlegislative favors are useful because policy goals are only one of the many objectives of members of Congress. Other objectives include assignment to a prestigious committee, getting reelected, running for higher office, obtaining larger office space and staff, or even being selected to attend a conference abroad. The wide variety of these nonpolicy objectives creates numerous bargaining opportunities—particularly for party leaders, who can dispense many favors—from which coalitions can be built. As Senate majority leader from 1955 to 1961, Lyndon B. Johnson of Texas was known for his skill in using his powers to satisfy the personal needs of senators to build support for legislation Johnson wanted.

> For Johnson, each one of these assignments contained a potential opportunity for bargaining, for creating obligations, provided that he knew his fellow senators well enough to determine which invitations would matter the most to whom. If he knew that the wife of the senator from Idaho had been dreaming of a trip to Paris for ten years, or that the advisers to another senator had warned him about his slipping popularity with Italian voters, Johnson could increase the potential usefulness of assignments to the Parliamentary Conference in Paris or to the dedication of the cemeteries in Italy.[39]

In this way, Johnson made his colleagues understand that there was a debt to be repaid.

THE CONGRESSIONAL CYCLE

Every bill introduced in Congress faces the two-year deadline of the congressional term. (The term of the 104th Congress, elected in November 1994, began at noon on January 4, 1995, and will expire at noon on January 3, 1997.)

Legislation introduced must be passed by both the House and the Senate in identical form within the two-year term in order to become law. Congress normally adjourns prior to the end of the two-year term; thus bills usually have less than two full years. Bills that have not completed the required procedural journey prior to final adjournment of a Congress automatically die and must be reintroduced in a new Congress. Inaction or postponement at any stage of the process can mean the defeat of a bill. This book repeatedly focuses on the various delaying and expediting tactics available to members during the legislative process.

Many measures considered by Congress come up in cycles. Much of Congress's annual agenda is filled with legislation required each year to continue and finance the activities of federal agencies and programs. Generally, this kind of legislation appears regularly on the congressional agenda at about the same time each year. Other legislation comes up for renewal every few years. Often, there are emergencies that demand immediate attention. Other issues become timely because public interest, international events, or the president has focused on them; health care, Bosnia, domestic terrorism, and welfare reform are examples of such issues in the 1990s.

Complex legislation often is introduced early because it takes longer to process than a simple bill. A disproportionately large number of major bills are enacted during the last few weeks of a Congress. Compromises that were not possible in July can be made in December. By this time—with the two-year term about to expire—the pressures on members of the House and Senate are intense, and lawmaking can become frantic and furious. "It is a time when legislators pass dozens of bills without debate or recorded votes, a time when a canny legislator can slip in special favors for the folks back home or for special-interest lobbyists roaming Capitol corridors."[40] Needless to say, members plan purposefully to take advantage of the "end game" in lawmaking.

Finally, many ideas require years or even decades of germination before they are enacted into law. Controversial proposals—reintroduced in successive Congresses—may need a four-, six-, or eight-year period before they win enactment. Many of the 1960s policies of Presidents Kennedy and Johnson, for example, first were considered during the Congresses of the 1950s. Landmark immigration reform legislation required the action of three 1980s Congresses before it eventually surmounted hurdles and roadblocks to become public law. However health care reform is handled in the mid-1990s, legislation to revise, refine, or revamp the health care system will likely occupy center stage into the next century.

SUMMARY

Rules and procedures affect what Congress does and how it does it. They define the steps by which bills become law, decentralize authority among numerous specialized committees, distribute power among members, and permit orderly consideration of policies. Above all, the rules and organi-zation of Congress create numerous decision points through which legisla-tion must pass in order to become law. As a result, congressional decision making presents many opportunities for members to defeat bills they oppose. Proponents, by contrast, must win at every step of the way. At each procedural stage, they must assemble a majority coalition. Throughout the legislative process, time is a critical factor as members maneuver to enact or defeat legislation under the pressure of numerous scheduling deadlines and the two-year period of each Congress. "Any time you want to legislate around here you have to convince an awful lot of people over a long period of time to get something accomplished," declared Sen. Sam Nunn, D-Ga.[41]

NOTES

1. Benjamin Fletcher Wright, ed., *The Federalist by Alexander Hamilton, James Madison, and John Jay* (Cambridge, Mass.: Belknap Press of Harvard University Press, 1961), 356 (Federalist No. 51).

2. Paul L. Ford, ed., *The Federalist: A Commentary on the Constitution of the United States by Alexander Hamilton, James Madison and John Jay* (New York: Henry Holt, 1898), 319 (Federalist No. 47). James Madison wrote this commentary on "Separation of the Departments of Power."

3. Thomas Jefferson, "Notes on Virginia," in *Free Government in the Making*, ed. Alpheus Thomas Mason (New York: Oxford University Press, 1965), 164.

4. See Woodrow Wilson, *Congressional Government* (Boston: Chapman, 1885), and James MacGregor Burns, *Presidential Government* (Boston: Houghton Mifflin, 1966).

5. Donald Bruce Johnson and Jack L. Walker, eds., "President John Kennedy Discusses the Presidency," in *The Dynamics of the American Presidency* (New York: John Wiley & Sons, 1964), 144.

6. *Washington Times*, June 4, 1987, 2B.

7. *Constitution, Jefferson's Manual and Rules of the House of Representatives*, 102d Cong., 2d sess., H Doc 102-405, 121-122.

8. *Congressional Record*, April 8, 1981, S3615.

9. Statement of Rep. Earl Pomeroy on the application of laws to Congress, hearing before the House Rules Subcommittee on Rules, March 24, 1994, 1.

10. Clarence Cannon, *Cannon's Procedure in the House of Representatives*, 86th Cong., 1st sess., H Doc 86–122, iii.

11. John M. Barry, "The Man of the House," *New York Times Magazine*, November 23, 1986, 109.

12. Testimony submitted to the Senate Rules and Administration Committee, March 10, 1994, 5.

13. Testimony before the GOP Task Force on Congressional Reform, House Republican Research Committee, December 16, 1987, 3.

14. *National Review*, February 27, 1987, 24.

15. *Los Angeles Times*, February 7, 1977, sec. 1, 5.

16. *Congressional Record*, March 9, 1976, 5909.

17. Robert S. Walker, "Why House Republicans Need a Watchdog," *Roll Call*, January 19, 1987, 10.

18. *Washington Post*, November 9, 1989, A14.

19. Richard E. Cohen, "Crumbling Committees," *National Journal*, October 6, 1990, 2416.
20. *National Journal*, October 6, 1990, 2416.
21. *New York Times*, March 25, 1994, A20.
22. CQ's *Congressional Monitor*, April 17, 1995, 1.
23. *Washington Post*, March 7, 1995, A1, A6.
24. Quoted in *Deschler–Brown Precedents of the United States House of Representatives*, vol. 1, 94th Cong., 2d sess., H Doc 94–661, iv.
25. *Wall Street Journal*, June 29, 1987, 54.
26. Richard F. Fenno, Jr., "Adjusting to the Senate," in *Congress and Policy Change*, ed. Gerald C. Wright, Jr., et al. (New York: Agathon Press Inc., 1986), 134–136. Also see Edward V. Schneier, "Norms and Folkways in Congress: How Much Has Already Changed?" *Congress & the Presidency*, Autumn 1988, 117–138; David W. Rohde, "Studying Congressional Norms: Concepts and Evidence," *Congress & the Presidency*, Autumn 1988, 139–145; and Chester W. Rogers, "New Member Socialization in the House of Representatives," *Congress & the Presidency*, Spring 1992, 47–63.
27. During the 96th Congress (1979–1981), a House reorganization panel found that there were eighty-three committees and subcommittees in the House alone that exercised some jurisdiction over energy issues. See *Final Report of the Select Committee on Committees, U.S. House of Representatives*, 96th Cong., 2d sess., H Rept 96–866, 334–355.
28. Alissa J. Rubin, "Members' Health Concerns Now Center on Turf Wars," *Congressional Quarterly Weekly Report*, October 9, 1993, 2734–2737.
29. Roger H. Davidson and Walter J. Oleszek, *Congress against Itself* (Bloomington: Indiana University Press, 1977), and Roger H. Davidson, "Breaking Up Those `Cozy Triangles': An Impossible Dream?" in *Legislative Reform and Public Policy*, ed. Susan Welch and John G. Peters (New York: Praeger, 1977), 30–53; Hugh Heclo, "Issue Networks and the Executive Establishment," in *The New American Political System*, ed. Anthony King (Washington, D.C.: American Enterprise Institute for Public Policy Research, 1978), 87–124; and Charles O. Jones, *The United States Congress: People, Place, and Policy* (Homewood, Ill.: Dorsey Press, 1982), 360. "Sloppy large hexagons," a phrase coined by Jones, refers to the large number of participants who shape policy issues.
30. Jeff Rainmundo, "Cool Whip," *California Magazine*, April 1987, 64.
31. Richard E. Cohen, "Sen. Mitchell, A Lame Duck, Sizes Up '94," *National Journal*, March 12, 1994, 598.
32. David S. Cloud, "Shakeup Time," *Congressional Quarterly Weekly Report*, March 25, 1995, 10.
33. *The Bill Status System for the United States House of Representatives*, Committee on House Administration, July 1, 1975, 19.
34. *New York Times*, Oct. 31, 1984, B6.
35. "President John Kennedy Discusses the Presidency," *The Dynamics of the American Presidency*, 144.
36. *Wall Street Journal*, February 15, 1985, 54.
37. *Congressional Record*, March 17, 1994, 1483.
38. *Congressional Record*, May 20, 1987, S6798.
39. Doris Kearns, *Lyndon Johnson and the American Dream* (New York: Harper & Row, 1976), 11.
40. *Los Angeles Times*, October 6, 1982, sec. 1, 1.
41. *Los Angeles Times*, July 15, 1990, A4.

CHAPTER 2

The Congressional Environment

While James A. Garfield served as a House member (1863-1880) and before he became the twentieth president of the United States, he provided this compelling observation of the legislative branch:

> Congress has always been and must always be the theater of contending opinions; the forum where opposing forces of political philosophy meet to measure their strength; where the public good must meet the assaults of local and sectional interests; in a word, the appointed place where the nation seeks to utter its thought and register its will.[1]

More than 125 years later it is safe to say that Congress, even when it is beset by dramatic and even traumatic changes, remains the nation's premier forum for addressing the economic, social, and political issues of the day.

Congress is an independent policy maker. This does not mean that it is impermeable to outside influences; nor does it mean that each member operates independently of every other member. Rather, there is a tangled, multifaceted relationship between Congress and the other governmental and nongovernmental forces. Similarly, there are complicated internal hierarchies and networks that affect the way Congress goes about its business. This chapter will focus on some of the conditions that mold the congressional environment, including the bicameral nature of Congress, the key actors in the congressional leadership, the outside pressures on Congress, and the procedural changes that swept through the House and Senate during the past few decades.

THE HOUSE AND SENATE COMPARED

The "House and Senate are naturally unlike," observed Woodrow Wilson.[2] Each chamber has its own rules, precedents, and customs; different terms of office; varying constitutional responsibilities; and differing constituencies. "We are constituted differently, we serve different purposes in the representative system, we operate differently, why should [the House and Senate] not have different rules," Sen. Wayne Morse, D-Ore. (1945-1969) once commented.[3] Table 2-1 lists the major differences between the chambers.

TABLE 2-1 Major Differences Between the House and Senate

House	Senate
Shorter term of office (2 years)	Longer term of office (6 years)
Adheres closely to procedural rules on floor activity	Operates mostly by unanimous consent
Narrower constituency	Broader, more varied constituency
Originates all revenue bills	Sole power to ratify treaties and advise and consent to presidential nominations
Policy specialists	Policy generalists
Less press and media coverage	More press and media coverage
Power less evenly distributed	Power more evenly distributed
Less prestigious	More prestigious
More expeditious in floor debate	Less expeditious in floor debate
Strict germaneness requirement for floor amendments	No general germaneness rule for floor amendments
Less reliance on staff	More reliance on staff
More partisan	Less partisan
Strict limits on debate	Unlimited debate on nearly every measure
Method of operation stresses majority rule	Traditions and practices emphasize minority rights

Probably the three most important differences are: (1) the House is more than four times the size of the Senate, (2) senators represent a broader constituency than do representatives, and (3) senators serve longer terms of office. These differences affect the way the two houses operate in a number of ways.

COMPLEXITY OF THE RULES

The factor of size explains much about why the two chambers differ. Because it is larger, the House is a more structured body than the Senate. The restraints imposed on representatives by rules and precedents are far more severe than those affecting senators. More than 1,250 pages are needed to describe the House rules for the 103d Congress. Its precedents from 1789 to 1936 are in eleven huge volumes; those from 1936 forward are recorded in the multivolume *Deschler-Brown Precedents*. In contrast, the Senate's rules and standing orders are contained in 1,038 pages and its precedents in one volume.

Where Senate rules maximize freedom of expression, House rules "show a constant subordination of the individual to the necessities of the whole House as the voice of the national will."[4] Furthermore, House and Senate rules differ fundamentally in their basic purpose. House rules are designed to permit a determined majority to work its will. Senate rules, on the other hand, are intended to slow down, or even defer, action on legislation by granting inordinate parliamentary power (through the filibuster, for example) to individual members and determined minorities. "Senate rules are tilted toward not doing things," remarked a former House Speaker (1987-1989), Jim Wright, D-Texas. "House rules, if you know how to use them, are tilted toward allowing the majority to get its will done."[5] Ironically, it is easier to move legislation in the larger House than the smaller Senate because of differences in their rules. A simple majority is sufficient to pass major and controversial legislation in the House. In the Senate, at least sixty votes (necessary to break a filibuster) might be needed—sometimes more than once—to move legislation to final passage. In short, the House acts on the basis of majority rule; the Senate emphasizes minority rule and often functions as a "supermajoritarian" institution where sixty votes are crucial to the enactment of legislation.

The Senate, as a result, is more personal and individualistic. "The Senate is run for the convenience of one Senator, to the inconvenience of 99," said Sen. J. Bennett Johnston, D-La.[6] It functions to a large extent by unanimous consent, in effect adjusting or disregarding its rules as it goes along. It is not uncommon for votes on a bill to be rescheduled or delayed until an interested senator can be present. Senate party leaders are careful to consult all senators who have expressed an interest in the pending legislation, because "under the rules of the Senate any one Senator can hold up the works here," said Robert C. Byrd, D-W.Va., an acknowledged expert in Senate procedure.[7] In the House, the leadership can consult only key members—usually committee leaders—about upcoming floor action. No wonder bills often take longer to complete in the smaller Senate than the larger House. All senators can participate actively in shaping decisions on the floor given their unique prerogatives: unlimited debate and unlimited opportunities to offer floor amendments to virtually any bill. House members typically get involved on the floor only on measures reported from the committees on which they serve. To be sure, the "cosmic" issues (such as major health reform or anti-crime proposals) will trigger floor participation by many representatives.

POLICY INCUBATION

Incubation entails "keeping a proposal alive, while it picks up support, or waits for a better climate, or while the problem to which it is addressed grows."[8] Both houses fulfill this role, but it is promoted in the Senate particularly because of that body's flexible rules, more varied constituent pressures on senators, and greater press and media coverage. As the chamber of greater prestige, lesser complexity, longer term of office, and smaller size, the Senate is simply easier for the media to cover than the House.[9] The Senate is more involved than the House with cultivating national constituencies, formulating questions for national debate, and gaining general public support for policy proposals. The policy-generating role is particularly characteristic of senators having presidential ambitions, who need to capture headlines and national constituencies.[10]

However, when the House began televising its floor sessions in 1979 over C-SPAN (Cable-Satellite Public Affairs Network)—the Senate began gavel-to-gavel coverage in mid-1986—many activist representatives recognized the technology's "bully-pulpit" potential. For example, when Newt Gingrich, R-Ga., was elected to the House in 1978, he quickly saw C-SPAN's potential for mobilizing grass-roots support behind the GOP's agenda and for attacking Democrats and their decades-long control of the House. He organized floor debates and speeches, even when there was hardly anyone in the chamber, to highlight Republican ideas to the C-SPAN viewing audience and to persuade them that they ought to put the House in Republican hands. He was successful. As Speaker of the 104th Congress (1995-1997), Gingrich set out to transform the "speakership into a powerful pulpit from which he hopes to continue to displace [the president] as the primary source of ideas and vision about where the country should be heading."[11]

Many Senate Republicans who had previously served in the House with Gingrich began to emulate their former colleague by conducting organized, often early morning, speeches to a largely empty chamber. For example, the eleven Senate Republican freshmen elected to the 104th Congress (seven of whom had served in the House) organized a "Freshman Focus" to emphasize their commitment to changing the way Washington works. The GOP freshmen began presenting twice-weekly speeches, aimed at C-SPAN viewers, on timely and major issues—mindful that, as freshman senator James M. Inhofe, R-Okla. stated, "a lot of people out there are watching what's going on here."[12]

SPECIALISTS VERSUS GENERALISTS

Another difference between the chambers is that representatives tend to be known as subject matter "specialists" while senators tend to be "generalists." "If the Senate has been the nation's great forum," a representative said, then the "House has been its workshop."[13] Indeed, the House's greater work force and division of labor facilitate policy specialization. "Senators do not specialize as intensively or as exclusively in their committee work as House members do" because senators must spread their "efforts over a greater span of subjects than the average representative."[14] During the 104th Congress, for example, the average senator served on about ten committees and subcommittees, compared with about five for the average representative.

One reason for the specialist-generalist distinction is that most senators represent a more heterogeneous constituency than House members. This compels the former to generalize as they attempt to be conversant on numerous national and international issues that affect their state. With their six-year term, senators are less vulnerable to immediate constituency pressures. Therefore, they can afford to be more cosmopolitan in their viewpoints than House members. Journalists tend to expect senators, more than representatives, to have an informed opinion on almost every important public issue. Senators, too, suffer from what Senator Byrd called "fractured attention."[15] They are often away from the Senate raising campaign funds, appearing on television, giving speeches, or engaging in other activities that limit their ability to participate in floor deliberations.

A result of the generalist role is greater reliance by senators on knowledgeable personal and committee staff aides for advice in decision making. House members, on the other hand, are more likely to be experts themselves on particular policy issues. If not, they often go to informed colleagues rather than staff aides for advice on legislation. "House members rely most heavily upon their colleagues for all information," one study concluded, while senators "will often turn to other sources, especially their own staffs, for their immediate information needs."[16] Consequently, Senate staff aides generally have more influence over the laws and programs of the nation than do their House counterparts.

There are senators, to be sure, who can hold their own with knowledgeable House members. In some policy areas certain senators hold the specialization advantage. For instance, membership on the Senate Budget Committee is permanent, whereas the House Budget Committee has a limited tenure (or rotational) membership. This difference tilts the balance of expertise to the Senate during consideration of the annual concurrent budget resolution (see Chapter 3).

The House in 1995 adopted rules that limit members to six consecutive years of service as committee or subcommittee chairs. The purpose of this change, besides allowing additional majority party lawmakers to assume leadership posts, was "more importantly to prevent stagnation or too close a relationship to develop between committee leaders and the interests they oversee."[17] On the other hand, rotating committee leadership could limit the ability of the chairs to master the work of being a leader (such as negotiating compromises, setting the agenda, and managing the committee), foster short-term thinking when long-range planning may be necessary, and undermine the panel leaders' bargaining potency with the White House, the executive branch, and other groups and entities. (During the 104th Congress, Senate Republicans considered a six-year term limit for committee chairmen.)[18]

DISTRIBUTION OF POWER

Another difference between the two chambers is that power to influence policy is more evenly distributed in the Senate than in the House. Unlike most representatives, senators can readily exercise initiative in legislation and oversight, get floor amendments incorporated in measures reported from committees on which they are not members, influence the scheduling of bills, and, in general, participate more widely and equally in all Senate and party activities. Witness the ability of Sen. Bill Bradley, D-N.J., then a relatively junior member of the Finance Committee, to become known as the "father" of the landmark tax reform package of 1986 even though the chamber was in Republican hands. Every senator, too, of the majority party typically chairs at least one committee or subcommittee.

This ability to make a difference quickly is one reason why the Senate is so politically attractive to House members. In the 104th Congress, thirty-nine senators were former House members; by contrast, no representative served previously in the Senate. In the House, remarked Sen. Paul Simon, D-Ill., a former House member, "you are restricted by your committee. But in the Senate, you're not tied down. You have a lot more room to exert influence."[19] House procedures, in short, emphasize the mobilization of voting blocs to make policy; deference to individual prerogatives, including camaraderie across party lines, is the hallmark of senatorial decision making.

SIMILARITIES

There are many similarities between the House and Senate. Both chambers are essentially equal in power and share similar responsibilities in lawmaking, oversight, and representation. Both have heavy workloads, decentralized committee and party structures, and somewhat parallel committee jurisdictions. The roles and responsibilities of one chamber interact with those of the other. House and Senate party leaders often cooperate to coordinate action on legislation. Cooperation generally is made easier when both houses are controlled by the same party.

In recent years, the two chambers have become more similar in some unexpected areas. Today's House members are more dependent on staff than were their colleagues of a few decades ago, in part because issues are more complex and because more informed constituents look to Capitol Hill for assistance and information. Senators are much more involved in constituency service than ever before. Like House members, they travel frequently to their states to meet in diverse forums with their constituents. "I have averaged 48 weekends a year in going home to my State," remarked veteran Democratic senator Wendell Ford of Kentucky.[20]

Many senators, too, emulate their House colleagues by preparing to run for reelection almost immediately after being sworn into office. This situation reflects contemporary electoral developments unforeseen by the framers— the huge costs of campaigns, professionalization, the rise of campaign specialists, and the emphasis on videopolitics—that make senatorial races more competitive than most House contests. Sen. Dianne Feinstein, D-Calif., for instance, had to raise $14,000 per day (not the $12,000 per week over six years that most senators on average must raise to defend their seat) for her reelection campaign in 1994. Elected two years earlier to fill a senatorial vacancy, Feinstein narrowly defeated Rep. Michael Huffington, R, who spent a record $30 million—nearly all of it his own money.

House members enjoy more incumbent protection than senators because they attract fewer effective challengers (in part by scaring off opponents with their money-raising ability), receive more favorable press and media attention, and court their constituents assiduously. Thus representatives are more likely than senators to survive periodic electoral tides that oust numerous incumbents. But not always.

The mid-term election of 1994 was "nationalized" (rather than being a series of local elections), largely by Newt Gingrich's Contract with America, which found politically fertile soil given a seething public's dismay with the economy, the president, the government, and the direction of the country. The result: severe losses for the Democrats, among incumbents as well as candidates in formerly Democratic "open" districts. An electorate angry at the party that had controlled the House for forty years and the Senate for thirty-four of those years produced a nationwide surge of votes for Republicans with only Democrats targeted for defeat. Many incumbent Democrats, including Speaker Thomas S. Foley, Wash., were simply unable to insulate themselves from this electoral tide. "The combination of shrinking vote totals for the Democrats with an exploding GOP vote (nearly one-third larger than 1990) was unparalleled since the Democrats' own growth spurt during the Depression and early days of the New Deal."[21] The GOP triumph shifted party control from Democrats to Republicans in both chambers—something that had not occurred since the election of 1952—and transformed Congress's policy agenda.

A whole range of institutional, partisan, and policy connections makes bicameralism a force that shapes member behavior and policy outcomes. Along with traditional interchamber jealousies and rivalries, evident even when the same party controls both chambers, House members sometimes hold intense negative feelings against what they perceive as Senate obstructionism. Part of the explanation is House frustration and exasperation with the ability of even one senator to block legislation through extended debate or to force votes on unwanted nongermane amendments. Senators, of course, have their own complaints about House procedures and policy making. Suffice it to say that the within-chamber procedures of each body influence the policy-making activities of the other. The two are interlocked, with national policies fundamentally shaped by the interchamber connection.[22]

LEADERSHIP STRUCTURE OF CONGRESS

In both the House and the Senate, the party leadership is crucial to the smooth functioning of the legislative process. Leaders help to organize orderly consideration of legislative proposals, promote party support for or

FIGURE 2-1   Congressional Leadership

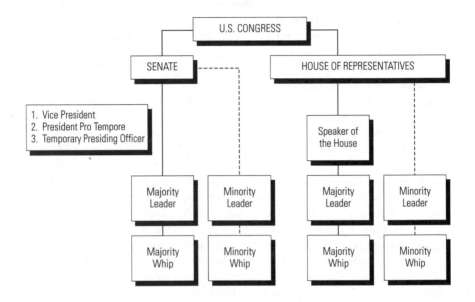

against legislation, attempt to reconcile differences that threaten to disrupt the chambers, plan strategy on important bills, consult with the president, and publicize legislative achievements (see Figure 2-1).

In the House, the formal leadership consists of the Speaker, who is both the chamber's presiding officer and the leader of the majority party; the majority and minority leaders; whips from each party; assistants to the whips; and various partisan (Democratic and Republican) committees that assist with party strategy, legislative scheduling, and the assignment of party members to the legislative committees.

In the Senate, there is no party official comparable to the Speaker. Under the Constitution, the vice president of the United States assumes the post of Senate president, and in his absence the president pro tempore or, more commonly, a temporary presiding officer of the majority party, presides; none of these individuals, however, has political power comparable to that of the Speaker. The Senate also has majority and minority leaders, whips, assistant whips, and party committees.

Party leaders may offer tangible incentives to shape the course of legislation. These include influencing committee assignments, sharing media attention with colleagues, raising money and campaigning for colleagues, selecting members to serve on special committees or panels, intervening with the White House, or mobilizing support or opposition to policy proposals.

For example, when Gingrich became Speaker in 1995 he took several steps to strengthen the authority of his office in a manner not seen since the era of Joseph G. Cannon, R-Ill. (Speaker, 1903-1911). To bolster his base within GOP ranks, Speaker Gingrich even assigned freshmen Republicans to several "power" committees: Appropriations, Commerce, Rules, and Ways and Means. As one scholar wrote:

> Putting freshmen on the four most important committees in the House is unprecedented. Three-fifths of the Republicans have been elected to the House in the last two elections; many feel they owe their seats to Gingrich and are naturally his backers. His appointment of the freshmen to important committee assignments reinforces this loyalty to the speaker.[23]

The Speaker also ignored seniority, as noted earlier, by reaching down the roster of three important committees to personally select their Republican chairmen: Appropriations (Robert L. Livingston, La.), Commerce (Thomas J. Bliley, Jr., Va.), and Judiciary (Henry J. Hyde, Ill.).

SPEAKER OF THE HOUSE

The position of the Speaker is established by the Constitution, but until the early nineteenth century the Speaker had little actual power. Henry Clay was the first really influential Speaker (1811-1814, 1815-1820, 1823-1825). The office reached its peak of power in the early 1900s, under a series of Speakers who extended and sometimes abused their prerogatives.

Drastic reform of the rules came about as a result of the 1910 "revolt" against Speaker Cannon, who was stripped of his authority to sit on the House Rules Committee, to appoint committee members, and to control all floor action.

Modern Speakers achieve their influence largely through personal prestige, mastery of the art of persuasion, legislative expertise, and the support of the members. Among the Speaker's primary formal powers are presiding over the House, deciding points of order, referring bills and resolutions to the appropriate House committees, scheduling legislation for floor action, and appointing House members to select, joint, and House-Senate conference committees. As Speaker Thomas P. "Tip" O'Neill, Jr., D-Mass. (1977-1987), once remarked:

> You know, you ask me what are my powers and my authority around here. The power to recognize on the floor; little odds and ends—like men get pride out of the prestige of handling the Committee of the Whole, being named the Speaker for the day; those little trips that come along—like those trips to China, trips to Russia, things of that nature; or other ad hoc committees or special committees, which I have assignments to; plus the fact that there is a certain aura and respect that goes with the Speaker's office [second in succession to the White House].[24]

THE VOTING SPEAKER

Newt Gingrich not only talks more than any Speaker in memory, he's also voting more.

The Georgian, the first GOP Speaker in four decades, cast his eighth vote February 10, 1995, just 38 days into the 104th Congress.

Traditionally, Speakers have voted infrequently. Texas Democrat Sam Rayburn cast only a handful of votes in his 20 years as speaker, and he did not vote at all in at least nine of those years. Massachusetts Republican Joe Martin, who twice interrupted Rayburn's tenure, never voted as Speaker. John McCormack, D-Mass., continued the tradition, voting only twice in his eight years as Speaker.

Carl Albert, D-Okla., was the first to break with the tradition. Every Speaker since his tenure (1971-77) has been less reluctant to vote. Tom Foley, D-Wash., for instance, voted 61 times in the 103rd Congress.

But Gingrich's record tops the early session mark set by Foley. Foley cast five votes in January 1991 on the Persian Gulf War, but he did not vote again until the end of March.

All but one of Gingrich's votes have come on items within the "Contract with America"—his first was a "present" vote for election of the Speaker—and most have been on final passage of bills.

"When I can," Gingrich said, "I'll try to show up on final passage of the contract items."

Still, Gingrich has a long way to go to match the modern-day record for most votes in a session. Albert set that mark in 1971, his first year as Speaker: He voted 92 times.

Source: CQ's Congressional Monitor, February 14, 1995.

BOX 2-1

Although the Speaker may participate in debate he does so infrequently, and usually only when his remarks may affect the outcome of a crucial vote. Most recent Speakers have seldom voted, usually only to break a tie. Here again, Gingrich has been an exception, not being shy about excercising his right to vote. (See Box 2-1, "The Voting Speaker.")

O'Neill's ten-year tenure as Speaker transformed the post in an important respect. He elevated the national visibility of the speakership and thus the office's potential to articulate and establish the House's agenda. "[Speaker] Sam Rayburn could have walked down the streets of Spokane [Wash.] without anybody noticing him," said then majority leader Foley. "Tip

O'Neill couldn't do that, and it is very unlikely that any future Speaker will be anonymous to the country."[25] In short, O'Neill ushered "in a new age in the House without ever being a new age politician."[26]

Speaker Gingrich, anything but anonymous, has exploited the New Age politics as no other Speaker before him. For instance, he went on prime-time national television after the House successfully completed action on the Contract with America, emulating presidents who address the nation; allowed talk radio announcers to broadcast from the Capitol; taught televised college classes and conducted town meetings; championed a "technological revolution" on Capitol Hill; co-hosted a weekly program on National Empowerment Television; and held daily televised news conferences while the House was in session (until the conferences were suspended, in part because of clashes between the Speaker and some journalists and concern in GOP ranks that the Speaker was getting overexposed in the media).[27]

MAJORITY AND MINORITY LEADERS

Both the majority and minority parties of the House and Senate appoint officials to shape and direct strategy on the floor. These officials, elected by their respective party caucuses, try to hold together their parties' loose alliances in hopes of shaping them into voting majorities to pass or defeat bills and amendments. Majority leaders have considerable influence over the scheduling of bills. The majority leader in the House ranks just below the Speaker in importance. In the Senate, the majority leader is the most influential officer because neither the vice president nor the president pro tempore holds substantive powers over the chamber's proceedings. Like the Speaker, the majority and minority leaders in both chambers receive larger salaries than other members as well as additional staff resources and other perquisites.

Duties of the House majority and minority leaders are not spelled out in the standing rules of the House. (House rules do state that the majority and minority leaders are ex officio members of the Permanent Select Intelligence Committee and that the minority leader, or a designee, is guaranteed the right to offer a motion to recommit with instructions—see Chapter 5—on legislation regulated by a "rule" from the Rules Committee.) In practice, the majority leader's job has been to formulate the party's legislative program in cooperation with the Speaker and other party leaders, steer the program through the House, work to ensure that committee chairmen take action on bills deemed of importance to the party, and act as party spokesman on the House floor. Speaker Gingrich, for example, assigned Majority Leader Dick Armey, R-Texas, responsibility for managing day-to-day decisions on the House floor with respect to enactment of the Contract with America.

Everyday duties of the minority leader correspond to those of the majority leader, except that the minority leader has no authority over scheduling legislation. The minority leader speaks for his party and acts as field general on the floor, promoting partisan cohesion and searching for votes on the majority side. It is the minority leader's duty to consult ranking minority members of House committees and encourage them to follow agreed-upon party positions. Minority Leader Richard A. Gephardt, D-Mo., worked with Senate Democrats and the White House during the 104th Congress to devise a legislative agenda that would highlight the fundamental aims of the Democratic party and portray "the Republican Contract as a mean-spirited attempt to benefit wealthy individuals and business interests."[28]

If the occupant of the White House is of the minority party, that party's leader in the House will be the president's spokesman. "It's a dual role," former House minority leader Robert H. Michel, R-Ill. (1981-1995) once noted. "On each decision, [the leader's job] makes you look at things from two perspectives—your own district's and the President's."[29]

The functions of the Senate majority leader are similar to those of his counterpart in the House. He can nominate members to party committees, influence the election of party officers, affect the assignment of members to committees, and appoint ad hoc party task forces to study and recommend substantive or procedural reforms. Traditionally, the "primary role of the majority leader remains similar to that at its inception, namely, to program and to expedite the flow of his party's legislation."[30] All Senate floor business essentially is scheduled by the majority leader in consultation with the minority leadership. Scheduling is the bedrock on which the majority leader's fundamental authority rests. The majority leader is aided in controlling scheduling by many parliamentary and procedural precedents, such as the priority given him (and the minority leader) when he seeks recognition on the floor, and the ability to set the times and dates the Senate recesses (or adjourns) and reconvenes. These informal prerogatives can be useful, for instance in deciding what tactics to employ against filibusters.

If used aggressively by the majority leader, the task of scheduling, discussed in Chapter 7, can be transformed from a largely procedural responsibility to one with significant programmatic and political overtones. Legislation can be scheduled to suit party or White House interests; to facilitate comprehensive policy making through the sequential consideration of related topics; to expedite policies supported by the leadership; or to coordinate House-Senate decision making.

With the aid of the majority whip, the majority leader also is responsible for securing the attendance of party colleagues during important floor sessions and ascertaining in advance how senators are likely to vote on issues. Measures may be scheduled to maximize attendance by the bill's supporters and minimize attendance by the opponents. The leadership expends a great deal of effort to ensure that senators backing a measure favored by the party are on hand for important votes.

Occupying center stage in the Senate, the majority leader is best positioned institutionally to know the status of legislation, when a bill probably will be scheduled, how intensely committed its supporters and opponents are, what strategies are being formulated to pass or defeat it, and under what conditions the president will intervene to help secure the measure's enactment or defeat. A knowledgeable majority leader is in a good position to guide and advise his colleagues.

The Senate minority leader has important responsibilities, too. These include articulating minority criticism of the majority party's legislation, mobilizing support for minority party positions, and acting as Senate spokesman for the president if both are of the same party. Asked how to push ideas through Congress, Minority Leader Tom Daschle, D-S.D., replied: "Put your message together the same way you put a campaign together."[31] When Republicans lost the White House in November 1992, Bob Dole, Kan., then the Senate minority leader, quickly emerged as a forceful critic, and sometimes ally, of President Clinton. His skillful "loyal opposition" role as majority leader in the GOP-controlled 104th Congress was likely to be of help in his 1996 run for the presidency—his third such attempt.

WHIPS

Each party in the House and Senate elects a whip and appoints a number of deputy, assistant, or regional whips to aid the floor leader in implementing the party's legislative program. Senate Majority Whip Trent Lott, R-Miss., assists Majority Leader Dole in a variety of ways.

> The rough division of labor between the leaders is that Dole stays above the day to day fray, leaving floor managing, vote counting and intelligence-gathering to Lott. "Trent goes down there, tries to make sure things happen down on the floor. He'll say, 'Hey, let's hurry up and dispense with this bill and amendments,' " said a [Senate] aide. In addition, [because he served previously in the House as GOP whip], "He's a terrific conduit to the House," noted the aide.[32]

The diversity of whips provides greater geographical, ideological, and seniority balance in the party leadership structure. They can also take on specialized assignments for their party. House Chief Deputy Majority Whip Dennis Hastert, R-Ill., for example, is in charge of managing two GOP ad hoc groups working on overhauling Medicare and Medicaid.[33]

The whips' principal jobs are to aid the party leadership in developing a program; transmit information to party members; check attendance before key votes; conduct counts of party members for and against major bills; assist the leaders in interpreting the counts and developing strategy; build coalitions to pass amendments and bills; oversee and expedite floor activity generally; and publicize the party's accomplishments.[34] As House Minority Whip David E. Bonior, D-Mich., stated at the beginning of the 104th Congress: "My new role will not only be counting the votes by which we are going to lose.

My role will be to emphasize the message we are trying to convey to the American people."[35] In sum, the whips' job is to know where the votes are and to produce the votes on behalf of party objectives, even if this means negotiating substantive changes in the bill at hand.

PRESSURES ON MEMBERS

In making their legislative decisions, members of Congress are influenced by numerous pressures—from their constituents, the White House, the news media, lobbyists and interest groups, and their own party leadership and colleagues on Capitol Hill. These pressures are a central feature of the congressional environment; they affect the formal procedures and rules of Congress. All of these pressures are present in varying degrees at every step of the legislative process. The interests and influence of groups and individuals outside Congress have a considerable impact on the fate of legislation. This section highlights some major external influences on members.

THE PRESIDENT AND THE EXECUTIVE BRANCH

The president and executive branch are among the most important sources of external pressure exerted on Congress. Many of the president's legislative functions and activities are not mentioned in the Constitution. The president is able to influence congressional action through the manipulation of patronage, the allocation of federal funds and projects that may be vital to the reelection of certain members of Congress, and the handling of constituents' cases in which senators and representatives are interested.

For example, President Clinton worked feverishly to win a come-from-behind victory for congressional approval of the North American Free Trade Agreement. Clinton bartered for votes on such a grand scale that Olympia J. Snowe, R-Maine, an anti-NAFTA House member (now a senator) said, "They have practically given away the family silver." Another NAFTA opponent, consumer activist Ralph Nader, even established a "NAFTA Pork Patrol" to calculate "the cost of the deals to U.S. taxpayers."[36]

As leader of the Democratic or Republican party, the president is his party's chief election campaigner. The president also has ready access to the news media for promoting his administration's policies and commanding headlines. This "bully pulpit" role, as Theodore Roosevelt described it, enables presidents to mold public opinion and build popular backing for White House proposals. With advances in communications and the amplifying power of the media, the bully-pulpit role is arguably the president's most significant resource. "Teledemocracy" (satellite press conferences, cable TV, interactive technology, talk show formats, "800" telephone numbers, televised town hall meetings, Internet, and more) enables public officials to bypass traditional news outlets and communicate directly with the electorate. As Clinton pollster Stanley Greenberg put it, to enact the president's agenda "is not simply a matter of presenting a policy proposal, sending it to Congress and letting Congress do its work. Now you need an effort to keep the American public with you."[37]

The president's role as legislative leader derives from the Constitution. While the Constitution vests "all legislative Powers" in Congress, it also directs the president to "give to the Congress Information of the State of the Union, and recommend to their Consideration such Measures as he shall judge necessary and expedient." This function has been broadened over the years. The president presents to Congress each year, in addition to his State of the Union message, two other general statements of presidential aims: an economic report, including proposals directed to the maintenance of maximum employment, and a budget message outlining his appropriations requests and policy proposals. During a typical session, the president transmits to Congress scores of other legislative proposals, and ensures that his White House and executive agency liaison offices keep tabs on legislative activities and lobby for administration policies. To be sure, the president's constitutional power to veto acts passed by Congress, which requires a two-thirds vote in each house to override, often promotes legislative-executive accommodations.

THE MEDIA

Of all the pressures on Congress, none is such a two-way proposition as the relationship between legislators and the media.

While senators and representatives must contend with the peculiarities of the news-gathering business, such as deadlines and limited space or time to describe events, and with constant media scrutiny of their actions, they also must rely on news organizations to inform the public of their legislative interests and accomplishments. At the same time, reporters must depend to some extent on "inside" information from members, a condition that makes many of them reluctant to displease their sources lest the pipeline of information be shut off.

But Congress basically is an open organization. Information flows freely on Capitol Hill and secrets rarely remain secret for long. It has always been the case that an enterprising reporter usually could find out what was newsworthy. Moreover, Congress has taken a variety of actions during the past two decades to further open its proceedings to public observation. Recall the nationwide, gavel-to-gavel coverage over C-SPAN of House and Senate floor proceedings. Instead of relying on press accounts of congressional actions, many citizens now have an opportunity to watch the floor sessions via the "electronic gallery" and make their own legislative judgments.

The Congress-media connection has undergone recent changes that significantly affect individual lawmakers, Capitol Hill parties, and the legislative branch itself. From an individual perspective, lawmakers are exploiting a large array of technologies to communicate with their constituents, generate favorable publicity, and promote their policy proposals. As congressional scholar David E. Price (a former House member, D-N.C., 1987-1995) described this aspect of his legislative experience:

> We send a weekly five-minute radio program, in which I discuss an issue before Congress, to fifteen stations in the district. We may also send radio feeds and, occasionally, satellite television feeds to local stations from Washington, offering commentary about matters of current interest, and we arrange interviews on these topics when I am home. In addition, we provide a steady stream of press releases to newspaper, radio, and television outlets; most of these either offer news about my own initiatives or give some interpretation of major items of congressional business, often relating to North Carolina. We furnish copies of my statements and speeches and let stations know when they can pick up my floor appearances on C-SPAN. I also do a monthly call-in show on cable television, which is then distributed and rebroadcast on most cable systems in the district.[38]

Lawmakers, in short, employ a variety of high-tech devices—faxes, computers, electronic mail, teleconferencing ("meeting" constituents in their states or districts without ever leaving Capitol Hill), and more—in addition to their traditional means (newsletters, franked mail, radio and television) of contacting constituents or promoting issues. As a sign of the times, two advocates of the constitutional balanced budget amendment, Sen. Larry E. Craig, R-Idaho, and Rep. Charles W. Stenholm, D-Texas, fielded questions from users of the CompuServe computer network as part of their effort "to be armed with favorable comment from beyond the Beltway sent to them over the information superhighway."[39]

From a party perspective, Democratic and Republican leaders devote considerable attention to ways of using the media to frame the terms of public debate on substantive and political issues so as to promote the outcome they want. Regularly, House GOP leaders employ sophisticated high-tech and communications strategies to highlight their goals and message to the American public. Opinion polling, televised ads, the mobilization and coordination of interest groups, town meetings, airport rallies, radio and television interviews, op-ed articles, and more are employed to muster public support. There are also daily and weekly "theme team" meetings "to plan the message of the [day or] week for the speeches at the beginning and end of each legislative day" (see Figure 2-2).[40] Similarly, when Democrats lost control of the House, Minority Leader Gephardt created a new communications team to accomplish several goals: to plan and coordinate the daily themes the party wants to emphasize, "to stay ahead of the news curve, rather than continually playing catch-up to Republicans," and to assemble the best technology available to get their message out to the public. "We are going to use everything short of carrier pigeons" to get the Democratic message out as quickly and efficiently as possible, said Rep. Kweisi Mfume, D-Md.[41]

FIGURE 2-2 A Daily "Message" for House Republicans

CONFERENCE NOTES...

A daily publication for House Republicans

June 12, 1995

DEFENSE AUTHORIZATION:

message of the day

Cutting bureaucracy, smarter spending to preserve national security in a dangerous world.

featured issue: department of defense authorization

H.R. 1530, the Department of Defense Authorization Act, continues the Republican trend of trimming the fat while reinforcing the muscle. This bill cuts bureaucratic waste from the Department of Defense while it preserves and strengthens military readiness and modernization programs. Here are highlights of the bill:

- 30,000 personnel cut from acquisition workforce in FY '96.
- Cuts personnel by 25% from the Office of the Secretary of Defense.
- Republicans have taken a responsible approach to national security, maintaining our national defense with spending on par with other first-world nations. Measured by percentage of GDP, US defense outlays are about the same as France.
- Cuts over $2 billion from nondefense spending in Pentagon budget.

fyi

The rule for H.R. 1530 provides for two hours of general debate. In all, 56 amendments were ruled in order. Of the 56, 34 are Republican amendments and 22 are Democrat amendments.

"And I quote..."

"These initiatives will create a stronger defense posture and a leaner Pentagon, while providing a better standard of living for our troops and their families. They add up to a defense policy that makes sense for an era where we must maintain our global responsibilities while putting America's fiscal house in order."

--Rep. Floyd Spence (R-SC), Chairman
House National Security Committee

HOUSE REPUBLICAN CONFERENCE 202/225-5107

Senate Republicans even have their own internal cable channel, dubbed "R-TV," to conduct electronic staff meetings, to facilitate GOP policy development, and to air Republican views on issues. [42] Many of their leaders, especially Dole, are exceptionally skilled in using the airwaves to convey party positions and sentiments. Senate Democrats under Daschle's leadership established a Technology and Communications Committee, headed by Sen. John D. Rockefeller IV, W.Va. "Rockefeller's job is to examine the growing selection of communications technology available in an effort to improve the Democrats' ability to get their message out to the general public—and to receive feedback."[43] Senator Rockefeller also wants to improve internal communications among Democratic offices. Minority Leader Daschle emphasized the importance of keeping pace with the latest in telecommunications developments. "It's inevitable, or equally inevitable that we won't win."[44]

From an institutional perspective, Congress today is subjected to an unending barrage of criticism in the press and media. Some of it is deserved, some of it is the by-product of political, partisan, policy, or personal clashes, and some of it is simply wrong. From Mark Twain and Will Rogers to Johnny Carson and Jay Leno, Congress has been the butt of jokes, ridicule, and sarcasm. Today, critiques of the legislative branch seem especially caustic and pervasive in part because of competitive pressures in the news business (scandals, rumors, and misdeeds sell) and public anger and lack of confidence in a more visible yet little understood Congress.

Scholarly research has shown, noted one student of Congress, "that press coverage of Congress has declined in volume and increased sharply in negativity, while moving from coverage of what the institution does as a legislature to increased emphasis on reports, rumors, and allegations of scandal, individual and institutional."[45] The implications that flow from this development are several, including the contemporary emphasis on "reform," especially among newly elected lawmakers, some propensity for "quick-fix" solutions to complex problems, and a grass-roots movement to impose term limits on lawmakers. Citizens seem so "turned off" by Congress that they are skeptical about whatever it does. In the judgment of Sen. Frank Lautenberg, D-N.J.:

> Democracy simply cannot function in an atmosphere of distrust. After all, when citizens view everything the Congress does in the worst possible light, they are similarly skeptical about the legislation we propose. That makes it extremely difficult to build public support. And without public support, it becomes almost impossible to address major social problems in a meaningful way.[46]

In short, Congress and the media are interdependent institutions. As broadcast journalist Walter Cronkite once said: "Newspapers and broadcasting stations are to politicians as heavy guns to generals—weapons to be used or neutralized in the continuing battle for favorable public opinion."[47]

CONSTITUENT PRESSURES

Although there are many pressures competing for influence on Capitol Hill, it is still the constituents, not the president or the party or the congressional leadership, who grant and can take away a member's job.[48] A member who is popular back home can defy all three in a way unthinkable in a country like Great Britain, where the leadership of the legislature, the executive, and the party are the same.

The extent to which a member of Congress seeks to follow the wishes of his constituents is determined to a considerable degree by the issue at stake. Few members would actively oppose issues deemed vital by most constituents. A farm-state legislator, for instance, is unlikely to push policies designed to lower the price of foods grown by those who elect him or her. Noteworthy is the view of Senate Agriculture chairman and presidential candidate for the GOP nomination in 1996 Richard G. Lugar, Ind., that the federal government should gradually phase out farm subsidy programs so that competitive market forces can take hold to boost the agriculture industry.[49]

Likewise, few members would follow locally popular policies that would endanger the nation. Between these extremes lies a wide spectrum of different blends of pressure from constituents and from conscience. But it is in this gray area that members must make most of their decisions. (It is no coincidence that the committees on which senators and representatives seek membership often are determined by the type of constituency served.)

A fundamental change from a generation ago is the increased amount of time that lawmakers spend with the people they represent. Today, most members travel virtually weekly to their states or districts to meet with constituents. Lawmakers not only are in close and constant touch with voter sentiments back home, but also they may be even too hypersensitive to constituency opinion. From a member's perspective, it is understandable that doing a good job on constituency service is the road to electoral success. On the other hand, it tends to push lawmakers toward more of an "ombudsmen" role than a leadership role where citizens are educated about major problems and solutions and about the unpopular decisions and difficult choices that may be required to serve the national interest. As Walter Mondale (former senator, vice president, and currently ambassador to Japan) told the 1993 Joint Committee on the Organization of Congress:

> Good constituent service is, of course, necessary—and honorable—work for any member of Congress and his staff. Citizens must have somewhere to turn for help when they become victims of government bureaucracy. But constituent service can also be a bottomless pit. The danger is that a member of Congress will end up as little more than an ombudsman between citizens and government agencies. As important as this work is, it takes precious time away from Congress' central responsibilities as both a deliberative and a law-making body.[50]

Members, then, regularly confront the dilemma of how to maintain a rough balance between serving the often contradictory impulses of their constituents (provide more government services without raising our taxes, for instance) and the larger national interest.

WASHINGTON LOBBYISTS

Lobbyists and lobby groups play an active part in the legislative process. The corps of Washington lobbyists has grown markedly in number and diversity since the 1930s, in line with the expansion of federal authority and its spread into new areas. The federal government has become a tremendous force in the life of the nation, and the number of fields in which changes in federal policy may spell success or failure for special interest groups has been greatly enlarged. Thus commercial and industrial interests, labor unions, ethnic, ideological, and racial groups, professional organizations, state and local governments, citizen groups, and representatives of foreign interests—all from time to time and some continuously—have sought by one method or another to exert pressure on Congress to attain their legislative goals.

Pressure groups, whether operating at the grass-roots level to influence public opinion or through direct contacts with members of Congress, perform some important and indispensable functions. These include helping to inform both Congress and the public about problems and issues, stimulating public debate, opening a path to Congress for the wronged and needy, and making known to Congress the practical aspects of proposed legislation: whom it would help, whom it would hurt, who is for it, and who is against it.

Lobbyists also work closely with sympathetic legislators and their staffs drafting legislation, developing strategy, or preparing speeches. For example, House GOP Conference chairman John A. Boehner, Ohio, assembled a number of lobbyists and conservative groups, called the "Thursday Group" for their weekly meeting day, to mobilize grass-roots support for the Contract with America. Sen. Paul Coverdell, R-Ga., also participated in these meetings. Representative Boehner divided the Thursday Group "into various committees, each lobbying on separate provisions of the Contract With America, with companies and trade associations contributing money to pay for phone banks, advertising and other efforts."[51] "Electronic advocacy" by way of the Internet and other means is also being used today to generate grass-roots campaigns for or against legislation.[52]

Interest groups may, in pursuing their own objectives, lead the legislature into decisions that benefit a particular pressure group but do not necessarily serve other segments of the public. A group's ability to influence legislation is based on a variety of factors: the quality of its arguments; the size, cohesion, and intensity of the organization's membership; the group's ability to augment its political power by forming ad hoc coalitions with other associations; its financial and staff resources; and the shrewdness of its leadership.

With lawmakers increasingly being elected on their own— establishing personal organizations in their states or districts with little or no help from their parties and raising the funds to sustain them—interest groups have recognized the potency of grass-roots lobbying, mobilizing constituents to pressure lawmakers by phone calls, faxes and telegrams, letters, or personal visits. Even with "manufactured" grass-roots activity, members realize they cannot simply ignore these expressions of voter opinion. Hence, a crucial phase in determining whether a bill is passed, defeated, or amended on Capitol Hill is the struggle among contending interests in members' states or districts.

Paradoxically, the proliferation of interest groups and their sophistication in using campaign funds, expert information, and technology to affect legislative decisions has, on the one hand, added to the demands on lawmakers and created difficulties in organizing winning coalitions. On the other hand, the very proliferation of these groups often enables lawmakers to play one against another. "The power of interest groups is not, of course, exercised without opposition," wrote several scholars. "The typical issue has some interest groups on one side and some on the other, or many interest groups on many sides, not necessarily with an equal balance of power."[53] Although lawmakers must contend with more interest groups, no single one is likely to exercise dominant influence over policy formation as sometimes occurred in the past. For example, where tobacco interests once held sway on Capitol Hill, their efforts at avoiding smoking bans, regulation, and higher cigarette taxes are being undermined by a variety of antismoking interests that have stressed the health perils of both directly inhaled smoke and so-called secondhand smoke.[54]

CONGRESS IN FLUX

The contemporary Congress is strikingly different from its predecessors in a variety of ways. For instance, the House and Senate have stripped away many vestiges of the secrecy that once cloaked their committee and floor activities; committee and member offices have been provided with modern technology; staff resources have been augmented; power has shifted from seniority leaders to factional and individual leaders; party leaders have gained new authority, as Speaker Gingrich has in being able to appoint the chairs of important committees; and budgetary procedures have been revamped (see Chapter 3). These changes, in brief, have affected Congress's lawmaking processes, distribution of power, and policy-making capabilities.

External events and internal frustrations largely triggered these diverse developments. Congress began to change in the late 1960s and early 1970s. Of fundamental importance were the two overriding issues of the period: the Vietnam War and the Watergate scandal. Both forced Congress to reflect on the growing mistrust between the legislative and executive branches and to examine whether it had the tools, and the will, to handle those crises and others that might arise in the future. New members were coming to Congress—many brighter, more activist, and more ambitious than the people they replaced—determined to participate actively in legislative decision making and to restore Congress to a position equal with that of the presidency.

This era of change reinforced the decentralized and democratic tendencies of Congress. Power was diffused further throughout Congress's components—committees, subcommittees, party panels, task forces, staff aides, and informal groups—rather than concentrated (as during the 1950s) in a relatively few individuals. The object of the changes of the 1970s, said former Speaker O'Neill, "was to take power out of the hands of the few and give it to more people."[55] This development greatly increased the need for bargaining and coalition building to achieve legislative results.

Change is an iron law of politics, however. The diffusion of influence precipitated in the 1980s and 1990s, especially in the House, some recentralization of authority. Mention has already been made about the consolidation of influence in Speaker Gingrich's office. The forces that buffet Congress today are part of the ebb and flow of diverse conditions and circumstances that seem likely to shape the context of congressional policy making into the next century. Several are worth briefly noting because they and others will be reviewed in succeeding chapters. They include:

THE FISCAL DEFICIT. With a national debt of around $5 trillion (tripling in size during the past decade) and annual fiscal deficits hovering in the $200 billion to $300 billion range, it is no wonder that the politics of fiscal scarcity have dominated virtually all congressional policy making. Deficits and governance are inextricably linked. Lawmakers are hard-pressed to find the resources to initiate or expand programs. Frustration abounds on Capitol Hill because of the fiscally austere environment. Interestingly, fiscal politics on Capitol Hill have had the effect of augmenting the authority of party leaders, who are key actors in assembling budget packages.

SHARP PARTISANSHIP. There has been a resurgence of partisanship on Capitol Hill, especially in the House. On votes involving party priorities, large majorities of Democrats and Republicans frequently are on opposite sides of the issue. Various factors account for the polarization. Some argue that it is rooted in electoral and demographic forces that have produced greater ideological homogeneity within each major party. For example, the South, long the bastion of Democratic support, is now making a historic realignment to Republicanism. A case in point is the Georgia House delegation in the mid-1990s. The 1995 Democratic defection of Rep. Nathan Deal to the Republican party polarized that delegation racially and ideologically into three liberal African-American Democrats and eight conservative white Republicans.[56]

Ideologically, then, the divide between the parties has grown as each pushes its own policy preferences.[57] On some critical issues, intraparty blocs expect their colleagues to toe the party line. Witness the effort by conservative Senate Republicans to convene the party to discuss removing moderate Sen. Mark O. Hatfield, Ore., as chairman of the Appropriations Committee. Hatfield voted against a major GOP priority: the balanced budget constitutional amendment, which failed Senate passage by one vote. [58] Further contributing to the heightened partisanship is the use of procedural rules to accomplish party objectives, the emphasis on "attack politics" legislatively and electorally, and the use of ethics as a partisan weapon.

"INSIDE-OUTSIDE" POLICY MAKING. Given today's political environment where the news media and interest groups are major players, and where decision-making authority is fragmented among scores of individuals and entities, new policy-making developments were bound to follow. Today it is no longer sufficient to work behind the scenes to line up votes to pass legislation. This "inside game," while still important, by itself is unlikely to produce major legislation unless the "outside game" is added to it. Just as the president must use his "bully pulpit" effectively if he is to succeed, party leaders and members understand that they must also strive to influence public opinion and mobilize grass-roots support for their initiatives. "If you are going to pass important legislation," said House Democratic leader Gephardt, "you have to both deal with Members and put together coalitions in the country."[59] Scores of techniques associated with campaigning—speech making before specialized groups, television and radio appearances, or article writing for publication, for instance—are now important components of legislative policy making. The task of coordinating the inside game and outside game typically falls to party leaders.

COMPLEXITY OF ISSUES AND AGENDAS. A major challenge of the 1990s is how to reconcile divergent tendencies. Economically, the world is rapidly moving toward greater global integration. Politically, the electoral imperative compels lawmakers to represent local interests. Economic globalism and political localism are parallel developments that will be difficult to accommodate easily. Congress confronts a host of new, complex, interdependent and not easily resolvable problems (such as depletion of the ozone layer, deforestation, drug trafficking) that are transnational in character. Today, many issues do not neatly track domestic and international categories because national and foreign problems are intermingled in diverse ways. One effect on Congress is that no single panel is the "trade," "defense," or "energy" committee. This intertwining invites broad chamber and party participation in the resolution of issues. It contributes to the proliferation of task forces, informal groups, and other ad hoc arrangements for addressing crosscutting issues. The volume and complexity of today's issues mean that lawmakers must take into account diverse concerns and rely more extensively on expert advice in making decisions.

To be sure, there are many other important developments, such as the growing diversity of the congressional membership (more women, African Americans, Hispanics, and Asians) and the agenda implications (more concern for children's issues and so forth) that flow from that diversity; the "changing of the guard" as the World War II generation of lawmakers gives way to the "baby boomer" and "post-baby-boomer" era of lawmakers; and the renewed debate about the roles and responsibilities of different levels of government. Suffice it to say that Congress today is subject to a broader and wider range of inside influences and outside forces than ever before.

SUMMARY

This chapter has discussed the general environment in which members of Congress operate, the many influences on congressional procedures and decision making, including the party leadership and outside pressures—from the executive branch, members' constituents, the media, and lobbying groups. The chapter has also highlighted some of the similarities and differences in the House and Senate that affect the operations of the national legislature. This chapter completes a preliminary overview of Congress.

Chapter 3 turns to a detailed discussion of the congressional budget process. The power of the purse is one of Congress's fundamental constitutional prerogatives. Congress's revamped budgetary process has become an integrating mechanism in an institution that thrives on fragmented authority. Moreover, it imposes a web of relationships upon committees and members that affects action on almost all public policy. To examine the budget process at this stage should aid in understanding the fundamental thrust of the remaining chapters, which discuss what typically happens to bills as they follow the lawmaking route.

NOTES

1. James A. Garfield, "A Century of Congress," *Atlantic Monthly,* July 1877, 60.
2. Woodrow Wilson, *Constitutional Government in the United States* (New York: Columbia University Press, 1911), 87.
3. *Congressional Record,* February 7, 1967, 2838.
4. Asher C. Hinds, *Hinds' Precedents of the House of Representatives,* vol. 1, v.
5. Janet Hook, "Speaker Jim Wright Takes Charge in the House," *Congressional Quarterly Weekly Report,* July 11, 1987, 1486.
6. *New York Times,* November 22, 1985, B8.
7. *Congressional Record,* September 10, 1987, S11944.
8. Nelson W. Polsby, "Policy Analysis and Congress," *Public Policy* (Fall 1969): 67.
9. Michael Green, "Obstacles to Reform: Nobody Covers the House," *Washington Monthly,* June 1970, 62-70.
10. See Robert L. Peabody, Norman J. Ornstein, and David W. Rohde, "The United States Senate as a Presidential Incubator: Many Are Called but Few Are Chosen," *Political Science Quarterly* (Summer 1976): 236-258.

11. David S. Cloud, "Speaker Wants His Platform To Rival the Presidency," *Congressional Quarterly Weekly Report*, February 4, 1995, 331.
12. *National Journal*, April 15, 1995, 938. Also see, for instance, *Congressional Record*, April 6, 1995, S5277.
13. Charles Clapp, *The Congressman* (Garden City, N.Y.: Doubleday, 1963), 39.
14. Richard F. Fenno, Jr., *Congressmen in Committees* (Boston: Little, Brown, 1973), 172.
15. Robert C. Byrd, "Operations of Congress," Hearing before the Joint Committee on the Organization of Congress, February 2, 1993, 4.
16. Norman J. Ornstein, "Legislative Behavior and Legislative Structure: A Comparative Look at House and Senate Resource Utilization," in *Legislative Staffing*, ed. James J. Heaphey and Alan B. Balutis (New York: John Wiley & Sons, 1975), 175.
17. *Congressional Record*, January 4, 1995, H34.
18. See Mary Jacoby, "Now, Senate Chairs Face Term Limits," *Roll Call*, May 8, 1995, 1.
19. *Chicago Tribune*, July 21, 1983, 9.
20. *Congressional Record*, October 1, 1985, S12343.
21. Rhodes Cook, "Rare Combination of Forces May Make History of '94," *Congressional Quarterly Weekly Report*, April 15, 1995, 1076.
22. See, for example, Lawrence Longley and Walter Oleszek, *Bicameral Politics: Conference Committees in Congress* (New Haven: Yale University Press, 1989).
23. James Thurber, "Thunder from the Right: Observations About the Elections," *The Public Manager*, Winter 1994-1995, 16.
24. Michael J. Malbin, "House Democrats Are Playing with a Strong Leadership Lineup," *National Journal*, June 18, 1977, 942.
25. *Los Angeles Times*, October 19, 1986, sec. 1, 2.
26. Quoted in Janet Hook, "O'Neill Changed Speaker's Role and Helped Remake House," *Congressional Quarterly Weekly Report*, January 8, 1994, 16.
27. *Washington Times*, May 3, 1995, A6.
28. Albert Eisele, "House Dems poised to counterattack," *The Hill*, March 15, 1995, 1.
29. *Chicago Tribune*, August 16, 1982, 2.
30. Robert L. Peabody, *Leadership in Congress* (Boston: Little, Brown, 1976), 336.
31. Jamie Stiehm, "Daschle leadership tested," *The Hill*, April 12, 1995, 4.
32. Jamie Stiehm, "Dole-Lott: A marriage of convenience," *The Hill*, April 26, 1995, 8.
33. *National Journal's CongressDaily/PM*, April 10, 1995, 1.
34. Lawrence C. Dodd, "The Expanded Roles of the House Democratic Whip System: The 93rd and 94th Congresses," *Congressional Studies*, (Spring 1979): 27-56. See also Dodd and Terry Sullivan, "Majority Party Leadership and Partisan Vote Gathering: The House Democratic Whip System," in *Understanding Congressional Leadership*, ed. Frank H. Mackaman (Washington, D.C.: CQ Press, 1981), 227-260.
35. Gabriel Kahn, "Bonior Overhauls His Whip Operation," *Roll Call*, January 16, 1995, 16.
36. Both quotations are from Jackie Calmes, "How a Sense of Clinton's Commitment and a Series of Deals Clinched the Vote," *Wall Street Journal*, November 19, 1993, A7.
37. Thomas B. Rosenstiel, "Presidents' Pollsters: Who Follows Whom?" *Los Angeles Times*, December 28, 1993, A5.
38. David E. Price, *The Congressional Experience*, (San Francisco: Westview Press), 1992, 115-116.
39. Andrew Mollison, "Lawmakers for balanced budget take case to computer network," *Washington Times*, February 15, 1994, A8.
40. Robin Toner, "G.O.P. Mobilizes for Contract Deadline," *New York Times*, March 30, 1995, A21.

41. *Roll Call,* January 16, 1995, 16.
42. Mary Jacoby, "Ford Says Glitzy New `R-TV' Can Stay on Air, As Long as It's Not Broadcast Outside Senate," *Roll Call,* February 7, 1994, 12.
43. *The Hill,* March 8, 1995, 15.
44. *Washington Post,* April 24, 1995, A4.
45. Norman J. Ornstein, "If Congress Played a Better Host to Guests, Maybe It Would Improve a Crummy Image," *Roll Call,* March 31, 1994, 15.
46. *Congressional Record,* March 25, 1994, S4025.
47. Quoted in *The Mass Media and Politics,* ed. Mammes F. Fixx (New York: Arno Press, 1972), ix.
48. For a valuable discussion of constituent pressures, see David Mayhew, *The Electoral Connection* (New Haven: Yale University Press, 1974).
49. David Hosansky, "Lugar's Farm Plan Poses Test For Fellow Republicans," *Congressional Quarterly Weekly Report,* April 29, 1995, 1167-1170.
50. Testimony of Walter F. Mondale, Hearing before the Joint Commmittee on the Organization of Congress, July 1, 1993, 33.
51. Stephen Engelberg, "100 Days of Dreams Come True for Lobbyists in Congress," *New York Times,* April 14, 1995, A12.
52. Alice Love, "The Age of CyberLobbying," *Roll Call,* March 13, 1995, 3.
53. John P. Heinz, et al., *The Hollow Core: Private Interests in National Policy Making* (Cambridge, Mass.:Harvard University Press, 1993), 391. Also see Allan J. Cigler and Burdett A. Loomis, *Interest Group Politics,* 3d ed. (Washington, D.C.: CQ Press, 1991).
54. Eben Shapiro and Rick Wartzman, "Tobacco Lobby Finds Its Influence Waning As Health Issue Grows," *Wall Street Journal,* March 24, 1994, A1.
55. *U.S. News & World Report,* August 11, 1980, 24.
56. Deborah Kalb, "Georgia delegation polarized by race, politics," *The Hill,* May 10, 1995, 4.
57. See David W. Rohde, *Parties and Leaders in the Postreform House* (Chicago: University of Chicago Press, 1991).
58. *New York Times,* March 7, 1995, 14.
59. Quoted in *National Journal,* June 22, 1985, 1459.

CHAPTER 3

The Congressional Budget Process

The framers of the Constitution deliberately lodged the power of the purse in Congress because it is the branch of government closest to the people. The president, of course, exercises significant fiscal authority by using his constitutional power to veto measures (including money bills), his statutory responsibility under the Budget and Accounting Act of 1921 for preparing an annual national budget, and his wide-ranging influence on legislation. Only Congress, however, can constitutionally authorize the government to collect taxes, borrow money, and make expenditures. The executive branch can spend funds only for the purposes and in the amounts specified by Congress. As Article I, Section 9, proclaims: "No Money shall be drawn from the Treasury, but in Consequence of Appropriations made by Law."

Although these words have not been amended since they were written into the Constitution, the budgetary context of the 1990s—a persistent climate of fiscal austerity, the ballooning of so-called mandatory spending programs, and the shrinking size of appropriations subject to annual controls—has led to severe stresses and strains for Congress's "power of the purse." The framers would wonder about the effectiveness of the congressional purse strings today when about 70 percent of federal expenditures are relatively uncontrollable under existing law. This means that the national government is required to spend money automatically for certain purposes because of laws previously enacted by Congress. "Uncontrollables" include interest on the public debt (the debt currently is nearly $5 trillion); entitlements (laws that require mandatory payments to all eligible individuals, such as Social Security, Medicare, and government pension programs); and contract obligations that must be paid when due (such as the Defense Department's procurement arrangements with various businesses).

One consequence of uncontrollables is clear. On the day the 104th Congress convened on January 4, 1995, it could have adjourned the session immediately, without passing any laws, and spending by the federal government for that year still would have been around $1 trillion. Further, spending each year thereafter would continue—and increase—because many federal programs are indexed to the cost of living. In short, large portions of the federal budget operate on "automatic pilot." Congress, of course, can convert uncontrollables into controllables by changing the basic law that establishes governmental obligations and that authorizes automatic funding without regular legislative review. (There are different degrees of controllability, however. Interest on the national debt and the interest rates to finance that debt are largely beyond Congress's control.) But there are serious political risks for members who want to subject uncontrollables to annual budgetary scrutiny. The elderly, for example, are sensitive to any changes in Social Security and have the clout to quickly mobilize against legislators who arouse their ire.

Congress chooses to place programs in the uncontrollable category for a variety of reasons. Stability, certainty, and preferred status are among the values that accrue to such programs. Retired persons, for instance, would have "to live under a great deal of financial uncertainty" if Congress subjected Social Security to annual review.[1] Budgetary decisions of Congress profoundly affect the taxpaying electorate, the national and international economy, and the volume and variety of federal programs and activities. The federal budget itself reflects the president's and Congress's choices among competing national priorities and identifies where the nation has been, where it is now, and where the administration plans to make future fiscal as well as policy commitments. Thus the nation's budget is both an economic and a political document.

It is hardly surprising that Congress devotes a large percentage of its time to spending and taxing issues. This is particularly true during periods of fiscal scarcity and economic hardship, when the pressure and competition for funds are greatest. And it has been especially the case in the mid-1990s. Republicans controlled Congress for the first time since 1953, and they promised to produce a balanced budget by 2002. (The national budget was last in balance—with revenues matching spending—in 1969.)

In broad terms, federal budgeting is composed of four main phases (see Figure 3-1):

1. Preparation and submission of the budget by the president to Congress.
2. Congressional action on the president's budget proposals.
3. Execution of budget-related laws by federal departments and agencies.
4. Audits of agency spending.

The first and third steps are controlled primarily by the executive branch; the fourth is conducted largely by the General Accounting Office (GAO), a legislative support agency of Congress. The focus of this chapter is on the second stage, the basic elements and features of Congress's budgetary process. The first part of the chapter examines traditional procedures; the second discusses exceptions to the routine.

FIGURE 3-1 The Budget Process

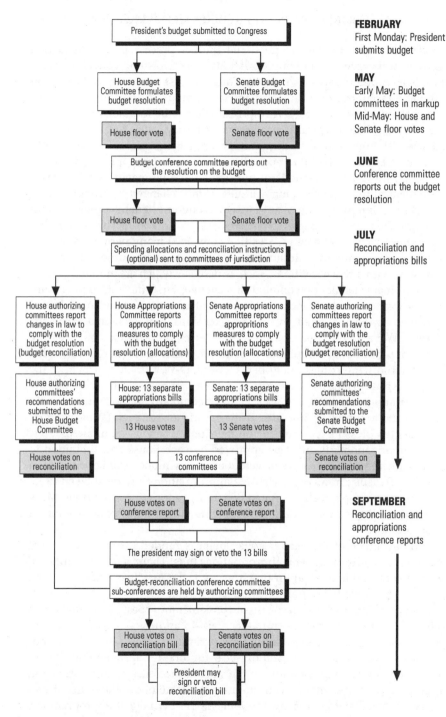

President's budget submitted to Congress

House Budget Committee formulates budget resolution

Senate Budget Committee formulates budget resolution

House floor vote

Senate floor vote

Budget conference committee reports out the resolution on the budget

House floor vote

Senate floor vote

Spending allocations and reconciliation instructions (optional) sent to committees of jurisdiction

House authorizing committees report changes in law to comply with the budget resolution (budget reconciliation)

House Appropriations Committee reports appropriations measures to comply with the budget resolution (allocations)

Senate Appropriations Committee reports appropriations measures to comply with the budget resolution (allocations)

Senate authorizing committees report changes in law to comply with the budget resolution (budget reconciliation)

House authorizing committees' recommendations submitted to the House Budget Committee

House: 13 separate appropriations bills

Senate: 13 separate appropriations bills

Senate authorizing committees' recommendations submitted to the Senate Budget Committee

House votes on reconciliation

13 House votes

13 Senate votes

Senate votes on reconciliation

13 conference committees

House votes on conference report

Senate votes on conference report

The president may sign or veto the 13 bills

Budget-reconciliation conference committee sub-conferences are held by authorizing committees

House votes on reconciliation bill

Senate votes on reconciliation bill

President may sign or veto reconciliation bill

FEBRUARY
First Monday: President submits budget

MAY
Early May: Budget committees in markup
Mid-May: House and Senate floor votes

JUNE
Conference committee reports out the budget resolution

JULY
Reconciliation and appropriations bills

SEPTEMBER
Reconciliation and appropriations conference reports

Source: Congressional Quarterly Weekly Report, May 13, 1995, 1305.

AUTHORIZATION-APPROPRIATIONS PROCESS

Fundamental to the congressional budget process is the distinction between authorizations and appropriations. This two-step, sequential procedure is intended to work as follows. Congress first passes an authorization bill that establishes or continues an agency or program and provides it with the legal authority to operate. Authorizations may be for one or more years, and such legislation typically recommends funding levels for programs and agencies. The bills also include statutory language (such as "hereby authorized to be appropriated") that permits the enactment of appropriations.

Until the 1950s, most federal programs were permanently authorized. Permanent authorizations remain in effect until changed by Congress and provide continuing statutory authority for ongoing federal programs and agencies. This situation began to change after World War II. The authorizing committees won enactment of laws that converted many permanent authorizations into temporary authorizations. (Today, most authorizations are multiyear with a few exceptions, such as defense, which are annual.)

Two major factors precipitated this change. First, the authorizing committees wanted greater control and oversight of executive and presidential activities, especially given interbranch tensions that stemmed from the Vietnam War and Watergate. Second, short-term authorizations put pressure on the appropriating committees to fund programs at levels recommended by the authorizing panels. As Robert C. Byrd, D-W.V., then chairman of the Senate Appropriations Committee, noted: "Those who criticize the Appropriations Committee so loudly and perennially for spending, should turn off the authorizing faucet. . . . [T]he enactment of each [authorization] increases the pressures for funding on the Appropriations Committee."[2]

Authorization bills must be approved by each house and submitted to the president for his signature or veto. Before any money can be withdrawn from the Treasury, however, a separate appropriations law must be enacted. "I think most people realize," stated Senate Appropriations Chairman Mark O. Hatfield, R-Ore., that an authorization "is only a hunting license for an appropriation."[3]

Today, much of the federal government is funded through the annual enactment of thirteen general appropriations bills. There is no constitutional requirement for annual appropriations, but the practice since the First Congress has been to appropriate for a single year.

Appropriations bills are of three fundamental types: (1) annual—also called regular or general; (2) supplemental—to address unexpected contingencies, such as emergency funding for natural disasters; and (3) continuing—to provide stop-gap or even full-year funding for agencies that did not receive an annual appropriation by the start of the fiscal year. A permanent appropriation makes monies continuously available under the terms of previously enacted statutes. Many entitlements are permanent appropriations;

some, such as food stamps and veterans pensions, are called "appropriated entitlements" because they are funded by annual appropriations. However, if the amount appropriated annually is not sufficient to provide the entitlements stipulated in law, Congress must meet the shortfall with a supplemental appropriation. About one-half of federal spending each year is subject to the congressional authorization-appropriations process. The other half gets its legal basis from laws that provide spending authority automatically, such as the entitlement programs just referred to. As a chairman of the House Appropriations Committee pointed out:

> [M]any people don't know that only about one-half of all Federal spending goes through the annual appropriations process. The remainder is mandatory or entitlement spending and interest on the debt. And even though one-half of all spending is appropriated—only 35 percent of the total is truly discretionary. [Virtually all activities of the federal government, such as all housing programs, all foreign aid, all national parks, and all research and development programs, are funded by discretionary appropriations.] The other 15 percent that is appropriated consists of appropriated entitlements [such as unemployment compensation and veterans' pensions] that we cannot easily adjust without changing the authorizing legislation.[4]

Appropriations approved by Congress provide "budget authority"; this allows government agencies to make financial commitments, up to a specified amount, that eventually result in the spending of dollars. As one budget analyst explains it:

> Congress does not directly control the level of federal spending that will occur in a particular year. Rather, it grants the executive branch authority (referred to as *budget authority*) to enter into *obligations*, which are legally binding agreements with suppliers of goods or services or with a beneficiary. When those obligations come due, the Treasury Department issues a payment. The amount of payments, called *outlays*, over an accounting period called the fiscal year (running from October 1 to September 30) equals federal expenditures for that fiscal year. Federal spending (outlays) in any given year, therefore, results from the spending authority (budget authority) granted by Congress in the current and in prior fiscal years.[5]

As a House member once said, "Budget authority is permission to spend; outlays are actual spending."[6] To state it differently, budget authority occurs when you put money in your checking account; budget outlays take place when you write a check.

The conversion of budget authority to budget outlays depends on a variety of factors, including the character of the program or activity. Budget authority granted annually to pay federal salaries is typically converted to budget outlays that same year. To build a highway takes many years. Budget authority, as a result, is converted to budget outlays at a variable rate over several years as highway planning costs give way to actual construction costs. Lawmakers require both figures so they can assess the projected total cost of a multiyear program or project compared with what will be spent on it annually.

Legislators are mindful of budget authority figures for these—rather than the outlay numbers—are the better predictors of an agency's growth or decline. Outlays, however, are reflected in each year's national deficit levels. With the escalation of annual deficits from about $75 billion at the start of the 1980s into the $200 billion range throughout that decade and into the 1990s, outlays have loomed large in legislative-executive efforts to constrain federal spending.

AUTHORIZING AND APPROPRIATING COMMITTEES

Whether agencies receive all the budget authority they request depends in part on the recommendations of the authorizing and appropriating committees. Each chamber has authorizing committees (Agriculture, Banking, Commerce, Small Business, and many others), which have responsibilities that differ from those of the two appropriating committees—the House and Senate Appropriations committees. The authorizing committees are the policy-making centers on Capitol Hill. As the substantive legislative panels, they propose solutions to public problems and advocate what they believe to be the necessary level of appropriations for new and existing federal programs.

The two Appropriations committees and their thirteen subcommittees have the job of recommending how much federal agencies and programs will receive in relation to available fiscal resources and economic conditions. In addition to the thirteen annual appropriation bills there are several (usually two) supplemental appropriations measures to meet unexpected contingencies, such as funding for emergencies. Each annual or regular appropriations measure is considered by a comparable pair of House and Senate Appropriations subcommittees (agriculture, defense, transportation, and so on). The twenty-six Appropriations subcommittee chairs are collectively known in their respective chambers as the "College of Cardinals" because of their large influence over spending issues.

For each program and agency subject to the annual appropriations process, these committees have three main options: (1) provide all the funds recommended in the previously approved authorization bill, (2) propose reductions in the amounts already authorized, or (3) refuse to provide any funds.[7] It is important to remember that a newspaper headline declaring that Congress has just authorized, for example, a new $3 billion antidrug program means that the program officially exists on paper. It still lacks money to operate until it receives an appropriation, and even then the program might be appropriated only half the amount authorized. In the fiscally austere 1990s, said David R. Obey, D-Wis., then the House Appropriations chairman, "We're going back to the days when authorizations are funded at 10, 20, 30 cents on the dollar."[8] Table 3-1 identifies some of the congressional committees or subcommittees that influence a particular agency's level of funding.

TABLE 3–1 Key Participants in Agency Funding

Federal Agency	Authorization Committees	Appropriations Committees
Park Service, U.S. Department of the Interior	House Resources; Senate Energy and Natural Resources	House Subcommittee on Resources; Senate Subcommittee on Energy and Natural Resources. Submitted to full committee in each house and reported.

To recapitulate, Congress requires authorizations to precede appropriations to ensure that substantive and financial issues are subject to separate and independent analysis. This procedure also permits almost every member and committee to participate in Congress's constitutional power of the purse. There are, to be sure, numerous exceptions to this two-step model, despite House and Senate rules that encourage separation of the authorization-appropriations stages. (See subsection "Exceptions to the Rules.")

CONSTITUTIONAL UNDERPINNING

The authorization-appropriation dichotomy is not required by the Constitution. Rather, it is a process that has been institutionalized by the rules of the House and Senate and in some cases by statute. Of the two steps, the appropriations stage is on firmer legal ground because it is rooted in the Constitution. An appropriations measure, which provides departments and agencies with authority to commit funds, may be approved even if the authorization bill has not been enacted. As long as "appropriations are enacted," wrote a budget scholar, "funds may be obligated by agencies, regardless of whether ... authorizations have been enacted."[9] Or, as one House Appropriations subcommittee chairman put it, "It's not the end of the world if we postpone the Clean Air Act or a tax measure. But the entire government will shut down if ... appropriations" are not enacted annually.[10]

Informally, Congress has employed this division of labor since the beginning of the Republic, as did the British Parliament in 1789 as well as the colonial legislatures. As Sen. William Plumer of New Hampshire noted in 1806: "Tis a good provision in the constitution of Maryland that prohibits their Legislature from adding any thing to an appropriation law."[11] Generally called "supply bills" in the early Congresses, appropriations measures had narrow purposes: to provide specific sums of money for fixed periods and stated objectives. Such bills were not to contain matters of policy.

There were exceptions to this informal rule even during the early days, but the practice of adding "riders," or extraneous policy provisos, to appropriations bills mushroomed in the 1830s. This practice often provoked sharp controversy in Congress and delayed the enactment of supply bills. "By 1835," wrote a parliamentary expert, the "delays caused by injecting legislation [policy] into these [appropriations] bills had become serious, and John Quincy Adams . . . suggested that they be stripped of everything save appropriations."[12] Two years later the House adopted a rule requiring authorization bills to precede appropriations. The Senate later followed suit.

SEPARATE POLICY AND FISCAL DECISIONS

Several major implications flow from Congress's efforts to separate policy from fiscal decision making—matters that usually are inextricably intertwined with each other. Among the major implications are flexibility, bicameral differences, and committee rivalries.

FLEXIBILITY. The authorization-appropriations rules, like almost all congressional rules, are not self-enforcing. Either chamber can choose to waive, ignore, or circumvent them or establish precedents and practices that obviate distinctions between the two. As one scholar has written:

> The real world of the legislative process differs considerably from the idealized model of the two-step authorization-appropriation procedure. Authorization bills contain appropriations, appropriation bills contain authorizations, and the order of their enactment is sometimes reversed. The Appropriations Committees, acting through various kinds of limitations, riders, and nonstatutory controls, are able to establish policy and act in a substantive manner. Authorization committees have considerable power to force the hand of the Appropriations Committees and, in some cases, even to appropriate.[13]

Recent Congresses, operating in a period of fiscal austerity, have witnessed an increase in unauthorized appropriations and in legislation in appropriations measures.

In short, there is flexibility in the authorization-appropriations procedure that allows it to accommodate stresses and strains. For example, a failure to enact authorization bills does not bring the appropriations process to a halt. The "must-pass" annual appropriations bills often become the vehicle for extending or revamping existing laws that did not make it through the authorization process. As Representative Obey stated:

> It seems to me what has happened in our system is that the authorization process has been jammed up many times, sometimes because of committee incompetence, sometimes because the issues are just . . . tough and we have issues that aren't resolvable over the short haul, and sometimes because the

TABLE 3-2 Authorization-Appropriations Rules Compared

House	Senate
No unauthorized appropriations are permitted except for public works in progress. The Appropriations Committee generally cannot report a general appropriations bill unless there is an authorization law.	Unauthorized appropriations are not permitted. There are exceptions: if the Senate has passed an authorization during that session; if an authorization is reported by any Senate standing committee, including Appropriations; or if an authorization is requested in the president's annual budget.
No legislation (policy) is permitted in an appropriations bill.	No legislation is permitted in an appropriations bill unless it is germane to the House-passed bill.
No appropriation is permitted in an authorization bill; floor amendments that propose appropriations are not in order in authorization bills.	There is no equivalent rule. By custom, the House initiates appropriations bills and objects to Senate efforts aimed at circumventing this arrangement.

White House has chosen to simply stiff the authorizing committee because they think they can get a better deal from us on appropriations.[14]

It is not uncommon for authorizers to ask appropriators to include policy proposals or legislation in annual appropriations bill.

BICAMERAL DIFFERENCES. Because the House and Senate are dissimilar, they have different rules governing the authorization-appropriations process. These differences are described in Table 3-2 and reflect each chamber's fundamental nature: the smaller Senate permits greater procedural flexibility than the larger House.

The dissimilar rules of the House and Senate affect each chamber's legislative behavior and policy deliberations. The Senate, for example, often gets off to a slower start on appropriations measures since, by tradition, it customarily waits for the House to originate those bills. Moreover, the multistage process creates numerous opportunities to shape issues. Policy debates may be resurrected again and again in different contexts in either chamber.

An issue of some concern to the House involves the committee assignment practices of the Senate. In the House, for both parties, service on the Appropriations Committee is, with very few exceptions, an exclusive assignment. Senators, by contrast, may serve simultaneously on both authorizing and appropriating committees. There even have been instances where the same senator chaired both the authorizing committee (or relevant subcommittee) and the comparable appropriations subcommittee. Fundamental bicameral imbalances are created, said former House Science chairman George E. Brown, Jr., D-Calif., when senators "are permitted to serve on both Committees. Inevitably, Members will prefer to legislate in appropriations bills (or the accompanying reports), which by their nature and by the rules of both Houses, are more protected from debate, amendment, and perfection than are corresponding authorization bills."[15] The committee's current chairman, Robert S. Walker, R-Pa., shares Brown's perspective.

> What we have seen happening is that, because the [Senate] appropriators find that it is easy to just throw everything into the appropriation bill, very often the authorizing bills simply don't get passed, and therefore authorization bills that pass the House are left sitting in the Senate. And we will sometimes go one, two, three, four years before we get an authorization bill passed in a very important policy area.[16]

In addition, members of House authorization committees often rail against Senate appropriators for invading their "turf" by including unauthorized language or policy provisos in appropriations conference reports. (See Chapter 9 on resolving House-Senate differences in legislation.) House authorizing chairmen, for instance, write the Rules Committee and urge that panel not to waive their right to raise points of order on the House floor against Senate-inserted provisions in conference reports that violate House rules.[17]

COMMITTEE RIVALRIES

Another consequence of the two-step system is that it breeds continuing conflict between the authorizing and appropriating committees. Predictably, the authorizing committees generally support high levels of spending for the programs they recommend and seek ways to bypass Appropriations Committee domination. The appropriating panels, on the other hand, often view themselves as "guardians of the purse." It is their job, they believe, to say no to many funding requests. There are occasions, however, when maximum funding is the preferred objective of the Appropriations committees.

The traditional tension between authorizers and appropriators was highlighted by a House jurisdictional disagreement between Transportation and Infrastructure Chairman Bud Shuster, R-Pa., and Appropriations Chairman Robert L. Livingston, R-La. Shuster's panel approved legislation to require designated revenues to go into a self-sustaining "trust fund" (federal funds that are collected and used for specific governmental purposes). The trust fund would be used exclusively for financing the construction and maintenance of highways, airports, inland waterways, and harbors. As one account noted:

> The Shuster plan would effectively do away with the present role of Livingston's Appropriations Committee in approving spending [for transportation projects]. Now transportation projects have to compete with other government spending programs for their share of the $540 billion in discretionary funds available to Livingston's committee.[18]

Exempting transportation projects from annual scrutiny by the appropriators forces the other discretionary programs to absorb deeper spending cuts if deficit-reduction targets are to be met.

More generally, authorizers devised ways to circumvent the annual appropriations process. These "backdoor" authorization measures (avoiding the appropriators' "front door") blur the distinction between authorizations and appropriations because backdoors permit spending by the federal government. Three common forms are (1) *borrowing authority* (a federal agency, for instance, is authorized by law to borrow specific sums of money from the Treasury or the public, through commercial channels, to build low-cost homes or make student loans); (2) *contract authority* (for example, a federal agency is statutorily permitted to enter into contractural agreements with private companies for the construction of municipal sewage treatment plants. Appropriations must be provided in the future to honor these commitments.) And, as mentioned earlier, (3) *entitlement authority* (federal programs such as Social Security, Medicare, and Medicaid that allow eligible recipients to be automatically entitled to federal payments). Entitlements (along with interest on the national debt) constitute the fastest growing parts of the federal budget and will be discussed later in this chapter. Unsurprisingly, appropriators often suggest that various entitlement programs be taken off "automatic pilot" and be subjected to annual appropriations review.

EXCEPTIONS TO THE RULES

There are many exceptions to the authorization-appropriations rules. For instance, the House rule that forbids legislation in any general appropriations bill explicitly permits such policy making if it is a retrenchment (reduction) and if it is "germane to the subject matter of the bill." The ostensible purpose of this rule (called the Holman rule after Rep. William S. Holman of Indiana, who formulated it in 1876) is to encourage economy in government. Over the years members seldom have used the Holman rule to make policy. Instead, they have relied heavily on "limitation" riders.

Legislative provisions find their way into appropriations bills notwithstanding the strictures of the rules—for instance, if no member raises a point of order against the practice or if either chamber waives its rules. The House by precedent also permits unauthorized programs to be included in continuing resolutions (see p. 69 for further discussion) that provide interim funding for agencies whose general appropriations bills have not been enacted by the start of the fiscal year.

Senate rules, unlike those for the House, grant wide leeway to appropriators to authorize projects, programs, or activities (see Table 3-2). "I'm not about to start hunkering down and running like a scared rabbit because somebody says it's got to be authorized," said Senator Byrd when he headed Appropriations. "If this committee wants to authorize demonstration grants, it has the authority."[19]

LIMITATION RIDERS. *Limitations* are provisions in general appropriations bills or floor amendments to those measures that prohibit the spending of funds for specific purposes. Always phrased in the negative ("None of the funds provided in this Act shall be used for . . . "), limitations are based on scores of House precedents that collectively uphold the position that because the House can refuse to appropriate funds for programs that have been authorized, it also can prohibit the use of funds for any part of a program or activity.

House members and staff aides may devote endless hours to carefully drafting provisions that make policy in the guise of limitations. For guidance they turn to the House rule book, which is replete with precedents that have interpreted permissible from impermissible limitations. There are three basic criteria. Limitations cannot (1) impose additional duties or burdens on executive branch officials, (2) interfere with these officials' discretionary authority, or (3) require officials to make judgments or determinations not required by existing law.

The 1977 antiabortion amendment remains a classic example of a limitation and the impact that procedure can exert on policy. The Labor-Health Education and Welfare (now Health and Human Services) appropriations bill for that year contained a limitation on the use of funds "to perform abortions except where the life of the mother would be endangered if the fetus were carried to term." A point of order was raised and sustained against that amendment on the ground that it was legislation in an appropriations bill. The limitation required officials in the executive branch to determine when the life of a pregnant woman would be endangered. The language then was amended to read: "None of the funds appropriated by this Act shall be used to pay for abortions or to promote or encourage abortions, except when a physician has certified the abortion is necessary to save the life of the mother." Again, a point of order was raised that the amendment was legislation in an appropriations bill. And again the chair ruled in favor of the parliamentary objection, this time on the ground that the federal government employed many physicians and that they would be required to make "life-deciding" judgments.

Finally, the sponsor of the proposal, Rep. Henry J. Hyde, R-Ill., said he had no choice but to offer the following language: "None of the funds appropriated under this Act shall be used to pay for abortions or to promote or encourage abortions." There was no point of order because the amendment required no judgments by executive officials. The Hyde amendment then was adopted.[20]

When the Labor-HEW bill, now containing the Hyde amendment, reached the Senate, Edward W. Brooke, R-Mass. (1967-1979), offered an amendment that permitted abortions "where the life of the mother would be endangered if the fetus were carried to term, or where medically necessary, or for the treatment of rape or incest." Barry Goldwater, R-Ariz. (1953-1965, 1969-1987), said the amendment was legislation in an appropriations bill and raised a point of order. The Senate has its own procedural devices to obviate such points of order, however, and Senator Brooke used them successfully on the abortion issue. He raised what is called a "question of germaneness" before the presiding officer had ruled on the Goldwater point of order.

DECIDING GERMANENESS QUESTIONS. Senate rules require that amendments be germane to general appropriations bills. And once the question of germaneness is raised, those rules require that the issue be submitted to the entire membership for resolution by majority vote and without debate. If the Senate decides that the proposed amendment is germane, the point of order automatically falls. In the abortion case described above, the Senate declared Brooke's amendment germane by a 74-21 vote. To be sure, in such situations senators typically vote on the policy issue and not on the procedural question. As Ted Stevens, R-Alaska, noted, Senate rules prohibit legislation on appropriations, but if senators raise the defense of germaneness on their amendments, "we will have a vote on germaneness, and that will be equivalent to adopting the amendment."[21] Technical objections, in short, can be waived to achieve preferred policy outcomes.

The House experienced a rapid increase in the number of limitation amendments—from eleven in 1965 to eighty-six in 1980. Many of those dealt with so-called social issues, particularly school busing, school prayer, and abortion. These controversial issues were repeatedly bottled up in the authorizing committees, and members wanting action on them turned increasingly to limitations as a vehicle to force House consideration. Frustrated by the sharp controversies and long delays these limitations were causing, the House changed its rules in 1983 to restrict the opportunities for members to offer limitation riders to appropriations bills.[22] The change authorized limitation amendments only if the motion to rise from the Committee of the Whole (see Chapter 5) was either rejected or not offered after the regular amendment process was completed on an appropriations bill.

When Republicans took control of the 104th Congress, they again changed House rules by allowing the majority leader or a designee to have

By THE BOOK AND . . .

In the June 30, 1993, debate over public funding of abortion, nothing was more important than knowledge of the complex parliamentary rules that govern House floor debate. In the end, the ace in the hole for Henry J. Hyde, R-Ill., an abortion opponent, was his knowledge of how many members would support his position and how to use an eighty-five-year-old precedent to make his measure meet House rules.

Going into floor action, abortion rights supporters wanted to strip language from the health and human services spending bill that would restrict federal funding for abortion; abortion opponents wanted to retain it.

Because the amendment was on an appropriations bill, abortion rights supporters had the edge: House rules prohibit "legislating on an appropriations bill," putting policy language into a bill that is supposed to deal only with money. The bill's section on abortion funding counted as legislation because it set out conditions under which the government could pay for abortions.

At the outset, abortion supporters struck the abortion funding section from the bill on the grounds that it was legislating on a spending bill. The bill then had no restrictions on the use of federal funds to pay for abortions through Medicaid, the federal-state health insurance program for the poor.

The challenge at this point for Hyde was to find a way to get the restrictive language back into the bill without "legislating." Because Hyde's amendment set conditions for funding, under House rules it was considered a "disfavored" form of amendment. It could not be offered until lawmakers—meeting as the Committee of the Whole, where the House handles most amendments—finished all other amendments and had a chance to "report" the bill to the House for final action.

BOX 3-1

precedence in offering the motion to rise. "The intent of the new rule is to permit the offering of limitation amendments at the end of the reading [for amendment], subject only to a motion to rise offered by the majority leader or a designee."[23] The effect of this change is to enhance the majority leadership's control over the offering of limitation amendments.

Certain limitations continue to arouse substantive and procedural controversy. Sixteen years after the initial Hyde amendment, the House once

. . . FOR THE BOOKS

If the Committee of the Whole defeated the motion to rise and report the bill, then Hyde would be permitted to offer his amendment. The committee defeated the motion to rise 190-244.

Hyde's next obstacle was to find a way to word his amendment to avoid the charge that it was legislating on an appropriations bill. To do that, he drafted the amendment according to a 1908 precedent that allows an amendment to set conditions on the use of funds if it is worded in the passive voice—and therefore doe not require federal officials to do anything. His amendment read:

> None of the funds appropriated under this act shall be expended for any abortion except when it is made known to the federal entity or official . . . that such procedure is necessary to save the life of the mother, or that the pregnancy is the result of an act of rape or incest.

The key words were "made known." This construction passes the "legislating" test because it does not impose new duties on the federal officials named in the bill. A similar construction has been used a few times in recent years. In 1988 Robert S. Walker, R-Pa., used it to attach an amendment about drug-free workplaces to the energy and water development appropriations bill.

When Hyde offered his amendment, abortion-rights members said they were advised that it would not be struck on parliamentary grounds because of the precedents.

Source: Adapted from *Congressional Quarterly Weekly Report*, July 3, 1993, 1736.

again became embroiled in this issue. Even with a political climate thought to be more supportive of abortion rights, given the influx after the November 1992 elections of twenty-three more women and sixteen more minority representatives as well as a new president, the Hyde amendment still prevailed in the House after artful parliamentary moves (see Box 3-1).

The House has other rules with fiscal implications worth noting. Among them is the stricture that no committee except Ways and Means may report tax or tariff proposals. This rule was first used on October 27, 1983, when Dan Rostenkowski, D-Ill., then Ways and Means chair, raised a point of order against a proposition in a general appropriations bill that concerned the duty-free entry of certain products from the Caribbean countries. The chair sustained the point of order by ruling that the provision "is a tariff measure in violation" of House rules. Just as authorizing committees may not report appropriations, appropriating and authorizing panels may not report tax and tariff proposals.

A controversial rule adopted at the start of the GOP-controlled 104th Congress requires a three-fifths (rather than a simple majority) vote to pass measures containing an income tax rate increase. The objective is to make it difficult to pass tax hike legislation. As House Rules Chairman Gerald Solomon, R-N.Y., said: "The three-fifths majority vote to raise taxes will stand as a hindrance to any Democratic attempt to foist more taxes on the American people."[24] To promote public accountability, a related rules change requires an automatic roll call vote on final passage of bills and conference reports that raise taxes (or make appropriations).

House Democrats brought suit in federal court challenging the rule's constitutionality on the ground that except in those seven instances where the Constitution requires a supermajority vote (such as overturning presidential vetoes) a majority of a quorum is sufficient to pass legislation.[25] House Democrats also protested this rules change by urging the Speaker to repeal it, challenging it on the floor, and raising points of order against some GOP revenue proposals on the ground that they constitute a "phantom tax" on the public.[26]

House Republicans in the 104th Congress also temporarily suspended a rule put in place during the 96th Congress. Called the "Gephardt Rule," after Democratic leader Richard A. Gephardt, Mo., its purpose is to provide for the automatic passage (without a separate vote) of legislation raising the national debt ceiling when the House adopts the concurrent budget resolution. Traditionally, votes to raise the debt ceiling are politically dangerous, because challengers can characterize incumbents as "out-of-control spenders" if they vote for the debt-raising legislation. This is "must-pass" legislation. Republicans have said they may want to "Christmas tree" it (adding various extraneous measures) with GOP bills that President Clinton might veto. "The president knows if he doesn't sign [the debt-ceiling increase], the government shuts down," said House Majority Whip Tom DeLay, R-Texas. "Republicans are very anxious to raise the ceiling if we have a lot of good things to attach to it."[27]

PRELUDE TO BUDGET REFORM

Congress's continuing struggle to control expenditures precipitated a comprehensive overhaul of its budgetary process. Titled the Congressional

Budget and Impoundment Control Act of 1974 (CBA), the enactment came about largely for three reasons. First, the congressional Appropriations committees gradually lost control of budget expenditures as the legislative, or authorizing, committees turned to backdoor financing techniques to accomplish their policy objectives. The result was that Congress lacked a central body to coordinate budgetary decisions, relate governmental revenue to expenditures, or calculate the effect of individual spending actions on the national economy. National fiscal policy reflected whatever emerged from Congress's excessively fragmented budget process. Second, the annual deficit had been on an upward spiral and many lawmakers believed that a revamped budgetary process would enable Congress to gain better control of fiscal decisions.

Finally, presidents sometimes took advantage of Congress's piecemeal process. President Richard Nixon, in particular, clashed with Congress over national spending priorities and frequently impounded (refused to spend) monies for programs initiated by Democrats in Congress. Conflict raged between the Nixon White House and Congress over the president's impoundment of appropriated funds. "Far from administrative routine,"wrote a budget scholar, "Nixon's impoundments in late 1972 and 1973 were designed to rewrite national policy at the expense of congressional power and intent."[28]

The combination of these three factors, along with growing public concern about the state of the national economy, led to enactment of the landmark 1974 CBA. That act established a congressional budget process that encouraged coordination and centralization. However, it did not institute this fiscal reorganization by abolishing the traditional authorization-appropriations process. Such an attempt would have pitted the most powerful committees and members against one another and jeopardized any chance of realizing substantive budgetary changes. Instead, Congress added another budget layer to "the existing revenue and appropriations process" of the House and Senate.[29] In brief, the act was a "shotgun marriage"—an effort to accommodate Congress's chronic fragmentation with its felt need for budgetary integration.

THE 1974 BUDGET ACT

Passage of the 1974 budget act had a major institutional and procedural effect on the legislative branch. Not unexpectedly, many of the act's original requirements have been modified in response to new developments. More than two decades later it is still worthwhile to describe the main features of the act, because they remain generally intact—the institutional entities, the timetable for budget decisions, the concurrent budget resolution, controls on backdoors and impoundments, reconciliation and the Byrd rules, and enforcement of the budget resolution.

NEW ENTITIES

The budget act created three new entities: the House Budget Committee, the Senate Budget Committee, and the Congressional Budget Office (CBO). The two budget committees have essentially the same functions, which include (1) preparing annually a concurrent budget resolution, (2) reviewing the impact of existing or proposed legislation on federal expenditures, (3) overseeing the Congressional Budget Office, and (4) monitoring throughout the year the revenue and spending actions of the House and Senate. The last function listed here is called "scorekeeping" and is shared with the CBO.

The two panels, however, are constituted differently. The House Budget Committee is required to have a rotating membership: most members may not serve more than eight years during a period of six consecutive Congresses. The committee must be composed of members drawn mainly from other standing committees, including five each from Appropriations and Ways and Means, and a leadership member from each of the two parties. While rotation allows many lawmakers over time to serve on this panel, it also has the effect of inhibiting cohesion (members' loyalty is to other committees), thus making it difficult at times for committee members to reach consensus on issues. Further, although the jurisdiction of the House Budget Committee was expanded in 1995 to include budget legislation generally and measures affecting budget totals and controls over the federal budget, the committee's fundamental task remains focused on one critical, visible, and often sharply partisan function: producing a budget resolution that reflects differing Democratic and Republican views on the role and priorities of the national government.

By contrast, the Senate Budget Committee has no restrictions on tenure, nor are its members required to come from other designated committees. A consequence of the membership difference is that key career-oriented senators are sometimes more knowledgeable about budgetary matters than their House Budget counterparts and, therefore, are better equipped to shape conference committee deliberations to their own liking. Moreover, the Senate Budget Committee "has standing on a par with any other committee in the institution, the result being more centralized budget control in the Senate" compared with the House.[30] The Congressional Budget Office is Congress's principal informational and analytical resource for budget, tax, and spending proposals. With about two hundred thirty aides, CBO performs important services for the House and Senate Budget committees and other congressional panels.

> Scoring bills for their budgetary impact . . . , making economic and budget projections, analyzing program and policy issues affecting the budget and—since 1979—printing a widely distributed book of options for reducing the deficit.[31]

CBO, for example, played a vital and highly visible role in the congressional debate on President and Mrs. Clinton's proposal to curtail the rising costs of health care. CBO's cost estimates indicated that the "Clinton plan would increase Federal budget deficits through the year 2000, rather than reducing them as the President had asserted."[32] CBO's cost estimates also angered congressional Republicans, who promised the citizenry that they would balance the budget by the year 2002. A proposed GOP change to Medicare designed to save millions of dollars was called unrealistic by CBO's director (who serves a four-year term). In response, House Budget Chairman John R. Kasich, R-Ohio, declared: "I think they have some very stupid ways of doing things."[33] With budgetary issues dominating much Capitol Hill activity, CBO's role in "scoring" the fiscal impact of proposals is especially significant.

TIMETABLE

To promote order and coordination in the budget process, Congress established a budgetary schedule as shown in Figure 3-1. The timetable has been periodically changed, and it is quite common for Congress to miss some of the target dates. For example, Congress is supposed to enact its concurrent budget resolution on or before April 15 of each year, but it is not uncommon for Congress to miss this deadline. "In fact," noted Senator Byrd, "Congress has met the deadline only three times since enactment of the 1974 Budget Act; namely for fiscal years 1976, 1977, and 1994."[34] Disagreements over priorities and between the chambers, parties, and branches are among the considerations that account for the missed deadlines. In 1995, because Congress focused initially only on legislation associated with the Contract with America, action on the budget resolution was delayed in each chamber until mid-May.

It is worth noting that whenever Congress cannot complete action on one or more of the thirteen regular appropriations bills by the start of the fiscal year, it provides temporary funding for the affected federal agencies through a joint resolution called a *continuing resolution* or a *continuing appropriation*. Traditionally, continuing resolutions were employed to keep a few government agencies in operation for short periods, typically one to three months. Continuing resolutions, however, have sometimes become major policy-making instruments of massive size and scope. In 1986 and 1987, for example, Congress packaged all thirteen regular appropriations bills into continuing resolutions. Such measures are often called "megabills"; they authorize and appropriate money to operate the federal government and make national policy in scores of diverse areas.

CONCURRENT BUDGET RESOLUTION

The core of Congress's annual budget process centers on the adoption of a *concurrent budget resolution*. This measure is formulated by the Budget committees and is composed of two basic parts. The first deals with fiscal aggregates: total federal spending (budget authority and outlays), total federal revenue, and the public debt (or surplus) for the upcoming fiscal year (October 1 through September 30). (The budget resolution also sets multiyear targets for these fiscal aggregates.) The second part subdivides the spending aggregates into twenty functional categories, such as national defense, energy, and agriculture. This fiscal blueprint, in brief, establishes the context of congressional budgeting; guides the budgetary actions of the authorizing, appropriating, and taxing committees; and represents Congress's spending priorities.

The 1974 act originally required the adoption of at least two concurrent budget resolutions—one in the spring (by May 15) that served as a guidepost or target for committee actions and one in the fall (by September 15) that was binding on Congress. *Reconciliation* legislation was to follow if Congress's individual fiscal decisions—made during the rest of spring, summer, and early autumn—did not match the budgetary totals agreed to in the second budget resolution. Reconciliation directed appropriate committees to report additional savings or revenues to meet the fiscal requirements of the second resolution. Congress informally abandoned the second resolution in the early 1980s when it became clear that the first was the fundamental vehicle of congressional budgeting. This informal change was later embodied in law (now April 15 for passage of the budget resolution) when Congress passed a significant revision of the 1974 act—the Balanced Budget and Emergency Deficit Reduction Act of 1985 (or Gramm-Rudman-Hollings, after the measure's sponsors). Discussion of Gramm-Rudman-Hollings will follow.

Because of its importance to congressional policy making, the budget resolution is considered in the House and Senate under special procedures that expedite its consideration. In the House, the budget resolution is considered under a "rule" issued by the Rules Committee that lays out the conditions for debating and amending the measure. Since the early 1980s, when Democrats controlled the House, the rule specified a "king-of-the-hill" procedure (see Chapter 5) for considering major amendments to the budget resolution. When Republicans took control of the House in the mid-1990s, they followed the normal amendment process.

For instance, in 1995 the GOP-controlled Rules Committee permitted House action on several alternative budget plans with the added requirement that each had to balance the budget by the year 2002 to be eligible for floor consideration. First to be acted upon was a plan put forward by conservative Democrats, then another by a group of Republicans, and then a budget drafted by the Congressional Black Caucus. Rules Chairman Solomon pointed out that the order of consideration is important, "because if any one of these pass, then the debate immediately ceases and we go right to final passage."[35] (Parliamentary principles stipulate that it is not in order to re-amend something that has already been amended. A substitute budget plan, if adopted, would amend the entire text of the concurrent budget resolution leaving nothing left to further amend.) In the end, the House rejected all three fiscal alternatives and agreed to the GOP-crafted budget blueprint that promised a balanced budget by the year 2002 and drastically cut back on the size of government (recommending the elimination of 3 cabinet departments, 13 agencies, 284 programs, and 60 commissions).[36]

Senate floor procedure is regulated by the statutory requirements of the 1974 act and unanimous consent agreements (see Chapter 8) negotiated by the party leadership. Significantly, the 1974 act changed traditional Senate procedures in two fundamental ways. First, budget resolutions carry a fifty-hour statutory debate limitation (twenty hours for reconciliation bills), which means that they cannot be filibustered to death. Second, the 1974 act imposes a germaneness (somewhat akin to a relevancy) requirement on amendments to budget resolutions. The act permits the germaneness standard to be set aside, but it requires at least sixty votes, rather than a simple majority, to obtain the waiver. The Senate, unlike the House, has no general germaneness rule.

The budget resolution is not submitted to the president. It is a concurrent resolution approved by both houses and is intended as an internal guide for Congress. Hence, it cannot be vetoed; nor does it carry legal effect. (Some lawmakers want to amend the 1974 Budget Act and make the concurrent resolution a legally binding joint resolution, thus requiring presidential involvement in formulating the budget plan.) Presidents, of course, may veto tax or appropriations bills that follow the guidelines established in the budget resolutions.

To assemble the resolution, the budget panels employ several sources: annual "views and estimates" reports from the other standing committees outlining each panel's fiscal plans for programs under its jurisdiction; committee hearings; the president's annual budget; informal consultations with members and staff; CBO analyses; and assessments of what the national interest and the economy require.

When the House and Senate pass budget resolutions that contain different aggregate and functional totals, which is normal practice, the disagreements usually have to be resolved by a conference committee. The conferees prepare a report that provides a "bank account" for the various House and Senate committees. This account distributes the total agreed-upon spending for the year among twenty functional categories.

This allocation procedure, called a "budget crosswalk," involves two steps. First, section 302a of the 1974 budget act (now called section 602a under the act as amended by Gramm-Rudman-Hollings) requires the joint statement that accompanies the conference report to divide the budget totals among the House and Senate committees with budgetary jurisdiction for the programs reflected in the various functional categories. The crosswalk is necessary because Congress chooses to employ functional category designations developed by the White House's Office of Management and Budget. These designations do not correspond exactly to many House and Senate committees, with their overlapping jurisdictions.

In the second step, under section 302b (now 602b), the House and Senate committees subdivide their spending allocations among the appropriate subcommittees or programs. (If the concurrent budget resolution is not passed by the required April 15 date, then to avoid delays in the appropriations process the allocation to committees is based on the discretionary spending amounts included in the president's budget.) The suballocations are reported by the committees to their respective chambers and they are enforceable by members raising points of order against bills that exceed a committee's total allocation and the suballocations assigned its subcommittees. And in the Senate, such points of order can be overturned only by a 60 percent supermajority vote.

The whole section 602b process is important because it is employed by committees and members to ensure compliance with the financial totals specified in the budget resolution. Further, the suballocation process among the thirteen Appropriations subcommittees in each chamber is crucial in influencing funding for various policy priorities. Rather little is known about how the Appropriations committees actually divide their "spending pie" among the subunits. "The allocation of the [discretionary] federal budget among the thirteen Appropriations subcommittees is the most closed, the least understood, and the most consequential annual process within the Congress," wrote a congressional budget analyst.[37] No doubt hard bargaining permeates the activities of the "college of cardinals" as each subcommittee chair strives to maximize his or her share of spending authority.

In an unprecedented move before the Democrats lost control of Congress, House Appropriations Chairman Obey held a bipartisan caucus of committee members to discuss the 602b subcommittee allocation process. "It's the first time we've ever been called in for a 602b discussion—usually we're just presented with the numbers," said C. W. Bill Young, R-Fla., the third-ranking Republican on Appropriations.[38] The move was part of Obey's effort to promote bipartisanship and to remove some of the secrecy that surrounds committee deliberations. In another unprecedented development, the committee even issued a press release that publicly announced the allocations among the various subcommittees. Previously, reporters "had to convince a cardinal to leak the numbers to them."[39] Livingston, Obey's successor as chairman, went even further when he appointed Appropriations' first-ever "communications director" to deal with the media and journalists and to publicize the panel's work.[40]

RECONCILIATION

Reconciliation is an important procedure that enables Congress to implement its comprehensive fiscal policy (as reflected in the budget resolution) by requiring House and Senate authorizing committees to comply with the entitlement, revenue, and deficit reduction targets specified in the budget resolution. The two-step process is designed to reconcile the parts with the whole or, put differently, to bring existing law into conformity with the current budget resolutions. In practice, reconciliation is used to reduce spending, primarily through entitlement savings, and to increase revenues (or to accomodate tax cuts provided sufficient savings are derived from reductions). It does not address funding that is established in annual appropriations bills. The Appropriations committees are bound by the discretionary spending limits set forth in the budget resolution.

Although it was intended to be employed at the end of Congress's budget cycle, the reconciliation procedure has been moved since 1980 to the front of the cycle, where it has proved to be an effective device for making budgetary savings.

The first step in reconciliation calls for congressional approval of a budget resolution that instructs House and Senate committees to report legislation making cuts in spending (and/or increases in revenue) on programs and agency operations by a certain date. The panels' recommended budget savings, which are supposed to meet or exceed the amounts designated for each committee in the resolution, are transmitted to the respective House and Senate Budget committees. The second step involves the packaging of the recommendations into an omnibus reconciliation bill, followed by floor action in each chamber. The Budget committees cannot make substantive changes in the savings proposals received from each instructed committee.

In 1981 President Ronald Reagan persuaded Congress to employ reconciliation to achieve massive cuts in domestic programs (totaling about $130 billion over three years). Never before had reconciliation been employed on such a grand scale. The entire two-step process was put on a "fast track" that short-circuited regular legislative procedures. A highly charged atmosphere produced a legislative result, wrote Howard H. Baker, Jr., R-Tenn., then Senate majority leader, "that would have been impossible to achieve if each committee had reported an individual bill on subject matter solely within its jurisdiction."[41] Reconciliation forced nearly all House and Senate committees to make unwanted cuts in programs under their jurisdiction.

The irony was that Congress's budget process, designed in 1974 to advance and reassert the legislative branch's power of the purse, was captured by the White House in 1981 and used to achieve President Reagan's objectives. On the other hand, reconciliation can be used by either branch or party provided they have the votes to implement their objectives. In 1995, when congressional Republicans seized the policy initiative from President Clinton, reconciliation was employed to eliminate scores of governmental entities and programs, to scale back the size of others, and to chart a GOP course toward a smaller government. In sum, reconciliation's proven effectiveness in compelling fiscal retrenchment has made it an important and regular part of the budget process. And like the budget resolution, reconciliation legislation is accorded procedural protections in the Senate against nongermane amendments and filibusters (there is a debate limit of twenty hours).

THE BYRD RULE

The *Byrd Rule,* named after Senator Byrd of West Virginia, fundamentally states that reconciliation provisions must reduce the deficit. Because reconciliation requires committees with policy-making responsibilities—the tax-writing and authorizing committees—either to raise revenues or cut mandatory spending programs, these panels sometimes report policy provisions that have no bearing on reducing the deficit, and which may even increase its size. Reconciliation has been used, for example, to expand Medicaid coverage, reinstate the broadcast fairness doctrine, and provide funds for the trade adjustment assistance program. Such provisions are inserted in reconciliation bills in part "because the budget committees are specifically prohibited from making any substantive changes in the recommendations from each committee."[42]

The addition of extraneous matter to reconciliation bills has proven to be more of a problem in the Senate than in the House. The House has the Rules Committee (see Chapter 5) which can, for example, permit members to offer motions to strike extraneous matter from these bills. In the Senate, reconciliation measures are taken up, as noted earlier, under procedures that limit the normally unfettered debate and amendment process. Committees, as a result, may deliberately add new initiatives to reconciliation bills to gain procedural protections for proposals that if taken up separately would be subjected to unlimited debate and amendment, including the offering of nongermane amendments.

The Byrd Rule's objective, then, is to exclude extraneous (unrelated to deficit reduction) matter in reconciliation bills. To maximize its potency, the rule can be waived only by a three-fifths vote of the Senate; similarly, it takes sixty votes to overturn a ruling of the Senate's presiding officer that a provision in a reconciliation bill (or a floor amendment to it) is extraneous. What is extraneous, however, is not always easy to determine. The Senate has evolved a dozen criteria for making that evaluation. For instance, a provision is considered extraneous if it is outside the jurisdiction of the committee reporting it or if the provision causes the reporting committee to miss its deficit target. On the other hand, a provision is not extraneous, for example, if it results not in immediate spending cuts or revenue increases but does so in future fiscal years.

> The application of the [Byrd] rule can be tortuous. Take food stamps, for example. The House approved $7.3 billion in extra spending for food stamps in its reconciliation bill; the Senate did not. Conferees . . . agreed to include up to the House amount in the conference report, but [Senate]

Republicans hope to strip it out, arguing that it violates the Byrd rule because it would force the [Senate Agriculture] committee to miss its deficit-cutting target. The Senate Agriculture Committee's target was $3.2 billion. [Senate] Democrats argued behind the scenes that it was impossible to apply the Byrd rule to a conference report. What was the relevant "committee"? House Agriculture? Senate Agriculture? The conference committee? The House's Committee of the Whole? [The Senate] parliamentarian agreed that the rule could not properly apply [in this case], clearing the way for the food stamps provision to remain [in the conference report].[43]

Because the Byrd Rule also applies to House-Senate conference reports, it has become a source of heightened conflict between the chambers. House committee chairmen charge that the Byrd Rule, "by allowing Senators to rise on points of order and strike extraneous provisions [from conference reports], gives the Senate the power to dictate House actions."[44] Where House members recommend the elimination of the Byrd Rule insofar as it applies to conference committees, senators have recommended that the rule be strengthened.

CONTROL ON BACKDOORS AND IMPOUNDMENTS

The 1974 budget act tightened control over some new types of backdoor financing, excluding those already in effect when the measure was enacted. Legislation providing new contract or borrowing authority must indicate that the authority becomes effective only to the extent provided in appropriations acts. Members can raise points of order against such legislation, including amendments and conference reports, to enforce this requirement.

Title X of the 1974 act permits Congress to review executive impoundments of appropriated funds. The act divides impoundments into two categories—*deferrals* (a temporary delay in the expenditure of funds to achieve savings made possible through greater efficiencies or to provide for contingencies) and *rescissions* (the permanent cancellation of budget authority)—which are considered under separate procedures. Presidents are obligated to inform Congress of their proposed deferrals and rescissions and to set forth the reasons for them. The General Accounting Office (GAO), a legislative support agency of Congress, is authorized to review these special messages to ensure that impoundments are not misclassified and to challenge misclassifications in federal court.

Today, unless both houses pass legislation within forty-five days of continuous session approving the rescission proposal, the president must spend the money. Inaction, in short, makes the funds available for obligation. To strengthen the president's ability to control spending, various lawmakers have proposed legislation calling for either an "enhanced" or "expedited" rescission procedure. Both require express congressional action and represent a modified form of a constitutional line-item veto. Under the enhanced procedure, the president could cancel budget authority and Congress would have to pass legislation to reinstate it. Such legislation could be vetoed, requiring each house to muster the two-thirds vote needed to override. The expedited procedure simply changes the current process by requiring each house, by majority vote, to approve (or disapprove) the president's rescission recommendations.[45]

Neither change has yet been enacted into law. However, the line-item veto was part of the Republicans' Contract with America (the agenda for the first 100 days of the 104th Congress). Both chambers passed divergent versions of the proposed statute so the likelihood of enactment by the end of the Congress appeared good. Congress, it is worth noting, initiates rescission legislation on its own and, over time, "the share of total enacted rescissions which were originally proposed by the president has fallen and the share originating in the Congress has increased."[46]

ENFORCEMENT OF THE BUDGET RESOLUTION

The House and Senate enforce the goals and policies set forth in the budget resolution through several devices already mentioned (for example, scorekeeping, spending allocations to committees and subcommittees, reconciliation, budgetary information provided by CBO, and the monitoring role of the budget committees) as well as through points of order (such as the Byrd Rule) raised on the House or Senate floor. Points of order under the budget act are either substantive or procedural in character. Substantive points of order are raised to ensure compliance with the budget resolution. For example, a lawmaker can challenge a floor amendment that would cause a standing committee to exceed its allocation of new discretionary spending authority. Procedural points of order are raised to ensure compliance with features of the 1974 budget act and companion legislation. "Perhaps the most important of these," wrote three budget experts, "is Section 303, which bars consideration of any revenue, spending, entitlement, or debt-limit measure prior to the adoption of the budget resolution. However, the rules of the House permit it to consider regular appropriations bills after May 15 . . . even if the budget resolution has not yet been adopted."[47]

The House and Senate permit waivers of any points of order. The House usually does this in a "rule" issued by the Rules Committee. The Senate, by contrast, must waive most points of order by a three-fifths vote of all senators. A common feature of Senate floor activity is efforts by senators to attract sixty votes to waive some feature of the budget act so as to accomplish a policy objective, especially when there is a broad consensus to pass a bill or amendment. Alternatively, proposals that can attract a majority—but not the sixty votes to waive a budget requirement—frequently arouse controversy. In 1989, for instance, the Senate Democratic leadership stymied President George Bush's efforts to cut the capital gains tax rate by invoking a sixty-vote budgetary point of order against the tax-cut amendment

Republicans wanted to offer on the floor. (The capital gains tax cut ran afoul of the Byrd Rule as "extraneous" matter because it caused a shortfall in revenues.) Unable to attract the sixty votes, Bush's capital gains proposal died in the Senate.[48]

EVOLUTION OF THE BUDGET PROCESS

Change is ever present in congressional procedures and politics. This is certainly the case with the congressional budget process. Dropping the requirement for a second budget resolution, moving reconciliation into the first budget resolution, and expanding the scope of the budget resolution to include such matters as federal credit activities are a few examples of how the 1974 act was changed in some procedural ways. In the mid-1980s and later, moreover, Congress enacted significant statutory changes to its budget process. These changes emerged from a new political climate: the politics of deficit reduction.

Many factors explain the dramatic increase in deficits: the annual gap between spending and revenue. (The accumulation of annual deficits translates into our national debt.) Certainly the public wants more governmental services than it is willing to pay for. As former Senate Finance chairman Russell Long, D-La., used to quip: "Don't tax me. Don't tax thee. Tax that fellow behind the tree." Two other factors in the deficit explosion are noteworthy: divided government (one party controls the White House and the other controls one or both chambers of Congress) and the growth in entitlement spending. As Figure 3-2 highlights, the composition of our national budget has been dramatically transformed by growing entitlement expenditures, cuts in domestic discretionary spending, and increases in interest payments on the national debt.

When Ronald Reagan began his tenure as president in 1981, his principal objectives were threefold: slash domestic spending, increase defense expenditures, and cut taxes. With the Senate (at that point in GOP hands) spearheading the effort, Congress generally went along. Major problems soon arose, however. The revenue losses caused by the tax cuts, combined with rising defense spending and insufficient funding reductions in other areas, soon produced annual budget deficits in the $200 billion range. Never before had the nation seen such huge deficits during peacetime and during an economic expansion (following the 1982 recession). (See Figure 3-3 for actual and projected federal deficits as a percentage of gross domestic product.)

DIVIDED GOVERNMENT

The mushrooming deficits of this period, some suggested, enabled advocates of smaller government to "undercut support for starting new government programs, and even for sustaining old ones, less by discrediting the

FIGURE 3-2   Proposed Federal Spending, Fiscal 1996 (in billions)

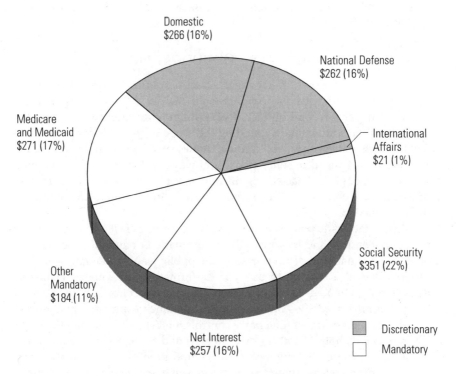

Domestic
$266 (16%)

National Defense
$262 (16%)

Medicare
and Medicaid
$271 (17%)

International
Affairs
$21 (1%)

Social Security
$351 (22%)

Other
Mandatory
$184 (11%)

Net Interest
$257 (16%)

Discretionary

Mandatory

Source: Congressional Quarterly Weekly Report, April 11, 1995, 404.

programs than by pitting them against the need to reduce a huge and grow-ing national debt."[49] Certainly the fiscal legacy of this period hemmed in the Clinton administration. The intense squeeze on federal spending left little discretionary money to fund all the new program initiatives that President Clinton or even lawmakers wanted. The shortage of money and the urge to act prompted Congress to require states, localities, and businesses to take cer-tain actions—such as providing access ramps for the handicapped—without providing funds to pay for them.

Unsurprisingly, the issue of these "unfunded mandates" became a source of contention between the states and federal government. For exam-ple, it was estimated that during the 1990s "state and local governments will spend more than $200 billion to comply with current federal waste water mandates alone."[50] In response, the 104th Congress enacted legislation that discourages the imposition of new unfunded mandates on state and local

FIGURE 3-3   The Federal Budget Deficit, 1970–2000 (in billions)

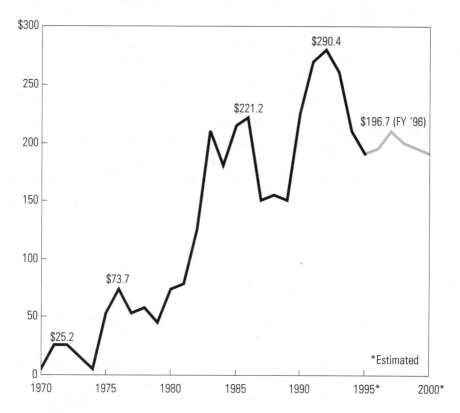

Source: Congressional Quarterly Weekly Report, April 11, 1995, 406.

governments. The statute establishes procedural hurdles—cost estimates and specific votes—before Congress can impose such mandates.

Concern with growing deficits mounted, but there was no consensus between the branches on how to address the problem. The budgets of several presidents (Reagan and Bush, for instance) even came to be viewed as unrealistic (described by some lawmakers as "dead on arrival" or "dead before arrival" because of their rosy economic assumptions); instead, the president's budget became a negotiating device used by the administration to bargain with Congress over budgetary priorities.[51]

Sharp disputes over spending priorities among the branches, chambers, and parties, plus intraparty disagreements, impeded progress in reducing the deficit. Legislative-executive deadlock that characterized much of the fiscal politics of the 1980s and early 1990s led to wide use of "budget summits" where Democratic congressional leaders negotiated with Republican presidents over the national budget.[52] With the political situation reversed since 1995, "divided government" remained a formidable obstacle to budgetary agreement.

For instance, congressional Republicans produced a budget plan in 1995 that promised to shrink big government and slash the federal deficit to zero. President Clinton waited several months before he produced a "counter budget" to eliminate the federal deficit. At first he tried instead "to shift the topic away from the deficit, force the public to confront the kind of cuts the Republicans wanted and paint the GOP as heartless vandals who would loot Medicare and student loans to give tax cuts to the wealthy."[53] A related aspect of the president's initial strategy was to compel Republicans to negotiate a budgetary compromise with the Democratic White House. For their part, GOP lawmakers taunted Clinton for not providing budgetary leadership. Switching tactics, in a June 13, 1995, address to the nation, President Clinton unveiled his own ten-year plan to balance the budget. His fiscal blueprint highlighted spending differences between the parties, but it also emulated the GOP's objective of downsizing the national government.

ENTITLEMENTS

Until the mid-1960s Great Society era, there were few entitlement programs other than Social Security and veterans' pensions. As a result, the Appropriations committees were well situated to balance competing program claims against available financial resources. For example, in 1932 "the Appropriations Committee in each chamber was responsible for 90 percent of federal spending."[54] Today, as noted previously, that share has fallen to around 33 percent, with entitlements consuming 50 percent of current federal expenditures and interest on the debt constituting the remainder. The dominant role of the federal budget, as one scholar wrote, has now become "transferring money to recipients outside the government rather than financing the operations of the government."[55] To be sure, appropriators are strong supporters of gaining more control over these open-ended mandatory spending programs; skyrocketing entitlement expenditures constrict their share of available monies and their annual bills become handy targets for lawmakers who want to offer floor amendments cutting discretionary spending programs.

Although there are about 410 entitlement programs, four cost the most: Social Security, Medicare (a health program for the elderly and disabled), Medicaid (a health program for the poor), and government retirement programs for civil servants and the military. As the Senate Finance chairman exclaimed:

> You think they are growing? Boy, are they growing. You take those four . . .
> plus interest [on the national debt], in 1964 those four, plus interest, were 23

percent of all of the money that the Federal Government spends—23 percent. Ten years later, in 1974, they were 39 percent. In 1984 they were 48 percent. In 1994, they were 56 percent. In the year 2004, they will be 67 percent.[56]

Clearly, there has been a dramatic reversal between the amount of money controlled through yearly appropriations and that subject to mandatory spending (entitlements). However, not all entitlements are exploding in growth. In fact, only Medicare and Medicaid are real budget-busters. These entitlements are growing rapidly for a variety of reasons, including the aging of the population and the high cost of medical technology. The Clinton administration tried but failed to enact comprehensive health care reform in part to control escalating expenditures in this area. Unless costs are contained, by 1998 health costs "are projected to take 22 cents of each dollar, surpassing both Social Security and national defense to become the government's largest single account."[57]

With Medicare facing insolvency by the year 2002, the GOP-controlled 104th Congress proposed savings of more than $250 billion over seven years through various cost-cutting devices. Republicans argued that Medicare reforms were required to save the program from bankruptcy; Democrats charged that the reductions were being made to offset GOP-planned tax cuts. In his counterproposal, Clinton offered $127 billion in Medicare cuts to be achieved through more emphasis on managed care and home care.

Social Security, while huge in cost, "is not expected to grow substantially [as a share of the federal budget] until the baby boom generation [those born between 1946 and 1964] reaches retirement age in the next century."[58] When that occurs, however, Social Security is projected to go broke by the year 2029 unless steps are taken to ensure that retirement benefits will continue to be available for eligible recipients. As Sen. Bob Kerrey, D-Neb., who cochaired a 1990s entitlement reform commission, said: "Mathematics is not on our side. Demographics is not on our side."[59]

Heightened concern with the need to curb entitlement costs now and in the future prompted consideration of various recommendations to revamp entitlement programs that were driving up the deficit.[60] As Sen. Judd Gregg, R-N.H., said: "[T]he naked truth of the matter is that the budget deficit cannot be dealt with in an honest manner without addressing the runaway growth of entitlement programs."[61]

Congress considered various options to rein in entitlement spending, including a balanced budget constitutional amendment, converting some entitlements into block grants to the states (an indirect way to cap mandatory spending), scaling back or eliminating benefits, establishing harder eligibility standards, and subjecting entitlement programs to income taxes. In sum, the debate surrounding entitlement raises many fundamental issues, such as balancing governmental limits and obligations against individual rights and responsibilities.[62]

GRAMM-RUDMAN-HOLLINGS

Escalating deficits and budgetary gridlock between the legislative and executive branches triggered enactment in 1985 of major financial management legislation. The measure was designed to force a specific policy objective: deficit reduction.

The Gramm-Rudman-Hollings Act (GRH) established a statutory pathway to "zero out" deficits and have a balanced federal budget after six years, by 1991. It mandated that a set amount—$36 billion—be chopped yearly from the allowable deficit ceilings established in GRH. For instance, the allowable deficit for fiscal 1987 was $144 billion, for fiscal 1988 was $108 billion, and so on down to the zero deficit of fiscal 1991.

To ensure that Congress and the president met the successive installment payments on the deficit, GRH included an automatic deficit-reduction mechanism called "sequestration." Sequestration is the core concept of GRH. Its objective was to change the political dynamics between the branches. If there is no legislative-executive success in meeting the deficit target, then the president must make across-the-board spending cuts (sequestration), evenly divided between domestic and defense programs, to achieve the prescribed GRH target. No further action is required of Congress. In effect, inaction produces action. "Without an automatic spending cut, you don't guarantee an outcome," noted House Democratic leader Richard Gephardt. "And that's what [GRH] is all about, guaranteeing an outcome."[63]

To be sure, the operative assumption of those who advocated the sequestration mechanism was that it would never be used. As one senator explained: "The whole idea behind sequester was to force Congress and the President to work together and find a responsible way to reduce the Federal deficit. Sequester was intended to be the price we would have to pay for failure."[64] The threat of sequestration loomed over both branches as a contrived crisis to force concessions from each: consideration of more revenues and a defense slowdown from the president's side in exchange for deeper cuts in domestic social programs from Congress. Unless a fiscal accord was reached between the branches, sequestration would indiscriminately cut defense and domestic programs.

As a blueprint for deficit reduction, GRH had mixed results. The legislation was revised in 1987 to accommodate a constitutional defect and to extend from 1991 to 1993 the target date for reaching zero deficit. On the one hand, its "deficit-neutrality" requirement continues to have a noticeable impact on lawmaking. Deficit neutrality means that when legislators propose spending more in one area they have to cut somewhere else or find new revenues to offset the proposed increase. When the 104th Congress began, for example, Speaker Newt Gingrich declared that there would be offsetting cuts for all supplementary spending.[65]

On the other hand, GRH had two major weaknesses. First, the act exempted nearly 70 percent of federal spending from sequestration. While defense and many domestic programs were subject to automatic cuts, popular entitlement programs were exempt. Deficit reduction is difficult to achieve when so much of the budget is excluded from cutbacks. Second, with rosy economic scenarios, fiscal gimmicks, and unrealistic revenue proposals GRH's deficit levels were met—but only on paper—while the actual deficit continued to grow far beyond expectations.

THE BUDGET ENFORCEMENT ACT OF 1990

Because GRH's system of fixed deficit targets did not effectively achieve spending reductions, and with the prospect of a huge sequestration looming, Congress and the White House negotiated in October 1990 a five-year budget agreement entitled the Budget Enforcement Act (BEA). (The BEA was Title XIII of an omnibus reconciliation bill.) Once again Congress changed its fiscal procedures. The legislation outlined a binding, multiyear deficit-reduction plan (almost $500 billion over five years) and established complex procedural controls to restrain federal spending. When President Clinton signed the Omnibus Reconciliation Act of 1993 into law, the BEA was extended through 1998 (and likely through 2002 by further amendment of the law).

Where GRH emphasized deficit reduction, the BEA's fundamental focus was on spending and revenue controls. Two enforcement mechanisms undergird the BEA. First, the BEA set strict spending caps for three discretionary categories—defense, domestic, and international—and prohibited Congress for the first three years from shifting money from one category to another. The prohibition against shifting money among categories (dubbed "firewalls") was designed to prevent Congress from raiding the defense category to fund domestic programs. However, for 1994 to 1998 the three categories were merged into one pot of discretionary money, with all programs competing for scarce dollars. (There is congressional discussion about reducing further the discretionary spending caps so as to achieve a balanced budget by 2002.) Discretionary appropriations, moreover, were denied increases to keep pace with inflation. With such strict spending limits, any increase for one program has to be offset by decreases in another. In short, this is zero-sum budgeting.

Under BEA, Congress was prohibited from breaching the spending caps; otherwise, a sequestration could occur in the offending category or, after 1993, in all discretionary programs. However, no longer was there a threat of an automatic fiscal guillotine if conditions beyond Congress's control (such as inflation or the need for emergency funding) pushed the deficit upward. As Robert Reischauer, the former director of CBO, and Philip Joyce, a CBO analyst, pointed out: "We have reached the era of no-fault deficits. Neither party nor branch of government is responsible for the deficit, and no one has to do anything about it when changed economic or technical conditions cause it to grow."[66] But since the 1992 elections, when presidential candidates Ross Perot and Paul Tsongas placed deficit reduction on the national agenda, and the 1994 elections, with the Republican takeover of Congress, the House and Senate have been filled with "deficit hawks" who want to slash spending and balance the budget. (There is little support in the current Congress for tax hikes.)

The second major enforcement mechanism in the BEA makes taxes and entitlements subject to a pay-as-you-go (PAYGO) procedure, which requires that any tax reductions or increases in mandatory spending programs must be offset by tax hikes or reductions in other mandatory spending programs. Otherwise, there would be a sequester of those mandatory spending programs not exempt under the terms of the BEA. (Existing entitlements are not subject to PAYGO requirements; only new ones are. Further, there are efforts under way to permit tax cuts to be offset by reductions in the discretionary caps.) As the chief counsel of the Senate Budget Committee put it, "The `pay-as-you-go' label implies that Congress and the President may cut taxes or create new programs—that is `go'—if they also agree to provide offsetting increased revenues or spending reductions—that is `pay.'"[67] (See Box 3-2 for a summary of the current budget rules.) If Congress and the president declare there is an "emergency," then spending or revenue legislation that exceeds the spending caps or the PAYGO limits is exempt from BEA procedures. The emergency designation, for example, was used to fund Operation Desert Storm (the military rollback of Iraq's 1990 invasion of Kuwait) and to provide domestic disaster assistance.

The budget rules put in place by the BEA shape policy deliberations in significant ways. For instance, the Clinton administration negotiated the General Agreement on Tariffs and Trade (GATT), which lowered tariffs worldwide on imported goods. Because lower tariff rates reduced federal tax revenue by $12 billion, PAYGO rules required that the lost revenue be offset either by higher taxes or spending cuts. Congress and the administration struggled for months to come up with a politically and fiscally acceptable way to replace the lost revenue without arousing the ire of voters or lawmakers.[68]

A BRIEF ASSESSMENT

There is little question that Congress's budgetary procedures are complex, time consuming, and often confusing to members and citizens alike. It is fairly safe to predict that they will undergo change again in the future. Congressional budgeting seems to be a moving target; innovations are always being suggested to improve its performance. In the 104th Congress House freshman Steve Largent, R-Okla., received a green light from Speaker Gingrich to form a bicameral budget reform task force. Largent said he was

---

LIVING BY BUDGET RULES

DISCRETIONARY CAPS. The rules set ceilings for discretionary spending—the money the appropriators control directly. In fiscal 1993 there were separate caps for domestic, foreign, and defense spending; in 1944-1995, there was a single cap on all discretionary spending.

PAY-AS-YOU-GO RESTRICTIONS. Any changes that Congress makes in taxes and mandatory spending ("entitlement" programs such as Medicare and food stamps) must be deficit neutral. Tax cuts or entitlement increases must be paid for by tax increases or cuts in entitlement programs.

AUTOMATIC CUTS. If Congress exceeds the discretionary caps or violates the pay-as-you-go rule, the Office of Management and Budget must order an across-the-board spending cut, or sequester, targeted to that part of the budget where the violation occurred. Such mini-sequesters can also be triggered by supplemental spending bills.

EMERGENCIES. Congress can take actions that violate the caps or the pay-as-you-go rules without triggering a sequester if both Congress and the president agree that the situation is an emergency.

Source: Adapted from *Congressional Quarterly Weekly Report*, December 21, 1991, 3729.

BOX 3-2

moved to act when a senior Budget Committee member did not know that "D" and "M" next to budget numbers stood for discretionary and mandatory spending. If a veteran had to ask that question, Largent said, "I could see the total chaos that was going on in members' minds."[69]

Part of the explanation for so many changes in the budget process is the difficulty of downsizing the deficit. Unexpected developments, such as a sluggish economy, natural disasters, or higher-than-anticipated costs for various entitlement programs, seem to overwhelm the best-laid procedural plans for controlling spending and reducing the deficit.

A former CBO director once said, "The problem is not the process, the problem is the problem."[70] Although any process is subject to improvements, the message here is that continual rewrites of budgetary procedures will not, by themselves, resolve the deficit issue. A growing economy, the willingness to make hard choices to kill ineffective programs protected by influential constituencies, and legislative-executive cooperation are among the factors required to deal with the deficit on a sustained basis. To be sure, there are scholars and others who contend that the deficit is not a big problem. They suggest that its size is mismeasured, that economic growth will bring it down, or that there is good debt (for investment purposes) and bad (for consumption only) debt, and that the deficit as percent of gross national product is much lower than in past, especially during WWII.

One thing appears clear. Many lawmakers believe that process changes can resolve the deficit issue. There are scores of proposals introduced each Congress on this topic. Examples are the aforementioned proposals for expedited rescission, placing yearly caps on entitlements and requiring legislative action if spending exceeds the caps, constitutional balanced budget amendments, or eliminating the use of "baselines" in developing the budget resolution and reconciliation instructions.

The baseline estimates the future costs of programs, assuming no policy changes, by taking into account such considerations as inflation and cost-of-living adjustments. Hence, virtually every program has yearly automatic increases built into them by the baseline projections even before Congress considers any spending reductions. "Cuts" in programs are often decreases from the inflation-adjusted baseline rather than from the amount the program received the previous year. As Rep. Charles Stenholm, D-Texas, put it, "It's like a worker who makes $25,000 a year assuming he will get a $4,000 raise and, if he gets only a $3,000 raise, calling that a cut."[71] On the other hand, if prices are being driven upward by inflation and other factors, then spending the same amount this year as last means that it is unlikely that agencies can continue to provide the same level of services. (The House amended its rules at the start of the 104th Congress to require committee reports on measures to compare an inflation-adjusted baseline with the amount spent the year before on the program.)

In short, there are often heated political debates in Washington about the meaning of two simple words: "cut" and "increase." Fundamentally, the disagreement revolves around cutting or increasing from what, the dollars spent last year or the level of services purchased with those dollars. When Republicans proposed savings in the Medicare program, they argued that the program would continue to grow but at a slower rate (Medicare expenditures are projected to increase by about 10 percent a year; Republicans recommended several program changes that would limit the growth rate to 7 percent.) Democrats charged that the GOP plan would impose real pain because there will be insufficient funds to address the health needs of the growing elderly population. "You can't make cuts of that order and not hurt people," declared Senate Minority Leader Tom Daschle, D-S.D.[72]

The arithmetic for addressing the deficit seems plain: raise revenues, cut spending, or devise an acceptable combination of the two. A dilemma for lawmakers is that although constituents may dislike the deficit, they dislike taxes even more yet favor spending for programs that benefit them. More than economics or politics or procedures are involved in taxing and spending questions. They raise the age-old philosophical issue about what ought to be the appropriate size and role of the national government. The challenge ahead for policy makers, then, appears at least three-fold: persuade the electorate to accept some fiscal belt-tightening so as to minimize "passing the buck" to subsequent generations, determine what level of government citizens are willing to support with taxes, and devise a program of economic growth that ensures the nation's future prosperity.

SUMMARY

Legislative changes are notable for producing mixed results and unexpected consequences. The budget process has been no exception to these conditions. Its procedures, and those applicable generally to congressional policy making, can produce whatever can attract a majority or, in some cases, an extraordinary majority. Legislative procedures, in short, define the context in which policies are made and influence the choice of strategies to advance or frustrate legislation, including budget resolutions.

Chapter 4 turns to the initial steps of the legislative process: the introduction and referral of bills to House and Senate committees and committee action on legislation. The executive branch and pressure groups usually are given most of the credit for initiating ideas that Congress eventually formulates and passes in legislative form. But Congress also initiates numerous proposals. And ideas for legislation frequently are discussed in academic circles, private associations, federal advisory committees, national commissions, citizens' groups, professional societies, and by knowledgeable individuals. In essence, legislation "is an aggregate, not a simple production," Woodrow Wilson once wrote. "It is impossible to tell how many persons, opinions and influences have entered into its composition."[73]

NOTES

1. *Congressional Control of Expenditures,* House Committee on the Budget, January 1977, 6. The study was prepared by Allen Schick.
2. *Congressional Record,* April 13, 1994, S4218.
3. *Congressional Record,* April 9, 1987, S4919.
4. Budget Process: Testimony of William H. Natcher, Hearing before the Joint Committee on the Organization of Congress, March 11, 1993, 2.
5. John William Ellwood, ed., *Reductions in U.S. Domestic Spending* (New Brunswick, N.J.: Transaction Books, 1982), 21.
6. *Congressional Record,* November 2, 1987, E4279.
7. Absent an authorization law, the Appropriations committees typically base their financial recommendations on the president's budget requests.

8. Helen Dewar and Barbara Vobejda, "Clinton Signs Head Start Expansion," *Washington Post,* May 19, 1994, A1.
9. Roy T. Meyers, "Biennial Budgeting," staff working paper, Congressional Budget Office, November 1987, 42.
10. Richard Munson, *The Cardinals of Capitol Hill* (New York: Grove Press, 1993), 6.
11. Everett Somerville Brown, ed., *William Plumer's Memorandum of Proceedings in the United States Senate, 1803-1807* (New York: Macmillan, 1923), 490.
12. Robert Luce, *Legislative Problems* (Boston: Houghton Mifflin, 1935), 425-426.
13. Louis Fisher, "The Authorization-Appropriation Process in Congress: Formal Rules and Informal Practices," *Catholic University Law Review* (Fall 1979): 53.
14. *Operations of the Congress: Testimony of House and Senate Leaders,* Hearing before the Joint Committee on the Organization of Congress, January 26, 1993, 75-76.
15. Budget Process: Hearing Before the Joint Committee on the Organization of Congress, March 16, 1993, 52.
16. Operations of the Congress: Testimony of House and Senate Leaders, Hearing Before the Joint Committee on the Organization of Congress, January 26, 1993, 70.
17. Mary Jacoby, "Turf Wars: House Chairmen Bid to Protect Their Fiefdoms from Senate Appropriators," *Roll Call,* October 11, 1993, 11.
18. Dan Morgan, "Transportation Funding Yields House GOP Dispute," *Washington Post,* May 9, 1995, A4.
19. Jon Healey, "Lautenberg Moves to Reduce Transportation Earmarks," *Congressional Quarterly Weekly Report,* October 2, 1993, 2625.
20. Fisher, "The Authorization-Appropriation Process in Congress," 74-75. The House considered the issue on June 17, 1977, and the Senate on June 29, 1977. See Roger H. Davidson, "Procedures and Politics in Congress," in *The Abortion Dispute and the American System,* ed. Gilbert Y. Steiner (Washington, D.C.: Brookings Institution, 1982), 30-46.
21. *Congressional Record,* October 20, 1993, S13966.
22. *Congressional Record,* January 3, 1983, H5-H22.
23. *Congressional Record,* January 4, 1995, H37.
24. *Congressional Record,* February 9, 1995, H1469.
25. Mary Jacoby, "Lawsuit Challenges GOP's Tax-Hike Rule," *Roll Call,* February 9, 1995, 17. Also see David Broder, "The Three-Fifth Rule: A Dangerous Game," *Washington Post,* December 18, 1994, C7, and Bruce Fein, "In Defense of Supermajorities," *Legal Times,* February 6, 1995, 30.
26. See *Roll Call,* May 8, 1995, 10; *Congressional Record,* April 5,1995, H4315-H4319.
27. *CQ's Congressional Monitor,* May 22, 1995, 1.
28. Allen Schick, *Congress and Money,* (Washington, D.C.: Urban Institute Press), 46.
29. Ibid., 59.
30. Daniel P. Franklin, *Making Ends Meet: Congressional Budgeting in the Age of Deficits* (Washington, D.C.: CQ Press, 1993), 40.
31. Viveca Novak, "By the Numbers," *National Journal,* February 12, 1994, 349.
32. Robert Pear, "Second Thoughts on Health Data," *New York Times,* May 9, 1994, A14. Also see Dana Priest and Spencer Rich, "Health Plan Will Swell Deficit, Hill Office Says," *Washington Post,* February 9, 1994, A1; James Risen, "Budget Office Sees Health Plan Widening Deficit," *Los Angeles Times,* February 9, 1994, A1; and Robert Pear, "Congress Asserts Health Proposals Understate Costs," *New York Times,* February 9, 1994, A1.
33. Marcia Gilbert, "GOP leaders feuding with CBO chief," *The Hill,* May 3, 1995, 1, 29.
34. *Congressional Record,* May 8, 1995, S6228.
35. *Congressional Record,* May 17, 1995, H5107.
36. *Congressional Record,* May 18, 1995, H5309.

37. Munson, *Cardinals of Capitol Hill,* 19.

38. *National Journal's CongressDaily,* April 29, 1994, 1.

39. *National Journal's CongressDaily,* May 12, 1994, 10.

40. *National Journal's CongressDaily/AM,* May 4, 1995, 4.

41. Howard H. Baker, Jr., "Essay, An Introduction to the Politics of Reconciliation," *Harvard Journal on Legislation* (Winter 1983): 2.

42. Stanley E. Collender, *The Guide to the Federal Budget, Fiscal 1995* (Washington, D.C.: Urban Institute Press, 1994), 60.

43. George Hager, "The Byrd Rule: Not an Easy Call," *Congressional Quarterly Weekly Report,* July 31, 1993, 2027.

44. Karen Foerstel, "Byrd Rule War Erupts Once Again," *Roll Call,* February 24, 1994, 13.

45. Viveca Novak, "Defective Remedy," *National Journal,* March 27, 1993, 749-753.

46. Harry Havens, assistant comptroller general, "Use and Impact of Rescission Procedures," Testimony before the Subcommittee on Legislative Process, House Committee on Rules, September 25, 1992, 5.

47. Allen Schick, Robert Keith, and Edward Davis, *Manual on the Federal Budget Process,* Congressional Research Service, Report No. 91-902, December 24, 1991, 72.

48. *Congressional Quarterly Almanac,* vol. XLV, 1989, 116. Also see Susan F. Rasky, "G.O.P. Senators Warn of Tie-Up Over Gains Tax," *New York Times,* October 5, 1989, A1.

49. Alan Brinkley, "Reagan's Revenge," *New York Times Magazine,* June 19, 1994, 36.

50. William Claiborne, "Unfunded Mandates Occupy Center Stage," *Washington Post,* May 18, 1994, A21. Also see Adam J. Rombel, "Mandate Medicine," *State Government News,* July 1994, 23-24; Christine Wnuk, "Foiling Federal Mandates," *State Legislatures,* May 1993, 13; and Tommy Neal, "Just Another Mandate," *State Legislatures,* July 1993, 59, 61.

51. See Louis Fisher, "Federal Budget Doldrums: The Vacuum in Presidential Leadership," *Public Administration Review,* November/December 1990, 693-700.

52. See Allen Schick, *The Capacity to Budget* (Washington, D.C.: Urban Institute Press, 1990), 184-189.

53. *Los Angeles Times,* May 22, 1995, A9.

54. John F. Cogan, *Federal Budget Deficits: What's Wrong With the Congressional Budget Process* (Palo Alto, Calif.: Hoover Institution, Stanford University, 1992), 14.

55. Schick, *The Capacity to Budget,* 37.

56. *Congressional Record,* February 10, 1995, S2447.

57. David Lauter, "Rising Health Costs May Erase Cuts in Deficit" *Los Angeles Times,* April 9, 1993, A7.

58. Ibid.

59. *National Journal's CongressDaily,* May 18, 1995, 1.

60. George Hager, "Entitlement Reform Panel Convenes in Pessimism," *Congressional Quarterly Weekly Report,* June 18, 1994, 1583-1584. Also see George Hager, "Entitlements: The Untouchable May Become Unavoidable," *Congressional Quarterly Weekly Report,* January 2, 1993, 22-30.

61. Judd Gregg, "No More Sacred Cow," *Washington Post,* February 8, 1995, A19.

62. See, for example, Robert J. Samuelson, "How Our American Dream Unraveled," *Newsweek,* March 2, 1992, 32-39.

63. *New York Times,* October 16, 1985, A22.

64. *Congressional Record,* October 14, 1987, S14257. See, for example, Harry S. Havens, "Gramm-Rudman-Hollings: Origins and Implementation," *Public Budgeting and Finance* (Autumn 1986): 4-24; and Lance T. LeLoup, Barbara Luck Graham, and Stacey Barwick, "Deficit Politics and Constitutional Government: The Impact of Gramm-Rudman-Hollings," *Public Budgeting and Finance* (Spring 1987): 83-103.

65. *Congressional Record,* April 6, 1995, H4344.
66. Philip Joyce and Robert Reischauer, "Deficit Budgeting: The Federal Budget Process and Budget Reform," *Harvard Journal on Legislation,* Summer 1992, 441.
67. William G. Dauster, "Budget Process Issues for 1993," *Journal of Laws & Politics,* vol. IX: 9, 1992, 26.
68. David S. Cloud, "Clinton Seeks Action on GATT Pact, Proposes Financing Package," *Congressional Quarterly Weekly Report,* July 16, 1994, 1919-1911.
69. "Gingrich Gives OK To New Task Force on Budget Process," *CQ's Congressional Monitor,* May 15, 1995, 6.
70. *Washington Post,* July 18, 1984, A14.
71. Patrice Hill, "Built-in increases face `cut' in House," *Washington Times,* May 18, 1994, A4.
72. Barbara Vobejda and Spencer Rich, "Medicare War Opens With Skirmishes Over Terms: What Constitutes a Cut?" *Washington Post,* May 11, 1995, A6.
73. Woodrow Wilson, *Congressional Government* (Boston: Houghton Mifflin, 1885), 320.

CHAPTER 4

Preliminary Legislative Action

The introduction of a bill in Congress usually is a simple procedure. In the House, members just drop their bills into the "hopper," a mahogany box near the clerk's desk at the front of the chamber. In the Senate, members generally submit their proposals and accompanying statements to clerks, or they may introduce their bills from the floor. Measures may be introduced only when the chamber is in session. All House and Senate bills are printed and made available to members and the public.

There are occasions when standing committees battle behind the scenes to assert jurisdiction over bills before they are formally introduced. This was the case with President Bill Clinton's massive and unsuccessful health care reform legislation that he submitted to the 103d Congress. Several House and Senate committee leaders wanted the bulk of the health plan referred to their panels.

> The stakes are large. If a committee could gain solid recognition as having the main jurisdiction, it would have control over legislation affecting a major segment of the economy for years to come, perhaps permanently. That would boost power and political clout immeasurably for members of the winning committee [and garner them political contributions as well].[1]

Preintroductory jockeying over the health bill in the House led to the whole package's referral to three standing committees; an additional seven committees received parts of the bill. In the other body, the Clinton plan was assigned to the Senate Calendar; the two prime health committees—Finance and Labor and Human Resources—drafted their own version of health care reform. The majority party leaders in each chamber then worked, respectively, to meld the products reported by the various committees into a health bill "that can secure broader and stronger coalitions than any put together by the chairmen."[2]

The act of introducing a bill sets off a complex and variable chain of events that may or may not result in the final passage of a bill by Congress. Most bills follow a path in which the various steps, governed by rules and convention, are fairly predictable, but the outcome usually is uncertain. This chapter considers some of the factors that affect the probable route a bill will take and focuses on the early stages in the life of a bill: its referral to committee and, of utmost importance, its consideration in committee.

Although thousands of pieces of legislation are introduced in every Congress, a relatively small number become law. Figure 4-1 shows that of the roughly ten thousand measures introduced during the 102d Congress (1991-1993), 1,405 (13.8 percent) were reported from committee and only 590 (5.8 percent) became public law. Of the thousands of measures introduced since 1965, the number emerging from committee in any one Congress never exceeded 4,200 and the number that became law never exceeded 810. Committees clearly are the primary graveyard for most bills that die in Congress. Stated positively, committees select from the vast number of bills introduced those that they feel merit further consideration.

Quantitative data on legislative output require careful interpretation. Although the number of laws that Congress enacts annually has dropped in recent years, the number of pages per law has increased significantly (from 2.5 pages on average in the 1950s to nearly 13 pages in the early 1990s), a reflection of wider use of so-called megabills, measures that are hundreds of pages in length (Clinton's health care proposal, for example, was more than thirteen hundred pages). The contemporary Congress may pass fewer laws than before, but they are, on average, about four times longer.

The productivity of Congress cannot be measured only by the number of laws it enacts annually. Today Congress devotes considerably more time and effort to its other principal functions: representation and oversight. The surge of legislative activity in both areas is considerable. Finally, the very complexity and interconnectedness of many contemporary issues slows down the law-enacting process.

CATEGORIES OF LEGISLATION

The winnowing process that occurs in committee suggests that the thousands of bills introduced in each Congress may be broken down roughly into three categories: bills having so little support that they are ignored and die in committee; noncontroversial bills that are expedited through Congress; and finally, major bills that are generally so controversial that they occupy the major portion of Congress's time. Legislative proposals take four forms: *bill, joint resolution, concurrent resolution,* and *resolution.* (See Glossary.)

BILLS LACKING WIDE SUPPORT

Bills having little support usually are introduced with no expectation that they will be enacted into law. Members introduce such bills for a variety of reasons: to go on record in support of a given proposal, to satisfy individual constituents or interest groups from the member's district or state, to convey a message to executive agencies, to publicize an issue, to attract

FIGURE 4-1   From Bill to Law: House and Senate Statistics for the
102d Congress, 1991–1993

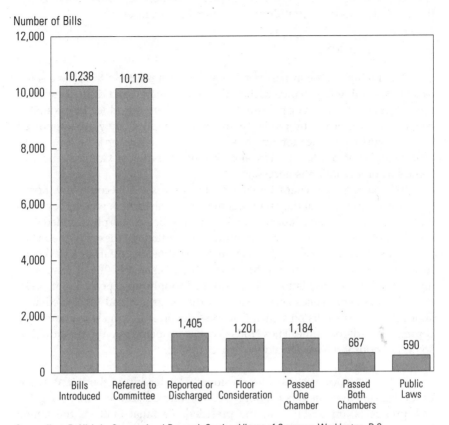

Source: Ilona B. Nickels, Congressional Research Service, Library of Congress, Washington, D.C.

Note: Statistics represent only bills and joint resolutions. Simple resolutions, concurrent resolutions, and private bills are excluded.

media attention, or to fend off criticism during political campaigns. Once a member has introduced a bill, he or she can claim "action" on the issue and can blame the committee to which the bill has been referred for its failure to win enactment. Most of the bills introduced in each Congress fall into this category.

NONCONTROVERSIAL BILLS

Noncontroversial bills make up another large segment of the measures introduced. Examples are bills that authorize construction of statues of public figures, establish university programs in the memory of a senator, rename a national park, or name federal buildings after former members of Congress. Committees in both chambers have developed rapid procedures for dealing with such measures. As shown in Chapters 6 and 8, these bills generally are passed on the floor without debate in a matter of minutes.

MAJOR LEGISLATION

Bills taking up the largest percentage of a committee's time have some or all of the following characteristics: they are prepared and drafted by executive agencies or by major pressure groups; they are introduced by committee chairmen or other influential members of Congress; they are supported by the majority party leadership; or they deal with issues on which a significant segment of public opinion and the membership of Congress believe some sort of legislation is necessary.

Bills having such characteristics do not necessarily become law; nor is there any assurance that they will become law in the form in which they originally were introduced. Indeed, sentiment may be so sharply divided that they do not even emerge from committee. Nevertheless, these are the major bills before Congress each year. They may affect the wage earner's paycheck (taxes and Social Security) and the consumer's pocketbook (health insurance and natural gas deregulation); they may be brought up repeatedly at presidential news conferences and covered in the electronic and print media. In short, they are the bills on which Congress devotes the largest portion of its committee and floor time. These bills account for perhaps only a hundred or so of the thousands introduced in each Congress.

EXECUTIVE BRANCH BILLS. The president's leadership in the initial stages of the legislative process is pronounced. The administration's major legislative proposals are outlined in the president's annual State of the Union address, nowadays televised nationally during prime time and delivered before a joint session of Congress. In the weeks and months following the address, the president sends to Congress special messages detailing his proposals in specific areas, such as "reinventing" government, welfare, and health. Bills containing the administration's programs are drafted in the executive agencies, and members of Congress, usually committee chairmen, are asked to introduce them simultaneously as "companion" bills in both chambers. Only representatives and senators, not the president or executive officials, may introduce legislation in Congress.

INFLUENTIAL MEMBERS' BILLS. Bills supported by influential members stand a good chance of receiving attention in committee. During the past decade, for example, the House and Senate on several occasions debated immigration reform bills. Because of the mounting public concern about the flood of illegal aliens into the country, two key members, Sen. Alan K.

Simpson, R-Wyo., and Rep. Romano L. Mazzoli, D-Ky., sponsored companion bills to revamp the nation's immigration laws. Simpson and Mazzoli each chaired his chamber's Judiciary subcommittee that handled immigration measures. Because of their strategic leadership posts, the two members were successful in advancing the legislation to the House and Senate floor during the 97th and 98th Congresses. Finally, after being given up for dead several times, the landmark measure became law at the end of the 99th Congress. Simpson and Mazzoli (who voluntarily retired at the end of the 103rd Congress) had worked diligently to develop tradeoffs and compromises among colleagues and lobbyists to enhance the measure's prospects for passage.

"MUST" LEGISLATION. As lawmakers, members of Congress may not want to deal with controversial "no-win" public issues such as abortion or gun control. As politicians answering constituent mail, responding to inquiring journalists, and, of course, facing reelection, they may not be able to ignore them. Hence, it frequently occurs that members are in basic agreement that legislation must be enacted to deal with a given problem but are in sharp disagreement over the solution. Under these circumstances, most members work hard to compromise their differences because they realize that some type of legislation is desirable or unavoidable. Money bills, to be sure, fall into the category of "must-pass" legislation, as did the measures associated with House Republicans' ambitious "Contract with America"—the first-100-day agenda of the 104th Congress.

Many of the factors determining a bill's probable route, therefore, are apparent by the time the legislation is introduced. Bills having little support will be buried in committee; noncontroversial legislation will move quickly through Congress; major bills may or may not become law but in any case will command the greatest portion of Congress's time.

Especially for major bills will lawmakers contemplate a variety of pre-introductory considerations. Timing is always important. When should a bill be introduced: early or late in a legislative session; if late, what strategies might be employed during the "end game" (the rush to adjournment) to gain enactment of the measure? For example, a bill likely to be filibustered in the Senate might be introduced early so there is plenty of time to overcome any "talkathon." What should the bill be called? An attractive title (such as the Freedom of Information Act) might garner a bill useful media coverage. (To be sure, opponents of legislation will try to attach an unattractive label to it. For instance, the *New York Times* called the Gramm-Rudman-Hollings bill discussed in Chapter 3 the "Balanced Budget Baloney Act," but it passed anyway.) Should companion bills (identical legislation) be introduced simultaneously in the House and Senate to expedite legislative action? How many cosponsors (members who join together to introduce the bill) should be sought and who should they be? As Sen. Edward M. Kennedy, D-Mass., said

---

FOR THE RECORD

Under clause 5 of Rule X and clause 4 of rule XXII, public bills and resolutions were introduced and severally referred as follows:

By Mr. DeFazio (for himself, Mr. Bilbray, Mr. Metcalf, Mr. Rohrabacher, and Mr. Sensenbrenner):

H.R. 1709. A bill to amend the Military Selective Service Act to suspend the registration requirement and the activities of civilian local boards, civilian appeal boards, and similar local agencies of the Selective Service System, except during national emergencies, and to require the Director of Selective Service to prepare a report regarding the development of a viable standby registration program for use only during national emergencies; to the Committee on National Security.

By Mr. Hyde (for himself, Mr. McCollum, Mr. Smith of Texas, Mr. Gekas, Mr. Canady, Mr. Hoke, and Mr. Bono):

H.R. 1710. A bill to combat terrorism; to the Committee on the Judiciary.

By Mr. Bachus:

H.R. 1711. A bill to improve the administration of the Fair Debt Collection Practices Act; to the Committee on Banking and Financial Services.

By Mr. Collins of Georgia (for himself and Mr. Kingston):

H.R. 1712. A bill to amend the Harmonized Tariff Schedule of the United States with respect to imports of civil aircraft; to the Committee on Ways and Means.

Source: Congressional Record, May 25, 1995, H5607.

BOX 4-1

about Sen. Strom Thurmond, R-S.C., "Whenever Strom and I introduce a bill together, it is either an idea whose time has come, or one of us has not read the bill."[3] The art of drafting a bill to ensure its referral to the proper committee may be crucial to its fate and thus merits separate discussion.

BILL REFERRAL PROCEDURE

Once a bill is introduced it receives an identifying number. Measures introduced in the House are identified by the letters "HR" and an accompanying number (see Box 4-1, "For the Record"); Senate bills are identified by the letter "S" and a number. Usually, bills are assigned numbers according to the chronological order in which they are introduced. Occasionally, however, members will request the bill clerk to reserve a particular number. During consideration of statehood for Alaska and Hawaii, various bills were introduced as S 49 or HR 50, representing the new states. H J Res 51, introduced by the District of Columbia delegate in the 103d Congress (1993-1995), would admit the District as our fifty-first state.

Bill numbers also may be assigned for political and symbolic purposes. Customarily, party leaders of the House and Senate reserve the first several numbers for measures that are important party initiatives. Former Speaker Jim Wright, D-Texas, even organized his nationally televised remarks in response to the president's 1988 State of the Union message around the first five measures introduced ("House bill number 1, our first legislative act, was the clean water bill . . . "). When the 103d Congress began, with a Democrat in the White House for the first time in a dozen years, the Senate Democratic leadership introduced as their first five priority bills (S 1, S 2, and so on), such as the family and medical leave act, legislation that had been vetoed the previous Congress by GOP president George Bush. Every measure in Speaker Newt Gingrich's Contract with America received top billing during the 104th Congress, starting with H R 1, the Congressional Accountability Act (to apply federal workplace safety and other laws to Congress).

Some measures are assigned the same number for several Congresses. This is often done to avoid confusion among legislators and others who have grown accustomed to referring to a proposal by its bill number. Informally, many bills also come to be known by the names of their sponsors, such as Gramm-Rudman-Hollings, discussed in Chapter 3.

With few exceptions, bills are referred to the appropriate standing committees.[4] The job of referral formally is the responsibility of the Speaker of the House and the presiding officer of the Senate,[5] but usually this task is carried out on their behalf by the parliamentarians of the House and Senate.[6] Precedent, public laws, turf battles, and the jurisdictional mandates of the committees as set forth in the rules of the House and Senate determine which committees receive what kinds of bills. As an example, the jurisdiction of the House Economic and Educational Opportunities Committee is listed in Table 4-1.

The vast majority of referrals are routine. Bills dealing with farm crops are sent to the House Agriculture Committee and the Senate Agriculture, Nutrition and Forestry Committee; tax bills are sent to the House Ways and Means Committee and the Senate Finance Committee; and bills dealing with veterans' benefits are sent to the Veterans' Affairs committees of each chamber.[7] Thus, referrals generally are cut-and-dried decisions. (Under Republican control, the House changed the names of several committees in 1995. House and Senate standing committees as currently named are listed in Box 4-2.)

Yet there are usually notable cases in each Congress where committees will clash over their jurisdictional prerogatives. The early 1990s, for example,

TABLE 4-1 Jurisdiction of House Committee on Economic and Educational Opportunities

---

1. Child labor.
2. Columbia Institution for the Deaf, Dumb, and Blind; Howard University; Freedmen's Hospital.
3. Convict labor and the entry of goods made by convicts into interstate commerce.
4. Food programs for children in schools.
5. Labor standards and statistics.
6. Measures relating to education or labor generally.
7. Mediation and arbitration of labor disputes.
8. Regulation or prevention of importation of foreign laborers under contract.
9. United States Employees' Compensation Commission.
10. Vocational rehabilitation.
11. Wages and hours of labor.
12. Welfare of miners.
13. Work incentive programs.

Source: *Rules of the House for the 104th Congress* (1995-1997).

witnessed sharp clashes between two House committees over financial securities and insurance matters. When Energy and Commerce Chairman John D. Dingell, D-Mich., wrote to Speaker Thomas S. Foley, D-Wash., and complained about the Banking, Finance and Urban Affairs Committee's assertion of jurisdiction over these issues, Banking Chairman Henry B. Gonzalez, D-Texas, responded in kind that it is "incredible that we are constantly subjected to the perverse claim that legislative issues not expressly listed with [House] Rule X [which sets out the jurisdictions of committees] . . . somehow automatically fall within the purview of the Energy and Commerce Committee."[8]

Even in the revamped House committee system of the 104th Congress, turf struggles were not uncommon. For instance, the Commerce (renamed from Energy and Commerce in the previous Congress) and Judiciary Committees clashed over telecommunications policy. Judiciary Chairman Henry J. Hyde, R-Ill., stated that he planned discussions with Commerce Chairman Thomas Bliley, R-Va., over their differences. "I don't think we have a lot of middle ground," said Chairman Bliley.[9] Jurisdictional border wars, in brief, may influence the expansion or contraction of committees' authority. Some committees may even have "staffers called `border cops,' whose jobs involve protecting turf and looking for new areas to conquer."[10]

STANDING COMMITTEES, 104TH CONGRESS

SENATE

Agriculture, Nutrition and Forestry	Environment and Public Works
Appropriations	Finance
Armed Services	Foreign Relations
Banking, Housing and Urban Affairs	Governmental Affairs
	Judiciary
Budget	Labor and Human Resources
Commerce, Science and Transportation	Rules and Administration
	Small Business
Energy and Natural Resources	Veterans' Affairs

HOUSE

Agriculture	Judiciary
Appropriations	National Security
Banking and Financial Services	Resources
Budget	Rules
Commerce	Science
Economic and Educational Opportunities	Small Business
	Standards of Official Conduct
Government Reform and Oversight	Transportation and Infrastructure
House Oversight	Veterans' Affairs
International Relations	Ways and Means

BOX 4-2

In the House, a member is not permitted to appeal referral decisions to the entire membership except in rare instances of erroneous referral. In the Senate, the rules do permit an appeal to the full Senate by majority vote, but in practice such appeals do not take place. Disputes over referral in the Senate are resolved informally through negotiation prior to the introduction of the bill in question.

LEGISLATIVE DRAFTING, REFERRAL STRATEGY

Occasionally, a bill's sponsors may have the opportunity to draft legislation in such a fashion that it will be referred to a committee likely to act favorably on it rather than one where members are known to be less sympathetic. One technique is to draft the measure ambiguously so that it can legitimately fall within the jurisdiction of more than one committee, thus presenting the Speaker or the presiding officer with some options in making the referral.

The House and Senate parliamentarians regularly meet with congressional staffers (and even receive briefs from lobbyists regarding bill referrals) who are interested in having their measures referred to one committee rather than another. The parliamentarians provide general advice on what language or terms to include in legislation so it will be referred to preferred committees. "A great deal of our time in the office is spent dealing with drafts of bills," stated the Senate parliamentarian, "the committee to which they would be referred, advising staff on what to include and what to delete if in fact they have a preference in terms of committee referral."[11] Another drafting technique by members is to introduce legislation that amends statutes over which their committees have jurisdiction. Noted Rep. Bob Eckhardt, D-Texas (1967–1981):

> You can phrase your new bill as an amendment to some Act that the Committee has previously dealt with, and then the bill will go to that Committee. For instance, I had the Open Beaches Bill. I had a strong interest in it. By phrasing it as an amendment to certain legislation involving estuarine matters, I could get my bill referred to Merchant Marine and Fisheries, because that Committee [now abolished] had previously processed the statute my bill amended. Had I amended certain bills dealing with land use, I could have got it referred to the [Resources] Committee.[12]

Other examples of bill drafting that resulted in a favorable referral could be cited. Nevertheless, it is important to understand that these are the exceptions and not the rule. Committees guard their jurisdictional turfs closely, and the parliamentarians know and follow the precedents. Only instances of genuine jurisdictional ambiguity provide opportunities for the legislative draftsman and referral options for the Speaker and the presiding officer of the Senate to bypass one committee in favor of another.

REFERRAL TO SEVERAL COMMITTEES

Many bills obviously cut across the jurisdiction of several committees so that it sometimes is difficult for the House Speaker or Senate presiding officer to decide where to refer a bill. Particular sections, for example, may fall outside the main jurisdiction of the appropriate committee. Other committees may assert their jurisdiction over those bills, refusing to be bypassed on referrals. Committees' jurisdictional mandates often are ambiguous or overlap in various issue areas. For example, House rules assign the Committee on International Relations jurisdiction over "international economic policy";

Commerce handles "foreign commerce generally"; and Ways and Means considers "reciprocal trade agreements." Committees, in brief, often share jurisdiction—formally or informally. At the start of the 104th Congress, for instance, the GOP-controlled House abolished several standing committees, including the Committee on Merchant Marine and Fisheries. The respective chairmen of the National Security and the Transportation and Infrastructure committees developed a "memorandum of understanding" explaining their agreement as to how matters involving the merchant marine would be divided between them. As the chairmen wrote: "In general, matters relating to merchant marine activities will be referred to the National Security Committee if the national security aspects of the matter predominate over transportation and other merchant marine aspects."[13] This type of intercommittee referral agreement will be honored by the parliamentarian.

The Senate has long permitted the practice of *multiple referral*, assigning legislation to two or more committees. There are three types of multiple referral: joint referral of a bill concurrently to two or more committees; sequential referral successively to one committee, then a second, and so on; and split referral of various parts of a bill to different committees for consideration of each part.

The Senate nevertheless makes infrequent use of multiple referrals. Measures normally are sent to a single committee as determined by the panel that has jurisdiction over the "subject matter which predominates," the referral criterion specified for the Senate in the Legislative Reorganization Act of 1946. However, multiple referrals can be implemented either by unanimous consent or upon a joint motion made by the majority and minority leaders (to date never employed). An example of the unanimous consent method occurred on March 1, 1994, upon a request made by the majority whip:

> Mr. President, I ask unanimous consent that Calendar No. 330, S. 687, the Product Liability Fairness Act be sequentially referred [from the Commerce Committee] to the Committee on the Judiciary for a period not to extend beyond April 11, 1994, that if the Committee on the Judiciary has not reported the measure within that time, then the bill be automatically discharged and returned to the Calendar.

No senator objected to this sequential referral. The Senate normally grants such requests because senators who offer them usually have worked out an agreement previously with all interested parties—committee chairmen, party leaders, and other members concerned about the bill. By the time the bill is introduced the appropriate bases have been touched; thus no senator is likely to object to the multiple referral.

Until 1975 House precedents dictated that the Speaker could refer a bill to only one committee. That year, flexibility was injected into the bill-referral process by two changes in the rules. First, the Speaker was permitted to refer a bill to more than one committee through joint, sequential, or split referral.

This authority augments the Speaker's authority by enabling him to delay (sending a bill to several panels) or expedite (fixing committee reporting deadlines) action on legislation. Second, the Speaker, subject to approval of the House, was permitted to create ad hoc committees to consider measures that overlap the jurisdictions of several committees.

Speaker Thomas P. O'Neill, Jr., D-Mass., exercised this ad hoc committee option in 1977 by creating an Ad Hoc Energy Committee to expedite action on the Carter administration's complex energy proposals. The ad hoc committee was composed of members selected from the five committees to which various parts of the energy proposal initially had been referred.[14] In the Senate, the administration's 1977 energy proposals were referred to the Finance Committee and the Energy and Natural Resources Committee. There is no Senate provision for the creation of ad hoc committees by party leaders.

In 1977 House rules were amended to permit the Speaker to impose committee reporting deadlines during the initial referral of measures. Further, the Speaker announced on January 3, 1983, his intention "in particular situations to designate a primary committee among those to whom a bill may be jointly referred, and may impose time limits on committees having a secondary interest following the report of the primary committee."

At the beginning of the 104th Congress, the majority Republicans abolished joint referrals (retaining sequential and split references) and added to House rules the requirement that the Speaker shall "designate a committee of primary jurisdiction upon the initial referral of a measure to a committee."[15] This change was designed in part to achieve greater committee accountability for legislation while retaining significant flexibility for the Speaker in determining whether, when, and how long additional panels will receive the legislation. The House parliamentarian refers to this new form of multiple referral as an "additional initial referral." Such referrals occur in this way:

> H.R. 2. A bill to give the President item veto authority over appropriation acts and targeted tax benefits in revenue acts; to the Committee on Government Reform and Oversight, and in addition to the Committee on Rules, for a period to be subsequently determined by the Speaker, in each case for consideration of such provisions as fall within the jurisdiction of the committee concerned.[16]

For H R 2, the Committee on Government Reform and Oversight is the primary committee of jurisdiction; Rules obtains the measure on an additional initial basis.

Today, it is quite common in the House and Senate for party leaders or caucuses to establish ad hoc task forces to draft legislation, modify committee-reported measures, or monitor issues and areas. Speaker Gingrich, for example, has created so many task forces that it is difficult to keep track of them all. Some of these entities are partisan and others bipartisan. His Task Force on Immigration Reform is composed of 47 Republicans and 7

Democrats and charged with producing a comprehensive report on ways to deal with the problem of illegal immigration.[17] Committees, in short, may be bypassed in whole or in part as informal arrangements are devised (as previously noted on health care) to draft or redraft priority legislation.

Several observations may be made about multiple referral. First, contemporary problems tend to have repercussions in many areas; thus more and more of the major bills coming before Congress—particularly those in new problem areas—will be candidates for multiple referral. Second, to the extent that multiple referral is chosen as an option, the decentralized nature of congressional decision making is reinforced. Third, every time another committee is added to the legislative process there is one more hurdle for a bill to overcome and additional opportunities for delay, negotiation, compromise, and bargaining. Fourth, multiple referrals may promote effective problem solving as several committees bring their expertise to bear on complex issues. Finally, multiple referrals are a growth area in the House. From 6 percent of all House measures introduced during the 94th Congress (1975–1977), multiple referrals climbed to 18 percent of all measures introduced by the 102d Congress (1991–1993). Even with the multiple referral change instituted during the 104th Congress, about 23 percent (347 of 1,510) of the measures introduced during the first 100 days were assigned to two or more committees. Moreover, as Table 4-2 indicates, multiple referrals constitute a significant portion of many committees' workload with some panels (Agriculture and Rules, for example) in the 102d Congress considering more multiply referred bills than singly referred measures. "One bill, one committee" no longer applies to the extent that it once did. With growing frequency, the processing of legislation has become "one bill, many committees," including multiple subcommittee review within the parent committees.

CONSIDERATION IN COMMITTEE

Once a bill has been referred, the receiving committee has several options. It may consider and report (approve) the bill, with or without amendments or recommendation, and send it to the House or Senate. It may rewrite the bill entirely, reject it, or simply refuse to consider it. Failure of a committee to act on a bill usually is equivalent to killing it. When a committee does report a bill, the House or Senate often accepts its main thrust even when the chamber amends the bill on the floor.

There are several reasons for this general deference to the committee's decisions. Committee members and their staffs have a high degree of expertise on the subjects within their jurisdiction, and it is at the committee stage that a bill comes under its sharpest congressional scrutiny. It is understandable, therefore, that a bill that has survived the scrutiny of the experts will be given serious consideration on the floor by the generalists of the House and Senate.

TABLE 4-2 Number of Single and Multiple Referrals of Measures to Selected House Committees, 102d Congress (1991–1993)

Committee	Total Referrals	Single Referrals (% of Total)		Multiple Referrals (% of Total)	
Agriculture	290	138	(48)	152	(52)
Appropriations	151	136	(90)	15	(10)
Armed Services					
[National Security]	388	204	(53)	184	(47)
Banking	454	272	(60)	182	(40)
Energy and Commerce					
[Commerce]	1094	558	(51)	536	(49)
Foreign Affairs					
[International Relations]	637	413	(65)	224	(35)
Natural Resources					
[Resources]	605	381	(68)	183	(32)
Judiciary	999	736	(74)	263	(26)
Rules	200	78	(39)	122	(61)
Ways and Means	1988	1406	(71)	582	(29)

Source: Background Materials: Supplemental Information Provided to Members of the Joint Committee on the Organization of Congress (Washington, D.C.: Government Printing Office, 1993), 504.

Note: Names in brackets are as known in the 104th Congress.

Recent Congresses, however, have seen more floor challenges to some committee-reported measures. Defense and foreign aid bills, for instance, have been subject to extensive floor "markups" in both chambers. Hundreds of amendments are sometimes offered to these measures. At one point in 1987 Sen. Sam Nunn, D-Ga., then Armed Services chairman, noted that "[W]e have had 118 amendments on this bill. That is more amendments than any Department of Defense authorization bill since the Senate first started the [Pentagon] authorizing process."[18] Contrast this development with the situation a few decades ago when legislation reported by the Armed Services committees was enacted in each house within a day or so and with few amendments proposed from the floor. Today's consideration of military measures may stretch over several weeks. Similarly, a House member pointed out "that it is not uncommon to see 100 amendments on a foreign aid bill."[19]

Several factors account for this stepped-up floor amending activity and its success. Much of it is aimed at committees that deal with the most important or controversial bills and it may come from outside the committee and even from the panel's own membership. First, deference to committee prerogatives has been weakened with the influx of many activist and independent legislators who are not reluctant to challenge seniority leaders. Second, the composition of committees may be substantively or ideologically imbalanced, as compared with their respective chambers. Hence, rank-and-file members propose changes in the committees' handiwork. Third, there are electoral incentives for entrepreneurial lawmakers to offer floor amendments that can garner them publicity back home, especially given today's wide array of media outlets, including nationally televised gavel-to-gavel coverage of House and Senate floor proceedings. Fourth, lawmakers have ample staff and analytical resources to craft substantively attractive or politically friendly (or unfriendly) floor amendments. Finally, the increase in floor amendments sometimes reflects legislative mistrust of the executive. Many amendments are offered and written in great detail to limit or define executive behavior and activity.

It is true that a committee's decision not to report a bill generally will be respected by the chamber as a whole. After all, if the experts have decided not to approve a bill, why should their decision be second-guessed? Furthermore, since all members of Congress are members of committees and dislike having their committee's decisions overturned, they normally will reciprocate by not undermining the actions of another committee. Finally, the general impact of the rules in both chambers—particularly those of the House—is to "protect the power and prerogatives of the . . . committees . . . by making it very difficult for a bill that does not have committee approval to come to the floor."[20]

There are procedures, to be examined in Chapters 5 and 8, for overturning committee decisions or even bypassing committees, but these procedures are employed infrequently and are seldom successful.

When a committee decides to take up a major bill, the full committee may consider it immediately. But more often the chairman assigns the bill to a subcommittee for study and hearings. The subcommittee usually schedules public hearings on the bill, inviting testimony from interested public and private witnesses. Or the subcommittee may decide not to schedule hearings if there is strong opposition from executive branch officials or interest groups. After the hearings have concluded, the subcommittee meets to *mark up* the bill—that is, to consider line by line and section by section the bill's specific language before sending it to the full committee. The subcommittee may approve the bill unaltered, amend it, rewrite it, or block it altogether. It then reports its recommendations to the full committee.

When the full committee receives the bill, it may repeat the subcommittee's procedures, in whole or in part, or it may simply ratify the subcommittee action. If the committee decides to send the bill to the House or Senate, it justifies its actions in a written statement called a *report*, which must accompany the bill.[21]

On a major legislative proposal the entire committee process may stretch over several Congresses, with a new bill (containing identical or similar provisions) introduced at the beginning of each Congress. For example, the struggle to enact the aforementioned immigration reform measure took several consecutive Congresses. Indeed, decades may pass before some bills become public law.

On the other hand, the process can be compressed into a very short time. In less than twenty-four hours, both houses passed and the president signed into law legislation stopping a nationwide rail strike in 1991 "by mandating further mediations between labor and management."[22]

The start of a new Congress usually is marked by a slow legislative pace while committee and party leaders attend to matters such as filling vacancies on the committees. Needless to say, the start of the 104th Congress was anything but slow. The pace of work during its first three months was record-breaking in comparison with other Congresses. The "House was in session 528 hours [during its consideration of the Contract with America], more than double that of the first 13 weeks of the last Congress and nearly triple that of the same period in the 102nd Congress."[23] The physical and political fatigue of the 100-day marathon led Speaker Gingrich to say, "I'll be strung up by my troops if I say there's a second 100 Days."[24]

The remainder of this chapter will focus on the key steps in committee consideration of a major bill: hearings, the markup, and the report. To simplify the discussion, assume that the committee chairman is also the chairman or an ex officio member of the subcommittee to which the bill is referred, and assume further that the full committee merely ratifies the subcommittee decisions. Because the committee chairman is a central figure in the legislative process, it is first necessary to focus on the chairman's role.

THE COMMITTEE CHAIRMAN'S ROLE

To a large extent, the options available to a committee in dealing with a bill are exercised by the chairman, who has wide discretion in establishing the committee's legislative priorities. The chair's sources of authority include: (1) control of the committee's legislative agenda, (2) control over referral of legislation to the subcommittees, (3) management of committee funds, (4) control of the committee staff, and (5) the designation of majority party conferees. According to former House Banking chairman Gonzalez, the "real power" of the chairmen is "to set the agenda, mark the course and lead."[25]

The chairman usually has had a long period of service on the committee and is likely to be better informed than most other members on the myriad of issues coming before the committee. (When the 104th Congress began, the majority Republicans amended House rules to limit committee and subcommittee chairmen to six years of consecutive service.) The chairman often is privy to the leadership's plans and policies, especially the Speaker's or the

Senate majority leader's legislative objectives. Chairmen can use these and other resources to delay, expedite, or modify legislation.

A chairman who opposes a bill may simply refuse to schedule hearings on it until it is too late to finish action on the bill during the session. The same result can be achieved by allowing the hearings to drag on. A chairman having strong negative feelings about a bill can instruct the committee staff to "stack" the witnesses testifying on it. He may ask witnesses holding favorable views to submit statements rather than appear in person.[26] In the case of welfare reform hearings in the 104th Congress, some opponents of the legislation were almost excluded from the process. "We had to fight to testify," remarked a staff aide for Catholic Charities, "and when we did it was 8 o'clock at night after almost all the members and all the press had gone."[27]

Committee members who are likely to raise dilatory questions or employ obstructive tactics may be recognized before others. Through control of committee funds and the power to hire and fire most staffers, the chairman can block action on a bill by directing the staff to disregard it.[28]

A chairman who favors a bill can give it top priority by mobilizing staff resources, compressing the time for hearings and markups, and, in general, encouraging expeditious action by committee members. Several items on the GOP's Contract with America went directly to full committee markup, bypassing the public hearing stage entirely. In sum, chairmen are typically the chief "agenda setters" of committees. They employ this prerogative to powerfully influence the form in which bills are reported to the House or Senate as well as the timing of floor action on their bills.

The ranking minority party member on a committee also has certain prerogatives. He or she controls the hiring and firing of minority staff aides; recommends minority party conferees; acts as the minority side's spokesperson to the press and media; influences, depending on his or her relationship with the committee leader, the panel's agenda of activities; and designates the minority floor manager for legislation reported by the committee. Newt Gingrich of Georgia, then in line to be House GOP leader in the 104th Congress, told the ranking committee members of the 103d Congress "not to take their jobs for granted" because "seniority alone won't be enough to win or retain" those leadership positions in the new Congress. They must, he implied, work to advance and broaden GOP interests so Republicans could become the majority party. As it turned out, the Republicans did win control of Congress and Gingrich, instead of becoming minority leader, became Speaker in 1995.[29]

THE CHAIRMEN IN PERSPECTIVE

The general picture of a committee chairman as an almost omnipotent figure underwent modification during the 1970s. Until then, the chairmen were the central figures in the legislative process, holding power equaled only by a few party leaders of great influence, such as House Speaker Sam Rayburn, D-Texas (1913–1961; Speaker 1940–1947, 1949–1953, 1955–1961), or Senate Majority Leader Lyndon B. Johnson, D-Texas (1937–1961; majority leader 1955–1961). Beginning about 1970, however, the chairmen's power was gradually trimmed under pressure from newly elected members and from some senior members who wanted to equalize the distribution of power. During that decade, Congress approved several fundamental changes that ended the nearly absolute authority enjoyed by committee chairmen.

The most significant change came when both parties modified the seniority system, specifically the practice of automatically selecting as chairman the majority party member with the longest continuous service on the committee. Seniority meant that chairmen normally came from safe congressional districts, were repeatedly reelected, and served until their retirement or death. Because many safe districts during the 1950s and 1960s were in the conservative Democratic South, chairmen often were sharply at odds with Democratic presidents, congressional leaders, and northern Democrats. Nevertheless, as seniority then was practiced, the chairmen could not be removed. They were able to use their entrenched positions to block civil rights and social welfare legislation proposed by Democratic administrations.

Today, because of party rules changes made by Democrats and Republicans in each chamber, all committee chairmen (and ranking minority committee members) are subject to secret ballot election within the confines of their party caucus or conference. Chairmen and ranking minority committee members are now accountable for their actions to at least a majority of their party's caucus or conference. When Democrats were in charge of the House, they even deposed committee and subcommittee chairmen and elected other party members in their stead. With the GOP takeover of Congress following the 104th Congress, the House, as noted above, amended its rules to impose term limits on committee and subcommittee chairmen. (Senate Republicans, too, took up the issue of term limits for committee chairmen.) Speaker Gingrich, backed by overwhelming party support, ignored seniority and named committee chairmen who were ideologically in sync with the leadership's views and agenda.

The one-person rule that previously characterized many House and Senate committees has evolved toward greater bargaining and negotiation among the chairman, other members of the committee, and party leaders. Nevertheless, committee chairmen remain crucial figures in the legislative process. As House Commerce Chairman Thomas J. Bliley, Jr., of Virginia stated, "The chairman controls the staff, the chairman has the right to name the subcommittee chairmen and has much more power than the . . . Democratic chairmen [had] when they were in the majority."[30] In brief, Congress functions primarily through its committees, the person who heads one has considerable influence over the advancement or defeat of legislation.

HEARINGS

Ostensibly, hearings are important primarily as fact-finding instruments. Witnesses from the executive branch, concerned members of Congress, interest group spokesmen, academic experts, and knowledgeable citizens appear before the committee to give it their opinions as to the merits or pitfalls of a given piece of legislation. From this encounter the committee members gather the information needed to act as informed lawmakers. Hearings also aid members in determining whether new laws are needed or whether changes in the administration of existing laws will be sufficient to resolve problems. "Legislation need not always be the answer," remarked then senator and later vice president Albert Gore, Jr., D-Tenn. "In many areas, the most important missing ingredient is attention, and an elevated awareness of the problem can be a very successful outcome of hearings."[31]

Much information is available to committee members long before the hearings take place. Major bills usually have been the subject of public debate and media coverage. The positions of the administration and the special interest groups are well known, and, in all likelihood, executive branch officials and pressure group lobbyists have already presented their views to committee members and staff aides well in advance of the hearings. The members themselves often have strong partisan positions on the legislation and thus may have little interest in whatever additional information emerges from the hearings.[32] Hearings often are poorly attended by committee members, and interruptions are common because of floor votes or quorum calls.

HEARINGS FORMAT

Staff research and preparatory work precede committee hearings. Committee aides, for example, may interview witnesses in advance, compile research and documentary materials, and prepare notebooks for committee members to use at the hearings. These notebooks may list questions—and the answers—used in probing the witnesses. Explained a committee staff director:

> We write the question. Under the question we write the answer. This is the answer we expect to get on the basis of the staff research that has gone before. The Member who asks the question knows what the witness has told us in the weeks and weeks of preparation; and he knows he should get the same information. If he does not get that information, then he has the answer in front of him and he can ad lib the questions that solicit that information or refute it.[33]

Hearings can be perfunctory, particularly where similar legislation has been before the committee for several years in succession. Witnesses usually read from prepared texts, while the committee members present often feign interest or simply look bored until the statement has been read. Once the formal testimony is completed, each committee member, usually in order of seniority, will ask the witness questions. House rules allot at least five minutes per member to question witnesses. Senate rules have no such provision. Instead, each committee establishes its own rules governing internal procedures. For example, the rules of the Senate Energy and Natural Resources Committee give each member five minutes to question witnesses until all members have had an opportunity to ask questions.

The traditional format for questioning witnesses in the House and Senate does not lend itself to opportunities for extended exchanges between members and witnesses, for analysis of different points of view, or for in-depth probing of one witness's views by another. "I've testified before Congress several times," said an automotive executive, "and I've always come away a little frustrated by the limits on the dialogue."[34] This is changing, however, as numerous committees today structure their hearings to ensure that conflicting viewpoints are heard. Committees often hold panel sessions where members and witnesses of different persuasions sit in round-table fashion to discuss the merits of particular policies.

Committees also conduct joint hearings (with other panels or with the "other body") or "field" hearings (away from Capitol Hill). The House Judiciary Subcommittee on the Constitution, for example, conducted field hearings during mid-1995 to receive testimony and generate public support for a school-prayer constitutional amendment.[35] Congress is experimenting with "video teleconferencing" where witnesses located around the United States or around the world can testify before House or Senate committees without ever leaving their locale.[36] Committees even hold "prehearings" to assess privately issues that witnesses will discuss later during the public sessions.

Purposes of Hearings

Despite their limitations, hearings remain an integral part of the legislative process. They provide a permanent public record of the position of committee members and the various interested groups on a legislative proposal. Preparation of congressional testimony is regarded as an important function by executive agencies and interest groups. Above all, hearings are important because members of Congress believe them to be important. The decision to hold hearings is a critical point in the life of a bill. Measures brought to the floor without first being the subject of hearings are likely to be the targets of sharp criticism. (There are, of course, many instances of policies not subject to hearings becoming public law. Offering legislative proposals as floor amendments, incorporating them into conference reports, or burying them in megabills are among the techniques for bypassing committee hearings.) The sanctity of the committee stage is based on the assumption that the experts— the committee members—carefully scrutinize a proposal, and hearings provide a demonstrable record of that scrutiny.

Hearings are perhaps the most orchestrated phase of policy making and are part of any overall strategy to get bills enacted into law. Committee members and staff typically plan with care who should testify, when, and on what issues. Ralph Nader's testimony before several congressional committees on his 1965 best-selling book, *Unsafe at Any Speed,* led to passage of the Traffic Safety Act of 1966. The testimony of celebrity witnesses, such as movie stars, is a sure-fire way to attract national attention to issues. "I haven't seen anything like this in the 30 days we have had hearings," declared a Senate subcommittee chairman about the extensive press coverage when actress Elizabeth Taylor testified on the need for more money for AIDS research.[37]

Witnesses who have experienced issues or problems first-hand and can tell their stories to lawmakers are especially sought after, because they put a human face on public problems.

> Speaking to a congressional committee [considering the issue of child care], a 10-year-old girl whose parents could no longer afford day care said, "Some things scare me when I'm alone—like the wind, the door creaking, and the sky getting dark fast." "This may not seem scary to you," she told the committee of adults, "but it is to young people who are alone."[38]

Committees, in brief, often want witnesses who will provide a broad coalition of endorsements for their predetermined position and promote political and public support for this course of action.

Hearings serve other functions as well. They may be used to assess the intensity of support or opposition to a bill, to gauge the capabilities of an executive agency official, to publicize the role of politically ambitious committee chairmen and members, to allow citizens to express their views to their representatives, and to promote new ideas or agendas. The Senate's constitutional duties mean that it holds hearings on advising and consenting to treaties and nominations. The Judiciary Committee's televised hearings on the controversial nomination of Robert H. Bork to the Supreme Court dominated the headlines in 1987, as did its hearings in 1991 on the selection of Clarence Thomas, who was accused by Anita Hill of sexual harassment, to replace Thurgood Marshall as the sole African American on the Court.

Congress also uses investigative hearings to explore problems and issues. These hearings serve several purposes. They promote efficient program administration, secure information needed to legislate, and inform public opinion. Millions of American households watched on television the unfolding drama of the 1954 Army-McCarthy hearings, the 1957 hearings into corruption of the Teamsters Union, the Senate Foreign Relations Committee's hearings during the 1960s on the Vietnam War, the Watergate hearings of the 1970s, the 1987 Iran-contra hearings, and the mid-1990s Whitewater hearings. Investigative hearings often prompted the drafting of legislation to deal with the problems that were uncovered and subsequently led to more hearings on the legislation itself. On occasion, individual members conduct ad hoc, or "informal," investigative hearings of their own.

IMPORTANCE OF TIMING

The chairman's control over the timing and duration of hearings is an important factor in deciding a bill's fate. Postponing or dragging out hearings is an obvious ploy if the chairman is opposed to a bill or wants it extensively modified. There are times, too, when a delay will help the bill's chances. This might be true if sentiment in favor of the bill is much stronger in the other chamber than in the chairman's. Another possibility is that both House and Senate chairmen supporting a bill may want to expedite hearings because of time pressures.

In short, committee chairmen take into account a variety of factors when scheduling hearings. Among the more important are the positions of the White House, pressure groups, executive agencies, the other chamber, party leaders, and principal legislators; the climate of public opinion; the intensity of feeling of the major participants; and the mix of witnesses who can create momentum and support for legislation.

THE MARKUP

Some time after the conclusion of the hearings, the committee or subcommittee meets to mark up the bill. (The origin of the word *markup* probably stems from lawmakers making "marks" on the bill—changing its terminology and phraseology). Here committee members decide whether the legislation should be rewritten, either in whole or in part. The chairman's task is to keep the committee moving, getting unanimous agreement on as many sections of the bill as possible, trying to resolve differences through compromise, and sensing when to delay or speed up matters.

METHODS OF ACCELERATION

To expedite action on President Clinton's health proposal, Senator Kennedy, then chairman of the Labor and Human Resources Committee, presided over marathon markup sessions for nearly three weeks—daily from 8 a.m. to as late as 9 p.m.[39] Marathon markup sessions were certainly the order of the day during House consideration of the Contract with America. When Rep. Barney Frank, D-Mass., complained to Judiciary Chairman Hyde about abbreviated markups and the speed with which legislation was moving through the committee, Chairman Hyde responded: "I am a transmission belt for the leadership. Either I don't live up to the contract, or I move faster than both I or the Democrats want."[40]

Committee chairmen regularly line up leadership backing for their committee's bill, insert special provisions in legislation to win members' support, or accommodate interest group or agency officials by permitting them to make presentations during committee markup. Senate chairmen may even collect *proxy* votes to win key issues—quite often to the chagrin of the minority committee members who are in attendance. Proxy voting permits a committee member to cast a vote for an absent colleague. (Proxy voting is prohibited on the House or Senate floor.) As one account of a Senate markup noted:

> [The subcommittee chairman's] preparation paid off. The committee had been in session for more than five hours and about half the members had left. But when the vote was taken, [the chairman] could supplement the eight votes he had in the room with nine proxies. The vote was 17–12.[41]

In the GOP-controlled 104th Congress, the House banned proxy voting in committees and subcommittees. During their forty years in the minority, Republicans long chafed under a system where their members attended committee markups yet the GOP members were always outvoted by the handful of Democrats present because the chairman voted the proxies of absent colleagues. However, during the hectic 100-day contract period, and given the narrow GOP majority on many committees, the ban on proxy voting made life difficult for the new majority. Many GOP lawmakers with multiple assignments had to sprint to cast votes in committees marking up bills simultaneously. Moreover, because Republicans often voted to waive the House rule prohibiting committee meetings while the House floor was considering amendments, lawmakers had to run back and forth from committee markup sessions and the floor to cast votes.

Because the chairman is likely to be responsible for managing the bill on the floor, he or she will try throughout the markup to gather as much support within the committee as possible. A sharp split among the committee members will seriously damage chances of passing the bill in the House or Senate.

Chairmen may schedule pre-markup sessions to discuss possible revisions of the legislation and to develop a consensus on the bill. These informal and private sessions on major legislation are commonplace for many congressional committees. On the Clean Air Act, for instance, the Senate chairman of the Environment and Public Works Committee "scheduled several seminars prior to formal markup, to educate the members on the major issues and to try to develop a consensus among the members on the issues."[42] The chairmen also usually decide which legislative vehicle will be used for markup purposes (the so-called chairman's mark): the bill as introduced, a related proposal drafted by the chair, a staff proposal, or the administration's plan. Tactically, it often is easier to retain something already in a bill than to add it by amendment.

North American Free Trade Agreement . . .

Congressional consideration of trade agreements is dictated by a Byzantine set of [statutory] rules known as the fast track. The rules specify that Congress cannot amend a trade agreement submitted for its approval and must vote on the agreement within 90 days of its submission by the president. The idea is to prevent Congress from rewriting the terms of a trade deal after it has been negotiated.

But the fast track also allows for congressional input before the president formally sends the trade agreement to Congress. That is what is happening now to the North American Free Trade Agreement (NAFTA).

The House Ways and Means and Senate Finance committees, which have jurisdiction over trade, hold what are called "mock" or "shadow" markups of NAFTA. Essentially, these are drafting sessions at which lawmakers put together a bill to make the changes necessary to bring U.S. law into conformity with the terms of the agreement. They do it informally to make sure they get it right, because, under fast track, the bill that implements the agreement cannot be amended once it is introduced.

Other committees with jurisdiction over NAFTA—and there are many in an agreement of such complexity—also will suggest draft language, but they do not have to conduct "mock" markups.

Ways and Means and Finance will do most of the work, and they are aiming to complete the informal drafting by the end of October. If there are any differences between the bills drafted by the two committees, members will hold an informal conference to produce a compromise version.

BOX 4-3

The markup, then, is where committee members redraft portions of the bill, attempt to insert new provisions and delete others, bargain over final language, and generally determine the final committee product. A unique type of markup is associated with trade or other measures considered under statutes that mandate so-called fast-track (or expedited) legislative procedures (see Box 4-3, "North American Free Trade Agreement on the Fast Track").

Most markups today are conducted in open session. During consideration of President Clinton's major health care reform bill, the House Republican leader announced:

. . . On the Fast Track

The final product is then sent back to the White House, where President Clinton will review it, and, as one official put it, if it stays "within the letter and the spirit" of NAFTA, it will be introduced in Congress as the NAFTA-implementing bill. Practically speaking, there is little room for lawmakers to massage the terms of NAFTA.

Where members do have latitude is in making add-ons to the agreement as long as they do not require renegotiation with Mexico. For example, lawmakers could conceivably attach an amendment providing benefits for workers who lose their jobs as a result of NAFTA. The only restriction is that amendments be "necessary or appropriate." Then Clinton will have to decide whether to accept the provision, substitute his own version or drop it entirely in the final bill.

Clinton is not required to introduce a NAFTA-implementing bill that is identical to the one presented by Congress, but previous presidents have done so as long as the provisions are consistent with the underlying trade agreement. There is a political consideration: If the president ignores Congress' suggestions, it could endanger the bill's passage.

Once the implementing bill is introduced, the House must act first and do so within 60 days. House committees with jurisdiction over aspects of NAFTA have 45 working days to send the bill to the floor, or it is brought up automatically. In the Senate, committees must act within 15 days after the House vote. Then the full Senate has another 15 days to vote on the bill. Administration officials say they want the House and Senate to vote on NAFTA by the end of November.

Source: David S. Cloud, *Congressional Quarterly Weekly Report,* October 1, 1993, 262.

In order to insure that the [health] markup process remains as open as possible, and that information on all votes in [the various] Committees is made public, it is my intention to place in the *Congressional Record* on a daily basis each and every committee roll call vote, broken down by members. This will help to ensure that members are fully accountable to their constituents for the way they vote in committee.[43]

When Republicans won control of the 104th Congress, the House amended its rules to require committee reports accompanying legislation to contain the names of members voting for and against any amendments and motions to report the bill. Republicans also made committee reports more easily available to the public over the Internet.

However, important measures (tax, defense, and appropriations, for example) are still discussed in private without much protest from the press, media, or others. Even proponents of openness admit that members can reach compromises and make tough decisions more easily when they are away from the glare of lobbyists sitting in the audience. Moreover, with scores of journalists and media representatives covering Capitol Hill, the results of closed sessions become quickly known once the committee opens its doors. "Closed sessions don't necessarily mean bad legislation and sunshine doesn't guarantee good laws," remarked a journalist. "Openness just makes the process and the results slightly easier to discern."[44]

STRATEGIES DURING MARKUP

Members use various strategies during the markup. One ploy, sometimes used by opponents of a bill, is to add amendments to strengthen the measure. During markup of a gun control measure by the House Judiciary Committee, the National Rifle Association, the major lobbying group opposed to gun control, told its supporters in Congress that it would be easier to defeat a strong firearms proposal. "The way we look at it," said an NRA lobbyist, "the stronger the bill that comes out of committee, the less chance it has of passing on the floor."[45] Conversely, proponents of a strong bill might try to weaken it in committee so that it stands a better chance of winning majority support on the floor. Supporters then can try to persuade the other chamber or the House-Senate conference committee to strengthen the measure.

Another approach used by a bill's opponent is to offer a flurry of amendments to make a bill complicated, confusing, and unworkable for the executive branch agencies that would have responsibility for administering the law. Moreover, offering scores of amendments, or offering one huge amendment and insisting that it be read—slowly—in full, may stall the markup and grant opponents additional time to lobby against the legislation. For example, Sen. William V. Roth, Jr., R-Del., sought to delay markup of a federal employees bill "by reading—slowly and deliberately—a lengthy statement explaining his opposition. He then offered seven amendments" and launched into a long explanation of each.[46] To prevent Republicans from conducting committee markups, minority House Democrats sometimes boycotted the meetings to delay or prevent drafting sessions from proceeding.

Mobilizing grass-roots support and targeting the states or districts of key committee members is often critical to the outcome of markups. During markup by Congress's tax-writing panels, special interests work diligently to shape the thinking of these committees. As one account noted:

For several months, the lobbyists have been working behind the scenes trying to influence the outcome by personally talking with members and aides
of the tax committees in both chambers and getting members of their lobbying coalitions to write and phone their Congressmen. To bolster their
arguments, the lobbyists have hired independent research firms to produce
analyses that show the impact of the proposed tax changes, and they have
tried to mold public opinion through press releases and advertising campaigns.[47]

To win over opponents or skeptics, chairmen often willingly accept
numerous amendments from their committee colleagues. In this way, these
members develop a stake in the legislation and may stand united behind it
on the House or Senate floor. The reverse strategy is to load down a bill with
scores of costly "add-ons" so the legislation might sink of its own weight.
"We might just as well kill the president's [health reform] bill with kindness"
by adding costly and untenable amendments, said Rep. Marge Roukema, R-
N.J., during a markup of the House Education and Labor (now Economic and
Educational Opportunities) Committee. "I'm not going to kill it with kindness." She voted against the amendments.[48]

An important factor affecting markup strategies in the Senate is the
smaller size of its panels. "To get an amendment adopted [on my Senate sub-
committee]," wrote Sen. Paul Simon, D-Ill., "I need only two other votes of
the five-member subcommittee. In the House, subcommittees with more than
20 members are common," which means greater effort in forging winning
coalitions.[49]

Equally significant is that Senate rules permit legislation that has been
blocked in committee to be considered on the floor. Senators can offer to
pending legislation nongermane amendments that embody bills pigeonholed
in committee. The opportunity to offer such amendments on the Senate floor
indicates a significant difference between House and Senate committee procedures: efforts to block legislation in committee are less successful in the
Senate than in the House. Senate floor procedures provide various ways to
bypass committees if they refuse to report measures (Chapter 8).

Nevertheless, bypassing a Senate committee occurs infrequently. All
senators have an interest in seeing that the prerogatives of their own committees are respected. Thus they will make every effort to resolve their differences within the committee.

Compromise during the committee markup—indeed, at any stage of
the legislative process—is more likely when the members recognize that
some sort of legislation is necessary. The outcome of markups, with their
tradeoffs, compromises, and complexities, may not represent perfection, but
it does reflect what attracted at least a majority vote of the panel members.
As former Rep. Dan Rostenkowski, D-Ill., then Ways and Means chairman,
said after a tax markup: "We have not written perfect law. Perhaps a faculty
of scholars could do a better job. A group of ideologues could have provid-

TABLE 4-3 Procedural Differences at Preliminary Stages

House	Senate
Bills are usually introduced before committee or floor action can proceed.	Bills may originate from the floor.
No effective way to challenge the Speaker's (parliamentarian's) referral decisions.	Referrals are subject to appeals from the floor.
The Speaker is granted authority by House rules to refer bills to more than one committee.	Multiple referrals occur by unanimous consent, although the majority leader and minority leader can jointly offer a motion to that effect.
The Speaker is authorized, subject to House approval, to create ad hoc panels to consider legislation.	Neither the majority leader nor the presiding officer has authority to create ad hoc panels to process legislation.
Difficult to bypass committee consideration of measures.	Bypassing committee consideration of measures occurs more easily.
Floor action is somewhat less important for policy making than committees.	Floor action is as important as committee action in decision making.

ed greater consistency. But politics is an imperfect process."[50] Rep. Barney Frank, D-Mass., emphasized this point in describing coalition building on a controversial measure: "Our goal is to find something that's 60 percent acceptable to 52 percent of the members and I think we have a 75 percent chance of doing that."[51] Table 4-3 lists several major House-Senate differences regarding the introduction, referral, and committee consideration of legislation.

THE REPORT

Assuming that major differences have been ironed out in the markup, the committee then meets to vote on reporting the bill out of committee. House and Senate rules require a committee majority to be present for this purpose; otherwise, a point of order may be made on the floor that will force the bill to be returned to committee.

Bills voted out of committee unanimously stand a good chance on the floor. A sharply divided committee vote presages an equally sharp dispute on the floor. A bill is rejected if the committee vote is a tie.

Committees have several options when they vote to report, or approve, a bill. They may report the bill without any changes or with various amendments. Or a committee that has extensively amended a bill may instruct the chairman to incorporate the modifications in a new measure, known as a *clean bill.* This bill will be reintroduced, assigned a new bill number, referred back to the committee, and reported by the panel. Only the full House or Senate, of course, can amend legislation; committees formally recommend revisions to measures.

The clean-bill procedure is employed for various reasons, such as expediting floor consideration of legislation. Another factor involves germaneness. Provisions already in a bill are ipso facto considered to be germane; hence they are protected against points of order (germaneness rules apply to proposed floor amendments and not to provisions in the bill itself). Finally, a clean bill may reflect negotiated agreements between key committee members and executive officials.

Committees may take other actions besides favorably reporting a bill. They may report out a bill adversely (unfavorably), recommending that the bill not be passed by the full chamber, or they may report legislation without a formal recommendation, allowing the chamber to decide the bill's merits. In either case, though, the bill may be sent to the full chamber and scheduled for floor action. Committees adamantly opposed to a measure may decide, of course, not to take any action at all, thus blocking further consideration except through special procedures (see Chapters 5 and 8).

After the bill is reported favorably, or unfavorably, the chairman instructs the staff to prepare a written report. (House rules require a written report to accompany legislation; Senate rules do not impose that requirement, but it is informally observed in most cases.) The report will describe the purposes and scope of the bill, explain the committee revisions, note proposed changes in existing law, and, usually, include the views of the executive branch agencies consulted. Committee members opposing the bill often will submit dissenting, or minority, views. Any committee member may file minority, supplemental, or additional views, which are printed in the committee report. House and Senate rules also require committee reports to contain certain information, such as five-year cost estimates, oversight findings, and regulatory impact statements. Measures are open to points of order on the floor if their committee report fails to contain this material. A report may be more than a thousand pages long.

Reports are directed primarily at House and Senate members and seek to persuade them to endorse the committee's recommendations when the bill comes up for a floor vote. The reports are the principal official means of communicating a committee decision to the entire chamber. Committee reports

---

104TH CONGRESS *1st Session*	HOUSE OF REPRESENTATIVES	REPORT 104–88

COMPETITIVE BIDDING IN GRANTING LICENSES AND PERMITS

MARCH 23, 1995.—Committed to the Committee of the Whole House on the State of the Union and ordered to be printed

---

Mr. BLILEY, from the Committee on Commerce,
submitted the following

REPORT

together with

MINORITY VIEWS

[To accompany H.R. 1218]

[Including cost estimate of the Congressional Budget Office]

The Committee on Commerce, to whom was referred the bill (H.R. 1218) to extend the authority of the Federal Communications Commission to use competitive bidding in granting licenses and permits, having considered the same, report favorably thereon without amendment and recommend that the bill do pass.

CONTENTS

99–006

FIGURE 4-2

are also used by executive officials to fathom legislative intent when they are interpreting ambiguous statutory phrases. Federal judges, too, examine committee reports and other aspects of legislative history (hearings, floor debates, and conference reports) when laws are challenged in court.

Some federal justices, most notably Supreme Court Justice Antonin Scalia, argue that legislative history should be minimized in the interpretation of ambiguous statutes. Instead of examining staff-written committee reports to determine what Congress intended, Justice Scalia contends, judges should consider only the exact text of the statute because it is that and not "legislative history" that lawmakers vote on. Justice Stephen G. Breyer, by contrast, answers "that no one claims that legislative history is in any strong sense `the law,' but rather that it is useful in ascertaining the meaning of words in the statute."[52]

Reports are numbered, by Congress and chamber, in the order in which they are filed with the clerk of the House or Senate. (Thus, in the 104th Congress the first House report was designated H Rept 104-1 and the first Senate report as S Rept 104-1. The first page of a sample report is shown in Figure 4-2.) Both the committee-reported bill and its accompanying report are then assigned to the appropriate House or Senate calendar to await scheduling for floor action. Once committees conclude their markups, members often mobilize to achieve their objectives, such as lobbying colleagues and organizing pep rallies on Capitol Hill. Chapters 5 and 7 discuss the House and Senate calendars and scheduling legislation for floor action in each chamber.

SUMMARY

Of the thousands of bills introduced in each Congress, the vast majority have little support and provoke little controversy. Congress routinely either ignores these measures or rushes them through the legislative process, reserving the bulk of its time for the relatively small number of bills that deal with the nation's major problems and programs.

Once a bill is introduced, it usually is referred to a single committee, the one having jurisdiction over its subject area. In cases of overlapping jurisdiction, a bill may be referred to several committees.

In committee the critical decision is made either to ignore, expedite, or carefully examine a legislative proposal. Since committee members and their staffs have more expertise on matters within their jurisdiction than members of Congress as a whole, the fundamental outlines of committee decisions generally will be accepted. As one senator explained in objecting to a pending bill on the floor:

> [This bill] did not emerge from the crucible of the committee process, tempered by the heat of debate. The committees are important because, like

them or not, they do provide a means by which legislation can be carefully considered, can be exposed to public view and public discussion by calling witnesses before the committee.[53]

The rules and precedents of both chambers reinforce committee prerogatives. Exceptions to these rules exist, but members of Congress generally are reluctant to see the committee system weakened by frequent recourse to extraordinary procedures. Hence, members are encouraged to resolve their differences within the committees.

The key stages in committee consideration of a bill are hearings, the markup, voting, and the report. This process is controlled largely by the subcommittee and committee chairmen, who have many resources at their disposal to expedite, delay, or modify legislation. Chairmen choose tactics on the basis of their assessment of the many political and legislative factors present and their long-range objectives for the bill. Opportunities for a chairman to act arbitrarily have been trimmed somewhat by recent procedural reforms, particularly the abandonment of seniority as an automatic system for choosing chairmen.

When a bill has been reported from committee, it is ready to be scheduled for floor action. Like the winnowing process that occurs in committee, scheduling involves the budgeting of congressional time. Important political choices must be made in determining the order in which bills will be considered on the floor, how much time will be devoted to each measure, and to what extent the full chamber will be permitted to re-examine a committee decision. House scheduling of legislation is discussed in the next chapter and Senate scheduling in Chapter 7.

NOTES

1. Spencer Rich and Dana Priest, "Three House Panels Move to Assert Primacy Over Health Bill," *Washington Post*, October 24, 1993, A20. Also see Spencer Rich, "Senate Chairmen in Tug of War Over Health Plan," *Washington Post*, November 24, 1993, A1, and Alissa J. Rubin, "Members' Health Concerns Now Center on Turf Wars," *Congressional Quarterly Weekly Report*, October 9, 1993, 2734–2737.
2. Beth Donovan, "Leaders To Forge New Bill From Committee Efforts," *Congressional Quarterly Weekly Report*, July 2, 1994, 1792.
3. Julie Rovner, "Senate Committee Approves Health Warnings on Alcohol," *Congressional Quarterly Weekly Report*, May 24, 1986, 1175.
4. On rare occasions a member introducing a bill may ask unanimous consent that it be passed. Unanimous consent is more likely to be granted in the Senate than in the House and only on a noncontroversial measure or one on which all members agree that immediate action is required.
5. Article I, Section 3, of the Constitution provides that the vice president is president of the Senate, but he infrequently presides over that body. The Constitution also provides for a president pro tempore, a largely honorary position elected by the majority party. By custom, that position nowadays is held by the most senior

member of the majority party. Usually, however, junior members designated by the majority leader preside over the daily sessions of the Senate.

6. Each chamber has a parliamentarian, who is an expert on rules of procedure. During a session, the parliamentarians or one of their assistants always are present to advise the chair on all points of order and parliamentary inquiries. They also provide technical assistance to members in drafting bills or motions.

7. Committee structure and jurisdiction are not identical in the House and Senate. There are nineteen standing (permanent) committees in the House and seventeen in the Senate.

8. Richard Cohen, "Capitol Hill Watch," *National Journal*, March 27, 1993, 765.

9. Jon Healey, "Panel Vote Sets Up Clash," *Congressional Quarterly Weekly Report*, May 20, 1995, 1412.

10. David C. King, "The Nature of Congressional Committee Jurisdictions," *American Political Science Review*, March 1994, 49.

11. "Senate Parliamentarian Can Control Course of Bills," *C-Span Update*, January 14, 1990, 6. See Lawrence E. Filson, *The Legislative Drafter's Desk Reference* (Washington, D.C.: CQ Press, 1992).

12. Bob Eckhardt and Charles L. Black, Jr., *The Tides of Power* (New Haven: Yale University Press, 1976), 146.

13. *Congressional Record,* January 30, 1995, H849.

14. See Bruce I. Oppenheimer, "Policy Effects of U.S. House Reform: Decentralization and the Capacity to Resolve Energy Issues," *Legislative Studies Quarterly* (February 1980): 5–30; and David J. Vogler, "Ad Hoc Committees in the House of Representatives and Purposive Models of Legislative Behavior," *Polity* (Fall 1981): 89–109.

15. *Congressional Record,* January 4, 1995, H36.

16. *Congressional Record,* January 4, 1995, H122.

17. *The Hill,* May 17, 1995, 4.

18. *Congressional Record,* October 2, 1987, S13438.

19. *Congressional Record,* May 23, 1995, H5391.

20. Randall B. Ripley, *Congress: Process and Policy (New York: W.W. Norton, 1975)*, 75.

21. There is no formal requirement in the Senate for written reports to accompany legislation voted out of committee.

22. Mike Mills, "Hill Moves with Alacrity to End Rail Strike," *Congressional Quarterly Weekly Report,* April 20, 1991, 981.

23. *Congressional Monitor,* April 17, 1995, 1.

24. *Wall Street Journal,* April 7, 1995, A16.

25. *Congressional Record,* May 9, 1994, H3181.

26. "Stacking" was modified somewhat by the Legislative Reorganization Act of 1970, which gives the minority party on a committee at least one day in which to call witnesses. On issues where the committee members of both parties share similar views, however, opposing witnesses have limited opportunities to testify.

27. *Washington Post,* May 21, 1995, A4.

28. Members of Congress rely heavily on committee staff for assistance in organizing hearings, selecting witnesses, and drafting bills, as well as for many other key support functions. The chairman's control of committee staff therefore is an important resource in his control of the legislative process.

29. Timothy Burger, "Gingrich Warns All Ranking Members Not To Take Their Posts for Granted Next Year," *Roll Call,* March 24, 1994, 3.

30. Kirk Victor, "Mr. Smooth," *National Journal,* July 8, 1995, 1759.

31. *Wall Street Journal,* April 11, 1986, 54.

32. Members unable to attend a committee session frequently assign committee

staffers to attend the meeting and brief them later. Staff aides can ask questions of witnesses if authorized by committee rules or by the chairman.

33. *Workshop on Congressional Oversight and Investigations*, 96th Cong., 1st sess., H Doc 96–217, 25.
34. *Congressional Record*, May 7, 1987, E1789.
35. *Washington Times*, May 30, 1995, A2.
36. Curt Suplee, "Eliminating Witnesses," *Washington Post*, November 7, 1991, A21.
37. *Washington Post*, May 9, 1986, D8.
38. *Christian Science Monitor*, November 27, 1985, 28. Also see Barbara Vobejda, "Children Show Congress Scars of Gun Violence," *Washington Post*, March 11, 1993, A16.
39. Ceci Connolly, "Kennedy's Politics, Policy Collide," *Congressional Quarterly Weekly Report*, June 11, 1994, 1523.
40. Gabriel Kahn, "Hyde Battles Away on Judiciary Panel," *Roll Call*, February 20, 1995, 15.
41. *Congressional Quarterly Weekly Report*, October 3, 1987, 2409.
42. *State Government News*, April 1982, 4.
43. *Congressional Record*, March 16, 1994, H1418.
44. *Washington Post*, May 6, 1984, F5. See Jacqueline Calmes, "Few Complaints Are Voiced as Doors Close on Capitol Hill," *Congressional Quarterly Weekly Report*, May 23, 1987, 1059–1060.
45. *Washington Post*, February 6, 1976, A6.
46. Elizabeth Palmer, "Roth's Parliamentary Moves Halt Hatch Act Reform," *Congressional Quarterly Weekly Report*, March 7, 1992, 534.
47. *New York Times*, October 15, 1985, D25.
48. Dana Priest and Spencer Rich, "Key Hill Committees Take Up Health Care Legislation," *Washington Post*, May 19, 1994, A23.
49. Paul Simon, "Trying on the Senate for Size," *Chicago*, November 1985, 150.
50. *Washington Post*, November 25, 1985, A4.
51. *Washington Post*, February 24, 1988, A22.
52. Robert A. Katzmann, "Justice Breyer: A Rival for Scalia On the Hill's Intent," *Roll Call*, May 30, 1994, 5. See Joan Biskupic, "Congress Keeps Eye on Justices As Court Watches Hill's Words," *Congressional Quarterly Weekly Report*, October 5, 1991, 2863–2867, and Joan Biskupic, "Listening In on the `Conversation' Between Court and Congress," *Washington Post*, May 1, 1994, A4.
53. *Congressional Record*, September 26, 1986, S13769.

CHAPTER 5

Scheduling Legislation in the House

"The power of the Speaker of the House is the power of scheduling," stated Thomas P. "Tip" O'Neill, Jr., D-Mass., who served more consecutive years as Speaker (1977-1987) than anyone else.[1] Scheduling floor activities in the House is fundamentally the prerogative of the Speaker and the majority party leadership. Consequently, the politics of scheduling can strongly influence a bill's fate. Determining when (if at all), what, how, and in which order measures are brought to the floor is part of the arsenal of legislative tools that the leadership uses to produce winning coalitions, provide political protection to members, mobilize bipartisan support, engineer a record of accomplishment, or advance their own partisan agenda.

Through adroit use of his scheduling prerogatives, Speaker Newt Gingrich, R-Ga., was able to deliver on having the House act on the GOP's legislative agenda, entitled "Contract with America" (a balanced budget constitutional amendment, a moratorium on federal regulations, cutting taxes, and so on), within the first hundred days of the 104th Congress (1995-1997). Besides providing an agenda that Republicans campaigned on during the historic November 1994 election, when they won control of the House after forty years as the minority party, the contract provided the focal point for all House Republicans to rally around when the new Congress convened and enabled them to capitalize on their electoral momentum by bringing a specific program to the floor in rather short order.

Scheduling legislation for House floor debate may be simple or complex. Priorities for floor consideration of the bills reported from committee are established by the majority leadership (the Speaker, the majority leader, and the majority whip), sometimes in consultation with the minority leader. Numerous factors influence their decisions: House rules, budgetary timetables, bicameral considerations, election-year activities, the pressure of national and international events, the administration's programs, the leadership's policy and political preferences, and the actions of the Rules Committee. All these elements interact as legislators, pressure groups, and executive agencies maneuver to get favored legislation on the floor.

Scheduling involves many considerations: advance planning of annual recesses and adjournments, coordinating committee and floor action, providing a steady and predictable weekly agenda of business, regulating the flow of bills to the floor during slack or peak periods, and devising a workload that takes into account members' family needs. Before the 104th Congress began, for example, Speaker Gingrich appointed a bipartisan "Family Friendly Advisory Committee" to consider ways to make the House's schedule correspond more closely to family interests, such as scheduling recesses around school vacations or having one day a week set aside for early adjournment so families could have dinner together.[2] Even some "mystery" is involved in scheduling as majority party leaders assess the political climate. A former Speaker, Jim Wright, D-Texas (1987-1989), once noted:

> In scheduling the program for the Congress one must be constantly aware of the importance of maintaining a little suspense. I learned this from Agatha Christie. Always hold something back and keep people guessing a little bit. And that is what we are doing with this bill, quite frankly. We are maintaining a little suspense in the schedule [while we determine the best time for taking up this legislation].[3]

The procedures for managing the flow of bills to the floor have evolved throughout the history of Congress and still undergo frequent change. At first glance, they may appear needlessly complex and cumbersome, but they have an internal logic and over the years have served the needs of the House.

The focus in this chapter is on how bills reach the floor through one of three basic scheduling procedures: (1) special calendar days for speedy action on minor and noncontroversial legislation; (2) privileges (facilitated access to the floor) for certain categories of important legislation; and (3) actions of the Rules Committee, which is charged with the responsibility of scheduling most major legislation.

THE HOUSE LEGISLATIVE CALENDARS

Measures reported from committee are assigned by the clerk of the House to one of four regularly used *calendars*. These list bills in the chronological order in which they are reported from the various committees. The calendars are *Union, House, Corrections,* and *Private*.

Legislation dealing with raising, authorizing, or spending money is assigned to the Union Calendar. Non-money measures of major importance are put on the House Calendar. Noncontroversial measures are assigned to the Corrections Calendar. Bills of a private nature ("for the relief of"), those not of general application and usually dealing with individuals or small groups, are assigned to the Private Calendar. In addition, there is a *Discharge Calendar*, which lists bills removed from committees through special, and infrequently successful, procedures. All of these are discussed below.

MINOR AND NONCONTROVERSIAL BILLS

Legislation on the Corrections and Private calendars is in order only during special calendar days. The House also processes noncontroversial measures that are on the Union or House calendars under procedures that grant them privileged access to the floor during certain designated days of the month. These include bills dealing with the District of Columbia and measures brought to the floor under the suspension of the rules procedure. Each of these expedited procedures for processing relatively minor legislation also is discussed in this chapter.

It is worth noting that any lawmaker can ask unanimous consent at almost any time the House is in session to pass legislation. In 1984, however, the Speaker announced a policy that remains in effect today regarding recognition for such requests.

> [The Speaker] has established a policy of conferring recognition upon Members to permit consideration of bills and resolutions by unanimous consent only when assured that the majority and minority floor leadership and committee and subcommittee chairmen and ranking minority members have no objection.[4]

The Speaker's power of recognition ("For what purpose does the gentleman [or gentle lady] rise?") is an unchallengeable prerogative of the chair. The Speaker can, in brief, deny recognition to lawmakers who ask unanimous consent to pass legislation without having secured in advance the approval of the majority and minority floor and committee leaders.

When the House is in session, members receive a daily document, the *Calendars of the United States House of Representatives and History of Legislation* (see Figure 5-1), which lists all House as well as Senate measures that have been reported from committee. The document is a handy reference source, but not every measure listed is called up and considered by the House.

CORRECTIONS CALENDAR

On June 20, 1995, the House amended its rules and abolished the Consent Calendar and replaced it with a new Corrections Calendar.[5] The Consent Calendar originated in 1909 as a way to expedite action on noncontroverial measures. Legislation on this calendar was in order on the first and third Mondays of the month and adopted quickly without amendment by unanimous consent. However, in recent Congresses (the 102d and 103d, for instance), the Consent Calendar was never used; instead, the House relied increasingly on unanimous consent and suspension of the rules to process noncontroversial or relatively noncontroversial measures.

The idea for a Corrections Calendar was highlighted early in 1995 by Speaker Newt Gingrich. Crediting the concept to Gov. John Engler of

ONE HUNDRED FOURTH CONGRESS

FIRST SESSION { CONVENED JANUARY 4, 1995

SECOND SESSION {

CALENDARS

OF THE UNITED STATES
HOUSE OF REPRESENTATIVES

—————————— AND ——————————

HISTORY OF LEGISLATION

LEGISLATIVE DAY 73   CALENDAR DAY 73

Thursday, May 25, 1995

HOUSE MEETS AT 10 A.M.

SPECIAL ORDERS

(SEE NEXT PAGE)

PREPARED UNDER THE DIRECTION OF ROBIN H. CARLE, CLERK OF THE HOUSE OF REPRESENTATIVES:
By the Office of Legislative Operations

Calendars shall be printed daily—   *Index to the Calendars will be printed the first legislative day of each week*
Rule XIII: clause 6   *the House is in session*

FIGURE 5-1

Michigan, the Speaker stated that he wanted to establish a "Corrections Day" procedure for repealing "the dumbest things the federal government is currently doing."[6] After the Speaker's idea was considered and refined by a party task force and two standing committees, the House voted 236 to 185 to accept the Corrections Day concept.

The Corrections Calendar is in order the second and fourth Tuesdays of the month, at the Speaker's discretion. Only bills that have been favorably reported by committees and assigned to either the House or Union calendars are eligible for placement on the Corrections Calendar. The Speaker has sole authority to determine whether a bill is to be on the agenda for Corrections Day. Bills are debated for one hour, equally divided between the majority and minority; no amendments are permitted except if proposed by the committee or chairman of the primary committee of jurisdiction; a motion to recommit, with or without instructions, may be offered by a minority member; and a three-fifths (or 261) vote is required to pass corrections legislation. A bipartisan advisory group of seven Republicans (named by the Speaker) and five Democrats (named by the minority leader) assists the Speaker in determining which corrections bills are to be taken up.

SUSPENSION OF THE RULES

Another legislative shortcut and increasingly utilized source of agenda control by the Speaker, which may be used for important as well as minor public bills, resolutions, and conference reports, is through *suspension of the rules.* ("I move to suspend the rules and pass HR 1234.") By a two-thirds majority vote, the House may suspend its regular procedures for any bill. To ensure that opponents control half the time, the Speaker, if asked by a lawmaker, is obliged under House rules to inquire if the minority floor manager actually opposes the legislation. Absent an affirmative response, the Speaker will then allocate the twenty minutes to a real opponent of the bill.

A vote to suspend the rules is simultaneously a vote to pass the measure in question. Before the vote, debate is limited to forty minutes, evenly divided between proponents and opponents. Suspension motions formerly required a seconding motion, which required majority approval, but that requirement was dropped in 1991 to eliminate an extra vote. The motion to suspend the rules and pass a bill may include amendments, if they are stipulated in the motion ("I move to suspend the rules and pass HR 1234, as amended."), but floor amendments are not permitted. Bills that fail to gain the necessary two-thirds support may be considered again under regular House procedures. The House rules that govern legislation considered under the Corrections Calendar and suspension procedure are summarized in Table 5-1.

Until the 94th Congress (1975-1977), motions to suspend the rules were in order only during the first and third Mondays of the month and during the last six days of a session when the backlog of bills awaiting floor debate is

TABLE 5-1 The Corrections Calendar and Suspension of the Rules

Corrections Calendar	Suspension of the Rules
Second and fourth Tuesdays	Every Monday and Tuesday, and during the last six days of the session
Bills must be on the Corrections Calendar for three legislative days before House consideration	No deadline
Bills may not be amended unless offered by the primary committee jurisdiction	No floor amendments; 40 minutes of debate
Bipartisan advisory group to advise Speaker	No such group
For bills repealing laws or regulations viewed as unnecessary, obsolete, or overly burdensome	No restrictions on substance of bills ($100 million limit established by GOP Conference)
Three-fifths vote required for passage	Two-thirds of the members voting, a quorum being present, is required for passage

heavy. In 1975 the number of days for suspension of the rules was doubled by adding the first and third Tuesdays. In addition, the House instituted "cluster" voting to save more time and to accommodate lawmakers' constituency activities. (Many members travel to their district on Friday and return late the following Monday.)

Under the most recent version of the cluster voting rule, the Speaker announces that recorded votes on a group of bills considered under the suspension procedure will be postponed until later that day or until the next day. The bills then are brought up in sequence and disposed of without further debate. On the first clustered vote in a series, members have a minimum of fifteen minutes in which to vote; on the remaining votes the Speaker may reduce the time on each one to a minimum of five minutes.

In 1977 the suspension rule was changed again—over the objections of many Republicans—to permit the Speaker to entertain motions to suspend the rules every Monday and Tuesday. The Republican minority saw this as an effort by Democrats to steamroll legislation through the House. Democrats argued that the change facilitated action on the House's business. House Republicans sharply criticized this change, calling it "anti-deliberative" because of the procedure's restrictions on floor debate and amendments.

The Speaker is in complete charge of the measures considered under the suspension procedure. The Speaker "has the discretion whom to recognize for a motion to suspend the rules," the chair noted in response to a question about "why it is impossible to proceed with a suspension bill." I am "exercising that discretion" on this bill, declared the Speaker.[7]

Committee chairmen, usually with the concurrence of their ranking minority colleagues, write the Speaker requesting that certain bills be taken up via the suspension route. (By custom, veterans' bills are brought to the House floor under suspension procedure.) Typically, these are bills that committees have reported. But any measure—reported or not, previously introduced or not, including conference reports or constitutional amendments (which must attract a two-thirds vote)—can be brought to the floor under suspension of the rules if the Speaker chooses to recognize the representative offering the suspension motion. Speaker O'Neill, for example, brought an Equal Rights Amendment (ERA) to the Constitution to the House floor in 1983 under suspension procedure to prevent opponents from offering controversial floor amendments on abortion and the military draft. The ERA failed to attract the required two-thirds vote in part because even its supporters objected to taking up such a significant issue under procedures that limited debate and prevented amendments.

When Republicans won control of the 104th Congress, they (as the Democrats did in 1979) adopted guidelines governing the consideration of measures under the suspension method. Under GOP Conference rules, the Speaker "shall not schedule any bill or resolution for consideration under suspension of the Rules which fails to include a cost estimate, has not been cleared by the minority, was opposed by more than one-third of the committee members [who] reported the bill, and exceeds $100,000,000." To be sure, the leadership "does not ordinarily schedule bills for suspensions unless confident of a two-thirds vote."[8]

The suspension procedure enables the House to bypass normal floor procedures and quickly pass legislation that can attract an overwhelming voting majority. Committee chairmen generally support the suspension of the rules because they can bring measures to the floor under a procedure that protects their bills from floor amendments and points of order. Party leaders, too, use the suspension route to "fast track" emergency legislation or to move their issue agenda. No wonder there was a surge in the use of suspension motions, from 421 during the 98th Congress to 613 in the 102d.

However, with the GOP-controlled 104th Congress, there has been some disinclination to employ suspensions as extensively as in the past. Often prevented from offering floor amendments during the Democratic years of House control, Republicans want to encourage a more open process for considering legislation. The suspension procedure "actually does restrict Members from having the opportunity to participate," stated Rep. David Dreier, R-Calif.[9] Not until more than two months into the 104th Congress (on

March 14, 1995) did Republicans schedule eight noncontroversial measures for consideration under suspension of the rules. Of course, legislation associated with the contract dominated lawmakers' attention during this period.

During the hectic last days of a congressional session, suspension of the rules has been used more frequently and even on important measures. Dozens of bills may be scheduled daily for suspension votes. The parliamentary situation also is somewhat different during this period. Members who at an earlier time in the session might vote against a bill brought up under suspension because they had no opportunity to offer amendments to it or because it was a major bill, might vote for the legislation during the end-of-the-session crunch on the argument that it was that version or nothing.

The minority party's role is also enhanced during this pressure-packed, rush-to-adjourn period, because suspension votes virtually always require some bipartisan support. For example, during the closing days of the 103d Congress, House GOP leaders agreed with Democratic leaders that they would support moving the Safe Drinking Water Act under suspension of the rules to avoid lengthy floor fights. The bill easily passed the House.[10] By contrast, GOP leaders informed then Democratic Speaker Thomas S. Foley, Wash., that their membership opposed moving Superfund legislation (involving the cleanup of hazardous waste sites) through suspension procedure. Given the pressures of the clock and calendar, alternative routes to the floor were not practicable and the bill died with the end of the 103d Congress.[11]

In summary, the great bulk of legislation that goes before the House is passed by means of either unanimous consent requests or the suspension procedure. And measures that fail under suspension may pass the House under a "rule" (see below) granted by the Rules Committee.

DISTRICT OF COLUMBIA LEGISLATION

The federal capital is a unique governmental unit. Residents of the District of Columbia have no voting representation in Congress. (They have a nonvoting delegate in the House and no representation in the Senate.)

In a rules change initiated by D.C. Delegate Eleanor Holmes Norton, the 103d Congress permitted Norton and the four territorial delegates, all Democrats, to vote in Committee of the Whole (see Chapter 6) with the proviso that if their votes determined the outcome of an amendment, there would be an automatic revote without the five delegates' participation. Republicans vehemently protested granting the delegates and resident commissioner the right to vote in Committee of the Whole. In a good example of the majority rule principle in action, they dropped this provision from the House's rulebook for the GOP-controlled 104th Congress.[12]

Despite "home rule" for the capital, the House exercises control over the District principally through two committees, Appropriations and Government Reform and Oversight. Both have a District of Columbia subcommittee. Speaker Gingrich even appointed a party task force to develop plans to transform the District of Columbia into a "world-class" city.[13]

House rules set aside the second and fourth Mondays of each month for District legislation reported by the Government Reform and Oversight Committee. Appropriations bills for the District, however, do not come up during those special days. Instead, they are considered under the privilege given all legislation reported by the Appropriations Committee (see below, "'Privileged' Legislation").

THE PRIVATE CALENDAR

Private bills are designed to provide relief to persons or entities adversely affected by laws of general applicability. Most deal with immigration issues and claims against the federal government. For example, general immigration requirements may be waived or expedited to permit foreign-born athletes to be part of the U.S. Olympic team or to allow a Philadelphia woman to marry a Greek man. Most private bills are referred to the House and Senate Judiciary committees for review and, like other bills, private bills passed by both chambers are sent to the president for signature or veto.

Under House procedures, the Speaker is required to call private bills on the first Tuesday of each month (unless the rule is dispensed with by a two-thirds vote or unanimous consent is obtained to transfer the call to some other day of the month) and, at his discretion, on the third Tuesday as well. Because few lawmakers have the time to review private bills, that job is done by an informal committee of official objectors. It is composed of three members from each party appointed by the majority and minority leaders.

Bills must be placed on the Private Calendar seven days before being called up to give the objectors time to screen them for controversial provisions. (Committee reports on private measures must also be available to the objectors for three calendar days.) The objectors attend House sessions on Private Calendar days to answer any questions about the pending measures. If two or more members of the House object to a bill on the first Tuesday, it automatically is sent back to the committee that reported it, although at the request of a member it may at this time be "passed over without prejudice" for later consideration.

Private bills are considered in "the House as in Committee of the Whole." This is a special forum into which the House transforms itself to consider private bills and some public bills. Here, general debate on legislation is not permitted and amendments are considered under expedited procedures.

Over the years there has been a sharp decline in the number of private bills introduced each Congress. From 1,269 private claims bills introduced during the 80th Congress (1947-1949), the number has fallen to fewer than a hundred in recent Congresses. Among the factors that account for the dropoff are these: First, scandals associated with the introduction of private bills for pay (in the so-called Abscam scandal of 1980, FBI agents dressed as Arab sheiks paid several lawmakers to introduce private immigration bills for them) led to stricter procedures for their consideration. Second, Congress authorized administrative agencies and the U.S. Court of Claims to handle the bulk of these cases. Third, private bills often require an enormous amount of time to handle and in the end the claims can prove to be incorrect or fraudulent. Finally, the current climate of fiscal austerity is not conducive to their introduction. Congressional staff aides suggested that "the prominence of the budget deficit made legislators uncomfortable passing [private claims] bills that paid money to a few individuals when so many other programs affecting larger numbers were being cut."[14]

"PRIVILEGED" LEGISLATION

Under House rules, five standing committees have direct access to the floor for selected bills. These measures may be called up when other matters are not already pending on the House floor. The committees and the types of legislation eligible to be called up for immediate debate are listed in Table 5-2. Despite the privilege, consideration of most of these bills must wait at least three days to give members time to read the committee reports. Special rules from the Rules Committee, however, must lay over only one day, while reports on budget resolutions must be available to members for ten days before those resolutions can go to the floor. (See below, "Traditional Types of

TABLE 5-2 Committees with Direct Access to the Floor for Selected Legislation

Committee	Legislation
Appropriations	General appropriations bills; continuing appropriations resolutions if reported after September 15
Budget	Budget resolutions and reconciliation bills under the Congressional Budget and Impoundment Control Act of 1974
House Oversight	Printing resolutions and expenditures of the House contingent fund
Rules	Rules and the order of business
Standards of Official Conduct	Resolutions recommending action with respect to the conduct of a member, officer, or employee of the House

Special Rules.") Privileged measures are matters of special import to the House as an institution or to the federal government. The Appropriations and Budget panels report measures to finance the operations of the government; the Standards of Official Conduct Committee is concerned with matters involving the public reputation of the House; the House Oversight panel handles necessary housekeeping proposals; and the Rules Committee plays a major role in determining which measures the House considers.

Even privileged measures are subject to points of order (parliamentary objections that any member may raise at an appropriate time) on the ground that they violate certain rules of the House. If upheld, such points of order return the measure to the committee that considered it. It is not uncommon, therefore, that committees with privileged access will ask the Rules Committee to waive points of order against their bills. The Appropriations Committee, for example, may violate House rules banning unauthorized appropriations or legislative provisions (policy provisos) in general appropriations bills and will protect the panel's bills from points of order by persuading the Rules Committee to issue waivers.

MAJOR LEGISLATION

Most major bills do not go directly from committee to a calendar and then to the House floor. Because they are important and usually controversial, they cannot reach the House floor by way of the Corrections Calendar, unanimous consent requests, or suspension procedure. (See Table 5-3 on the use of procedural routes to the floor.) Instead, such measures are given special review by the Rules Committee.

This section on the role of the Rules Committee in scheduling major legislation will review five topics. First, there will be a brief overview of the panel's history; then it will highlight the various roles of the committee; third will be a review of the traditional types of rules granted by the panel; fourth will be a discussion of "creative" rules and the controversy they have engendered in the modern House; and, finally, there will be a look at House adoption of rules.

BRIEF OVERVIEW

The Rules Committee is among the oldest of House panels. The First Congress in April 1789 appointed an eleven-member rules body to draw up its procedures. With a few early exceptions, each succeeding Congress has done the same, although for nearly a century the Rules panel was a select (temporary) committee that prepared procedures for the incoming Congress and then went out of existence.

In 1858 the Speaker became a member and chairman of the Rules Committee. In 1880 the Rules Committee became a standing (permanent)

TABLE 5-3 Procedural Methods by Which Bills Are Called Up in the House

Method	Congress					
	98th	99th	100th	101st	102d	103d
Under Suspension of the Rules	421	428	617	572	613	483
As Privileged Matter	296	277	270	280	282	289
By Unanimous Consent	494	546	459	416	265	160
By Rule	136	91	97	103	143	108
By Private Calendar	64	50	6	37	45	6
By D.C. Calendar	14	4	0	1	7	0
By Consent Calendar	46	34	26	3	0	0

Source: Adapted from Ilona Nickles, Congressional Research Service.

committee, and in 1883 it initiated the practice of reporting special orders, or rules, which, when agreed to by majority votes of the House, controlled the amount of time allowed for debate on major bills and the extent to which they could be amended from the floor.

From 1858 to 1910 the Speaker determined which bills reached the House floor. He also appointed the other members of the Rules Committee and thus ensured a favorable attitude toward his policy preferences. Speakers during this period permitted the Rules Committee to acquire overwhelming authority over the House's agenda and the order of business. Speaker Joseph G. Cannon, a Republican from Illinois who was Speaker from 1903 to 1911, abused these and other powers, with the result that the House "revolted" in 1910 and removed the Speaker from the Rules Committee. The House majority leadership, however, retained—and still retains, in cooperation with the Rules Committee—fundamental control over the flow of legislation reaching the floor.

It has not always worked that way, however. There have been maverick Rules chairmen. One of the best known was Rep. Howard W. Smith, D-Va. (1931-1967), who presided over the committee with an iron hand from 1955 to 1967. Smith was no traffic cop simply regulating the flow of bills to the floor. He firmly believed the committee should "consider the substance and merits of the bills," and he often blocked measures he disapproved of and advanced those he favored, sometimes thwarting the will of the majority.[15]

The Rules Committee lacks authority to amend bills, but it can bargain for changes in return for granting rules. Smith frequently did this. In an attempt to lessen the power of the conservative coalition of southern Democrats and Republicans that controlled the committee from the mid-1930s to the early 1960s, House liberals succeeded in adopting a series of rules changes beginning in the late 1940s. But the independent power of the chairman was not effectively curbed until the membership of the committee was expanded in 1961.[16] (This resulted from a truly titanic battle between Speaker Sam Rayburn, D-Texas, and Rules Chairman Smith. Newly elected president John F. Kennedy directly intervened in an internal matter affecting House rules—a rare event for any president. Kennedy supported Rayburn's successful effort to enlarge Rules to change its ideological complexion so conservative members could not kill the president's "New Frontier" program.)

The committee's current composition is nine Republicans and four Democrats. Traditionally, the panel has had a disproportionate partisan ratio to ensure majority control. Today, the committee is one of the few centralizing panels in a decentralized House. Hence the importance of its rule-writing responsibilities.

By the 95th Congress the Rules Committee had become closely linked to the Speaker. In 1975 the Democratic Speaker was authorized to appoint, subject to party ratification, all majority party members of the Rules Committee. In 1989 House Republicans authorized their leader to name all the GOP members of the Rules Committee. Small wonder, then, that the panel is often the scene of sharp partisan battles.

This kind of institutional change has reduced the Rules panel's independence. As former Speaker Wright stated:

> The Rules Committee is an agent of the leadership. It is what distinguishes us from the Senate, where the rules deliberately favor those who would delay. The rules of the House, if one understands how to employ them, permit a majority to work its will on legislation rather than allow it to be bottled up and stymied.

Or as GOP Rules member Porter Goss, Fla., said about the panel's relations with Speaker Gingrich: "How much is the Rules Committee the handmaiden of the Speaker? The answer is, totally."[17]

Still, the Rules Committee's power should not be underestimated. The Speaker cannot track every major and minor bill or issue instructions constantly to the panel. The history of the Rules Committee is "one of the committee's accommodating the leadership on the one hand and seeking independent status on the other."[18] For the time being, at least, the emphasis is on sharing power with the Speaker.

ROLE OF THE RULES COMMITTEE

The power of the Rules Committee lies in its scheduling responsibilities: its "traffic cop" or even "police chief" role. Besides deciding whether to grant a rule, the committee must craft rules to accomplish diverse purposes, such as promoting orderly consideration of major policy alternatives on the floor, protecting partisan objectives, or expediting action on priority measures.

As public bills are reported out of committee, they are entered in chronological order on one of two calendars, the Union Calendar (technically, the Calendar of the Committee of the Whole House on the State of the Union) or the House Calendar. On the former are placed all revenue bills, general appropriations bills, and measures that directly or indirectly appropriate money or property (including all authorization measures); all remaining public bills, which generally deal with administrative and procedural matters, go on the latter.

If all measures had to be taken up in the order in which they were listed on the calendars, as was the practice in the early nineteenth century, many major bills would not reach the House floor before Congress adjourned. Instead, major legislation reaches the floor in most instances by being granted precedence through a special order (rule) obtained from the Rules Committee. A rule is really a simple resolution (H Res). A written request for a rule usually is made to the Rules chairman by the chairman of the committee reporting the bill.

The Rules Committee holds a hearing on the request with witnesses limited to members of Congress and debates it in the same manner that other committees consider legislative matters. One congressional scholar called hearings the "dress rehearsal" function of the Rules Committee.

> Rules members comprise the first audience for a piece of legislation outside the narrow confines of the committee and subcommittee that reported it. As such, the hearing on a rule request serves as a "dress rehearsal" for bill managers before they take the legislation to the House floor. The hearing on a rule is an opportunity for them to present their case and test the reaction from Rules members.[19]

Following the hearings, Rules members craft their rule and vote it out of committee. A sign of the partisanship that exists on the Rules Committee is the surge in the number of its roll call votes. Where the panel used to vote out a rule by voice vote or unanimous consent, there has been an increase from eighteen recorded votes during the 100th Congress to more than five hundred in the 103d.[20]

The rule, if granted, then is considered on the House floor and voted on in the same fashion as regular bills. A rule serves two principal purposes:

1. It bumps a bill up the ladder of precedence, eliminating the waiting time that would be needed if chronological order were observed. The Rules Committee, in effect, shuffles the Union and House calendars by holding back rules for some bills and reporting them for others.
2. It governs the length of debate permitted once the bill reaches the floor and the extent to which a measure can be amended.

In blocking or delaying legislation from reaching the floor, the Rules Committee is not necessarily playing an obstructionist role. It actually may be providing "political cover" by drawing fire away from the leadership, certain committees, and individual members. It is not uncommon for representatives to request the Rules Committee to prevent unwanted bills or amendments from reaching the floor. As former Speaker O'Neill once said, "It takes the heat for the rest of the Congress, there is no question about that."[21] For example, Speaker Gingrich directed the Rules Committee to disallow any floor amendment on abortion to a welfare reform bill; abortion is an especially divisive issue for the Republican party.[22]

The committee also acts as an informal mediator of disputes among other House committees and members. Because of overlapping jurisdictions, one committee may report a measure that trespasses on the authority of another. In such a case, the Rules Committee may resolve the dispute by authorizing the second committee to offer amendments or by refusing to waive points of order on the floor, thus giving members of the second committee an opportunity to attempt to delete the offending matter. Intraparty conflicts are mediated, too, by Rules so majority party members are not hanging their "dirty linen" in public when contentious issues reach the floor. To be sure, interparty differences are reconciled to the extent that bills enjoy cross-party support.

The Rules Committee also plays a jurisdictional arbitration role on multiply referred legislation. As a precondition for a rule, the committee may urge or require competing committees to agree on the vehicle—one of the committee's reported bills, some consensus product, or something else—for floor debate and amendment. "Prior to the Rules Committee consideration" of the water resources bill, said former chairman [and now ranking minority member] Joseph Moakley, Mass., "the four committees responsible for this bill negotiated a substitute text to be used as the basis for [floor] consideration."[23]

This practice limits floor fights among rival committees, simplifies floor decision making, expedites the processing of legislation, and avoids putting Rules in the position of deciding that one panel's bill rather than another's will be the vehicle for floor discussion.

The Rules Committee also has substantive responsibilities. It reported out such major measures as the Legislative Reorganization Act of 1970, the Congressional Budget and Impoundment Control Act of 1974, and resolutions providing for the creation of a permanent Select Intelligence Committee and the televising of House floor sessions. In 1994 the committee reported a package of rules changes, which the House adopted, that applied to House employees the broad protections of ten workplace safety and antidiscrimination laws. The objective was to ensure House employees the same protections under these laws, such as the Fair Labor Standards Act of 1938 and the Occupational Safety and Health Act of 1970, that were "currently enjoyed by private sector and executive branch employees."[24] (On the first day of the GOP-controlled 104th Congress, and the first item in the Contract with America that was signed into law, legislation was enacted applying these statutes to *all* congressional employees.)

TRADITIONAL TYPES OF SPECIAL RULES

The Rules Committee traditionally grants three basic kinds of rules: *open, closed,* and *modified.* The distinction among them goes solely to the question of the amendment process. All three types almost always provide a fixed number of hours for general debate. In addition, any of these types also may contain waivers of points of order. An example of a rule from the Rules Committee is shown in Box 5-1.

OPEN RULE. Prior to the 93d Congress (1973-1975), most bills were considered under open rule (see Table 5-4 and the section on creative rules for a discussion of the shift in the proportion of open and closed rules). As Bob Michel, R-Ill., wrote at the end of his thirty-eight-year career in the House, the last dozen as GOP leader: When Democrats controlled the House, they "clamped down on the granting of open rules, making it more and more difficult for Members to offer amendments to legislation."[25] Given their frustrating and even embittering experience with rules that often restricted their right to offer amendments, when Republicans took control of the House, the Rules Committee provided more amendment opportunities for all lawmakers.

Under an open rule, any germane amendment to a bill may be offered from the floor. Amendments may be simple or complex. For example, an amendment may simply extend the funding of a program from two to four years or it may rewrite whole sections of a bill. Some committees, such as Science, customarily request the Rules Committee to grant an open rule for their legislation.

Although open rules permit any and all germane amendments, they do have a downside in the length of time it may take to complete action on legislation and in the unpredictable character of the many amendments that might be offered. After two weeks of debate and with nearly 170 amendments still pending to one of their Contract with America measures, Republicans began to have some doubts about open rules. They believed Democrats were offering scores of amendments to an unfunded mandates bill to prevent Republicans from considering all their Contract bills within the first 100 days

AN OPEN RULE

HOUSING FOR OLDER PERSONS ACT OF 1995

Mr. DIAZ-BALART. Mr. Speaker, by direction of the Committee on Rules, I call up House Resolution 126 and ask for its immediate consideration.

The Clerk read the resolution, as follows:

H. RES. 126

Resolved, That at any time after the adoption of this resolution the Speaker may, pursuant to clause 1(b) of rule XXIII, declare the House resolved into the Committee of the Whole House on the state of the Union for consideration of the bill (H.R. 660) to amend the Fair Housing Act to modify the exemption from certain familial status discrimination prohibitions granted to housing for older persons. The first reading of the bill shall be dispensed with. General debate shall be confined to the bill and shall not exceed one hour equally divided and controlled by the chairman and ranking minority member of the Committee on the Judiciary. After general debate the bill shall be considered for amendment under the five-minute rule. It shall be in order to consider as an original bill for the purpose of amendment under the five-minute rule the amendment in the nature of a substitute recommended by the Committee on the Judiciary now printed in the bill. Each section of the committee amendment in the nature of a substitute shall be considered as read. At the conclusion of consideration of the bill for amendment the Committee shall rise and report the bill to the House with such amendments as may have been adopted. Any Member may demand a separate vote in the House on any amendment adopted in the Committee of the Whole to the bill or to the committee amendment in the nature of a substitute. The previous question shall be considered as ordered on the bill and amendments thereto to final passage without intervening motion except one motion to recommit with or without instructions.

BOX 5-1

of the 104th Congress, as promised. Hence, the GOP voted to limit debate to ten minutes for each of the approximately 170 pending amendments. Added Rules Chairman Gerald Solomon, R-N.Y., "It looks like we're going to have to increasingly restrict rules if the Democrats won't cooperate."[26]

TABLE 5-4 Open Versus Restrictive Rules, 95th-103d Congresses

Congress	Open Rules		Restrictive Rules	
	Number	Percent	Number	Percent
95th	179	85	32	15
96th	161	75	53	25
97th	90	75	30	25
98th	105	68	50	32
99th	65	57	50	43
100th	66	54	57	46
101st	47	45	57	55
102d	37	34	72	66
103d	31	30	71	70

Source: Congressional Record, October 5, 1994, H10862.

Open rules, in brief, raise the important issue of where the fundamental deliberations on legislation should take place: in the committee setting among a relatively small number of lawmakers who specialize in the subject area, or on the House floor with the entire membership having a say in policy formulation?

CLOSED RULE. A closed rule prohibits floor amendments, but rarely are such "pure" closed rules reported by the Rules Committee. Instead, closed rules in the contemporary House usually forbid floor amendments except those offered by the reporting committee or committees. On occasion, a closed ruled will be reported that requires a bill to be considered in the House and not in the Committee of the Whole (see Chapter 6) under procedures where debate is limited to one hour and amendments are prohibited because the rule automatically orders the previous question on the bill. Critics say closed rules (also called "gag" rules) hamper the legislative process and violate democratic norms. Rep. Charles W. Stenholm, D-Texas, put it this way:

> In most cases, closed rules say that we as individual Members are willing to allow a small portion of the whole decide what information we need to consider, what complexities our minds are able to master, and from what alternatives we should choose. Furthermore, many times closed rules indicate either an arrogance on the part of the proponents of a bill or an insecurity about the bill's merits or abilities to stand up against competing ideas.[27]

Supporters of closed rules say they are necessary in the case of very complex measures subject to intense lobbying. In addition, national emergency legislation sometimes needs to be expedited by the closed rule procedure.

Tax bills provide a good illustration of the pressures surrounding closed rules. For decades and still today the House considers tax measures under closed rules, agreeing with the argument of Wilbur D. Mills, D-Ark. (1939-1977), chairman of the Ways and Means Committee from 1959 to 1974, that tax legislation was too complex and technical to be tampered with on the floor. If unlimited floor amendments were allowed, Mills argued, the internal revenue code soon would be in shambles and at the mercy of pressure groups.

MODIFIED RULE. A third category of special orders is the modified rule. There are two versions of this rule: modified open and modified closed. A modified open rule specifies that all parts of the bill are open to amendment except a specific title or section. A modified closed rule states that the entire bill is closed to amendment except a certain title or section. Modified closed rules may also identify the specific floor amendments that are permitted and identify the lawmakers who may offer them. The fundamental feature of a modified rule is that some parts of the bill will be open to amendment and some parts will not be.

WAIVER RULES. Finally, there are rules waiving points of order. Under these rules, which appear in open, closed, and modified rules, specific House procedures may be temporarily set aside. Without such waivers, measures in technical violation of House procedures could not be dealt with rapidly, and important parts of bills could be deleted for technical reasons during floor debate. "If we went strictly by the House rules," remarked a House member, "I am sure this body would have a very difficult time operating."[28] Waivers permit timely floor action on those measures. There are even rules that are exclusively "waiver" in character. Their purpose is typically to waive points of order against the consideration of legislation that is "privileged" (it has a right-of-way to the floor), such as conference reports, but which has also violated various House rules.

Generally, waivers are of two types: exemptions from *specific* House rules and procedures or *blanket* waivers of all points of order against pending legislation. There has been a surge of blanket and specific waivers in recent Congresses. For example, from the 96th Congress (1979-1981) to the 102d Congress (1991-1993) there was a jump from 8 percent to 14 percent in the number of times the Rules Committee waived the House rule requiring committee reports on legislation to be available to lawmakers for at least three calendar days (excluding Saturdays, Sundays, and legal holidays) before the House can take up a measure. The Republicans, then in minority, objected strenuously to the increase of waivers. When they assumed majority control of the House in the mid-1990s, Republicans amended the rules of the House to require the Rules Committee, to the maximum extent possible, "to specify in any special rule providing for the consideration of a measure any provisions of House rules being waived."[29]

There are occasions, however, when blanket waivers are essential to law-making. "Under the circumstances in which this bill is brought to the floor," exclaimed a GOP lawmaker, "I do not see how we could possibly proceed without the [blanket] waivers that are being asked for."[30] Unsurprisingly, minority Democrats complain when Republicans bring legislation to the floor with blanket waivers. "They have," stated Rep. Barney Frank, D-Mass., "exactly the same view of rules and waivers that we had."[31]

"CREATIVE" RULES FOR THE HOUSE

Fundamental changes in the workings of the House that began during the 1970s and continue into the 1990s triggered the rise of so-called creative rules. The House witnessed a dramatic redistribution of internal influence from powerful, seniority-chosen committee chairmen to scores of individual lawmakers, including subcommittee chairmen, factional leaders, and rank-and-file members. Party leaders and caucuses gained influence, too, as with the Speaker's multiple referral authority and the role of party caucuses in approving (or disapproving) committee chairmen (or ranking minority members).

In addition, great substantive and procedural complexity triggered the need for creative rules. Not only did measures become bigger and more complex, but also new procedures—multiple referrals, the requirements of the 1974 Budget Act, and various statutory provisions providing special procedures for certain bills—required the Rules Committee to sort through the complications and devise an orderly procedure for debating and amending legislation. The House also amended its rules in ways that encouraged lawmakers to ask for more recorded votes. The House permitted recorded votes in the Committee of the Whole (votes were unrecorded in this main amending forum until 1971, see Chapter 6), and electronic voting was authorized two years later.

These changes, combined with outside developments such as the heightened role of the news media in politics, produced a basic shift in the political culture of the House. It went from the "to get along, go along" spirit of Speaker Rayburn's era to an entrepreneurial and participatory style where even freshman lawmakers have wide opportunities to voice their views and exert their influence in all phases of lawmaking. (The role of the seventy-three GOP freshmen in the 104th Congress has been especially large; they are among the most active lawmakers in efforts to downsize the role of the federal government.) The Rules Committee responded to the new climate by providing members with wide-open amending opportunities on the floor. As one scholar pointed out:

Fewer than 900 amendments were offered in the 91st Congress (1969–1970) and fewer than 800 were offered in the 92d Congress (1971–1972), but over

1,400 were offered in the 93d Congress (1973–1974) and nearly 1,400 were offered in the 94th (1975–1976). In the 95th, floor amendments peaked at nearly 1,700. Clearly, the incentive to put oneself or one's opponents on the record helped to stimulate more amending activity. . . . [Further, a] group of Republicans—John Ashbrook of Ohio, Robert Bauman of Maryland, and John Rousselot of California—deliberately badgered Democrats with many amendments and requests for recorded votes.[32]

By the end of the 1970s, Democratic leaders and lawmakers wanted the Rules Committee to exert greater control over floor procedures. Members wanted greater predictability in an environment grown more conflict-ridden and unpredictable. The open amendment process produced longer sessions, disruptions in members' schedules, more dilatory tactics, and numerous challenges to committee-reported measures that often undercut carefully crafted compromises that had been negotiated in advance of floor consideration. For example, when President Jimmy Carter's proposal to create a Department of Education went to the floor in June 1979, "Republican opponents prepared nearly 200 amendments, for the express purpose of delaying a final vote and blocking passage."[33]

Other factors, too, contributed to the need for creative rules and the procedural crackdown that limited members' amendment opportunities. They included the aforementioned use of multiple referrals, which required Rules to play a larger coordinative role in arranging floor action on legislation reported by several committees; the rise of megabills hundreds of pages in length that contained Democratic priorities that the Speaker did not want picked apart on the floor; and the escalation of sharp partisanship, especially in the aftermath of Republican Ronald Reagan's election as president in November 1980 while the House remained in Democratic hands. GOP lawmakers, for example, sponsored floor amendments designed to embarrass Democrats and to supply Republican House challengers with campaign ammunition.

In response to these diverse circumstances, the Democratic controlled Rules Committee tightened opportunities for floor amendment and devised a variety of innovative and procedurally creative rules, which remain available to the GOP-controlled 104th Congress. Their primary objectives are to expedite floor decision making, focus member attention on the major policy alternatives, enhance partisan goals, and strengthen committee prerogatives. Among these creative procedures are structured, self-executing, king-of-the-hill, and multiple-stage rules.

STRUCTURED RULES. Structured rules limit the number of floor amendments, establish a specific order in which those amendments are to be offered, frequently identifying the member who can offer each amendment, and typically prohibit any change in the amendments made in order. These rules may also prescribe debate limits on the entire amendment process or on each amendment made in order. Structured rules may require that all amendments be published in the *Congressional Record* prior to floor action on the legislation. This requirement aids the floor managers. "Newer chairmen are kind of unsure of themselves," said former Rules chairman Moakley. "They ask for amendments to be printed [in advance, in the *Record*] so they can be ready for anything."[34]

On the one hand, the thrust of these rules is to restrict members' general right to offer floor amendments. This result frequently arouses the ire of minority party members. On the other hand, structured rules can expand the range of policy options put before the membership. Issues that are not eligible under normal parliamentary procedures can be made eligible for floor consideration. The Rules Committee can allow consideration of nongermane amendments, legislation stuck in committee, or even measures that have never been introduced.

Whether restrictive, expansive, or both, a fundamental thrust of structured rules is to define the sequence in which specific amendments are to be voted upon. Sometimes the purpose is to benefit the committee that reported the legislation; sometimes it grants other members an opportunity to revamp the reporting committee's priorities. There is little question, however, that the Rules Committee's ability to determine the sequence of action can influence the ultimate outcome.

For example, the majority leadership may support an expensive initiative over a less costly one advocated by the minority leadership. The Rules Committee could fashion a rule that permits votes on only three policy alternatives: the costly version; the less costly version; and a compromise midway between the other two, advanced by the majority leadership and designed to attract broad support. Members can then explain to constituents who opposed both the "budget-buster" and "inadequate" alternatives that they voted for the "reasonable" option.

SELF-EXECUTING RULES. Traditionally used to expedite consideration of Senate amendments to House-passed legislation, self-executing rules now appear in more complex guises. Self-executing rules stipulate a two-for-one procedure: adoption of the rule simultaneously enacts another measure, amendment, or both. The House, in short, is deemed to have passed a separate proposition when it adopts the rule. Controversial proposals, as a result, are never voted on separately in either the House or the Committee of the Whole. This type of rule "saves the House time by avoiding multiple subsequent votes that can be taken care of by the rule,"[35] and it allows members to avoid taking a direct recorded vote on a controversial issue. The majority Republicans, too, have employed this kind of rule.

KING-OF-THE-HILL RULES. Completely new to Capitol Hill are king-of-the-hill (or king-of-the-mountain) rules. "As far as I know," said Rules Chairman

Richard W. Bolling, D-Mo., during May 1982 debate on a rule governing consideration of the concurrent budget resolution, this procedure is "unique."[36] The rule is unusual in a parliamentary sense for two major reasons. First, it permits the House to vote on an array of major policy alternatives—so-called substitutes that are the equal of new bills—one after the other. Significantly, no matter the outcome—yea or nay—on any of the substitutes, the king-of-the-hill rule typically stipulates that the vote on the last substitute is the only one that counts for purposes of accepting or rejecting a national policy. As a Democratic Rules member explained in describing a rule on a concurrent budget resolution to which major alternatives would be proposed:

> Each substitute will be in order notwithstanding the prior disposition of any one of them. The amendments will be considered under the so-called king-of-the-mountain procedure whereby the last amendment . . . will be considered to have been finally adopted in the Committee of the Whole and reported back to the House.[37]

Speaker Gingrich, then House minority leader, highlighted the partisan importance of structuring the choice situation for lawmakers. "[If] you are the Democratic leadership, what you do is you set up the bills and you say to your [partisan] Members, vote for anything you want to, but when you get to the last one, vote for ours."[38] Several advantages flow from the king-of-the-hill rule. One is that it provides "political cover" to legislators who can cast votes on several policy alternatives and explain their actions to constituents in any manner they choose. Another is that the rule limits criticism of the Rules Committee. The panel can allow votes on major policy alternatives advocated by different House factions without taking sides among them.

Finally, the king-of-the-hill rule waives scores of procedures and precedents. For instance, parliamentary principles state that once part of a bill is amended, it is not generally in order to reamend that part unless another amendment, broader in scope, changes the part by taking a "bigger bite" of the legislation. The massive substitutes made in order by the king-of-the-hill rule amend literally everything in the pending legislation. Technically, nothing is left to be changed and the amending process automatically terminates under traditional House procedures. Traditional procedures, however, are not followed when this type of rule is used, because political and policy objectives are of overriding concern.

MULTIPLE-STAGE RULES. The Rules Committee will sometimes issue several rules for the same bill (multiple-stage rules) to facilitate coherent consideration of issues or to expedite action on legislation. Defense legislation, for instance, has often been considered with a series of rules that separates general debate from the amendment process. For example, the initial rule on a defense bill will govern the terms for general debate. The objectives are to focus House deliberation on the major issues and to apportion debate fairly among the interested parties. Then a second rule will be granted to govern the amendment process on the principal military issues. All related amendments might be grouped together and be debated under specific time limits. A third or even fourth rule might then regulate how all the remaining amendments will be considered by the membership. (The time lapse among multiple-stage rules can be hours, days, or even weeks.) For example, the GOP-controlled Rules Committee crafted a rule that only provided for general debate on a welfare reform measure; the next day, the committee reported another rule to govern the amendment process on the bill.[39]

GOP Innovations

When Republicans assumed majority control of the House in 1995, they promised, as noted earlier, to provide a fair and open amendment process. This goal, however, sometimes clashed with a fundamental objective of any majority party: passage of priority measures even if that means restricting lawmakers' amendment opportunities. Democrats, trying to hold the GOP firmly to the new openness they promised, regularly chastised Republicans for providing anything less than a completely open and unrestricted amendment process. Republicans returned the rhetorical fire, as the following exchange between ranking Democrat Moakley and Rules Chairman Solomon demonstrates.

> Mr. Moakley. [Y]ou said you were going to come forward with open rules so everybody could fully participate. I say to the gentleman, if you want to emulate our Congress, fine, but I thought you were coming in with a new broom, that you were going to sweep clean and give all open rules.

> Mr. Solomon. I say to the gentleman, you never had it so good. We are treating you twice as fairly as you treated us. Never in the history of this Congress has a minority been treated as fairly as we are treating you.[40]

Throughout the 104th Congress, Republicans and Democrats prepared "dueling statistics" on the number of open versus restrictive rules.[41] During the period when the Contract with America was considered by the House, Republicans said they reported open rules 72 percent of the time; Democrats claimed that it was only 26 percent. Their differences stemmed from how each defined an open rule and what measures were included in their calculations. Republicans, for instance, included three noncontroversial bills brought to the floor with open rules. Democrats deleted those from their count. They argued that Republicans granted open rules to the bills solely to pad their figures; the measures were so noncontroversial they should have been brought up under suspension of the rules procedure.[42]

There is little question, however, that change has characterized the GOP-run Rules Committee. Speaker Gingrich, for instance, appointed one freshman, two women, and three sophomores to the committee. Not since 1915 had a GOP freshman been assigned to this influential panel.[43] Significantly, at least two creative rules employed by the panel merit discussion: queen-of-the-hill and time-structured rules.

QUEEN-OF-THE-HILL. When they were in the minority, Republicans regularly lambasted Democrats for use of the king-of-the-hill procedure. Once in the majority, GOP Rules Chairman Solomon objected to this rule because it "allowed lawmakers to be on both sides of an issue and violated the democratic principle that the position with the strongest support should prevail."[44] As a result, Republicans rejected the king-of-the-hill rule in favor of the queen-of-the-hill rule, which means that whichever substitute amendment wins the most votes in the Committee of the Whole (see Chapter 6) is forwarded to the full House for a vote on final passage. In the event that two or more amendments receive the same number of affirmative votes, then the last one voted on is considered as finally approved.

The Rules Committee employed the queen-of-the-hill rule on a proposed constitutional amendment to establish term limits for lawmakers. (As part of their Contract with America, Republicans wanted to replace career politicians with citizen legislators.) The rule made in order two GOP substitutes (each imposed a limit of twelve years for senatorial service but differed on the length of House service) and one Democratic alternative (applying any new term limits to current members) to the base bill (a six-term limit for House service) supported by the GOP leadership. None of the substitute amendments even attracted minority support, and, in an outright rejection of a contract item, the congressional term limits proposal failed to attract the two-thirds vote required to enact constitutional amendments.[45] On May 22, 1995, in a 5 to 4 ruling, the Supreme Court said that states could not impose term limits on federal lawmakers (*U.S. Term Limits Inc. v. Thornton*).

TIME-STRUCTURED RULES. To accommodate their pledge for open rules with their need to act on priority bills, the Rules Committee issues rules that establish debate limits on the entire amendment process. A ten-hour cap for debating and voting on amendments is an example of such a rule. (These rules, too, commonly include the stipulation that members who pre-print their amendments in the *Congressional Record* should be accorded priority recognition for offering those amendments by the chair.) As David Dreier, R-Calif., the vice chairman of the Rules Committee, explained:

> The [GOP] majority . . . on the Committee on Rules has reported a large number of rules in which a time cap has been used. The reason is very simple, Mr. Speaker. After years in the minority, during which time the 9 to 4

[Democratic] majority structured rules to stack the deck politically for the majority, we learned how unfairly structured rules can be. Time limits, I will acknowledge, are not perfect. However, it is possible with time limits for the chairman and ranking member of a bill's committee of jurisdiction to minimize the drawbacks of those time limits. They are recognized for amendments before other Members . . . [and they can] largely set the course of debate.[46]

For their part, Democrats lambast these rules as not being genuinely open. Because the time for voting on amendments is counted against the cap, a ten-hour restriction may actually leave only seven hours for debating amendments. Limits, they say, encourage dilatory tactics. Recorded votes may be called on amendments that could pass by voice vote "in order to consume time allotted for considering amendments."[47] Republicans respond, as noted by Rep. Dreier, that Democrats should consult in advance with their leaders to identify priority amendments that need to be offered inside the cap. There are occasions when GOP lawmakers get upset with caps, because they may be foreclosed from offering their amendments.[48]

Creative rules, in summary, impact House operations in important ways. They enable the majority party to advance its policy and political agenda and to cope effectively with today's substantive and procedural complexities. They exacerbate partisan tensions when minority lawmakers are shut out from proposing their favorite amendments. They promote greater certainty and predictability in floor decision making and in the overall scheduling of House activities. And, in this era of "videopolitics" and attack ads on television, creative rules may protect lawmakers from casting politically troublesome votes.

ADOPTION OF THE RULE

All rules must be approved by a majority of the House. Rules are reported to the House by the Rules Committee and are debated for a maximum of one hour, with the time equally divided by custom between the Rules chair, or a designee, and the ranking minority member of the committee, or a designee. The *hour rule* is the basic rule of floor debate in the House. Theoretically, it permits each member one hour of debate on any question. The hour rule is never followed in practice, however. A member who controls the debate time under the hour rule, in this case the Rules chairman or his designee, always moves the *previous question* at the end of this hour (or before the full hour is used if no member seeks time for debate). Adoption of this motion by majority vote stops all debate, prevents the offering of amendments, and brings the House to an immediate vote on the main question, the rule itself in this context.

The main strategy, then, for a member wishing to amend a rule is to defeat the previous question. "I am urging my colleagues to vote against the previous question on this rule so that we can offer a substitute rule" is a common refrain from members who oppose the rule. Under House precedents, the member who led the fight against approval of the previous question is recognized by the Speaker to propose a substitute rule. In short, the significant vote here often is not on adoption of the rule but on approval of the previous question.

If there is no controversy, rules are adopted routinely by voice vote after a brief discussion. Under a 1977 procedural change, the Speaker may postpone votes on rules and permit them to be voted on at five-minute intervals later in the day or any time within the next two days. The procedure is similar to cluster voting under suspension of the rules.

The House seldom rejects a rule proposed by the Rules Committee. Speaker O'Neill once remarked, "Defeat of the rule on the House floor is considered an affront both to the Committee and to the Speaker."[49] The Rules Committee generally understands the conditions the House will accept for debating and amending important bills. Further, it is an expectation within the majority party that support for rules is a given and that deviations from this behavioral norm could be held against a lawmaker when, for example, plum committee assignments are handed out. The record number of rules defeated during the 103d Congress—seven—highlighted the fissures within Democratic ranks that doubtlessly contributed to their loss of the House in November 1994 after forty years of continuous control. (Six rules were rejected in the 100th Congress, three in the 101st, none in the 102d, and one, to date, in the GOP-run 104th.)

LEGISLATION BLOCKED IN COMMITTEE

What happens when a standing committee refuses to report a bill that many members support, or when the Rules Committee fails to grant a rule to legislation having substantial support? Several procedures are available to bring legislation to the floor that had been stalled in committee.

Which procedure to use depends on the nature of the legislation. Suspension of the rules, discussed earlier, is appropriate if the measure is relatively noncontroversial or minor. If a major bill is being blocked there are extraordinary procedures that can be employed to "spring" the bill from committee. These procedures are difficult to implement, but if the House is determined, committees can be compelled to yield legislation.

THE DISCHARGE PETITION

The discharge procedure, adopted in 1910, provides that if a bill has been before a standing committee for thirty legislative (a day on which the House meets) days, any member can introduce a motion to relieve the panel of the measure. A clerk of the House then prepares a discharge petition, which is made available for members to sign when the House is in session.

Until 1993 House precedents prohibited public disclosure of the names of lawmakers who signed discharge petitions until the required 218 signatures had been obtained. Then the names were published in the *Congressional Record*. Critics of this procedure successfully changed House rules to require the signers' names to be made public as soon as a discharge petition is introduced rather than when a majority is achieved. The sponsor, Rep. (now senator) James M. Inhofe, R-Okla., and backers such as Ross Perot, conservative talk show hosts, the *Wall Street Journal*, and freshmen lawmakers, including Democrats, argued that the change would help eliminate secrecy and hypocrisy by ending the practice whereby House members introduce, cosponsor, or publicly proclaim support for bills but then refuse to sign discharge petitions that might facilitate getting those same measures to the floor. Without public disclosure, they said, party and committee leaders can pressure members either not to sign or to remove their name if they had signed a discharge petition.

Opponents contended, unsuccessfully, that disclosure would permit lobbyists to pressure lawmakers to sign discharge petitions on their pet bills, encourage the filing of frivolous petitions, and encourage orchestrated public campaigns to expedite action on emotionally charged but unrealistic legislation, bypassing the scrutiny provided by the committee system. The change, too, reduced the power of the Speaker, the Rules Committee, or committee chairmen to stymie floor action on legislation favored by a majority of House members. Needless to say, the House was not persuaded by these arguments. As Rules Chairman Solomon put it, the "sunshine rule for discharging committees of popular legislation will make the House more responsive to the people."[50] (The House amended its rules at the start of the 104th Congress to require weekly publication in the *Congressional Record* of members who have signed a discharge petition; daily availability in the Clerk's office of the cumulative list of signers; and a study of how to make the list available over the Internet.)

When 218 members have signed the petition, the motion to discharge is put on the Discharge Calendar. After seven legislative days on the calendar, it becomes privileged business on the second and fourth Mondays of the month (but not during the last six days of a session). Any member who signed the petition may be recognized to offer the discharge motion. When the motion is called up, debate is limited to twenty minutes, divided between proponents and opponents. If the discharge motion is rejected, the bill is not eligible again for discharge during that session. If the discharge motion prevails, any member who signed the petition can make a motion to call up the bill for immediate consideration. It then becomes the business of the House until it is disposed of. A vote against immediate consideration assigns the bill to the appropriate calendar, with the same rights as any bill reported from committee.

Few measures are ever discharged from committee. From 1931 through 1994 (approximately the period during which the modern version of the rule has been in effect), more than five hundred discharge petitions were filed, but only forty-six attracted the required signatures and only nineteen bills actually were discharged and passed by the House.[51] Of those, only two became law: the Fair Labor Standards Act of 1938 and the Federal Pay Raise Act of 1960.

Several factors account for the general failure of the discharge procedure. Members are reluctant to second-guess a committee's right to consider a bill. The discharge rule violates normal legislative routine, and even members who support a bill blocked in committee may refuse to sign a discharge petition for this reason.

Legislators also are reluctant to write legislation on the House floor without the guidance and information provided in committee hearings and reports. Particularly in the case of complicated legislation, many members feel the need for committee interpretation. Then, too, it is not easy to obtain 218 signatures. Attempts to reduce the existing requirement occasionally are made, but none has been successful. Finally, members are hesitant to employ a procedure that one day may be used against committees on which they serve. For all its limitations, the discharge rule serves important purposes. It focuses attention on particular legislative issues, and the threat of using it may stimulate a committee to hold hearings or report a bill.

RULES COMMITTEE'S EXTRACTION POWER

The Rules Committee has an extraordinary authority that it seldom exercises: it can introduce rules for bills that the committee of jurisdiction does not want to report. The power of extraction is based on an 1895 precedent, which the committee has invoked rarely. Extraction is a highly controversial procedure and evokes charges of usurpation of other committees' rights.

One of the rare occasions when extraction was used occurred on February 9, 1972. The Education and Labor (now Economic and Educational Opportunities) Committee refused to approve a dock strike measure, but the Rules Committee went ahead and reported a rule for floor action on the bill. Despite the vigorous opposition of Speaker Carl Albert, D-Okla. (1947-1977), the House adopted the rule by a 203-170 vote, thus springing the bill from the committee. The House then proceeded to pass the bill.

The threat of extraction by the Rules panel in itself can break legislative logjams. In 1967 the Judiciary Committee balked at reporting an anti-riot bill. Rules Chairman William M. Colmer, D-Miss., announced that his committee would soon hold hearings on a rule for the bill. This was enough to prompt the Judiciary Committee to report the bill.[52]

A Rules Committee chairman can try to make any measure in order for floor action, even if it has not received committee consideration. Chairman

Claude Pepper, D-Fla., "used his position to circumvent Ways and Means and clear his home-care health bill for floor action without hearings, debate, or markup in the committee of jurisdiction—a rare use of the Rules Committee's chairman's power."[53]

More recently, when the GOP-controlled Government Reform and Oversight Committee rejected legislation changing the federal retirement system, the Rules Committee included the change as part of a major tax bill. "In what is clearly an extraordinary departure from usual procedures," declaimed Cardiss Collins, D-Ill., the ranking member on the Government Reform panel, "the Rules Committee has chosen to take a course of action which negates the very existence of the authorizing committees."[54] Despite her protest and that of others, the House agreed with the action of the Rules Committee.

DISCHARGING THE RULES COMMITTEE

The discharge rule, with several variations, also applies to the Rules Committee, with one significant difference: a motion to discharge the committee is in order seven legislative days, rather than thirty legislative days, after a measure has been before that panel. Any member may enter the motion, which is handled like any other discharge petition in the House.

Since the Rules Committee reports "rules" as a matter of original jurisdiction, members who wish to discharge a special rule must introduce one of their own so there will be something to discharge. Then, once a rule has been pending before the Rules Committee for seven legislative days, House precedents state, it is in order to bring before the House "a measure pending before a standing committee for 30 legislative days." In summation, when the Rules panel is discharged from a special rule, the bill to which it applies automatically is discharged from the legislative committee that is blocking it.

CALENDER WEDNESDAY

Under House procedures, every Wednesday is reserved for standing committees to call up measures (except privileged bills) that have been reported but not granted rules by the Rules Committee. The Speaker calls the roll of standing committees in alphabetical order. Each chairman (or designated committee member) either passes or brings up for House debate a measure pending on the House or Union calendars. The rule may be dispensed with by unanimous consent, that is, without objection, or by a two-thirds vote of the House. The Rules Committee may not report a rule setting aside Calendar Wednesday.

The Calendar Wednesday rule was adopted in 1909 in an attempt to circumvent Speaker Cannon's control of the legislative agenda. Today it is seldom employed and usually is dispensed with by unanimous consent. During the 98th Congress (1983-1985), however, a group of Republicans led by Rep.

Gingrich objected regularly to dispensing with Calendar Wednesday proceedings. Their purpose was to generate political heat on the majority leadership to schedule nonprivileged measures (a constitutional balanced budget amendment, school prayer measures, criminal code reform, and so on) pending on the Union or House calendars for floor action. Republicans called their list of priority measures "the Agenda of the American People." The House even adopted an agriculture bill under its Calendar Wednesday procedure.[55] Objections to dispensing with Calendar Wednesday gradually diminished because of inherent limitations with the procedure.

Since 1943, fewer than fifteen measures have become law under Calendar Wednesday proceedings.[56] House consideration of the aforementioned 1984 agricultural measure was the first time the procedure had been used in a quarter-century. Five factors account for the limited use of this procedure: (1) Only two hours of debate are permitted, one for proponents and one for opponents. This may not be enough to debate complex bills. (2) A committee far down in the alphabet may have to wait weeks before its turn is reached. (3) A bill that is not completed on one Wednesday is not in order the following Wednesday, unless two-thirds of the members agree. (4) The procedure is subject to dilatory tactics precisely because the House must complete action on the same day. (5) Only the chairman or a member authorized by the committee may bring up a bill under Calendar Wednesday. This requirement limits use of the procedure.

FINAL SCHEDULING STEPS

After a bill has been granted a rule, the final decision on when the measure is to be debated is made by the majority party leaders. The leadership prepares daily and weekly schedules of floor business and adjusts them according to shifting legislative situations and demands. A bill the majority has scheduled for consideration may be withdrawn if it appears to lack sufficient support. Or measures may be put on a fast track by the leadership. Some statutes, too, provide expedited procedures for processing certain measures. (Timetables established in law commonly provide for committee review for a specified time followed by an up-or-down vote—no amendments are permitted—on the floor, again within a specified time following committee consideration.)

Traditionally, trade laws contain so-called fast-track provisions. They are designed to expedite House and Senate committee and floor consideration of trade agreements negotiated by the president and any follow-on implementing legislation. Under these laws, Congress delegates trade negotiating authority to the president with the explicit understanding that he must consult with the Congress during the negotiations. When the trade agreement and implementing legislation are submitted to Congress, fast-track procedures prohibit any amendments by the House or Senate and impose a

One Hundred Fourth Congress
U.S. House of Representatives
Office of the Majority Whip
WHIP NOTICE
WEEK OF JUNE 26, 1995

MONDAY, JUNE 26

HOUSE MEETS AT 12:00 NOON -- NO LEGISLATIVE BUSINESS

TUESDAY, JUNE 27

TUESDAY, HOUSE MEETS AT 10:30 AM FOR MORNING HOUR
HOUSE MEETS AT 12:00 NOON FOR LEGISLATIVE BUSINESS

Suspension (1 Bill):
    1) H.R. 1565 -- Extension of Health Care to Veterans Exposed to Agent Orange

H.R. 1868 -- Foreign Operations Appropriations Act for FY96
    (Continue Consideration)

WEDNESDAY, JUNE 28 AND THE BALANCE OF THE WEEK

WEDNESDAY, THURSDAY AND FRIDAY, HOUSE MEETS AT 10:00 AM FOR LEGISLATIVE
BUSINESS

H.R. 1868 -- Foreign Operations Appropriations Act for FY96
    (Complete Consideration)

H.J.Res. 79 -- Proposing an amendment to the Constitution authorizing Congress and the states
    to prohibit the physical desecration of the flag
    (Subject to a Rule)

H.R. 1905 -- Energy and Water Appropriations Act for FY96
    (Open Rule, One Hour General Debate)

H.R. ___ -- Interior Appropriations Act for FY96
    (Subject to a Rule)

H.R. ___ -- Agriculture Appropriations Act for FY96
    (Subject to a Rule)

H.R. ___ -- 1995 Rescission and Disaster Supplemental Bill
    (Subject to a Rule)

       Members are reminded that votes will not be extended more than 2 additional minutes (17 minutes
total).
       Conference reports may be brought to the floor at any time. Any further program will be announced
later.

Sincerely,

Tom DeLay
Majority Whip

FIGURE 5-2

timetable for committee and floor action. For example, fast-track provisions may require the House to vote by a certain time and without amendment on implementing legislation. "The goal of fast track," wrote an analyst, "is to prevent U.S. trade agreements from being amended in Congress in ways that might be unacceptable to the other nation or nations that are parties to the agreements."[57] Some lawmakers object to fast-track devices because it undercuts the ability of Congress to review and amend trade agreements.

Nothing in the House rules requires the majority leadership to provide advance notice of the daily or weekly legislative program. This is done as a matter of longstanding custom in two principal ways. Announcements about floor action are made by majority party leaders, often in response to a query from the minority leader. The legislative program for the following day for both chambers also is published in each issue of the *Congressional Record*, in a section called the Daily Digest. The Friday *Record* contains a section called the Congressional Program Ahead, which lists the following week's legislative agenda and the dates on which floor action has been scheduled.

The majority leadership also sends "whip notices" to its members at the end of each week, or more frequently, if necessary. The whip notices contain information concerning the daily program for the following week. Although sent under the majority whip's signature, they are prepared mainly by the Speaker and majority leader. The schedule often is changed in response to unforeseen events or new circumstances. A whip notice is reproduced in Figure 5-2.

The majority and minority whip's offices have several phone recordings that announce the daily and weekly programs, legislative actions taken on the floor, and changes in the schedule. Democratic and Republican members obtain similar information from their respective cloakrooms (located just off the chamber floor) and from various partisan entities. The GOP party conference, for instance, publishes daily summaries of bills and amendments to be considered on the floor.

SUMMARY

Scheduling is a party function that the House majority leadership shares with the Rules Committee. Bills reported from committees are assigned to one of several calendars. (Committee reports on measures must also meet appropriate "layover" requirements—three calendar days excluding Saturdays, Sundays, and legal holidays in most cases—before legislation can be scheduled for floor action. To be sure, the Rules Committee can waive the layover requirement.) If measures are not brought up under the suspension of the rules procedure, most bills must receive a special rule, granted by the Rules Committee, giving the bill a green light to the floor and specifying the conditions under which it will be considered. Outside events and pressures often influence the timing of floor action on a particular bill. Upcoming congressional elections can be a critical factor in scheduling controversial bills. Congress's workload must be taken into account. Although they are seldom employed, there are special procedures to dislodge bills that are stalled either by a standing committee or the Rules Committee.

Bargaining and compromise are necessary at each stage of the scheduling process. Members, pressure groups, and executive officials all try to influence the shaping of the House agenda. Their efforts are directed principally at the Rules Committee and the majority leadership. Once an important proposal is granted a rule and placed on the House schedule by the Speaker, the focus shifts to the intricacies of floor procedure.

NOTES

1. *Congressional Record*, November 15, 1983, H9856.
2. Alice A. Love, "'Family Friendly' Survey Hits Hill," *Roll Call*, November 17, 1994, 1.
3. *Congressional Record*, July 2, 1980, H6106.
4. *Congressional Record*, January 5, 1993, H59. See *Congressional Record*, January 4, 1995, H111.
5. *Congressional Record*, June 20, 1995, H6104-H6116.
6. *Washington Post*, January 31, 1995, A13.
7. *Congressional Record*, September 22, 1986, H7893.
8. Martin Gold, et al., *The Book on Congress* (Washington, D.C.: Big Eagle Publishing Co., 1992), 124.
9. *Congressional Record*, February 7, 1995, H1305.
10. Catalina Camia, "House Passes a State-Friendly Drinking Water Act," *Congressional Quarterly Weekly Report*, October 1, 1994, 2783.
11. David Hosansky, "Superfund Bill's Supporters Look to Next Congress," *Congressional Quarterly Weekly Report*, October 8, 1994, 2865–2866.
12. See, for example, Karen Foerstel, "Delegates Decisive for First Time," *Roll Call*, March 21, 1994, 1.
13. *Washington Times*, May 10, 1995, A1.
14. Jeffrey S. Hill and Kenneth C. Williams, "The Decline of Private Bills: Resource Allocation, Credit Claiming, and the Decision to Delegate," *American Journal of Political Science*, November 1993, 1017.
15. *Nation's Business*, February 1956, 103.
16. See, for example, James A. Robinson, *The House Rules Committee* (Indianapolis: Bobbs-Merrill, 1963); Charles O. Jones, "Joseph G. Cannon and Howard W. Smith: An Essay on the Limits of Leadership in the House of Representatives," *Journal of Politics* (September 1968): 617–646; and Robert L. Peabody, "The Enlarged Rules Committee," in *New Perspectives on the House of Representatives*, 2d ed., Robert L. Peabody and Nelson W. Polsby, eds. (Chicago: Rand McNally, 1969).
17. *New York Times*, April 2, 1995, 20.
18. *New York Times*, December 18, 1987, A34.
19. *A History of the Committee on Rules*, 97th Cong., 2d sess. (Washington, D.C.: Government Printing Office, 1983). See Bruce I. Oppenheimer, "The Changing Relationship Between House Leadership and the Committee on Rules," in *Understanding Congressional Leadership*, ed. Frank H. Mackaman (Washington, D.C.: CQ Press, 1981).

20. *CQ's Congressional Monitor,* September 20, 1994, 4.
21. Spark M. Matsunaga and Ping Chen, *Rulemakers of the House* (Urbana: University of Illinois Press, 1976), 21. See also Alan Ehrenhalt, "The Unfashionable House Rules Committee," *Congressional Quarterly Weekly Report,* January 15, 1983, 151.
22. *New York Times,* April 2, 1995, 20.
23. *Congressional Record,* November 5, 1985, H9681.
24. *Amending the Rules of the House of Representatives to Apply Certain Laws to the House of Representatives and for Other Purposes,* H Rept 103–841, 103d Cong., 2d sess., 1994, 2.
25. Bob Michel, "Beyond the Political Wilderness: Reforming 40 Years of One-Party Rule," *Commonsense,* Fall 1994, 56.
26. Jonathan Salant, "Under Open Rules, Discord Rules," *Congressional Quarterly Weekly Report,* January 28, 1995, 277.
27. *Congressional Record,* December 15, 1987, H11436.
28. *Congressional Record,* July 14, 1987, H6282.
29. *Congressional Record,* January 4, 1995, H32.
30. *Congressional Record,* December 21, 1987, H11956. Implicitly, all special rules waive certain House rules and therefore potential points of order under them, such as the daily order of business rule. Explicitly, waivers are generally of two kinds: those waiving points of order that would prevent consideration of a bill and those waiving points of order against specific provisions in a bill or amendments to the bill that otherwise might be ruled out of order.
31. *CQ's Congressional Monitor,* March 2, 1995, 3.
32. *Floor Deliberations and Scheduling, Hearings Before the Joint Committee on the Organization of Congress* (Washington, D.C.: Government Printing Office, 1993), 216–217.
33. Alan Ehrenhalt, "O'Neill Studying Moves to Counter GOP `Obstructionism,' " *Washington Star,* August 5, 1979, A-3.
34. Janet Hook, "GOP Chafes under Restrictive House Rules," *Congressional Quarterly Weekly Report,* October 10, 1987, 2452.
35. Gold, *The Book on Congress,* 154.
36. *Congressional Record,* May 21, 1982, H2519.
37. *Congressional Record,* November 4, 1987, H1867.
38. *Congressional Record,* August 8, 1994, H7181.
39. See *Congressional Record,* March 21, 1995, H3343, and March 22, 1995, H3436.
40. *Congressional Record,* February 27, 1995, H2239. The order of this dialogue was reversed to make the partisan viewpoints stand out clearly.
41. See, for example, *Congressional Record,* May 23, 1995, H5390-H5394.
42. Mary Jacoby, "Three-Quarters `Open,' or Two-Thirds `Closed'? Parties Can't Agree on How to Define Rules," *Roll Call,* April 13, 1995, 7.
43. *Roll Call,* December 8, 1994, 10.
44. *National Journal,* January 21, 1995, 183.
45. Jennifer Babson, "House Rejects Term Limits; GOP Blames Democrats," *Congressional Quarterly Weekly Report,* April 1, 1995, 918.
46. *Congressional Record,* May 23, 1995, H5395.
47. *Congressional Record,* February 27, 1995, H2235.
48. See, for example, *Congressional Record,* February 24, 1995, H2211.
49. *Congressional Quarterly Weekly Report,* February 14, 1976, 313.
50. *Washington Times,* September 29, 1993, A4. See *Congressional Record* of September 28, 1993, for the debate and vote on the new discharge rule.
51. Figures were made available to the author by Richard Beth, Government Division, Congressional Research Service, Library of Congress.

52. Matsunaga and Chen, *Rulemakers of the House*, 25.
53. Julie Kosterlitz, "Still Going Strong," *National Journal*, January 2, 1988, 15.
54. *Congressional Record*, April 5, 1995, H4204.
55. *Congressional Record*, January 25, 1984, H126-H139.
56. Information compiled by Richard Beth, Government Division, Congressional Research Service, Library of Congress.
57. Bob Benenson, "Removal of `Fast Track' May Put GATT in the Fast Lane," *Congressional Quarterly Weekly Report*," September 17, 1994, 2561. Also see I.M. Destler, *American Trade Politics*, 2d ed. (Washington, D.C.: Institute for International Economics, 1992), 71–76.

CHAPTER 6

House Floor Procedure

To a casual observer, the House floor may appear hopelessly disorganized. Legislators talk in small groups or read newspapers while a colleague drones on. People come and go in an endless stream. Motions are offered, amendments proposed, points of order raised—all evoking little apparent interest from the members present. The scene may not make much sense to visitors in the gallery.

If the visitors are there to see their representatives in action, they are likely to be disappointed. Attendance is often sparse during floor debates. Members may be in committee sessions, meeting with constituents, or attending to numerous other tasks. Members can reach the floor quickly, however, to respond to quorum calls, participate in debate, or vote.

The House chamber has two levels. Above the floor itself are the galleries for visitors, diplomats, reporters, and other observers. Visitors sit on either side or facing the Speaker's rostrum; the press sits above and behind the rostrum. Unlike senators, representatives have no desks in the chamber. Their seats, which are unassigned, are arranged in semicircular rows in front of the Speaker. Aisles divide groups of seats, and a broad center aisle divides the majority and minority parties.

Traditionally, the majority party members sit to the Speaker's right, the minority to the left. In 1995, however, when Republicans took control of the 104th Congress after four decades of continuous minority status, they decided to remain seated where they were rather than switch sides with the Democrats. Hence, when Speaker Newt Gingrich, R-Ga., looks from the dais to his left, he sees his GOP colleagues; to his right are the Democrats (see Figure 6-1).

When a majority of the 435 members are present for a recorded vote, for instance, the floor becomes alive with activity. Normally, the House convenes daily at noon.[1] Buzzers ring in committee rooms, members' offices, and in the Capitol, summoning representatives to the floor. Rules and informal practices set the daily order of business: an opening prayer, approval of the *Journal* (a record of the previous day's proceedings), the pledge of allegiance (House rules adopted at the start of the 104th Congress), receipt of messages from the Senate or the president, one-minute speeches and insertions in the

FIGURE 6-1 Floor Plan of the House of Representatives

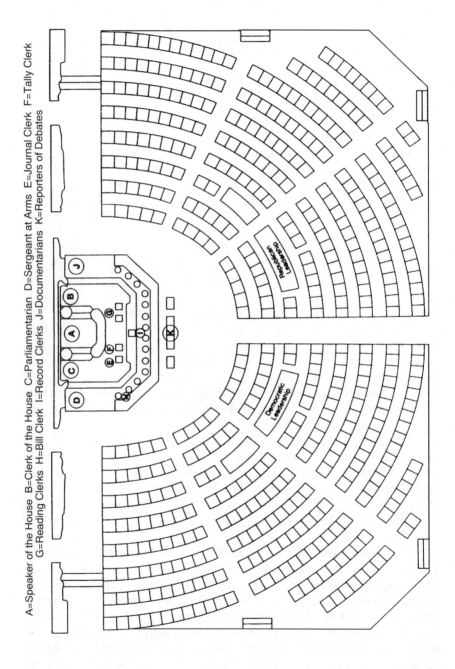

A=Speaker of the House B=Clerk of the House C=Parliamentarian D=Sergeant at Arms E=Journal Clerk F=Tally Clerk G=Reading Clerks H=Bill Clerk I=Record Clerks J=Documentarians K=Reporters of Debates

Congressional Record, and other routine business. There may also be a period of "morning hour" debate that occurs after the opening preliminaries but prior to the start of formal legislative business. The House will convene from an hour to an hour and a half earlier to accommodate lawmakers who want to discuss various issues of the day. The time is equally divided between the two parties.[2]

Under the rules, a majority of the House (218 members) must be present for business to be conducted. Whether or not a quorum has been established, it is assumed to be present unless officially discovered otherwise. A member may ask for a quorum call provided he or she is recognized for that purpose by the Speaker. Any member, however, may make a point of no quorum whenever a vote is pending. Informally, the House frequently operates with far fewer members.

The House usually is in session Monday through Friday. Mondays are reserved mainly for routine legislation. The workload on Fridays generally is light because many members want to return to their home districts on weekends. Most major business is concentrated in the period from Tuesday through Thursday (see Figure 7-1, p. 201). (Other scheduling arrangements are periodically employed during the year, such as providing for alternating four-day weekends with the House in session one week from Tuesday to Friday and the next from Monday to Thursday; five-day workweeks or more are common during the hectic last weeks of a legislative session.) The House has also tried for years, as noted in Chapter 5, to make its schedule more predictable and "friendly" to members' families (see Box 6-1).

The previous chapter outlined the normal procedure by which major legislation reported by standing committees is routed to the House floor through the Rules Committee, as well as certain legislative shortcuts to the floor, such as the Corrections Calendar, Private Calendar, and suspension of the rules. This chapter will focus on major bills, the most common route by which they reach the House floor (by way of a special "rule" granted by the Rules Committee), and basic floor procedures in the Committee of the Whole.

The basic steps in floor consideration for these bills are:

1. Adoption of the rule granted by the Rules Committee
2. The act of resolving the House into the Committee of the Whole
3. General debate
4. The amending process
5. Final action by the full House

Along the way we shall examine some of the strategies used by proponents of bills to secure passage of legislation and by opponents to defeat or modify bills, as well as examples of how the rules can be used to delay or expedite the proceedings.

WOLF'S "FAMILY FRIENDLY" MISSION

House members often complain that Little League games and ballet lessons are a lot more predictable than their work schedules. That's one reason House Republicans are trying to draft a more "family friendly" work schedule that maximizes productivity and efficiency.

Rep. Frank Wolf, R-Va., who was tapped by Speaker Newt Gingrich to chair the Family Friendly Advisory Committee, says he is confident he and his colleagues will be able to come up with recommendations that will satisfy legislators and their families.

Wolf says members can count on one thing: the congressional calendar will be more predictable. "We're going to really make sure that there is certainty in the schedule," said Wolf. "We are looking at ways we can work smarter, work better and much more efficiently."

Wolf said he has talked to dozens of legislators—both Democrats and Republicans—and has received more than 150 responses to a survey he circulated. He also has drawn input from past and incoming members as well as family members and staffers.

"The one thing I want to stress is that this isn't just for members only," he said. "It's for spouses, families, staffers, and for the American people who want us to live by the same rules we set for them."

Wolf, an advocate of telecommuting, on-site child care centers, and job- and leave-sharing for federal employees, said there is a preliminary consensus: Most members want to begin their days early, meaning before the customary noon or 2 p.m. And a majority appears to favor the current Tuesday-through-Thursday schedule. "What most people are saying is that they want to be able to count on a 4 p.m. adjournment time on Thursdays, and to start earlier in the day, say 10 a.m.," said David Whitestone, Wolf's spokesman.

In the past, Wolf said, countless hours have been lost waiting for votes to occur. If the 15-minute rule for members to cast votes were enforced, House members could save days' worth of time, Wolf said.

The committee also is exploring such ideas as coordinating Easter and summer recesses with school calendars, providing advance notice of dinner recesses to give families who live in Washington time to come to the Hill for meals, and installing dedicated phone lines in members' offices for use only by family.

Source: Adapted from Annie Tin, *CQ's Congressional Monitor*, December 12, 1994, 4.

BOX 6-1

ADOPTION OF THE "RULE"

As was noted in Chapter 5, the first step in bringing a major bill to the floor is to adopt the special rule issued by the Rules Committee. A rule, or special order, sets the conditions under which the measure is to be considered, decreeing whether floor amendments will be permitted and how much debate will be allowed.

The House rarely rejects a rule. Challenging the Rules Committee is an uninviting task; House members realize that at some future time they will need a rule from the committee for their own bills. Rejection of a rule usually reflects sharp divisions in the House; disagreements within the majority party (whose members are expected to support these procedural votes); heavy lobbying by pressure groups, the president, or federal agency officials; or general agreement that the reporting committee did a poor job of drafting the bill.

Voting down a rule is often a "procedural kill." During the 99th Congress, for example, Republicans organized to defeat the rule on the landmark tax reform bill.

> The rule was a tempting target for the Republicans. Members were hesitant to vote against the bill itself, fearing they might be straddled with the blame for killing reform, but the rule offered a chance, as [GOP Whip Trent] Lott put it, for members "to get rid of the bill without putting their fingerprints on the trigger."[3]

The defeat of the rule launched an intensive round of negotiations among the Speaker, party leaders, the Treasury secretary, and White House officials, including the president meeting privately with all House Republicans, to bring a second rule on the tax bill to the floor. Speaker Thomas P. O'Neill, Jr., D-Mass., even took the floor and successfully urged members in a moving speech to vote for the second rule. This incident shows how procedural matters can have a critical impact on policy making. Without favorable action on the second rule, tax reform would have been dead.

In another example, the House rejected a rule on a major 1994 crime bill in part because of procedure (the rule contained controversial waivers), policy (the charge was made that the bill contained more money for social programs than prison construction), and politics (GOP anger at being shut out of substantive discussions by Democratic leaders). The comprehensive crime bill was a top priority of President Bill Clinton and House Democratic leaders, but the rule on the bill was defeated by an "odd alliance of conservative pro-gun Democrats, anti-death penalty liberals and Republicans of every stripe."[4] In the end, after extensive lobbying and marathon discussions by the president and Democratic leaders with discontented lawmakers, the House passed a second rule ten days later during a rare Sunday session.[5] Clinton subsequently signed the $30 billion anticrime measure into law.

After the House votes to adopt the rule, the Speaker declares the House resolved into the Committee of the Whole. Under most rules, there is an hour of general debate, after which the bill is open to amendment under the five-minute rule. In other instances, a rule may permit more debate, restrict amendments, waive points of order, or grant priority to certain amendments. After all amendments are dealt with, the Committee of the Whole is directed to report the bill back to the House. There, after voting on any amendments reported (adopted) by the Committee of the Whole and on engrossment (printing the bill as revised by any changes made during floor consideration) and third reading (by title only), the House turns to a motion to recommit— returning the bill to the legislative committee that handled it, with or without instructions to revise the measure. Finally, the bill is voted on in its entirety. If the bill is passed, there also occurs an automatic pro forma motion to reconsider, which invariably is rejected ("laid on the table").

A typical rule from the Rules Committee is reproduced in Box 5-1, p. 141. This is an open rule for a bill providing for floor consideration of HR 660, the Housing for Older Persons Act of 1995. The decision-making process it outlines is used in the House for most major bills. The five principal procedural steps governing House consideration of major legislation are spelled out. These are:

1. Resolving the House into the Committee of the Whole
2. General debate
3. Consideration of amendments under the five-minute rule
4. A recommittal motion
5. Vote on final passage

COMMITTEE OF THE WHOLE

The Committee of the Whole is the House in another form. Every legislator is a member. House rules require all revenue raising or appropriations bills to be considered first in the Committee of the Whole. With its special authority for revenue and spending bills, wrote the staff director of the House Rules Committee, the Committee of the Whole "is the very essence of the House exercising its special [fiscal] powers and prerogatives under the Constitution."[6]

Technically, there are two such bodies. One is the "Committee of the Whole House," which debates private bills. The other and more important is the "Committee of the Whole House on the State of the Union," commonly shortened to Committee of the Whole, which considers public measures. (Further references to the Committee of the Whole in this chapter are to its meaning as the Committee of the Whole on the State of the Union.)

The Committee of the Whole has its origins, like many congressional practices, in the British Parliament. During the seventeenth century, the

TABLE 6-1 Major Characteristics, House and Committee of the Whole

House	*Committee of the Whole*
Mace raised	Mace lowered
Speaker presides	Chairman presides
More than half the House (218) is a quorum	100 is a quorum
One-hour rule for amendments	Five-minute rule for amendments
Previous question in order	Motion to limit debate on amendments, but not the previous question motion, in order
Forty-four members or one-fifth of the House trigger a recorded vote	Twenty-five members trigger a recorded vote
Motion to recommit in order	Motion to recommit not in order

Source: Adapted from *Manual on Legislative Procedure in the U.S. House of Representatives,* 6th ed., 99th Cong., prepared under the auspices of the House Republican leader, May 1986.

Parliament and the Crown regularly clashed over finances and taxes. To ensure that all members of the House of Commons participated in debates involving the expenditure of money, Parliament established the Committee of the Whole; the Committee acted to review and check the financial proposals made by parliamentary committees, which were sometimes "stacked" with the king's or queen's supporters. A further elaboration of the Committee of the Whole's origins is provided by a scholar and former member of the House of Representatives, De Alva Stanwood Alexander, R-N.Y. (1897–1911):

> It originated in the time of the Stuarts, when taxation arrayed the Crown against the Commons, and suspicion made the Speaker [of the House of Commons] a tale-bearer to the King. To avoid the Chair's espionage the Commons met in secret [in a Committee of the Whole], elected a chairman in whom it had confidence, and without fear of the King freely exchanged its views respecting [financial] supplies.[7]

The Committee of the Whole uses rules different from those of the House. They are designed to speed up floor action. A number of rules or customs distinguish the conduct of business in the full House from proceedings in the Committee of the Whole (see Table 6-1).

First, a quorum is only 100 members in the Committee of the Whole (218 constitute a quorum in the House). Second, the Speaker does not preside over the Committee of the Whole but appoints a colleague, who is a member of his own party, to chair it (a practice that can be traced to English precedent). The Speaker is permitted to remain in the chamber and take part in debate, but he rarely participates except to make closing remarks on closely contested major bills. By tradition, the Speaker seldom votes, except to break a tie. (Gingrich, however, has been going against this tradition; see Box 2-1, "The Voting Speaker," p. 34.) Third, it is in order to close or limit debate on sections of the bill by unanimous consent or majority vote of the members present. Fourth, various motions that are in order in the House are not permitted in Committee of the Whole, such as the "previous question" motion or motions to recommit, adjourn, or reconsider the vote by which an amendment was agreed to or rejected. Finally, amendments to bills are introduced and debated under the five-minute rule (discussed in this chapter under "the amending process") rather than under the hour rule.[8]

Visitors in the gallery can tell whether the House is in the Committee of the Whole by noting the position of the mace, a forty-six-inch column of ebony rods bound together by silver and topped by a silver eagle. The mace, symbol of the authority of the sergeant-at-arms, is carried by him, if called upon, to enforce order on the floor. It rests on a pedestal on a table at the right of the Speaker's podium. It is taken down from the table when the Speaker hands the gavel to the chairman of the Committee of the Whole. When the committee rises and the Speaker resumes the chair, the mace is returned to its place.[9]

GENERAL DEBATE

The first order of business in the Committee of the Whole is general debate on the entire bill under consideration.[10] One hour of debate usually is allowed, equally divided between the minority and majority parties. (In an unusual occurrence, a group of conservative Democrats who call themselves the Coalition, received a separate block of time during general debate on a clean water bill.[11]) For most bills, one hour is authorized; for very complex legislation, as many as ten hours may be scheduled.

Each party has a floor manager from the committee of original jurisdiction who controls time, allotting segments to supporters or opponents, as the case may be. Almost without exception, the floor manager for the majority party is the spokesman for the bill. Sometimes both sides favor passage of a bill, and both floor managers rise in support. During debate on controversial legislation, both floor managers may declare their support for the bill's aims but reflect differences of opinion on specific sections or amendments.

The term *general debate* can be misleading, as most members deliver set speeches and engage in a minimum of give-and-take. Because committees and subcommittees shape the fundamental character of most legislation, only a limited number of representatives actually participate in debate, and those who do usually are members of the committee that drafted the legislation. Yet general debate has an intrinsic value that is recognized by most House members and experts on the legislative process. (The House experimented with three Oxford-style floor debates in 1994 on agreed-upon national issues—health, welfare, and trade—where teams of lawmakers engaged each other in sustained discussions of these topics. There is some discussion in the 104th Congress to continue with this British debating format.)[12]

PURPOSES OF GENERAL DEBATE

General debate is both symbolic and practical. It assures both legislators and the public that the House makes its decisions in a democratic fashion, with due respect for majority and minority opinion. "Congress is the only branch of government that can argue publicly," noted a House Republican. "Debate appropriately tests the conclusions of the majority."[13] General debate forces members to come to grips with the issues at hand; difficult and controversial sections of the bill are explained; constituents and interest groups are alerted to a measure's purpose through press coverage of the debate; member sentiment can be assessed by the floor leaders; a public record, or legislative history, for administrative agencies and the courts is built, indicating the intentions of proponents and opponents alike; legislators may take positions for reelection purposes; and, occasionally, fence-sitters may be influenced.

Not all legislators agree on the last point. Some doubt that debate can really change views or affect the outcome of a vote. But debate, especially by party leaders just before a key vote, can change opinion. A 1983 speech by Speaker O'Neill on U.S. involvement in Lebanon, said a House Democrat, marked "one of the few times on the House floor when a speech changed a lot of votes."[14]

House Republican leader Robert H. Michel, Ill. (1981–1995) also highlighted the importance of having informed and persuasive speakers take part in floor debates.

> A classic example . . . occurred during our debate on the nuclear freeze in 1983. A Democratic colleague challenged my Illinois colleague, Henry Hyde, who had just criticized a prominent woman advocate of the freeze. The Democrat said: "Yes, she is, as you say the mother of the freeze. But President Reagan, through his lack of arms control progress, is the father of the freeze." And, without missing a beat, Henry Hyde shot back: "And that makes you a son of a freeze." The debate went our way after that.[15]

Rep. Hyde's eloquent and powerful speech against a constitutional term limits proposal, which was reported from the Judiciary Committee that he chaired, contributed to House rejection of the proposal. In defending experience against ignorance, Hyde declaimed: "I just cannot be an accessory to the dumbing down of democracy."[16] To be sure, a leader's exhortations may not be sufficiently persuasive. Speaker Gingrich's appeal to lawmakers to back a GOP-sponsored effort to repeal the War Powers Resolution of 1973 failed to persuade enough members.[17]

In sum, reasoned deliberation is important in decision making. Lawmaking consists of more than log rolling, compromises, or power plays. General debate enables members to gain a better understanding of complex issues, and it may influence the collective decisions of the House. The dilemma members often face, said a House member, "is to know what is right, and to make the right decisions" based upon skimpy, incomplete, or unavailable information.[18] This was certainly the case in 1991 when the House (and Senate) debated before a nationwide C-SPAN audience authorization for the president to use military force against Iraq following its invasion of Kuwait. The general debate on what amounted to a declaration of war, said then-Speaker Thomas S. Foley, D-Wash., was "the longest in the modern history of the House of Representatives, extending over 20 hours."[19]

FLOOR MANAGERS' ROLE

Longstanding customs govern much of the action on the floor. But the floor managers direct the course of debate on each bill. The manager for the majority side often is the chairman of the committee that reported the bill, or an appointed committee colleague. The ranking minority committee member, or an appointed surrogate, usually is the floor manager for the minority party. The floor managers are centrally located during debate at long tables near the center of the chamber, with the main aisle separating the Democratic from the Republican side.

The floor managers guide their bills through final disposition by the House. Their duties are varied. They must:

1. Plan strategy and parliamentary maneuvers to meet changing floor situations;
2. Respond to points of order;
3. Attempt to protect the bill from amendments the majority considers undesirable;
4. Alert supporters to be on the floor to vote for or against closely contested amendments;
5. Advise colleagues on the meaning and importance of the amendments;
6. Judge when amendments of committee members should be offered or deferred;
7. Inform party leaders of member sentiment and the mood of the House toward their bill;
8. Control the time for general debate and, if necessary, act to limit debate on amendments, sections or titles of the bill, or on the entire measure;

9. Arrange the sequence of speakers on major amendments to ensure that the best supporting orators are matched against those of the opposition; and

10. Mobilize outside support to build winning coalitions on the floor.

The fate of much legislation depends on the skill of the floor managers. Effective floor management increases the chances for smooth passage. The enactment of the landmark Congressional Budget and Impoundment Control Act of 1974 was credited in large part to its skillful floor manager, Rep. Richard W. Bolling, D-Mo. (1949–1983).

Floor managers are given several advantages over their colleagues. They customarily lead off debate in the Committee of the Whole and have the first opportunity to appeal for support. During debate they receive priority recognition from the chair. A floor manager may take the floor at critical moments ahead of other legislators to defend or rebut attacks on the bill, or they may offer amendments to coalesce support for the measure. The floor manager also is entitled, by custom, to close the debate on an amendment, thus having the last chance to influence sentiment.

Floor managers generally can count on support from their party leadership. They also are permitted to have up to five of their committee's staff members on the floor during debate, ready to research rules and precedents, draft amendments, answer technical questions about the bill, or prepare statements. Finally, as a result of committee hearings, discussion, and markup, the managers have a reservoir of knowledge about the technical details of a measure and are in a good position to judge which amendments to accept and reject, and the best arguments to employ for or against them.

DELAYING TACTICS

Despite the generally tighter rules on debate in the House than in the Senate, there are many ways to prolong or delay proceedings. Members may raise numerous points of order, make scores of parliamentary inquiries, or offer trivial amendments. For example, during consideration of a bill creating the Department of Education, an opponent offered two unsuccessful but dilatory amendments. One would have changed the department's name to the Department of Public Education (DOPE), the other to the Department of Public Education and Youth (DOPEY).[20] Members may also demand recorded votes on every amendment and motion, ask unanimous consent to speak for additional minutes on each amendment, make certain that all time for general debate is used, offer motions to adjourn the House, or move that the Committee of the Whole rise.

Until a 1971 rules change, a reading of the *Journal* was used as a delaying tactic. Before that time, the reading could be dispensed with only by unanimous consent or by a motion to suspend the rules, requiring a two-thirds vote. Since then, the Speaker has been authorized to examine the *Journal*, although a vote is often demanded on its approval. That often happens at the start of every day for various reasons: to determine which members are present, to break up committee meetings, or simply to vent partisan frustrations.

The purpose of delaying tactics is often to stall action on a measure to allow more time to gather support (if those using such tactics favor the bill) or to kill it (if they are opposed). Delay is intended sometimes to force action and other times to prevent it, or delay may be employed to protest actions of the majority. When Republicans were in the minority they used obstructionist tactics after a one-vote victory engineered, the GOP argued, by the unwarranted actions of Speaker Jim Wright, D-Texas, in permitting an extra ten minutes on a vote so that Democrats could lobby a partisan colleague to change his vote. To vent their anger and forge greater party rapport, Republicans retaliated by tying up the House for the next three days. The House found itself without a quorum (many legislators were in their districts) and could not conduct any business. The majority leader several times tried to adjourn the House but, because of Democratic absentees, Republicans kept voting against adjournment. Several hours elapsed before Democratic leaders rounded up enough partisan colleagues to adjourn the House.[21]

Minority Democrats in the 104th Congress have employed many of the parliamentary guerrilla warfare tactics used by Republicans when they were in the minority, such as raising parliamentary objections, clashing verbally with GOP lawmakers, demanding roll call votes, and offering floor amendments designed to foment reelection difficulties for GOP lawmakers who must vote against them.

THE AMENDING PROCESS

The amending process is the heart of decision making on the floor. Under an open rule, amendments determine the final shape of bills passed by the House. At times, amendments become more important or controversial than the bills themselves. A good example is the Hyde amendment on abortion funding discussed in Chapter 3.

THE FIVE-MINUTE RULE

House rules require all bills and joint resolutions to be "read" three times to give members every opportunity to become familiar with the measures they are considering. In practice, bills are not read word for word. Verbatim readings generally are dispensed with by unanimous consent, or by a rule that stipulates that each section of the bill is considered to have been read.

The first "reading" occurs when a measure is introduced and referred to committee. The bill is not read aloud; the bill's number and title are published in the *Congressional Record*. The second reading occurs in the Committee of the Whole. The third occurs by title (the name of the bill only) just before the vote on final passage.

Bills are considered, or "read," as specified in the rule from the Rules Committee, usually section by section. The Rules Committee might specify a reading by title rather than by section, to permit larger, interrelated parts of the measure to be open to amendment.

At the end of general debate, a bill is "read" for amendment under the five-minute rule. Under this rule, "any Member shall be allowed five minutes to explain any amendment he may offer, after which the Member who shall first obtain the floor shall be allowed to speak five minutes in opposition to it, and there shall be no further debate thereon."[22]

Actual practice differs from the rule. Amendments are regularly debated for more than the ten minutes allowed. Members gain the floor by offering pro forma amendments, moving "to strike the last word" or "to strike the requisite number of words." Technically, these also are amendments, although no alteration of the bill is contemplated by the sponsors; their purpose is to extend the debate. (Pro forma amendments are not in order under a closed rule.) In addition, members may ask for unanimous consent to speak longer than five minutes, and they may yield part of their time to other legislators.

Debate on amendments cannot extend forever, however, since the floor manager can move that discussion be terminated at a specified time. Time limits on amendments can be critical at times to the fate of legislation. On a Labor-Health and Human Services (HHS) appropriations bill, for example,

> a time limit on debate engineered by [the late] William H. Natcher, D-Ky., the [then] chairman of the Appropriations Subcommittee on Labor, HHS, and Education, effectively prevented amendments from being offered on sensitive social topics [abortion, for example] that in years past have mired the funding bill in controversy.[23]

There are occasions when the rule itself imposes specific time limits on amendments. Sometimes this can arouse sharp controversy. This occurred during the bitter House debate on revamping the welfare system. The rule from the Rules Committee allowed the majority floor manager, Ways and Means Chairman Bill Archer, R-Texas, in order to expedite floor action, to combine eleven individual amendments (each debatable for twenty minutes) in one en bloc (all together) amendment debatable for twenty minutes. When Chairman Archer proposed to do just that, his action infuriated the minority floor manager, Sam Gibbons, D-Fla., who asked unanimous consent that the en bloc amendment be debated for an hour. Republican Bill Emerson, Mo., objected. The following then occurred:

Mr. GIBBONS. Mr. Chairman, I ask unanimous consent for 59 minutes.
Mr. EMERSON. I object.
Mr. GIBBONS. Mr. Chairman, I ask unanimous consent for 58 minutes.
Mr. EMERSON. I object.
Mr. GIBBONS. Mr. Chairman, I ask unanimous consent for 57 minutes.
Mr. EMERSON. I object.

Minority floor manager Gibbons made several more attempts in this vein, and each time there was an objection. Gibbons was livid. He called the time limitation an "outrageous procedure." Chairman Archer stated that it was necessary "to expedite this debate." The discussion escalated into a frenzy of angry rhetoric. Gibbons, for instance, told Republicans: "You all sit down and shut up. Sit down and shut up." Finally, Chairman Archer asked and received unanimous consent to extend the time for debate for an additional thirty minutes.[24]

Amendments are in order as soon as the section to which they apply has been read, but they must be proposed before the clerk starts to read the next section. If the clerk has passed on to a succeeding section, a member must be granted unanimous consent to offer an amendment to the previous section. In addition to being timely, amendments must be germane to the bill and section under consideration. Reading by section or title helps structure rational consideration of complex bills, but on noncontroversial measures it is common for the floor manager to ask unanimous consent that the entire bill be considered as read. In that case, the entire measure is open to amendment at any point.

Reading amendments can be used to delay or prolong proceedings. Any member can object to a unanimous consent request to dispense with the reading of amendments. Opponents of a bill may draft lengthy amendments, perhaps the size of the Manhattan telephone directory, not with the expectation that they will be adopted, but to cause delays by having them read in their entirety.

House rules, however, permit a nondebatable motion to be made in Committee of the Whole to dispense with the reading of an amendment if it was either published in the *Congressional Record* or provided to the reporting committee at least one day prior to floor action on the bill. The Rules Committee, too, can obviate the reading requirement by requiring that amendments be published in advance in the *Record* or by specifying in its rules that amendments meet the terms of the aforementioned House rule that dispenses with the reading of amendments.

The Rules Committees, too, often request (or may require) that lawmakers have their proposed amendments to bills printed in advance in the "amendment section" of the *Congressional Record*. The special rule will then state that the "amendments so printed are to be considered as read." The prenotification of amendments strengthens the reporting committee's role on the floor by enabling it to prepare advance arguments, alternatives, or modifications to each prenoticed change; advance notice of amendments also provides some degree of predictability in floor decision making, an objective favored by the floor managers and the majority leadership.[25]

Opportunities for dilatory tactics, in brief, can be short-circuited by other actions. Moreover, the rules of the game and the expectation of retaliation in kind encourage moderation in the use of dilatory tactics.

RATIONALE FOR AMENDMENTS

Amendments serve diverse objectives. Some are offered in deference to pressure groups, executive branch officials, or constituents; others are designed to attract public notice, to stall the legislative process, to demonstrate concern for an issue, or to test sentiment for or against a bill. Some amendments are more technical than substantive; they may renumber sections of a bill or correct typographical errors. One common strategy is to load down a bill with so many objectionable amendments that it will sink of its own weight. Declared former Speaker Wright to proponents of an amendment he strongly opposed: "If that is your goal, if you just want to find a cynical way to burden down the committee bill and make it unpassable, then you might want to vote for this [amendment]."[26] Committee members themselves may vote against a bill they originally reported if objectionable or "irresistible," but inappropriate, amendments are added on the floor.

Committees, it is worth noting, do not have formal authority to amend bills or measures during their markups. Only the full House has the authority to approve or disapprove of proposed changes to legislation. "Committee amendments," then, are recommendations to the full House, where they are granted priority consideration ahead of amendments proposed by individual lawmakers. Committee amendments are themselves usually subject to amendment.

Three types of amendments are worthy of special attention: *committee amendments, riders,* and *substitutes.* These different amendments all propose to do one of three things: add or insert something into a bill, strike something from a bill, or both strike out and insert something that is not already in the measure.

COMMITTEE AND FLOOR AMENDMENTS. House precedents grant priority to amendments recommended by the reporting committee(s). "Committee amendments to a pending section," these precedents state, "are normally considered prior to amendments offered from the floor."[27] This condition is another example of the parliamentary advantage accorded committees by House rules and precedents. Recall, for instance, that committees receive most of the bills introduced in the House, influence the kind of "rule" their bills receive from the Rules Committee, and control general debate on the floor.

In the past, the House was inclined to defer to the committees' recommendations. That is changing. "When I came here ... [in 1965]," reflected Thomas Foley, then the majority leader, "most of the Members would follow the committee. Now ... the committee's `aye' or `nay' isn't enough."[28] The former committee monopoly over policy making has diminished during the past few decades as the Capitol Hill environment has become more permeable to outside influences. Committees have been bypassed in whole or in part by informal or leadership task forces established to draft legislation. The multiple referral of measures to several committees (modified by the rules change of the 104th Congress ending joint referrals but keeping sequential and split referrals) undercuts jurisdictional monopolies by involving several panels in the consideration of legislation.

The trend away from committee autonomy has been reinforced, wrote a congressional scholar, by the recent efforts of Republicans to further consolidate power in the office of the Speaker.

> Potentially the most powerful House leader in a generation, [Speaker] Newt Gingrich breached the seniority norm to place aggressive conservatives in key committee chairmanships. The terms of committee chairs have been limited to six years [by House rule], precluding the gradual accumulation power by senior committee leaders. And the remarkable consensus about policy among House Republicans provides Gingrich with the political support necessary to exert strong partisan leadership. As a key architect of the "Contract with America" [ten bills to revamp the role of the federal government], Gingrich's pledge to complete House action on the contract within the first hundred days of [the 104th Congress] necessarily limits the duration and thoroughness of committee deliberations.[29]

Speaker Gingrich is also utilizing many informal task forces to consider legislative issues and requiring each committee to submit to him a monthly "planning document."[30] With most committees being open to greater challenges on the floor (subject, of course, to the character of the "rule"), it is no surprise that chairmen may look to the suspension procedure as a way to protect their measures from floor amendments. Or the Rules Committee will make clear that if legislation gets bogged down during an open amendment process, the panel will reconvene and report another "follow-on rule" that limits amendments and expedites action on the bill.

RIDERS. Riders are amendments that are extraneous to the subject matter of the bill. They are more common in the Senate because House rules, in theory at least, require amendments to be germane or relevant to the bill itself. Any member can question the relevance of a proposed amendment by raising a point of order, on which the chair must rule. Such questions are not always raised, however, either because the rule from the Rules Committee may waive them, through oversight, or because members are in general agreement with the provision. "I don't make points of order on all [riders],"

Some Tests of Germaneness

When a Representative raises a germaneness point of order, the burden of proof rests with the sponsor of the amendment to establish its germaneness.

1. *Fundamental Purpose.* A basic test of germaneness is that the fundamental purpose of an amendment must be germane to the fundamental purpose of the bill. In determining this purpose, substantial reliance should not be placed upon the title of the bill as the title need not state the fundamental purpose of the bill, either as introduced or later amended. One must look rather to the text of the bill as the principal tool in determining purpose.
2. *Subject Matter.* The amendment must relate to the subject matter under consideration. One must determine "what is the subject matter under consideration?" Once it is clear just what the subject matter is, the next element . . . is whether or not the amendment relates to that subject matter.
3. *Committee Jurisdiction.* The jurisdiction of a committee is not necessarily controlling as to the germaneness of an amendment. When an argument has been advanced that the subject matter of an amendment lies within the jurisdiction of a committee other than the committee reporting the bill, the Chair has ruled that the germaneness of an amendment is based upon its relation to the bill in its amended form. In short, the subject matter of the bill is the controlling factor, not the description in the Rules of the House of the various committees' jurisdiction, May 1986.

Source: Excerpted from *Manual on Legislative Procedure in the U.S. House of Representatives,* 6th ed., 99th Cong., prepared under the auspices of the Republican leader, May 1986.

BOX 6-2

a member once observed, "because some may be necessary due to changing conditions."[31] In short, the House's strict rule requiring the germaneness of amendments is not self-enforcing.

A fundamental objective of the germaneness rule ("no motion or proposition on a subject different from that under consideration shall be admitted under color of amendment") is to focus the House's attention on one subject at a time. Brief though it is the germaneness rule, which applies to all amendments (committee and individual), is difficult and complex to apply. For example, if an amendment is proposed to a pending amendment, is the proposed change supposed to be germane to the pending amendment, to the bill, or to both? (The answer: to the pending amendment.) House members use scores of precedents and "tests" to defend their amendments from germaneness points of order (see Box 6-2). A dilemma for lawmakers is that these tests and "precedents do not set down perfectly distinct guidelines for analysis."[32]

Riders often encompass proposals that are less likely to become law on their own merits (as separate bills), either because of resistance in the Senate or the probability of a presidential veto. The strategy on such issues is to draft them as riders to important legislation—"must" bills that are almost certain to be enacted—such as appropriations measures funding the federal government or bills to raise the federal debt ceiling. If the House is tenacious enough in clinging to its rider, the chances are good that it will be accepted—grudgingly—by the Senate and the president.

SUBSTITUTE AMENDMENTS.   There are two kinds of substitutes: a "substitute amendment" and "an amendment in the nature of a substitute." The first type is an amendment that deals with *part* of a bill. When there is a proposal to change a section of a bill, a substitute amendment offers alternative language for that pending proposal. (By contrast, a "perfecting" amendment seeks to change, or perfect, the existing language in a bill.) The second kind recommends new language for the *entire* bill. Amendments in the nature of substitutes have increased in importance in recent years, in part because of the complexity and interrelatedness of contemporary issues and also because of multiple referrals.

For example, committees that consider the same bill may report dissimilar versions of it. Sometimes, such differences are resolved through intercommittee cooperation. Members and staff from each panel might blend their products into a consensus bill that will be offered on the House floor as an amendment in the nature of a substitute for the bill as originally introduced. Usually, the Rules Committee will accommodate the committees by giving such an alternative substitute special status by making it, rather than the original bill, the vehicle for House debate and amendment. The rule typically states that the consensus or substitute text will be considered an "original bill for the purpose of amendment."

DEGREES OF AMENDMENTS

A basic parliamentary principle permits only two degrees of amendments: an amendment and the amendment to it. Any further motion to amend is a third-degree proposal (an amendment to an amendment to an amendment) and is out of order. "The line must be drawn somewhere," Thomas Jefferson wrote, "and usage has drawn it after the amendment to the amendment."[33]

When a bill is open to revision in the House, only four forms of amendments are usually pending simultaneously. The four forms are:

1. An amendment to the bill itself
2. An amendment to the first amendment
3. A substitute amendment
4. An amendment to the substitute amendment

Once an amendment to a bill has been offered (the first degree), either an amendment to that amendment (the second degree), or a substitute amendment (another first-degree proposal under House rules) is in order.[34] Assuming that an amendment to the original amendment is offered, then members still may offer a substitute as well as an amendment to the substitute (second degree). A substitute amendment seeks not merely to modify the original first-degree amendment but to substitute entirely new language for it. If a substitute is adopted, its effect is to replace the language of the original first-degree proposal and any second-degree changes to it which might have been adopted.

The four amendments, with the degrees that are permissible and the order of voting on each, are shown in Figure 6-2. This representation of the "amendment tree" shows graphically that there are two first-degree amendments—the amendment to the text and the substitute amendment—and two amendments in the second degree. This amendment tree is quite common. As House Rule XIX states: "When a motion or proposition is under consideration a motion to amend and a motion to amend that amendment shall be in order, and it shall also be in order to offer a further amendment by way of a substitute, to which one amendment may be offered."

The numbered voting sequence on the "tree" shows that second-degree amendments are voted on first, and that the second-degree amendment to the original amendment to the bill is voted on before the second-degree amendment to the substitute. After consideration of the second-degree amendments, members then face a choice between two policy alternatives, with voting occurring first on the perfected substitute and then on the perfected original amendment. (Perfected amendments in this context are amendments that themselves have been amended by the second-degree proposals.) In sum, the final vote occurs on the originally offered amendment as modified by any of the subsequent amendments.

Strategically, the amendment procedure can be critical to policy formulation. Either side of an issue may be aided by the voting sequence: whether the amendment—a policy alternative—is voted upon first or last. During House consideration of a nuclear freeze proposal, the proponents wanted the

FIGURE 6-2   The Basic Amendment Tree

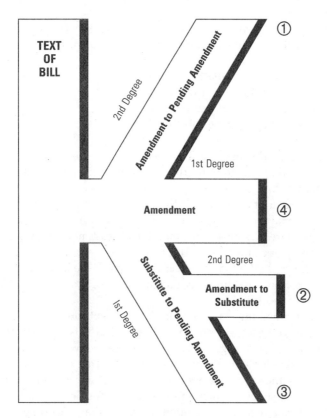

Note: Circled numbers indicate order of voting on amendments.

House to vote first on their policy recommendation. As a result, they waited for opponents to offer a first-degree amendment before they countered with a second-degree amendment to their liking. This approach gave backers of the freeze the opportunity "to formulate the final version of any amendment."[35] The first vote, therefore, was on the freeze backers' alternative amendment to the opponents' amendment revising the text of the freeze resolution. The strategy of "fighting fire with fire" means that "threatening amendments by opponents are . . . met with counteramendments" by proponents.[36]

MANEUVERING FOR ADVANTAGE: COMMON TACTICS

Proponents and opponents of bills constantly seek to advance their policy objectives through the amending process. Skillful use of various motions, dilatory tactics, or shrewd drafting of the wording of amendments can influence which side carries the day. Customarily, the minority party has self-appointed "floor watchdogs" who seek to protect party interests and stymie majority steamrollers by raising points of order or making parliamentary inquiries. Timing, too, is all important to the success of many floor maneuvers, especially preferential motions and amendments to "sweeten" bills. Even television can be a factor in prompting amendment activity.

"STRIKE THE ENACTING CLAUSE." Certain motions from the floor take preference over other House business. One is the motion to "strike the enacting clause." This clause is the opening phrase of every House and Senate bill and makes it an operative law once the bill is approved by Congress and signed by the president: "Be it enacted by the Senate and House of Representatives of the United States of America in Congress assembled,. . . " Under House rules, approval of a motion to strike the enacting clause is equivalent to rejecting the measure. A motion to strike the clause is in order at any time during the amending process. (The phrasing of the preferential motion is as follows: "I move that the Committee do now rise and report the bill to the House with the recommendation that the enacting clause be stricken out.") It is a privileged motion that must be disposed of before the House takes up any further business on the bill. The motion is in order only once, unless the bill is materially changed by adoption of major amendments, a determination the chair makes if a point of order is raised against a second motion to strike.

A motion to strike the enacting clause may cause considerable excitement in the chamber, and it may be used for psychological purposes by either opponents or proponents of a measure.[37] In 1974, for example, Representative Bolling, floor manager of the bitterly contested House committee reorganization bill, surprised foes of the plan by inviting them to offer a motion to strike the enacting clause. Bolling's plan was to defeat such a motion so resoundingly that it would be clear to all members that a committee reform plan was going to be considered in its entirety and adopted by the House.

Bolling gained an immediate psychological advantage when Rep. Joe D. Waggonner, Jr., D-La. (1961-1979), one of the opposition leaders, observed that his side did not have the votes to pass the motion. It might be made, he said, "at a point in time when we think there is a chance for it to succeed." Ironically, a supporter of committee reorganization, disappointed by the course of the debate on the floor, later offered a motion to strike. It was turned down overwhelmingly because most members did not want the measure abruptly killed.

As another example, Rep. David R. Obey, D-Wis., the ranking minority member on Appropriations, offered the motion to make a political point. Immediately after the Speaker declared the House to be in the Committee of the Whole for the further consideration of an appropriations bill that reduced spending for many programs supported by Democrats, Obey made the preferential motion to rise. He said: "What I would simply say to you [Republicans] is this: We believe that this bill is warped and we believe there is no underlying sense of decency in the way the cuts are focused in this bill." Appropriations Chairman Robert L. Livingston, R-La., responded that the bill represents "the first step toward fiscal sanity and a balanced budget and it must be taken."[38] Obey's motion was rejected, 187-228.

"SWEETENERS." Measures considered unpalatable can be made more acceptable, or "sweetened," by proposing changes to attract broader support. These might include amendments granting members more staff or additional office allowances, or "pork-barrel" provisions for construction of dams, highways, port facilities, airports, and the like, in various congressional districts. With the electorate currently in an antigovernment mood, many lawmakers have criticized "pork-barrel" spending. Amendment sweeteners, therefore, may need to broaden their focus to address topics that have wide appeal with voters, such as spending reductions, streamlining federal regulations, or cutting bureaucratic red tape.

Pot-sweetening is the opposite of a technique mentioned earlier, loading down a bill with enough unattractive amendments to kill it. There also are amendments that political scientists call "saving" and "killer" or "poison pill" amendments. The first is essentially a compromise amendment that, if adopted, enhances prospects for the measure's enactment. The second type deliberately strengthens a bill too much and turns a majority against the legislation.[39] Adoption of an amendment to include primaries in a congressional public financing bill, for example, is almost certain to kill the legislation because many House incumbents, particularly those from safe and one-party districts, oppose any measure that aids party challengers.

TELEVISION AND AMENDMENTS

Videopolitics has an effect on the amendment process. With the House in the television age, members sometimes craft amendments with the viewing public—or at least the voters in their districts—in mind. Proposing or debating amendments on the floor provides exposure for members and their ideas. Members who make articulate and forceful arguments may even find the footage of the House debates used on the national networks' evening news programs. Television and strategy are also linked. Democratic leader Richard A. Gephardt, Mo., was the chief sponsor of a tough trade amendment. "He fought for his amendment on the House floor, where proceedings are televised, rather than in the Ways and Means Committee," which considered trade legislation.[40] (New rules for the 104th Congress specify that committee and subcommittee meetings can be closed only for specific purposes, such as for national security; further, any open committee hearing or meeting must also be open to television coverage.) Members and staff can monitor the rhythm and pace of the amending process from their offices, which have television monitors to carry the proceedings.

IMPORTANCE OF THE AMENDING PROCESS

Attempts are almost always made to amend controversial bills when they are considered in the Committee of the Whole. The amending process is a critical stage for any bill and, as has been seen, quite complex. Some of the main features of the process are noted below:

- Amendments in the Committee of the Whole are usually offered section by section under the five-minute rule.
- All amendments must be offered from the floor in written form.
- Amendments may not be repetitious. When an amendment is rejected, a member may not offer exactly the same proposal later.
- Any amendment may be challenged on a point of order before debate on the amendment has begun.
- Committee amendments are considered before those introduced by other legislators.
- Pro forma amendments enable members to discuss the bill under consideration for five minutes, even though no change is intended.
- Amendments must be germane to the subject under consideration. Occasionally, nongermane amendments may slip by, either because members generally are agreed on their intent or because the Rules Committee has barred points of order against them.

VOTING

The House has a variety of methods of voting, with most votes occurring in the Committee of the Whole (see Box 6-3). A truly significant change in voting occurred on January 23, 1973, when electronic voting began. With electronic voting, which was authorized by the Legislative Reorganization Act of 1970, members insert a personalized card about the size of a credit card into one of the more than forty voting stations located on the House floor, and press one of three buttons: Yea, Nay, or Present. Each member's vote is displayed on panels above the Speaker's desk and on the walls of the House behind the press gallery. The system also is used to establish quorums. If electronic voting malfunctions, traditional methods are used. Former GOP House leader Michel, whom Gingrich replaced at the start of the 104th Congress, was not a fan of electronic voting because it quickened the pace of the House.

It eliminates the time for informal chats with other members. C-SPAN is even more of a problem. Members now follow the affairs of the House from their offices, rushing to the floor to vote only at the last minute. Again, valuable face-to-face contact is gone.[41]

METHODS OF VOTING . . .

The House regularly uses three main types of votes. Occasionally, the House takes several votes on the same proposition, using first simple and then more complex voting methods, before a decision is reached. The vast majority of votes are cast when the House sits as the Committee of the Whole, the session used for amending legislation.

A *voice vote* is the quickest method of voting, and the type usually used when a proposition is first put to the House. The presiding office calls for the "ayes" and then the "noes," members shout in chorus on one side or the other, and the chair decides the result.

If the result of a voice vote is in doubt or a single member requests a further test, a *division*, or *standing vote*, may be demanded. In this case those in favor of the proposal and then those against it stand up while the chair takes a head count. Only vote totals are announced; there is no record of how individual members voted. Few issues are decided by division vote. If an issue was important enough for members to seek a standing vote, then the losing side, hoping to reverse the outcome, usually will ask for a recorded vote. The recorded vote draws many more members to the chamber.

Recorded votes, which record how individual members vote on a bill or amendment, comprise the bulk of members' voting records. Since 1973 the House has used an electronic voting system for recorded votes. Members insert white plastic cards into one of forty voting boxes mounted on the backs of chairs along the aisles of the House chamber. When a member punches a button to indicate his position, a giant electronic board behind the Speaker's desk immediately flashes green for "yes" and red for "no" next to the legislator's name. Members may also vote "present," which shows up as a yellow light on the board. A recorded vote may be ordered upon demand of one-fourth of a quorum (twenty-five) when the House is meeting as the Committee of the Whole. One-fifth of a quorum (forty-four) is required when the House is meeting in regular session. Members have fifteen minutes to record their votes, although this time is sometimes shortened to five minutes if a number of votes have been clustered.

Until 1971 votes in the Committee of the Whole were taken by methods that did not record the stands of individual members. Many questions were decided by teller votes; the chair appointed tellers representing opposite sides on a vote and directed members to pass

BOX 6-3

. . . IN THE HOUSE

between them up the center aisle to be counted—first the "ayes" an then the "noes." Only vote totals were announced on teller votes.

In the 1960s moderate and liberal Democrats began to object to the unrecorded votes in the Committee of the Whole because members could not be held accountable for saying one thing to their constituents but voting the opposite way.

"A member can vote for any number of amendments which may cripple a water pollution bill or render ineffective a civil rights bill or fail to provide adequate funding for hospital construction or programs for the elderly, and then he can turn around on final passage and vote for the bill he has just voted to emasculate by amendment," Wisconsin Democrat David R. Obey said of the voting system.

A provision of the Legislative Reorganization Act of 1970 opened the way for "tellers with clerks," or *recorded teller votes*. This procedure made it possible to record the votes of individual members in the Committee of the Whole. When the change first went into effect, members were required to write their names on red or green cards, which they handed to tellers. After the electronic voting system was installed in 1973, the recorded teller vote process became known simply as a recorded vote.

Until the teller votes changes of the 1970s, yeas and nays were the only votes on which House members were individually recorded. Yeas and nays are ordered upon demand of one-fifth of those present, and they are not taken in the Committee of the Whole. During roll-call votes, members are required to vote "yea" or "nay." Representatives who do not wish to vote may answer "present." The Speaker's name is called only at his request. Unlike for the Senate presiding officer, the Speaker can vote to make or break a tie.

Use of the electronic system has blurred the distinction between yeas and nays and other recorded votes. Before the electronic voting system was installed, yeas and nays were taken by calling the roll, a time-consuming process in the 435-member House. Each roll call took about half an hour. The Speaker still retains the right to call the roll rather than use the electronic voting system. The old-fashioned method is used when the electronic system breaks down.

Source: Congressional Quarterly's Guide to Congress, 4th ed., 430.

These technological changes have placed additional pressures on the floor managers. Electronic voting cut balloting time in half, from about thirty minutes under the traditional roll-call method, to no less than fifteen minutes. Speaker Gingrich announced on the first day of the 104th Congress that to save time and expedite floor business he intended to enforce strictly a "policy of closing electronic votes as soon as possible after the guaranteed period of 15 minutes."[42] Further, recent changes in the rules have permitted the Speaker to postpone votes and schedule votes in clusters on matters such as passing bills or agreeing to suspension of the rules motions. The Speaker may reduce the time allowed for each vote in this procedure to five minutes.

Managers today have less time to coordinate floor activities during a vote. Members can enter the chamber through numerous doors, insert their cards and vote, leaving before the leadership has a chance to talk to them. As a result, both parties station monitors at all the doors to advise their colleagues when they enter and urge them to support the position of the floor manager or the party leadership.

From the floor managers' standpoint, there are advantages and disadvantages to the modern system. Managers have computer display terminals that show a continuous and changing record of the progress of a vote. However, there is less time to evaluate opposition to proposals and line up votes. Thus, floor managers today must work harder to build support before bills reach the floor. On the other hand, problems such as the absence of one member or the unexpected vote switch of another can be spotted quickly on the computer consoles. Absent members can be summoned to the floor, and vote-switchers can be approached by persuasive members of the party.

"PAIRS." On January 14, 1975, the House amended its rules to permit "pairs" in the Committee of the Whole. "Pairing" previously was limited to the House. Pairing is a voluntary arrangement between any two representatives on opposite sides of an issue. Wrote a noted House parliamentarian:

> A pair is essentially a "gentlemen's agreement," and the construction and interpretation of the terms, provisions, and conditions of a pair rests exclusively with the contracting Members. The rules do not specifically authorize them and the House does not interpret or construe them or consider questions or complaints arising out of their violation. Such questions must be determined by the interested Members themselves individually.[43]

Pairs are not counted in tabulating the final results of recorded votes. Pairs take three forms:

1. A *general* pair means that two members are listed without any indication as to how either might have voted.
2. A *specific* pair indicates how the two absent legislators would have voted, one for and the other against.
3. A *live* pair matches two members, one present and one absent.

In a live pair, the member in attendance casts a vote, but then withdraws it and votes "present," announcing that he or she has a live pair with a colleague and identifying how each would have voted on the issue. A live pair subtracts one vote, yea or nay, from the final tally and can influence the outcome of closely contested issues. Both parties have pair clerks to help arrange these informal agreements.

FACTORS IN VOTING

On any given day, legislators may be required to vote on measures ranging from foreign aid to abortion, from maritime subsidies to tax reform. It is nearly impossible for a member to be fully informed on every issue before the House. As one lawmaker said: "The sheer volume of votes is so great that there's no way you can weigh each and every issue."[44] Many lawmakers, as a result, follow the "rational ignorance" principle. They rely on "cue-givers" for guidance on matters beyond their special competence. These may be committee or party leaders, members of the state congressional delegation, trusted colleagues, staff aides, or floor managers.[45] "You want to know how Members are voting on an issue," a representative said, "you want to know how Members from your delegation vote, and you want to know how Members who always vote the opposite of you are voting."[46] Party loyalty, constituency interests, and individual conscience are primary factors in determining a member's vote on any issue, but they are not the only factors. It is not unusual for members to vote for proposals they actually oppose to prevent enactment of something worse, or in the expectation that somewhere along the line the proposal will go down to defeat. Members, too, might vote one way on an authorization bill and another on the corresponding appropriations measure.

To mobilize winning coalitions is no easy task on divisive issues. The art of vote counting can be crucial to policy outcomes. For example, former Speaker Foley extended the official voting period on a Clinton administration initiative to give him more time to persuade lawmakers to support the proposal. "At the end of the standard 15-minute roll-call period, opponents had a narrow majority, but the [Speaker] held the machines open for nearly 28 minutes while switching enough votes to prevail."[47] (The reverse charge— closing a vote with lawmakers still wanting to cast their ballot—reverberated through the House on June 21 and 22, 1995, during consideration of a closely contested amendment.) Members use their votes, too, as trading material. In exchange for voting yea or nay on an issue, they may receive some project or favor that benefits their district.

Finally, the voting records of members can become a campaign issue. Representatives who miss numerous votes might find their congressional attendance record an issue during the next campaign. Many interest groups contribute campaign funds to legislators whose votes are in accord with the groups' views. "If I cast a vote, I might have to answer for it," said a House member. "It may be an issue in the next campaign. Over and over I have to have a response to the question: Why did you do that?"[48]

Liberal Democrat Mike Synar, who represented a conservative Oklahoma district for sixteen years until his 1994 electoral defeat and who cast many votes that antagonized his constituency, put it this way: "If you don't like fighting fires, don't be a fireman ... and if you don't like voting, don't be a congressman."[49] It is worth noting that Rep. Natcher, who served continuously from 1953 until his death in 1994, never missed a vote and holds the congressional record for having cast 18,401 consecutive roll-call votes.

When voting on all amendments has been concluded, the Committee of the Whole "rises" (dissolves) and reports the bill back to the full House. (Rules from the Rules Committee typically provide that the Committee of the Whole rises automatically at the end of the amending process.) Then the chairman hands the gavel back to the Speaker, who resumes his place at the podium. The mace is returned to its pedestal on the table next to the podium, and a quorum becomes 218 members (a majority of the House). As prescribed in the rule, there is a standard sequence of events that takes place prior to the vote on final passage of a bill.

FINAL PROCEDURAL STEPS

After taking the chair, the Speaker announces that "under the rule, the previous question is ordered." This means that no further debate is permitted on the measure or on amendments, no amendments other than those reported by the Committee of the Whole may be considered, and previously adopted amendments are not subject to further amendment. Then members, sitting as the House, consider the decisions taken in the Committee of the Whole. (Recall that only the House can amend legislation; the Committee of the Whole is technically a parliamentary committee and its decisions must be approved or rejected by the chamber-at-large.)

The Speaker asks all the members to identify amendments on which they want separate recorded ballots. The remaining amendments are decided en bloc by voice vote, after which the contested amendments are voted on individually. Except for motions to send a measure back to the reporting committee with instructions, only first-degree amendments adopted in the Committee of the Whole can now be considered. Separate recorded votes are not usually requested on amendments previously adopted in the Committee of the Whole unless the earlier votes were very close and the amendments highly controversial (see, for example, Box 6-4). Votes on controversial amendments, needless to say, can be used against incumbents during congressional campaigns.

On occasion, the House rejects amendments adopted in the Committee of the Whole.[50] After all floor amendments are disposed of, there are two

GOP Decides Against Second "Star Wars" Vote

Blindsided by their first clear defeat on legislation rooted in the GOP's "Contract with America," House Republican leaders scrambled to turn around enough GOP votes to restore to their defense bill (HR 7) a nonbinding provision calling for the deployment of an antimissile defense of U.S. territory. But the leaders decided not to revisit the issue because the votes did not seem to be there.

The provision was deleted from the bill when 24 Republicans—including four committee chairs—broke party ranks to support an amendment offered by John M. Spratt, D-S.C. Spratt's amendment stipulated that antimissile defenses for U.S. territory rated a lower priority than maintaining the readiness of U.S. forces, modernizing their equipment, and creating defenses for U.S. troops in the field against short-range missiles, such as Iraq's Soviet-designed Scuds. Echoing the Clinton administration's policy, Spratt argued that short-range missiles posed a more immediate threat than potential future missile threats to U.S. territory. The Spratt amendment was adopted 218–212.

The 24 Republicans who supported the Spratt amendment included Budget Committee Chairman John R. Kasich, Ohio; Government Reform Committee Chairman William F. Clinger, Pa.; Banking Committee Chairman Jim Leach, Iowa; and Small Business Committee Chairwoman Jan Meyers, Kan.

Immediately after the amendment was approved, GOP defense experts tried to craft a strategy to reverse the defeat. Budget Chairman Kasich told reporters that his vote for the amendment had been inadvertent and that other Republicans had mistakenly taken their cue from him. The expectation was that, after switching enough Republicans to reverse the outcome, GOP leaders would simply demand a separate vote on the Spratt amendment when the Committee of the Whole reported the amended version of HR 7 to the House before final passage.

However, it became clear that the Republicans would not be able to pull it off. For one, it appeared that seven Democrats who voted against the Spratt amendment might have been persuaded to switch this time to defeat the proposal. The GOP defeat was only the third time House Republicans have lost on a vote pitting the two parties against each other.

Source: Adapted from *CQ's Congressional Monitor,* February 17, 1995, 5.

BOX 6-4

more steps before the final vote on passage. The first is *engrossment* and *third reading*. "The question is on engrossment and third reading of the bill," the Speaker declares. This is a pro forma question, which is approved automatically by unanimous consent. House rules provide that the bill be read by its title. (Before 1965 any legislator could demand that the bill be read in full, but the rules were changed to prevent this dilatory tactic.)

Engrossment is the preparation of a final and accurate version of the bill by an enrolling clerk, for transmission to the Senate. This can be a complicated process, particularly if numerous amendments were adopted.

The second step is the *recommittal motion*, provided for in the rule from the Rules Committee. This is a privileged motion, protected and guaranteed by the rules of the House, that gives the opponents one last chance to obtain a recorded vote on their own proposals. Recommittal is a motion to return the bill to the committee that reported it; it is always made by a member opposed to the bill. Recommittal is in order only in the House, not in the Committee of the Whole.

There are two forms of the motion: a simple, or "straight," motion to recommit, or a motion that contains instructions to the reporting committee. A simple motion to recommit the bill to committee, if adopted, in effect kills the bill, although technically it may be returned to the House floor later in the session. No debate is permitted on the simple recommittal motion.

Instructions in recommittal motions may embody amendments that were defeated in the Committee of the Whole. This is the only way amendments rejected earlier in the debate can be brought before the full House. Until 1970 no debate was permitted on a recommittal motion. The Legislative Reorganization Act of that year authorized ten minutes of debate on recommittal motions with instructions. On occasion, a rule from the Rules Committee will authorize longer debate on recommittal motions with instructions.

Although House rules prohibit the Rules Committee from excluding a motion to recommit from a special rule, partisan conflict over the recommittal motion with instructions escalated during the past dozen years when Democrats controlled the House. The Democratic-controlled committee issued rules with greater frequency that either eliminated or restricted the recommittal motion with instructions. The GOP staff director of the Rules Committee, Donald R. Wolfensberger, even wrote a report in 1990 entitled: "The Motion to Recommit in the House: The Rape of a Minority Right."

The GOP raged against special rules that prohibited Republicans from offering any floor amendments to legislation. The combination of restrictive rules and no recommittal motion with instructions meant that Republican policy alternatives never had an opportunity to be considered and voted upon. For their part, Democratic Speakers cited a 1934 precedent to overrule any GOP points of order against special rules that did not contain the recommittal motion with instructions. In brief, the precedent stated that under

House rules the minority was guaranteed the right to offer a simple, or straight, motion to recommit, but it was not guaranteed the recommittal motion with instructions. Noteworthy is that when the 104th Congress began, the new GOP majority amended House rules to guarantee the minority's right to offer a motion to recommit with instructions if offered by the minority leader or a designee.[51] (This rule change originally had been proposed in 1993 by the bipartisan Joint Committee on the Organization of Congress.)

Recommittal motions with instructions commonly provide that the committee report "forthwith." If the recommittal motion is adopted, the committee chairman immediately reports back to the House in conformity with the instructions, and the bill, as modified by the instructions, is automatically before the House again. The committee chairman states: "Mr. Speaker, pursuant to the instructions of the House on the motion to recommit, I report the bill, H.R. 1234, back to the House with an amendment." The House votes separately on this amendment, then again on the pro forma engrossment and third reading questions, and finally on passage of the bill.

Recommittal motions seldom are successful, but much depends on the size of the minority party in the House and political circumstances. Probably the most dramatic recommittal motion in recent Congresses occurred on September 25, 1984 (only a few weeks before national elections), when the Comprehensive Crime Control Act was enacted via the recommittal route. Rep. Dan Lungren, R-Calif., offered the recommittal motion with instructions, containing the recodification of the criminal code, debated it for five minutes, and urged members to pass a crime package that "has been languishing here in the House since March of this year."[52] A Democratic opponent of the recommittal motion then took the floor and urged rejection of the motion in his five minutes.

To the surprise of nearly everyone, the recommittal motion was agreed to by a 243–166 vote. Then the continuing resolution to which the crime bill was attached was agreed to by the House. Democratic leaders were chagrined that the crime package had passed in this manner. "I think it was the wrong way" to pass major crime legislation after only ten minutes of debate, declared Speaker O'Neill.[53] Interestingly, when the next Congress convened, the House changed its rules to permit the majority floor manager—but not the minority floor manager—to request up to an hour of debate, equally divided, on a motion to recommit with instructions. This is a good example of the "majority rule" principle that undergirds House operations. Another is the series of rules changes made by Republicans when they took control of the 104th Congress (see Box 6-5).

If the recommittal motion is rejected, the Speaker moves to the third step, the final vote on the whole bill. "The question is on the passage of the bill," he says. Normally, final passage is by a recorded vote. If the outcome is obvious, and the members are eager to be done with it, the measure

RULES CHANGES OPEN THE PROCESS . . .

The rules package approved by the House on January 4, 1995, contained a number of changes in House procedure that embody the GOP pledge to make the House a more open, accountable body that respects minority rights. It also contained several rules changes that centralize power in the Speakership and were designed to help Republicans carry out their legislative agenda.

COMMITTEES

- Three committees were abolished: District of Columbia, Merchant Marine and Fisheries, and Post Office and Civil Service. Several other committees were renamed.
- The jurisdiction of the Post Office and Civil Service Committee and the District of Columbia Committee was transferred to the Government Reform and Oversight Committee. Matters handled by the Merchant Marine and Fisheries Committee were split among three other committees. Several issues formerly handled by the Energy and Commerce Committee were parceled out to other committees.
- The total number of committee staff was cut by one-third.
- With three exceptions, no committee will be allowed more than five subcomcommittees.
- Staff hiring will be controlled by committee chairmen.
- Members may serve on no more than two standing committees and four subcommittees, except for chairmen and ranking members, who can serve ex officio on all subcommittees.
- A chairman or other designee may not cast an absent member's vote by proxy in committee.
- Committees must publish the members voting for or against all bills and amendments.
- Committees and subcommittees are barred from closing their meetings to the public (with certain exceptions).
- Committees must allow radio and television broadcasts, as well as still photography, of all open meetings.
- Bills that increase spending on existing programs must contain a cost estimate that shows the current cost of the programs.
- The Speaker may not send a bill to more than one committee simultaneously for consideration. The Speaker may refer a bill sequentially to other committees or parts of a bill to separate committees.

BOX 6-5

... *But Strengthen the Reins of Power*

Term Limits

- Speaker: no more than four consecutive two-year terms.
- Chairmen of committees and subcommittees: no more than three consecutive terms. The limits begin this Congress.

Floor Procedures

- A three-fifths majority of members voting will be required to pass any bill, amendment, or conference report containing an increase in income tax rates.
- No retroactive tax increases that take effect prior to the date of enactment of the bill are allowed.
- Delegates and resident commissioners may no longer vote in or preside over the Committee of the Whole.
- Members may no longer delete or change remarks made on the floor in the *Congressional Record* except for technical or grammatical corrections.
- Automatic roll call votes are required on bills and conference reports that make appropriations and raise taxes.
- Members are guaranteed the right to offer so-called limitation amendments, which specify that no funds may be spent for a particular purpose, without having to defeat a motion to end amendments—unless the majority leader offers that motion.
- The minority leader or his designee is guaranteed the right to offer a so-called motion to recommit with instructions on a bill under consideration in the House.
- Commemorative legislation may not be introduced or considered.

Administration

- The Office of the Doorkeeper was abolished.
- The House inspector general was instructed to complete an audit of the financial records of the House while it was under the control of the Democrats.
- Funding was abolished for more than 25 caucuses that received office space and budgets to operate in the House.

Source: Adapted from *Congressional Quarterly Weekly Report,* January 7, 1995.

may be passed by voice vote. When the results of the final vote have been announced, a pro forma motion to reconsider is made and laid on the table (postponed indefinitely) to prevent the bill from being reconsidered later. House rules state that a final vote is conclusive only if there has been an opportunity to reconsider it on the same day or the succeeding day.

SUMMARY

Although the House decision-making process may appear to be quite complex, it accommodates varied institutional interests and members' needs. There are numerous restraints on what legislators can and cannot do. Success often depends on one side's gaining an advantage through use of the rules. Infinite variations are possible within the process, but basic House procedures are the same on almost all important bills:

1. A "rule" reported by the Rules Committee
2. Adoption of the rule by the House
3. Consideration of the bill in the Committee of the Whole
4. General debate
5. Consideration of amendments under the five-minute rule
6. Recorded votes on major amendments
7. Reporting the bill to the House once floor action is completed in the Committee of the Whole
8. Separate recorded votes, if requested, on any amendment adopted in the Committee of the Whole
9. A recommittal motion, with or without instructions
10. Final passage vote.

The intensity of debate may vary, the complexity of the special rule may change, and a host of other factors may differ from issue to issue, but the pattern of decision making is the same regardless of the range or scope of the legislation.

After the House passes the bill it moves to the Senate. There, the legislative process is quite different. If the House is characterized by devotion to rules and parliamentary procedures, the Senate is much more informal, often transacting its business by gentlemen's agreements, with the rules ignored or set aside. Chapter 4 covered the introduction of a bill, referral, and committee action in the Senate. The following chapter begins with a bill that has been reported by a Senate committee and discusses the scheduling procedure for moving a bill to the Senate floor.

NOTES

1. During the 95th Congress (1977–1979), the House developed a regular system of scheduling floor sessions. This was done in response to the desires of members, committees, and party leaders. Members complained about problems in arranging their personal schedules and their inability to make firm commitments for meetings in their districts; committees wanted more time early in the session to work on legislation without being interrupted by floor meetings; and party leaders wished to better synchronize committee and floor action and use the time in session more effectively. As a result, the House by standing order varies its starting time: noon on Mondays and Tuesdays, 3 p.m. on Wednesdays, 11 a.m. on Thursdays and the balance of the week until May 15, when the convening time for Wednesdays through the balance of the week, including Saturdays if the House is in session, is advanced to 10 a.m. for the remainder of the session.

2. For guidelines on morning hour debate, see *Congressional Record*, May 12, 1995, H4901.

3. Jeffrey H. Birnbaum and Alan S. Murray, *Showdown at Gucci Gulch* (New York: Random House, 1987), 163.

4. Phil Kuntz, "Democrats' Defeat Raises Specter of Gridlock," *Congressional Quarterly Weekly Report*, August 13, 1994, 2311.

5. See Holly Idelson, "Clinton, Democrats Scramble To Save Anti-Crime Bill," *Congressional Quarterly Weekly Report*, August 13, 1994, 2340–2343; Holly Idelson and Richard Sammon, "Marathon Talks Produce New Anti-Crime Bill," *Congressional Quarterly Weekly Report*, August 20, 1994, 2449–2454; and David Masci, "$30 Billion Anti-Crime Bill Heads to Clinton's Desk," *Congressional Quarterly Weekly Report*, August 27, 1994, 2488–2493.

6. Donald Wolfensberger, "Committees of the Whole: Their Evolution and Functions," *Congressional Record*, January 5, 1993, H31.

7. De Alva Stanwood Alexander, *History and Procedure of the House of Representatives* (New York: Burt Franklin, 1916), 257.

8. In the House sitting as the House, an hour is permitted for debate on amendments. "No member," the rule states, "shall occupy more than one hour in debate on any question in the House." Technically, then, all matters could be debated for 440 hours—1 hour each for the 435 representatives, 4 delegates (from the District of Columbia, the Virgin Islands, American Samoa, and Guam), and 1 resident commissioner (from Puerto Rico). In practice, measures are debated for only one hour in total and then are voted on.

9. For a description of the seventeenth-century English origins of the Committee of the Whole, see Alexander, *History and Procedure of the House of Representatives*, 257–258.

10. Technically, the first order of business in the Committee of the Whole is the reading of the bill. This usually is dispensed with either by unanimous consent or by the terms of the "rule," which is the ordinary practice today.

11. See *Roll Call*, May 11, 1995, 26, and *Washington Times*, May 10, 1995, A6.

12. See Norman Ornstein, "A Forgotten Reform: Floor Debate, Too, Needs an Overhaul," *Roll Call*, January 30, 1995, 5 and *Roll Call*, May 29, 1995, 18.

13. *U.S. News & World Report*, August 20, 1984, 30.

14. *Washington Post*, October 22, 1983, A19.

15. *Congressional Record*, September 12, 1989, E3001.

16. *Congressional Record*, March 29, 1995, H3905. See E. Michael Myers, "Anatomy of a Speech: How Hyde Turned Tide," *The Hill*, April 5, 1995, 1.

17. *Congressional Record,* June 7, 1995, H5672-H5673 and *New York Times,* June 8, 1995, A11.
18. *Congressional Record,* May 24, 1983, H3257.
19. *Congressional Record,* January 12, 1991, H441. See Joseph M. Bessette, *The Mild Voice of Reason: Deliberative Democracy and American National Government* (Chicago: University of Chicago Press, 1994).
20. *Congressional Record,* June 11, 1979, 14213–14215.
21. See the *Congressional Record* for October 30, October 31, and November 2, 1987.
22. *Constitution, Jefferson's Manual and Rules of the House of Representatives,* 102d Cong., 2d sess., H Doc 102-405, 665.
23. Julie Rovner, "House Passes Labor-HHS Appropriations Bill," *Congressional Quarterly Weekly Report,* August 8, 1987, 1790.
24. *Congressional Record,* March 22, 1995, H3498-H3500.
25. The Legislative Reorganization Action of 1970 provided that amendments published in the *Congressional Record* at least one day prior to their consideration in the Committee of the Whole are guaranteed ten minutes of debate time, regardless of any Committee agreements to end debate on the bill. The objective is to prevent arbitrary closing of debate when important amendments are pending. The Rules Committee, of course, can waive this requirement, which is incorporated in House rules.
26. *Congressional Record,* May 25, 1982, H2824. The amendment was not adopted.
27. *Procedure in the U.S. House of Representatives,* 97th Cong., 4th ed. (Washington, D.C.: Government Printing Office, 1982), 526.
28. Michael J. Malbin, "House Democrats Are Playing with a Strong Leadership Lineup," *National Journal,* June 18, 1977, 946. See also John F. Bibby, ed., *Congress off the Record* (Washington, D.C.: American Enterprise Institute for Public Policy Research, 1983), 23–24.
29. C. Lawrence Evans, "Committees and Health Jurisdictions in Congress," in *How Congress Makes Health Policy,* ed. Thomas Mann and Norman J. Ornstein, forthcoming publication of the Brookings Institution.
30. Karen Tumulty, "Man With a Vision," *Time,* January 9, 1995, 30.
31. Richard F. Fenno, Jr., *The Power of the Purse* (Boston: Little, Brown, 1966), 74.
32. Martin Gold, et al., *The Book on Congress,* (Washington, D.C.: Big Eagle Publishing Co., 1992), 226.
33. *Constitution, Jefferson's Manual and Rules of the House of Representatives,* 226-227.
34. When amendments in the nature of substitutes are offered first, it is possible to have as many as eight amendments pending simultaneously on the House floor. Seldom does this situation occur because confusion is all too often the result.
35. Pat Towell, "After 42 Hours of Debate: Nuclear Freeze Resolution Finally Wins House Approval," *Congressional Quarterly Weekly Report,* May 7, 1983, 869.
36. Barry R. Weingast, "Fighting Fire with Fire: Amending Activity and Institutional Change in the Postreform Congress," in *The Postreform Congress,* ed. Roger H. Davidson (New York: St. Martin's Press, 1992), 165.
37. Customarily, the motion to strike also is used by members to obtain five more minutes of debate time.
38. *Congressional Record,* March 16, 1995, H3282.
39. See James M. Enelow and David H. Koehler, "The Amendment in Legislative Strategy: Sophisticated Voting in the U.S. Congress," *Journal of Politics* (May 1980): 396–413; and James M. Enelow, "Saving Amendments, Killer Amendments, and an Expected Utility Theory of Sophisticated Voting," *Journal of Politics* (November 1981): 1062–1089.
40. *Wall Street Journal,* April 30, 1987, 64.

41. Donnie Radcliffe, "Many Hits, One Era," *Washington Post,* March 9, 1994, C4.
42. *Congressional Record,* January 4, 1995, H18.
43. *Cannon's Procedure in the House of Representatives,* H Doc 86–122, 233. Cannon further notes: "It is obviously impossible for all Members to be present at every roll call, and in cases of unavoidable absence the privilege of pairing is invaluable in preserving the rights of Members and the representation of constituencies" (231).
44. *New York Times,* June 29, 1983, A14.
45. On factors influencing votes, see, for example, John W. Kingdon, *Congressmen's Voting Decisions* (New York: Harper & Row, 1973); and Donald P. Matthews and James A. Stimson, *Yeas and Nays* (New York: John Wiley & Sons, 1975).
46. *Congressional Record,* July 16, 1986, H4558.
47. David Rogers, "Plan to Create Line-Item Veto Survives a Vote," *Wall Street Journal,* April 29, 1993, A16.
48. *New York Times,* May 13, 1986, A24.
49. Jack Anderson and Michael Binstein, "Synar Stands His Ground," *Washington Post,* August 22, 1993, C7.
50. See, for example, Martha Bridegam and Pat Towell, "'Goodwill Games' Spark Sharp Exchange," *Congressional Quarterly Weekly Report,* June 27, 1987, 1386.
51. There was some controversy surrounding Minority Leader Richard Gephardt's motion to recommit with instructions to a tax bill. See *Congressional Record,* April 5, 1995, H4331-H4332 and April 6, 1995, H4340-H4341.
52. *Congressional Record,* September 25, 1984, H10129.
53. See Charles R. Wise, *The Dynamics of Legislation* (San Francisco: Jossey-Bass Publishers, 1991).

CHAPTER 7

Scheduling Legislation in the Senate

The pace of activity on Capitol Hill places enormous demands on the time of legislators. Representatives and senators work long days, not only on the floor and in committee but also in meetings with executive branch officials, constituents, pressure groups, and the media. They also must stay in contact with the diplomatic community, party leaders, and state and local officials. It is not uncommon for a representative or senator to average eleven or more working hours a day while in Washington. To that must be added periodic trips home to attend important political functions, to meet with constituents, or to be present at campaign fund-raising events.

Of legislators in the two branches of Congress, senators lead the more harried existence. There are fewer senators (100 compared with 435 House members), and in most cases senators represent a larger number of constituents. Senators are more often in the public eye and are called upon more frequently to comment on national and international policy. The legislative and committee workload is as heavy in the Senate as in the House, but it must be carried out by fewer lawmakers. During the 103d Congress (1993–1995), the Senate was in session 2,513 hours; the House, 1,887 hours.

The workload is heaviest for senators from the larger states, not only because of the greater number of constituents that need assistance, but also because of the multiplicity of political and economic interests in those states. "I don't see how senators from big states like New York and California, Illinois and Pennsylvania do it [all]," Majority Leader Mike Mansfield, D-Mont. (1953–1977), once said.[1] A typical schedule for Sen. Mike DeWine, R-Ohio, shows the varied and often conflicting demands that arise on any given day (see Box 7-1). As is true of all his colleagues, Senator DeWine frequently is expected to be in two or more places at the same time. In such a situation, a senator must select the top priority event to attend in person and delegate staff members to cover the rest or, as a last resort, rely on a fellow senator to fill him in on what took place.

"It's absurd when you get a computer readout from your staff and it shows that you have four meetings at the same time," Sen. Alan K. Simpson, R-Wyo., once exclaimed. "And that happens more often than you would imagine."[2]

SCHEDULE OF SEN. MIKE DEWINE
(Thursday, June 15, 1995)

8:30 a.m. INTERVIEW w/PAUL BARTON of CINCINATTI ENQUIRER
Location: Office
Note: This is your yearly one-on-one interview w/Ohio press corps on general issues.

9:30 a.m. SENATOR DOLE'S MEETING with FRESHMAN SENATORS
Location: S-230
Note: This is to discuss and update the Legislative agenda and priorities. SENATORS ONLY, NO STAFF.

9:30 a.m. JUDICIARY COMMITTEE
Location: SH-216
Note: This is a hearing by the subcommittee on Terrorism, Technology, and Government information on "The Militia Movement in the United States."

12:30 p.m. LUNCH, hosted by SENATOR JEFFORDS
Location: SH-708

2:00 p.m. LABOR COMMITTEE
Location: SD-430
Note: Full committee meeting on "Affirmative Action in Employment: Federal Contractor Requirements."

3:00 p.m. MEETING w/ISRAEL POLICY FORUM
Location: Office
Note: See paper for details, but the Israel Policy Forum is a leadership group of American Jews advocating support for the Middle East Peace Process.

3:15 p.m. MEETING w/CHARLIE BALLARD, President of THE INSTITUTE FOR RESPONSIBLE FATHERHOOD
Location: Office
Note: The Institute is a community service organization for absent or nonattentive fathers that Mr. Ballard founded in Cleveland in 1982. He is now extending the program nationwide and will open 5 new sites by the end of 1995. See paper for details.

3:30 p.m. MEETING w/CHARLIE HARGRAVE and the EAST CLINTON HIGH SCHOOL BAND (Sabina, Ohio)
Location: Office
Note: They just want to drop in and say hello.

4:00 p.m. 103rd/104th CLASS MEETING
Location: SR-449 (Sen. Inhofe's Office)

5:00 p.m. PRESIDE OVER THE SENATE
Note: You preside from 5 to 6.

7:00 p.m. STAFF RETREAT DINNER
Location: The Occidental Grill
            1475 Pennsylvania Ave.
Note: This is the get-to-know-each-other segment.

BOX 7-1

FLEXIBLE SCHEDULING SYSTEM

In response to the manifold pressures on members, the Senate has evolved a highly flexible legislative scheduling system that responds to the individual member's, as well as to institutional, needs. The system bears little resemblance to what the formal rules specify and rests largely on usage and informal practice. For example, senators' frustration with delays and uncertainty in scheduling prompted a change that sometimes may be observed, depending on legislative workload and political circumstances, such as when the Senate is scurrying to move a backlog of business. Under the change, the Senate is in session three weeks of each month and off one week. This "gives Senators some predictability, to schedule their trips back home to their constituencies, or to catch up on committee work here or other work here," said Robert C. Byrd, W.V., then the Senate Democratic leader, who instituted the change.[3]

The plan serves individual and institutional objectives. Senators can conduct their constituency-related business and other work during the Senate's week off without fear of missing senatorial votes. This feature is especially attractive to members who must campaign for reelection and to those from the western United States. The Senate is expected to work five days a week during the three-week segment, including votes on Mondays and Fridays. The changes are meant to enhance the "quality of senatorial life" and the "quality of senatorial work."

On the other hand, the three-week, one-week system is not regularly adhered to. As former majority leader George J. Mitchell, D-Maine, noted: "Because of its rules, the Senate schedule is inherently uncertain and not fully predictable."[4] One study found that the Senate infrequently followed the scheduling innovation, reverting instead to the "three-day workweek of the past—plus that new week off every month."[5] Figure 7-1 spotlights the concentration of Senate work in the Tuesday-Thursday period during the 102d Congress (1991–1993) and contrasts the Senate pattern with the House's. (This pattern is typical of senatorial activity today.)

Because senators still complain about scheduling conflicts and chaos ("[Senate] Life is miserable," lamented Bob Kerrey, D-Neb.), Majority Leader Bob Dole, R-Kan., appointed a GOP task force at the start of the 104th Congress to devise a more predictable and "family friendly" schedule.[6] For example, the task force, headed by Robert C. Smith, N.H., recommended that the Senate strive not to hold votes after 6 p.m. on Tuesdays, Wednesdays, and Thursdays. The press of Senate business, especially during the first 100 days of the 104th Congress when both chambers addressed measures associated with the GOP's "Contract with America," inhibited observance of the scheduling recommendations.

The best-laid scheduling plans can always go awry in the Senate because individual senators have the capacity through various dilatory devices to

FIGURE 7-1 Distribution of Senate and House Votes, 102d Congress, by Day of Week

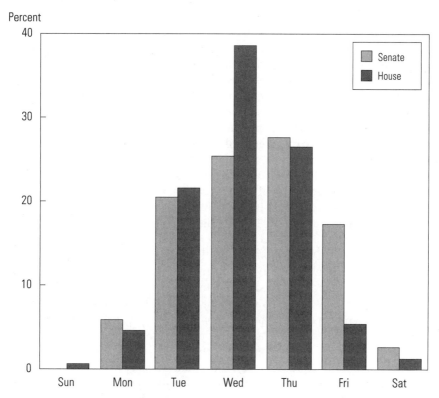

Percent

Legend: Senate, House

Source: Background Materials, Joint Committee on the Organization of Congress, 103d Congress, 1st Sess. (1993), 1092.

frustrate plans for moving the legislative agenda in a predictable fashion. Moreover, Senate leaders often require flexibility in determining the Senate's business; they understand that scheduling is a significant strategic and political resource. If the Senate is gridlocked on a measure because of various stalling tactics, for example, the majority leader can threaten to make members work long days, through the weekend, and even through a planned recess until the impasse is resolved. Or he might offer a "carrot" to his colleagues: if senators agree on the date for a final vote on controversial legislation, then a scheduled Senate recess would be extended another week. Majority Leader Dole pointed out, for instance, that the Senate had spent two straight weeks on a controversial balanced budget amendment to the Constitution. "We spent hours and hours and days and days on a couple of amendments" to the legislation, he said. "My view is that it is time that we bring this to a conclusion."[7] To encourage this result, Senator Dole said he would "extend the Presidents' Day recess if members make `substantial progress' on the balanced-budget measure this week."[8]

Strategic scheduling is part of deadline or "endgame" politics. Legislation may be scheduled during the closing weeks of a Congress to maximize political pressure for action. Lawmakers, too, are often willing to wait until the end of a Congress, "believing that he, she, or they will have maximum leverage at the end of the tunnel."[9] Or real or contrived "crises" can be generated as certain deadlines (the start of the fiscal year or the traditional August recess, for example) approach. The sense of urgency can heighten the pressure and stakes so members will act before the clock or calendar runs out.

Unlike House members, all senators have an opportunity to participate in scheduling legislation for floor action. As Dole once noted: "The Senate leadership convened a special meeting this morning for all 100 Senators—81 Senators attended to discuss [the schedule for] wrapping up the year's business before adjournment."[10] This condition reflects both the comity that is usually prevalent in the Senate and the power that every member has under senatorial rules. "One person can tie this place into a knot," said Senator Simpson. "And two can do it even more beautifully."[11] Minor or noncontroversial bills are expedited to save time for major and controversial measures. Insofar as possible, action on important bills is scheduled to suit the convenience of members and to minimize conflicts with legislative activity taking place off the Senate floor. "The Senate operates largely on the basis of unanimous-consent agreements, comity, courtesy, and understanding," said veteran senator Byrd.[12] (Byrd wrote a multi-volume Senate history and is widely regarded as the premier authority on the chamber's rules and precedents.)

The Senate's system for classifying measures for floor debate is simpler and more informal than the House system. In contrast to the House, with its five calendars, the Senate has only two: the *Calendar of General Orders* and the *Executive Calendar.* All legislation, major or minor, controversial or noncontroversial, is placed on the former; treaties and nominations under the Senate's "advice and consent" authority are placed on the latter.[13]

The Senate, by motion or unanimous consent, resolves into "executive session" to consider treaties or nominations. Within the course of a single day, the Senate may consider measures on both the Executive and General Orders calendars. It may go from executive session to legislative session before finishing the pending item on the Executive Calendar. (It is not in order to filibuster a motion to enter or exit an executive session; however, the nomination or treaty to be taken up is "filibusterable.")

As discussed in Chapter 5, relatively noncontroversial legislation in the House comes up under suspension of the rules procedure or by unanimous consent. Even specific days of the month are designated for consideration of legislation on the Corrections Calendar or Private Calendar. The Senate has no comparable procedures. Formal Senate rules for calling up legislation—both major and minor—are cumbersome and consequently are generally ignored. One of these rules, for example, requires a daily calendar call, with measures required to be brought up and debated in the order in which they appear on the calendar. (An example of a Senate calendar appears in Figure 7-2.) Were the Senate to follow that rule, it would lose virtually all flexibility in processing its workload.

NONCONTROVERSIAL BILLS

Practically all noncontroversial measures are "called up by unanimous consent and enacted without debate," observed Senator Byrd. "In this regard, I have reference to private bills, most nominations on the Executive Calendar—which run into the thousands—and bills that are not of general interest."[14] He estimated that "easily 98 percent of the business of the Senate is called up by unanimous consent."[15] The leaders and staff aides in both parties check with senators to clear minor or noncontroversial legislation before such measures reach the floor. A single dissent will hold up floor action until the roadblock is cleared away. Once cleared, minor and noncontroversial bills generally take from several seconds to a few minutes to pass. "Locomotive velocity may develop at this point, as bills come up and pass through with no objection," Byrd noted.[16] It is typically at the end of daily Senate sessions, the "wrap-up" period, when unobjected-to measures are quickly passed.

The Senate's small size, flexibility, and tradition of cooperation mean that the majority and minority leaders frequently can schedule noncontroversial legislation on a daily basis. Through informal floor discussions or colloquies, each examines the calendar to be sure the noncontroversial bills have been cleared by interested senators on their side. The measures then are passed quickly by voice vote.

Minor and noncontroversial measures also may reach the Senate floor on a motion of any senator. However, the majority and minority leaders normally try to reach agreement in advance on the floor schedule and are likely to oppose action that will bring bills to the floor without prior clearance from them. The leaders' prerogative of receiving preferential recognition from the presiding officer—first the majority leader, followed by the minority leader—enables them to control the agenda of activities on the floor. As Senator Byrd explained: "A majority leader has enormous power when it comes to the schedule of the Senate, the scheduling of bills and resolutions and the programming of the Senate schedule. The majority leader has the first recognition power and that is a big arrow in his arsenal. . . . Nobody can get recognition before the majority leader."[17] A senator who attempts to bring a measure or matter to the floor without consulting the majority leader in advance may find the proposal subject to a tabling motion. (The motion to table kills the action to which it is directed.)

SENATE OF THE UNITED STATES
ONE HUNDRED FOURTH CONGRESS

FIRST SESSION { CONVENED JANUARY 4, 1995   } DAYS OF SESSION 81

SECOND SESSION {   }

CALENDAR OF BUSINESS

Wednesday, May 17, 1995

(LEGISLATIVE DAY, MAY 15, 1995)

SENATE CONVENES AT 9:45 A.M.

(IN RECESS)

UNANIMOUS CONSENT AGREEMENT

WHITEWATER RESOLUTION

Ordered, That at 10:30 a.m. on Wednesday, May 17, 1995, the Senate proceed to the consideration of a D'Amato resolution regarding Whitewater, on which there shall be 2 hours debate, to be equally divided and controlled by the Chairman and the Ranking Minority Member of the Banking Committee.

Ordered further, That no amendments or motions be in order.

Ordered further, That upon the conclusion or yielding back of time, the Senate proceed to vote on the resolution, without any intervening action or debate. *(May 16, 1995.)*

PREPARED UNDER THE DIRECTION OF SHEILA P. BURKE,
SECRETARY OF THE SENATE

By R. SCOTT BATES, LEGISLATIVE CLERK

99–015

FIGURE 7-2

MAJOR LEGISLATION

Once major Senate bills are reported from committee, there are two main avenues by which they may be brought to the floor: through unanimous consent or by motion. Before they get there, however, the legislation may be subject to the one-day rule, the two-day rule, or to "holds."

ONE-DAY AND TWO-DAY RULES

The one-day rule states that bills and reports must lie over on the calendar for one *legislative* day before they are eligible for floor consideration. This rule is seldom enforced and commonly is waived by unanimous consent. To speed up action, the majority leader states, "I ask unanimous consent that [these bills] be considered as having been on the calendar 1 legislative day for the purpose of the rules of the Senate."[18] There rarely is an objection to the request.

The two-day rule requires that printed committee reports accompanying measures or matters be available to members for at least two *calendar* days before those proposals are eligible for floor action. (The two-day rule was a three-day rule until the Senate changed it in February 1986; Chapter 8 explains the difference between legislative and calendar days.) This rule, too, may be waived by unanimous consent or by joint motion of the majority and minority leaders. However, it is common for the Senate to observe this rule, sometimes to the chagrin of the majority leader, who has primary responsibility for scheduling the Senate's business.

When the Senate considered the controversial nomination of Robert H. Bork to the Supreme Court, Democratic leader Byrd wanted to facilitate floor action on the nominee. He repeatedly asked GOP leader Dole to join him in waiving the two-day rule. "Would the distinguished Republican leader indicate whether or not he is willing to join with me in waiving the 2-day rule?" asked Byrd. "I regret that I am not in a position now to waive the 2-day rule," answered Dole.[19] The discussion surrounding the two-day rule involved jockeying by both parties as they tried to expedite or stretch out debate on the Bork judgeship.

It is interesting that when the roles of the two senators were reversed during the 104th Congress, with Dole as majority leader and Byrd as the Senate's senior Democrat (he had voluntarily relinquished his party leadership role at the start of the 101st Congress), Dole hoped to act quickly on legislation curbing passage of unfunded federal mandates where the costs of national programs are passed on to state and local governments. To hasten floor action on the unfunded mandates bill, Dole requested the two committees with jurisdiction (Budget and Governmental Affairs) not to submit committee reports with the measure. The majority leader did not want the bill delayed by the two-day rule or the Senate rule granting committee members three calendar days to file supplemental, additional, or minority views for inclusion in the report. (Unlike the House, the Senate has no formal rule requiring committee reports to accompany legislation. Senate committees, however, usually file committee reports.) Despite protests from each committee's Democratic members, neither panel issued a formal committee report. Instead, the two GOP committee chairmen filed substitute statements in the *Congressional Record.*[20]

Senator Byrd quickly made a floor issue of the speed with which the bill whizzed through committee. "The Senate is not up against a deadline," he said. "We re not up against an adjournment *sine die.*" The measure, he argued, needed a thorough examination on the floor. He underscored the importance of formal committee reports noting, for instance, their value "to any court in determining what the legislative intent is with regard to a particular bill."[21] For two weeks Senator Byrd led the Democratic effort to delay action on the GOP proposal. "We have what we know as 'Byrd-lock,'" quipped Majority Leader Dole.[22] After fifty-nine hours of debate on the bill and forty-four roll call votes, the Senate finally enacted the legislation.[23]

"Holds"

"Holds" are an informal custom unique to the Senate. They permit any number of senators—individually or in clusters—to stop (sometimes permanently, sometimes temporarily) floor consideration of legislation or nominations simply by making requests of their party leaders not to take up such matters. For example, a Senate committee reports a measure by a 17–1 vote. The bill may even be slated for floor debate. Yet the dissenting senator can put a hold on the legislation and halt action on the measure. To be sure, party leaders can move ahead with the bill anyway, but then they face the daunting prospect of overcoming the probable filibuster. Unlike filibusters, which are ostensibly educational and occur in full view of everyone, holds require no public utterance and occur in shrouded circumstances. Sometimes called the "silent filibuster," they are especially effective on limited or special purpose measures that attract little public or political attention. "Must" legislation, such as continuing resolutions, cannot be killed by holds.

Relatively little is known about holds even among insiders in Washington. There is no public record of who places holds, how they are done (often by letter to the party leader), how many holds are placed on any bill, or how long they will be honored by the leadership. Most holds, noted Senator Byrd, are used so senators "might be assured that they will be informed or contacted so they can be present when the matter is called up, or have an opportunity to offer an amendment."[24] Yet secret holds can stymie action without anyone—press, constituents, interest groups, executive officials, or even other senators—knowing who is preventing consideration of a particular issue. "There is a hold on S. 1407," declared Sen. J. James Exon,

D-Neb., and "this Senator cannot even find out which Senator or the staff of which Senator has placed a hold on that bill."[25] With some sleuthing, senators and their aides are likely to track down who has placed the hold and what might be done to have the hold lifted.

Holds can forestall floor action because they are linked to the Senate's tradition of extended debate and unanimous consent agreements. Party leaders understand that to ignore holds can precipitate objections to unanimous consent requests and filibusters. Especially during the period when the Senate is rushing to adjourn, holds can be fatal. "At this stage in the year, you have a finite amount of time and an infinite amount of legislation. Either the hold goes away, changes are made to the legislation or the person with the hold wins," stated a Senate GOP leadership aide.[26] Holds are also used during the end-of-session rush by members who are searching for "must-pass" bills to which they can attach their favorite amendments. Sen. Phil Gramm, R-Texas, for example, placed a hold on the Export Administration Act "so he can attempt to attach [his] home equity loan amendment."[27]

Holds are a more prominent feature of today's Senate because assertive senators recognize the political and policy potential inherent in the concept. Holds "have come into a form of reverence which was never to be," declared Senator Simpson.[28] Periodically, party leaders assert that senators cannot put indefinite or anonymous holds on matters, but the practice still flourishes because senators recognize the tactical benefits. The Democratic and GOP leaders (Mitchell and Dole) in 1993 agreed on a uniform set of principles regarding holds; they remain in effect today (see Box 7-2, "Leadership Policy on Schedule Notifications").

Holds encourage bargaining not only among senators but also between the Senate and the executive branch. Sen. Jesse Helms, R-N.C., sometimes places holds on diplomatic and other nominations to extract concessions from the State Department and other federal agencies. Another senator blocked the confirmation of an undersecretary of the Commerce Department for three weeks because he wanted the "Commerce Department to award a $1 million grant for a marina development project in his home state."[29] The Reagan White House asked Sen. Mark O. Hatfield, R-Ore., to place a hold on a measure that would limit the perquisites afforded former presidents.[30] Lobbying organizations, and even House members, can ask sympathetic senators to place holds on legislation.

UNANIMOUS CONSENT REQUESTS

If the Senate strictly observed every rule, it would become mired in a bog of parliamentary complications. Instead, the chamber expedites its business by unanimously agreeing to set aside the rules. Any senator can object to a unanimous consent agreement. As former majority leader Mitchell once said: "I regularly propound unanimous-consent requests on the floor, and I

LEADERSHIP POLICY ON SCHEDULE NOTIFICATIONS

Over a period of time, the Democratic and Republican leadership have developed a system by which Senators ask the leaders to consult them regarding reservations or problems with particular legislation. These notifications are commonly called "holds".

The leaders will find it necessary to schedule matters on which Senators have requested consultation. When it is necessary to consider an issue, any Senator with an interest should be prepared to be on the Floor to defend his or her interests.

In order to develop a common understanding of what notifications mean, the leaders have agreed on the following principles.

1. It is the responsibility of every Senator to notify his or her respective leader, in writing, about any need to consult with that Senator on a bill or nomination. This notification should be made in a timely fashion. Each leader will develop his own notification system.
2. The leaders will respect the confidentiality of communications from Senators. However, in order to facilitate the scheduling of legislation, Senators, who ask to be consulted prior to the scheduling of a bill or nomination, should be prepared to discuss the issue with the relevant Committee Chairman and/or ranking member or sponsor of the measure. The leaders will encourage this type of consultation between Senators prior to Floor consideration.
3. The leaders will give as much advance notification as possible to any Senator who has asked to be consulted prior to the scheduling of legislation and nominations. Whenever possible, the leaders will announce a specific time for a unanimous consent request to go to a matter. Any Senator wishing to object to a unanimous consent request to go to legislation or to be involved in the arrangements under which a measure will be considered should be on the Floor at the announced time.

Source: Congressional Record, May 18, 1993, S5983.

BOX 7-2

can assure [the Senator] when Senators object we hear within seconds—within seconds. Frequently when I am in the middle of a sentence, the phone rings and staff comes running out to say, `Senator so and so objects.'"[31] Objections seldom occur because all members may participate in formulating these agreements, and senators usually concur in the need to keep legislation moving.

By longstanding tradition, the business of the Senate is "largely transacted through unanimous-consent agreements," Massachusetts Republican Henry Cabot Lodge said in 1913, and "not only the important unanimous-consent agreements which are reached often with much difficulty on large and generally contested measures, but constantly on all the small business of the Senate we depend on unanimous consent to enable us to transact the public business."[32] That statement holds true today. As one senator recently put it:

> [T]he way the Senate conducts its business hour after hour, day after day, week after week, and year after year, is Senators voluntarily waive the rights which they possess under the rules. I would guess in the course of a typical week we probably enter into anywhere from 10 to 200 unanimous consent agreements, literally, where Senators by unanimous consent, with 100 Senators agreeing to yield some right that they may have—the right to debate, to offer amendments, the right to do this, that or the other thing—waive their rights so that the body may proceed in a way that seems expeditious.[33]

Once accepted, unanimous consent agreements are as binding on the Senate as any standing rule and may be set aside or modified only by unanimous consent. There are two types of unanimous consent requests: *simple* and *complex*.

Simple requests are made from the floor by any senator; these almost always deal with routine business or noncontroversial actions. They are made orally and normally are accepted without objection. For example, senators regularly ask permission for staff members to be present on the floor during a debate. Committees may not meet after the first two hours of a Senate session except by unanimous consent or unless special leave is obtained from the majority and minority leaders. Simple unanimous consent agreements also may rescind quorum calls, add senators as cosponsors of bills, insert material in the *Congressional Record,* or limit the length of time members have to be recorded on roll-call votes.

Complex agreements usually set the guidelines for floor consideration of specific major bills. They are proposed orally—usually by the majority leader—often after protracted negotiations among other party and committee leaders and key senators.[34] Once agreed to, they are formally recorded. Such agreements may establish the sequential order in which measures will be taken up, pinpoint the time when measures are to reach the floor, and set rules for debate, including time limitations and, frequently, a requirement that all amendments be germane to the bill under consideration. Their two primary components are to impose limitations on debate and amendments. As a hypothetical example, they could restrict amendments by specifying that the Domenici amendment will have a time limit of twenty minutes equally divided between the two opposing sides or that the Hatch-Kennedy amendment will have a time limit of thirty minutes equally divided and controlled in the usual form (that is, between the mover of the amendment and an opponent).

Unanimous consent agreements are often worked out in advance of floor debate and then approved by the Senate and transmitted in printed form to all senators. Sometimes party leaders are able to negotiate only partial unanimous consent agreements (covering parts but not the entire bill) before they call up the bill for floor action. There are also plenty of piecemeal unanimous consent agreements—limiting debate on specific amendments or deciding when to call up a measure—hammered out on the floor (see Box 7-3). Party leaders and floor managers take what they can get when they can get it and work from there to more embracing unanimous consent agreements. It is "so hard to get these agreements," said one majority leader. "I find it is somewhat better to do them a little bit at a time."[35] Or as a congressional scholar wrote: "A dozen or more complex agreements are no longer uncommon for complicated contentious measures."[36]

An example of a unanimous consent agreement (also called a "time-limitation agreement") is shown in Chapter 8, p. 236. In addition to identifying the bills involved, such agreements indicate each bill's position (Order No.) in relation to all other measures on the General Orders Calendar.

The fundamental objective of unanimous consent agreements is to limit the time it takes to dispose of controversial issues in an institution noted for unlimited debate. These agreements, therefore, expedite action on legislation and structure floor deliberation. Typically, agreements impose time limitations on every debatable—and thus delaying—motion, including amendments and final passage, points of order, or appeals from the rulings of the presiding officer. These agreements, however, may allow an unlimited number of amendments to be offered, thus permitting what Sen. Ted Stevens, R-Alaska, once dubbed a "time agreement filibuster."

Of course, a unanimous consent agreement could ban certain amendments or place time limits on them, preventing a time agreement filibuster. Thus, depending on what the circumstances warrant, party leaders can craft highly detailed, complex, and creative unanimous consent agreements to accommodate the diverse procedural contingencies that might arise on the floor. Their fundamental problem is winning consent from senators reluctant to waive any of their procedural prerogatives. As former Democratic leader Byrd once said: "The leader is the prisoner of Senators, and always has been. Any Senator can object to time agreements, they can make it difficult for every other Senator."[37]

Other usual features of these agreements specify the senators who are to control the time for debate on the bill and all amendments, and provide that the time is to be controlled by senators on opposing sides of the issue. Common, too, is the requirement that amendments be germane. Senate rules

WINNING A UNANIMOUS CONSENT AGREEMENT

STAGE 1: THE ATTEMPT

Mr. DOLE. Mr. President, we are apparently stymied on S. 408, the Small Business Administration authorization bill. It was my understanding earlier that there would be no objection to a time agreement with reference to germane amendments to the SBA authorization proposal. Members on both sides had agreed to 2 hours on the bill and amendments offered by four or five Senators. With time agreements we thought we could dispose of that bill this afternoon.

It now appears that it is not possible, that there is objection to that agreement. There is a Senator who wants to offer a prayer amendment to the Small Business authorization bill.

STAGE 2: THE OBJECTION

A Congressional attempt to rescue the SBA from termination, as proposed by the White House, is being threatened by a resonant clash of Senate personalities, focused, at least ostensibly, on the issue of officially sanctioned prayer in the public schools.

Senator Lowell P. Weicker Jr., R-Conn., chairman of the Senate Small Business Committee, had drafted a compromise bill that would reduce the cost of the SBA by $2.5 billion over three years. He said the measure would continue the most important functions of the agency, had won support for it from Senate leaders, and was prepared to bring it to the floor. But then Senator Jesse Helms, R-N.C., introduced a proposal to legalize school prayer as an amendment to the Weicker bill. This had the effect of postponing floor action indefinitely. Under these circumstances, Senator Dole could not bring up the legislation without risking tying up the Senate for weeks on school prayer any time Senator Helms chose to call up his amendment.

Senator Weicker led the opposition to a school prayer amendment on its most recent appearance on the floor early in 1984, when it was defeated. Senator Helms, his opponents have discovered, never forgets.

STAGE 3: SUCCESS

Mr. DOLE. I am pleased to report that we have worked out an agreement with the distinguished Senator from North Carolina, Senator HELMS, who has an amendment to the SBA bill which he now . . . will not offer. In return, I have agreed to bring the amendment up as a freestanding resolution, a prayer resolution, sometime in September.

Sources: Adapted from *Congressional Record,* June 18, 1985, S8310 ("Stage 1"), July 16, 1985, S9538 ("Stage 3"); and *New York Times,* July 1, 1985, B8 ("Stage 2").

BOX 7-3

do permit nongermane floor amendments, but unanimous consent agreements often prohibit them to prevent extraneous issues from being taken up. Some agreements may also set the date and time for the vote on final passage of the measure. In brief, in an institution noted for procedural flexibility and sparseness (as compared with the House), unanimous consent agreements underscore the Senate's recognition that it needs to voluntarily impose additional rules on itself to dispatch its business.

In sum, complex unanimous consent agreements generally impose limitations on two of the most significant prerogatives associated with being a member of the Senate: the right of unlimited debate and the right to offer an unlimited number of floor amendments, even if they are nongermane. The irony of unanimous consent agreements is that, if they are accepted by everyone, the Senate can do almost anything it wants (unanimous consent agreements, however, cannot waive constitutional requirements, such as having recorded votes to pass a bill over the president's veto); yet, if even one senator objects, then it becomes difficult for the Senate to accomplish anything. Little surprise that in today's Senate, where individualism is perhaps its paramount feature, majority leaders must negotiate unanimous consent agreements that accommodate individual lawmakers' interests if they are to expedite the Senate's business.

THE TRACK SYSTEM

Another device used to move legislation to the floor is of relatively recent origin. The track system was instituted in the early 1970s by Majority Leader Mansfield with the concurrence of the minority leadership and other senators. It permits the Senate to have several pieces of legislation pending on the floor simultaneously by designating specific periods during the day when each proposal will be considered. The system is particularly beneficial when there are many important bills awaiting floor action or when there is protracted floor conflict on a particular bill.

Before the initiation of the track system, legislative business halted during filibusters. The "two-track system enables the Senate to circumvent that barrier," said Sen. Alan Cranston, D-Calif., then the majority whip. "[It] . . . can now continue to work on all other legislation on one `track' while a filibuster against a particular piece of legislation is . . . in progress on the other `track.'"[38] Use of the track system on certain legislation is implemented by the majority leadership after obtaining the unanimous consent of the Senate. Or the different tracks can be put into place by agreement between the majority leader and the minority leader. We have kept open "the possibility of double tracking" the constitutional balanced budget amendment and other matters, said one majority leader.[39]

On occasion, the Senate may operate on triple or quadruple tracks. "This means there would be about . . . four tracks going here with the Verity nomination to be the first. . . . Following that the war powers has next priority," said Senator Byrd. "Following that, catastrophic illness, and then, fourthly, the Labor-HHS appropriations bill."[40]

The use of unanimous consent agreements and the track system imposes a measure of discipline on the Senate. Formerly, senators could arrive in the midst of a debate on a banking bill, for example, obtain recognition from the chair, and launch into a lengthy discussion of the wheat harvest prospects. Today, complex agreements and the track system prevent that from happening. Now, senators generally know what measure will be considered on a specific day and at what time, when they are scheduled to speak on that bill, and how long they will have the floor.

SCHEDULING PROCEDURES COMPARED

As is probably clear to the reader by now, the Senate has nothing that compares with the scheduling function of the House Rules Committee.[41] That panel, as described in Chapter 5, regulates the flow of major bills to the floor, specifies the time for general debate, stipulates whether amendments can be offered, and decides if points of order are to be waived. The legislative route in the House is clearly marked by firm rules and precedents, but that is not so in the Senate. "Rules are never observed in this body," a president pro tempore once observed, "they are only made to be broken. We are a law unto ourselves, and it is entirely immaterial in my judgment whether we have a code of rules or not."[42]

Nonetheless, unanimous consent agreements and the special rules drafted by the Rules Committee are similar in several respects. Each waives the rules of the respective chamber to permit timely consideration of important measures and amendments. Each must be approved by the members— in the Senate by unanimous consent of all senators and in the House by majority vote of the representatives. Each effectively sets the conditions for debate on the legislation in question and on all proposed amendments. And rules and unanimous consent agreements are formulated with the involvement of party leaders, although such participation in the House is generally limited to the majority party leaders. And the House leadership generally plays a significant part only for rules on particularly crucial or controversial measures.

Among the more important differences between rules and unanimous consent agreements are that rules are drafted in public session by a standing committee, while unanimous consent agreements are often negotiated privately by senators and staff aides. Measures given a rule in the House commonly are taken up almost immediately, but unanimous consent agreements generally involve prospective action on bills.

The amendment process in each house also makes for important differences. Rules from the Rules Committee may limit the number of permissible

TABLE 7-1 Comparison of House Special Rules and Senate Unanimous Consent Agreements

House Special Rule	*Senate Unanimous Consent Agreement*
Specifies time for general debate	Specifies time for debating the bill and amendments offered to the bill
Permits or prohibits amendments	Usually restricts the offering of nongermane amendments only
Formulated by Rules Committee in public session	Formulated by party leaders informally in private sessions; occasionally on the Senate floor
Approved by majority vote of the House	Agreed to by unanimous consent of senators
Adoption generally results in immediate floor action on the bill	Adoption geared more to prospective floor action
Covers many aspects of floor procedure	Geared primarily to debate restrictions on amendments and final passage
Does not specify date and exact time for vote on final passage	May set date and exact time for vote on final passage
Effect is to waive House rules	Effect is to waive Senate rules

amendments or prohibit them altogether. Senate unanimous consent agreements, except those prohibiting nongermane amendments, do not usually limit or forbid floor amendments. Interestingly, Senate practices regard an amendment as germane if it is specifically enumerated in the unanimous consent agreement, even if it really is not germane at all. Of course, all senators must be willing to waive the germaneness requirement when the agreement is drawn up.

Finally, a special House rule specifies almost every significant floor procedure that will affect consideration of the bill. Complex agreements in the Senate focus on two points in particular: (1) setting limits on the debate time to be allowed for amendments, motions, points of order, and appeals from the rulings of the chair; and (2) setting limits on debate on final passage of the bill. In general, procedural experimentation is easier to accomplish in the smaller Senate than in the 435-member House. Table 7-1 briefly summarizes the principal characteristics of rules drafted by the Rules Committee and Senate unanimous consent agreements.

SENATE LEADERSHIP AND UNANIMOUS CONSENT

Complex unanimous consent agreements are formulated through informal negotiations among party leaders and interested senators. Bargains or informal understandings sometimes are struck on the Senate floor to win approval of unanimous consent agreements. A mid-1980s but still contemporaneous example of the intricate negotiations that sometimes are necessary appears in the Box 7-3, "Winning a Unanimous Consent Agreement."

The job of the leadership is to ensure that the interests of all senators are protected—a difficult assignment given the heightened individualism and openness of the contemporary Senate. One scholar has written: "Because the system of unanimous consent would collapse if even one senator were habitually mistreated, Senate leaders strive to identify those senators interested in a given measure and to give them ample opportunity to express their interest."[43]

If members were ever to lose confidence in the unanimous consent procedure, the Senate would be in danger of reverting to hidebound observance of cumbersome rules. It would almost certainly lose the informality and flexibility that sets it apart from the more rules-conscious House. Informal norms such as courtesy and fairness to all senators buttress trust in the wide use of unanimous consent agreements. The party leaders who negotiate complex unanimous consent agreements hold the key to the continued smooth operation of the Senate.

Two recent majority leaders—Democrats Mike Mansfield, who held the post longer than any other senator (1961-1977), and Robert C. Byrd (1977-1981; 1987-1989)—are largely responsible for refining and extending the use of unanimous consent agreements. Each had his own style. Mansfield was a mild-mannered leader who viewed himself as only "one among my peers." Byrd was an activist who worked diligently to control all procedural phases of floor action. The two approached negotiations on consent agreements in differing fashion, but each was successful in achieving agreements even, at times, in the face of fierce opposition to particular bills. During their tenure unanimous consent agreements became more complicated and governed floor action on a larger number of measures.

The personal styles of other majority leaders and the environmental context in which they served (the size of their majority, for example, or whether their party occupied the White House) also influenced how they employed unanimous consent agreements. As majority leader (1981-1985), Howard H. Baker, Jr., R-Tenn., brought measures to the floor without first obtaining comprehensive agreements. In many cases this was because he was unable to attract the unanimous approval of the Senate. With the Senate and White House in GOP hands, the Democrats were reluctant to enter into broad agreements restricting their floor options since they had no idea what amendments might surface. Thus, narrower agreements often were negotiated on the floor, typically regulating the consideration of a particular amendment or series of amendments.

Although of different parties, majority leaders Robert Dole (1981-1987, 1995-) and George Mitchell (1989-1995) operated with much the same styles. They forcefully took charge of the Senate's agenda and orchestrated floor actions to accommodate party goals and policy preferences. Each used his power of recognition to sequence and control the consideration of issues on the floor. And each often devised strategies for moving legislation through private meetings in their offices. "Much of the real work clearing legislative obstacles occurred in Mr. Dole's offices, where many problems were aired and resolved in private while out on the Senate floor quorum calls and recesses lasted hours."[44] Dole did not simply call the meetings; he participated actively in working out agreements that produced legislative results. Mitchell as majority leader functioned in a similar fashion. Here is what one account said about his role in the enactment of the Clear Air Act of 1990:

> Mitchell was the ringmaster of the clean air debate, both the private talks and the floor arguments. Although he did not often participate during the actual discussions, he set the daily agenda and cracked the whip on all sides [Senate Democrats, Senate Republicans, and White House officials], urging them to reach a deal.[45]

Needless to say, private negotiations of this sort facilitate reaching unanimous consent agreements on the Senate floor.

Mitchell did not seek reelection in 1994 and Dole, who became majority leader with the GOP takeover, was considering resigning that position if he obtained his party's presidential nomination in 1996.[46] Meanwhile, one of Dole's goals was to make the Senate run a bit more efficiently. "There ought to be some way with this modern technology—we do nothing all day and don't start voting until dark. Members should be disciplined enough to work in the daytime."[47]

The majority leader generally has an important ally in the minority leader. In contrast to the House, where scheduling is the sole prerogative of the majority leadership, Senate scheduling traditionally has been a bipartisan effort. The Senate system derives not merely from equity but also from necessity, because Senate rules confer on each individual member formidable power to frustrate the legislative process, including the right to object to any unanimous consent request.

The majority and minority leaders constantly consult with one another and with their top assistants, other senators, party colleagues, and key staff members on legislative scheduling. They also seek scheduling advice from committee leaders or receive it unsolicited from them. As Sen. William S. Cohen, R-Maine, noted about the Mitchell-Dole relationship: Mitchell's "been very cooperative with Bob Dole, works closely with him trying to alert the minority in order to keep us apprised of scheduling, so that there are no surprises."[48] As majority leader in the 104th Congress, Dole consults regularly with the leader of the Democratic minority, Tom Daschle, S.D., about the Senate's agenda.

Outside groups also lobby party leaders to bring favored legislation to the floor. Executive branch and White House officials importune party leaders to facilitate or delay action on certain legislation. Senators, too, might threaten to vote against "must" legislation unless proposals of great interest to them are also given an opportunity for passage.

In short, scheduling involves numerous considerations. Party leaders must balance their interest in planning the Senate's business on a daily, weekly, and annual basis with (1) the needs of committees, which require concentrated periods of time, particularly early in the session, to process legislation assigned to them, and (2) the needs of senators, who prefer some degree of predictability and certainty so they can schedule their time most efficiently. This often means that no matter how carefully Senate leaders plan the legislative agenda—the times and dates measures will be scheduled, and in what order they will be considered on the floor—they still must juggle bills to satisfy senators, take account of external events and political circumstances, and, where possible, influence policy outcomes in the interests of their own party. As former majority leader Mitchell once said:

> The ability of any Senator to speak without limitations makes it impossible to establish total certainty with respect to scheduling. When there is added to that the different and very demanding schedules of 100 Senators, it is very difficult to organize business in a way that meets the convenience of everybody.[49]

Majority leaders may also seek in election years to synchronize Senate action on measures to correspond with what their party's presidential candidate is emphasizing on the campaign trail or to schedule certain bills to underscore differences between the two parties.

BREAKDOWNS IN SCHEDULING

Party leaders work diligently to bring legislation to the floor by unanimous consent and are understandably reluctant to call up measures without time-limitation agreements or unless their proponents can guarantee the necessary votes to cut off any filibusters. After all, the Senate's time is finite and its workload immense. Still, there are measures that are too important to be delayed by the intense divisions and strong feelings that make unanimous consent impossible. "When you cannot get an agreement through, there is but one thing to do and that is just to put your head down and plow through," said former majority leader Baker.[50] When unanimous consent on scheduling cannot be reached, legislation is at the mercy of opponents, who

A PARLIAMENTARY WAR . . .

The Senate May 13 exploded into an angry partisan shouting match, as Republicans rolled out heavy parliamentary artillery to block action on a bill limiting testing for President Reagan's strategic defense initiative (SDI).

Republicans employed little-known Senate rules to outflank Majority Leader Robert C. Byrd of West Virginia, who in turn was resorting to a procedural maneuver to circumvent a threatened GOP filibuster.

The dispute paralyzed the Senate for four hours, while Byrd and GOP leader Robert Dole of Kansas deployed competing parliamentarians in what another senator aptly described as a "dueling banjos routine."

Caught in the snarl was the fiscal 1988 defense authorization bill (S 1174), which ended up exactly where Republicans wanted it—mired in a filibuster that prevented Byrd from officially bringing the bill to the floor.

Republicans vehemently oppose provisions of the bill that would, in effect, give Congress veto power over any move to speed up testing and deployment of SDI.

It was the second time this year that Republicans have stalled the Senate in parliamentary gridlock, reminding Democrats that being in the majority does not guarantee control of the Senate. In February, a similar brawl broke out over a bill (S 83) setting energy efficiency standards for household appliances that was opposed by the White House.

"MORNING HOUR" MANEUVER

The brouhaha over the defense bill erupted when Byrd tried to block Republican plans to filibuster his motion to bring the measure to the floor. He did so by arranging to call up the bill during the "morning hour"—a period within the first two hours of a legislative day during which, under Senate rules, any motion to proceed to a bill is non-debatable and therefore immune from filibusters.

To lay the groundwork for moving into morning hour, Byrd first called for a brief adjournment, so he could begin a new legislative day. He then called for the approval of the *Journal* of the previous day. Both moves were the subject of roll-call votes.

Republicans wanted to prevent Byrd from offering his motion to proceed to the defense bill for two hours—at which point morning hour would end and they would be able to filibuster.

With help from former [now current] Senate Parliamentarian Robert B. Dove, GOP leaders came up with an obscure rule that allows senators to ask to be excused from voting and to interrupt a roll call to explain why.

BOX 7-4

... ERUPTS OVER DEFENSE BILL

Beginning with the vote on the *Journal,* Republicans took turns invoking that rule and calling for votes on their request not to vote—thus preventing one roll call after another from being completed. After three Republicans asked to be excused from consecutive votes, Byrd tried to call a halt to the tactic. He objected to the third GOP request, saying it was out of order because it was "dilatory," being made only for the purpose of delaying the vote on the *Journal.* What followed was a procedural pileup of objections, roll calls, appeals and quorum calls, with Republicans and Democrats angrily accusing each other of parliamentary perfidy.

"Dictatorship!" cried Gordon J. Humphrey, R-N.H., after the presiding officer ruled in favor of the Democrats at one point.

"There is absolutely no precedent for this," Dole said at another point. "It is a strict flouting of the rules. Either we are going to play by the rules or not play by the rules."

Byrd charged that Republicans were trying to "drive me to the wall in my effort to carry out my responsibility to get a bill up."

He said his move to bring up the defense bill during "morning hour" would not have precluded Republicans from filibustering the bill itself.

"I often consider, in amusement, the explosion of interest in the arcane and esoteric rules and precedents of the Senate that occurs only when a situation such as we have seen occur today arises," Byrd said. "Suddenly there are many, many experts in the rules and precedents when a situation such as this arises."

An obviously baffled freshman, Timothy E. Wirth, D-Colo., was serving as the Senate's presiding officer during some of the most acrimonious exchanges. With the incumbent parliamentarian, Alan Frumin, whispering instructions to him, Wirth responded slowly and carefully to the repeated demands for rulings and clarification that were shouted at the chair.

As the situation deteriorated, Wirth was replaced by a savvy veteran, Wendell H. Ford, D-Ky., chairman of the Senate Rules and Administration Committee. He went so far as to declare Dole out of order with a blunt ruling: "You canot go on forever stating your reasons for not voting."

Dole didn't, but by the time the parliamentary knots were untied, the Senate had long since wound its way through morning hour, and the motion to proceed to the defense bill was once again open to debate.

The Senate duly staggered from its flap to its filibuster.

Source: Janet Hook, "Parliamentary War Erupts over Defense Bill," *Congressional Quarterly Weekly Report,* May 16, 1987, 977.

have a vast array of obstructionist tactics—including the filibuster—at their disposal.

A failure to reach an agreement delays bringing the legislation at issue to the floor. A dramatic and classic example occurred during the first session of the 100th Congress. Majority Leader Byrd tried to bring up the defense authorization bill by unanimous consent. Unable to proceed in that fashion, Byrd then tried to call up the legislation without triggering a filibuster on the motion to proceed. Republicans, however, immediately launched delaying actions that the Senate had seldom seen in decades (see Box 7-4). The GOP opposed a provision in the defense measure that required the White House to receive congressional approval before testing the antimissile Strategic Defense Initiative (SDI). Republicans vowed to prevent consideration of the Pentagon bill until Democrats deleted the offending provision. (It is worth noting that at the start of the 104th Congress, when an effort was made to change the filibuster rule, Senator Byrd vigorously opposed the revision and recommended use of the "morning hour"—which is discussed in Box 7-4—as the way to obviate filibusters on motions to proceed to legislation.)[51]

For months the Senate was stymied in its effort to call up the defense measure. After a four-month filibuster, Republicans relented and voted with Democrats to take up the bill. They took this action because Democrats had finally won enough GOP votes to win a scheduled cloture vote on the motion to proceed. Another three weeks passed before the Senate passed the Pentagon bill with the SDI language still in it. An effort that began on May 13 to call up the bill ended October 2 with Senate passage of the legislation. (Then followed weeks of House-Senate and Congress-White House negotiations before acceptable compromises could be signed into law.)

Unlike the House, where failure to secure a rule from the Rules Committee usually spells defeat for important bills, the Senate, with its greater flexibility, has a variety of ways to secure action on legislation. Any senator can move to take measures off the General Orders Calendar. (Normally, however, such motions are made by the majority leader or a designee.) If such a move has the backing of party and committee leaders and majority of the Senate, the proposal almost certainly will reach the floor. In situations were the leadership is blocking a bill, a senator has the option of offering it in the form of a nongermane floor amendment to another bill. Finally, a senator can threaten a filibuster or object to all unanimous consent requests until the leadership yields and schedules his or her measure for floor action.

KEEPING SENATORS INFORMED

At the start of each day, the majority leader often presents an overview of activities for the Senate, just as he announces the program for the next day or subsequent day at the conclusion of the daily session. Periodically, he indicates what the legislative agenda looks like for longer periods of time

WHIP NOTICE

United States Senate
OFFICE OF
SENATE REPUBLICAN WHIP
WASHINGTON, DC 20510–7012

Monday, May 15

The Senate will reconvene at 9:30 a.m. The Majority Leader has announced that it is his intention to turn to consideration of S. 395, which would authorize and direct the Secretary of Energy to sell the Alaska Power Administration. Roll call votes could occur with respect to a motion to proceed to the bill or amendments relative to S. 395.

Tuesday, May 16

The Senate will resume consideration of the Interstate Transportation of Municipal Solid Waste Act, S. 534, at 9:30 a.m.

At 9:30 a.m., Senator Murray will be recognized to offer an amendment on which there will be a time limit of one hour, equally divided. Following disposition of the Murray amendment, Senator Feinstein will be recognized to offer her amendment, on which there will be a 30 minutes of debate, equally divided. Following disposition of the Feinstein amendment, Senator Levin will be recognized to offer an amendment, on which there will be 30 minutes of debate equally divided. Following the Levin amendment, Senator Domenici will be recognized to offer an amendment relative to Title 3, on which there will be 30 minutes of debate equally divided.

A roll call vote could occur as early as 10:30 a.m. Additional votes are expected prior to the 12:30 p.m. recess for the weekly party caucuses. The Senate will stand in recess from 12:30 p.m. until 2:15 p.m. to accommodate the weekly party caucuses.

Balance of the Week

The Senate is expected to complete action on the Interstate Transportation of Municipal Solid Waste, S. 534. After disposition of S. 534, the Senate may turn to any item cleared for action. Possible items include the Ryan White reauthorization, the Medicare Select bill, the Telecommunications bill, and the Whitewater Resolution. Thursday the Senate may move to the Budget Resolution.

FIGURE 7-3

Senators are kept informed of the legislative program through a variety of means, such as weekly whip notices (issued more frequently as needed by each party) listing the measures likely to be considered during the week (see Figure 7-3). The Senate's whip notices are less detailed than the House's, because Senate rules limit predictability in scheduling.

Floor proceedings are telecast to senators' offices, where senators and staff aides often listen to floor debate while working on other matters. Both parties maintain a "hot line" (automatic telephone connection) to their members' offices to keep them abreast of impending floor developments. For example, during a typical session, a member of the GOP leadership announced that the hot line had "notified Senators on this side of the aisle [that] if we have not finished the bill by normal recess or adjournment hour . . . we will continue late into the evening."[52]

Senators and staff aides also monitor the *Congressional Record*, committee calendars, the daily Calendar of Business, newspapers, and other publications. Senate offices (like House offices) have computer terminals with access to an assortment of legislative information banks. These video terminals can call up summaries of bills describing key provisions and listing when the measures were introduced, their sponsors, the committees to which they were referred, and actions taken, such as hearings, markups, and floor action. Legislative support agencies, such as the Congressional Research Service, continually prepare reports for members, committees, and staff aides on current and prospective legislative activities. (When the 104th Congress began, Speaker Gingrich opened a new on-line information network in the Library of Congress called THOMAS, after Thomas Jefferson, to provide citizens across the country with information about the workings of Congress, such as weekly floor schedules and the full text of bills.)

SUMMARY

The informality of the unanimous consent process does not mean that Senate procedure is less complex than that of the House. On the contrary, unanimous consent requests are unique to each bill and are arrived at only after careful, patient, and often difficult negotiations. The differences between House and Senate scheduling procedures are summarized in Table 7-2. For example, the Senate, unlike the House, is filled with devices to stall action on legislation ("substantive delays"), and its party leaders frequently permit personal delays to accommodate individual senators. "I suppose at one time or another each Member of the Senate has asked to have his or her situation taken into account when votes are scheduled," said Sen. David Pryor, D-Ark. The dilemma arises "when the efforts to accommodate Members reach the point" where the Senate is prevented from accomplishing its workload in reasonable fashion.[53] The need to balance institutional with individual prerogatives is a permanent feature of senatorial scheduling.

TABLE 7-2 House and Senate Scheduling Compared

House	Senate
Important role for the Rules Committee	No equivalent body
Majority party leaders, especially the Speaker, are the predominant force in scheduling	Majority party leaders control the flow of legislation to the floor in close consultation with minority party leaders
More formal process	Less formal process
Only key members are consulted in scheduling measures	Every reasonable effort is made to accommodate the scheduling requests of all senators
Elaborate system of formal calendars and special days for calling up measures	Heavy reliance on informal practice and personal accommodation in scheduling
Party leaders can plan a rather firm schedule of daily and weekly business	Party leaders regularly juggle several measures to suit events and senators

Similarities in scheduling between the two chambers also are worth noting. Scheduling is essentially a majority party function in both the House and Senate. As in the House, privileged legislation, such as conference reports, bills vetoed by the president, or Senate bills with House amendments, could be brought to the floor at almost any time on the motion of any member.[54] But in the Senate, to a greater degree than in the House, party leaders decide when such motions will be made.

Standing committees provide the legislation considered by both chambers. Although majority party leaders largely set the agenda, they are dependent on committees to process the legislation. There are occasions, too, when majority leaders ask the committee chairmen to stop reporting out controversial legislation because there is insufficient time remaining in a session to consider such measures.

As in the House, there are a number of ways in the Senate to bring up stalled bills, including measures never considered in committee. Senate rules provide for discharging committees, suspending rules, placing measures directly on the General Orders Calendar, and offering nongermane amendments on the floor. These are discussed in Chapter 8, "Senate Floor Procedure." In the Senate, the extent of the support for or opposition to a bill is the critical factor in getting the bill to the floor. If a voting bloc is large enough, and intensely committed to a bill, it usually can overcome the resistance of even the most intransigent committee chairman. The process of gathering support is frequently done behind the scenes. As Sen. Ernest F. Hollings, D-S.C., put it: "The truth of the matter is all of us, 100 Members of this august body, understand that 95 percent of the activity and action, consideration, debate, decisions, and the formulation of legislation is done off the floor of the U.S. Senate and not on it."[55]

When there is a strong political consensus, bills may sail smoothly through the Senate. In the absence of such a consensus, the rules of that body can be applied to bring virtually any measure to a screeching halt. The art of legislating in the Senate requires an understanding of the procedural dynamics of floor action. The interplay of issues, rules, and personalities affect floor strategy and the eventual outcome of all bills. "Any time you want to legislate around here you have to convince an awful lot of people over a long period of time to get something accomplished," noted Sen. Sam Nunn, D-Ga.[56]

NOTES

1. *U.S. News & World Report,* August 16, 1976, 28.
2. *Christian Science Monitor,* August 2, 1983, 13.
3. *Congressional Record,* December 9, 1987, S17474.
4. *Congressional Record,* June 23, 1994, S7553.
5. Ilona Nickels, "Senate's `Three weeks on; One week off' Schedule," in *Background Materials: Supplemental Information Provided to Members of the Joint Committee on the Organization of Congress,* 103d Cong., 1st sess. (1993), 1050–1051; and Karen Foerstel, "Three-On, One-Off Senate Schedule: Where Did It Go?" *Roll Call,* July 1, 1991, 1.
6. See Kevin Merida, "Calling Time Out on Capitol Hill," *Washington Post,* May 16, 1993, A1; and Guy Gugliotta, "A New Senate Order?" *Washington Post,* February 21, 1995, A13.
7. *Congressional Record,* February 13, 1995, S2533.
8. Congressional Quarterly's *Congressional Monitor,* February 14, 1995, 3.
9. Norman Ornstein, "Let the End Games Begin," *Roll Call,* September 12, 1994, A23.
10. *Congressional Record,* November 17, 1989, S15948.
11. *New York Times,* May 21, 1987, B10.
12. *Congressional Record,* March 21, 1980, S2789.
13. Each calendar is printed separately. There also are separate executive and legislative *Journals.* The General Orders Calendar is found in the Senate *Calendar of Business,* which is printed each day the Senate is in session. Measures on the calendar are assigned a calendar order number. The Senate *Executive Calendar* appears whenever there is executive business on it.
14. *Congressional Record,* January 26, 1973, 2301. Byrd at the time was majority whip. It should be noted that according to Senate rules, "Any rule may be suspended without advance notice by unanimous consent of the Senate."
15. *Congressional Record,* August 5, 1987, S11293.
16. *Congressional Record,* April 8, 1981, S3618.
17. *Congressional Record,* January 4, 1995, S39.
18. *Congressional Record,* December 10, 1982, S14345.
19. *Congressional Record,* October 14, 1987, S14197.

20. *Congressional Record,* January 9, 1995, S646, and January 11, 1995, S783.
21. *Congressional Record,* January 12, 1995, S858–859.
22. Edwin Chen and Melissa Healy, "Byrd Dogs Republicans With Stall on GOP Proposals," *Los Angeles Times,* January 18, 1995, A5.
23. David Hosansky, "Chipping Away at Opposition, Senate Passes Mandates Bill," *Congressional Quarterly Weekly Report,* January 28, 1995, 276.
24. *Congressional Record,* February 24, 1986, S1512.
25. *Congressional Record,* October 5, 1984, S13779.
26. *CQ's Congressional Monitor,* October 4, 1994, 5. For an informative study of holds, see Toby McIntosh, "Senate 'Holds' System Developing As Sophisticated Tactic for Leverage, Delay," *Daily Report for Executives* (No. 165), Bureau of National Affairs, August 26, 1991, C1-C5.
27. *National Journal's Congress Daily/AM,* October 5, 1994, 5.
28. *Congressional Record,* December 5, 1985, S16916.
29. *Washington Post,* April 25, 1986, B9.
30. *Congressional Record,* July 25, 1984, S9129.
31. *Congressional Record,* August 6, 1992, S11692.
32. *Congressional Record,* January 11, 1913, 1388.
33. *Congressional Record,* September 25, 1990, S13803.
34. Unlike simple requests, which are formulated orally, complex unanimous consent agreements are formalized in writing and reported to senators by means of the *Congressional Record,* the front page of the daily *Calendar of Business,* and in party whip notices.
35. *Congressional Record,* September 13, 1994, S12793.
36. Steven S. Smith, *Call To Order* (Washington, D.C.: Brookings Institution, 1989), 115.
37. *Congressional Record,* June 1, 1989, S5939.
38. *Congressional Record,* January 21, 1975, 928.
39. *Congressional Record,* June 18, 1992, S8440.
40. *Congressional Record,* October 13, 1987, S14112.
41. The Senate's Rules and Administration Committee has jurisdiction over internal Senate matters but is not involved in scheduling bills for floor debate.
42. *Congressional Record,* December 18, 1876, 266.
43. Robert Keith, "The Use of Unanimous Consent in the Senate," *Committees and Senate Procedures,* A Compilation of Papers Prepared for the Commission on the Operation of the Senate, 94th Cong., 2d sess., 161.
44. See James A. Barnes, "Dole's Dilemma," *National Journal,* January 14, 1995, 80–82.
45. Richard E. Cohen, "The Judge's Trials," *National Journal,* July 13, 1991, 1729.
46. *Washington Times,* December 30, 1994, A8.
47. *New York Times,* November 13, 1994, 20.
48. *Christian Science Monitor,* July 3, 1989, 15.
49. *Congressional Record,* July 20, 1990, S10183.
50. *Congressional Record,* May 25, 1983, S7494.
51. *Congressional Record,* January 4, 1995, S38.
52. *Congressional Record,* August 11, 1982, S10154.
53. *Congressional Record,* October 31, 1985, 29990.
54. In general, privileged matter in the Senate means that such propositions are not subject to unlimited debate (the filibuster) on the motion to call them up for consideration; they are not referred to committee; they are in order at almost any time a senator can gain recognition from the presiding officer; they do not displace the pending business but rather suspend consideration of that measure temporarily; and they are not subject to the one-day layover rule.
55. *Congressional Record,* July 25, 1986, S9666.
56. *Los Angeles Times,* July 15, 1990, A4.

CHAPTER 8

Senate Floor Procedure

A visitor who moves from the House gallery to the Senate gallery is struck immediately by the contrast in atmosphere. The Senate chamber is more sedate, it is quieter, and business is conducted at a more relaxed pace. The chamber is smaller and more intimate. With fewer members milling about, senators are more easily recognizable than their House counterparts. Typically, only a handful of senators are present on the floor. The remainder are busy in committee meetings or occupied with constituent or other legislative business. All senators, however, generally arrive on the floor quickly in response to buzzers announcing roll-call votes or quorum calls.

There are four semicircular tiers of desks in the Senate (Figure 8-1). Each of the one hundred senators has an assigned desk, complete with snuffbox and open inkwell. There are no electronic voting machines in the Senate; each senator responds aloud as his or her name is reached during a roll call. Both the Senate and the House employ microphones on the floor, but, unlike representatives, each senator has a microphone.

The chamber is ringed by an upper level of galleries for the press, visitors, and dignitaries. On the floor, a broad aisle separates the Republicans, sitting on the right (facing the podium), from the Democrats, on the left. Depending on the makeup of the Senate, there may be more desks on one side than the other.

The senators face a raised platform. One of several persons may occupy the chair and preside over the session. When he is in attendance, the constitutional president of the Senate—the vice president of the United States—sits there. He may vote only to break a tie. During the struggle to pass the Clinton administration's 1993 deficit reduction package, the final tally stood at 50 to 50 until Vice President Al Gore (whose presence was assured because everyone expected the vote to be close) cast the tie-breaking vote. Usually, of course, the vice president is not present. During his service as vice president, John Adams (1789-1797) "cast 29 tie-breaking votes, more than any of his 44 successors in that position," observed Majority Leader Bob Dole, R-Kan.[1]

The Constitution also provides for a Senate president pro tempore, elected by that body, to preside in the vice president's absence. The president pro tem usually is the most senior senator of the majority party. (The Senate has also established the post of deputy president pro tempore.) In practice, each day's session is chaired by several temporary presiding officers—majority-party senators chosen by the president pro tem to serve for a particular period of time.

Neither the president pro tem nor the presiding officer is analogous to the Speaker of the House, in part because neither possesses the political resources to exert such wide-ranging influence in the Senate. (One consequence is that rulings of the Senate presiding officer are often appealed and overturned by the Senate; the Speaker's parliamentary rulings in the House are seldom appealed and virtually never overturned.) For example, the president pro tempore "has never been able to establish his authority as a party leader to the extent of the Majority Leader," said Sen. Robert C. Byrd, D-W.V. (Byrd served in both capacities, as president pro tem 1989-1995 and as majority leader 1977-1981, 1987-1989.) "This is partly the result of the President pro tempore's irregular appointments and uncertain tenure over the years while serving in the absence of the Vice President."[2]

The principal elective leaders of the Senate are to be found at the front two desks on the center aisle, those assigned to the majority and minority leaders. To the left of the majority leader and to the right of the minority leader sit the party whips, second in command in the Senate party hierarchy. These party leaders, or their designees, remain on the floor at all times to protect their party's interests. When Sen. Trent Lott, R-Miss., was elected majority whip for the 104th Congress, he even instituted the practice of having a "whip of the day" present on the Senate floor.

There is frequent contact between the leadership and individual senators. To a much greater extent than in the House, each member has the power to influence the course of the legislative process on a daily basis. Any senator can disrupt the Senate's consideration of a bill more easily and with more telling effect than any one representative in the House. That this does not occur on a regular basis is a tribute to the operation of the Senate's system of unanimous consent, the skill of party leaders, the long tradition of trust, accommodation, and reciprocal courtesy among members, which have survived periodic lapses into hard-line partisanship and confrontation.

Because it is smaller and can operate more flexibly, the Senate normally functions by setting aside many of its own time-consuming rules in order to process legislation efficiently. This chapter describes how the Senate processes legislation once it is readied for floor action. Four main topics are discussed: (1) the daily order of floor business, (2) consideration of major bills under a unanimous consent agreement, (3) consideration of bills without a unanimous consent agreement, and (4) special floor procedures that are used to bypass Senate committees.

Throughout this chapter various procedural devices used to delay or expedite legislation are examined, and comparisons with House procedure are highlighted. First, it is worthwhile to note what *day* means in the Senate.

FIGURE 8-1 Senate Floor Plan and Seating Chart (as of March 17, 1995)

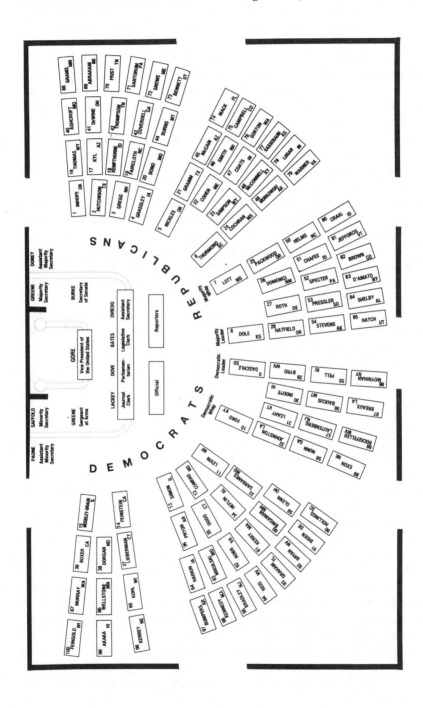

"LEGISLATIVE" AND "CALENDAR" DAYS

The Senate, unlike the House,[3] regularly distinguishes between a *calendar* and a *legislative* day. The former is the commonly understood notion of what constitutes a day. The latter refers not to a day when the Senate is in session but to the period between a *recess* and an *adjournment* of the Senate. Recesses and adjournments, in short, determine the sequence of legislative days and calendar days. If the Senate adjourns at the end of a daily session, the legislative day ends with that calendar day. If, however, it chooses to recess, the legislative day is carried over to the next calendar day. Senator Byrd once provided this illustration:

> The Senate has been recessing this year from day to day since January 3. There has not been an adjournment of the Senate since January 3. It has recessed over every day. So although today is calendar day Friday, March 28, 1980, we are still in the legislative day of January 3, 1980, because the Senate has never adjourned since it came in on January 3.
>
> If we should adjourn today until Tuesday . . . then, on Tuesday, the legislative day would have caught up with the calendar day, because we then would be in a new legislative day.[4]

As another example, the calendar day of March 1, 1995, was the legislative day of February 22, 1995. In brief, once the Senate adjourns after a series of recesses, the legislative day and calendar day become the same.

The distinction between the types of days is important because many of the Senate's rules are tied to the legislative day. For instance, the "word `day,' as used in the rules, unless it is specified as a calendar day, is construed to mean a legislative day," according to Senate precedents.[5] The decision to adjourn or recess is made either by unanimous consent or by majority vote on a motion made by the majority leader. If a quorum cannot be obtained, the Senate must adjourn. Adjournment favors senators trying to delay business since it may trigger a series of time-consuming tactics when the Senate next convenes. The majority leader's decision to ask for a recess or an adjournment, therefore, can have a significant effect on controversial legislation before the Senate. Party leaders generally prefer recesses to adjournments. Recesses grant the leadership greater flexibility in shaping the Senate's daily business. Senate rules prescribe a daily order of business, but it can be followed only when the Senate begins a new legislative day.

DAILY ORDER OF BUSINESS

Under resolutions adopted at the start of each Congress, the Senate generally convenes each day at noon. The leadership, by a unanimous consent request or motion, may modify the time on a day-to-day basis to stay abreast of the Senate's workload.

The regular order of business in the Senate, as in the House, begins with a prayer. This is followed by "leader's time" (usually ten minutes each to the majority leader and the minority leader). The majority leader, for example, might state what the Senate is expected to accomplish during that day or make a statement about a substantive matter. If neither leader wants any time, then the Senate typically either permits members who have requested time to make five-minute statements or it resumes consideration of business under the terms of an earlier unanimous consent agreement.

The Senate, too, must keep and approve a *Journal* of the previous day's activities. Commonly, the *Journal* is "deemed approved to date" by unanimous consent when the Senate adjourns or recesses at the end of each day. Any senator could object to the *Journal*'s approval and even propose amendments to it, but this is an exceedingly rare occurrence. (In 1986 the Senate amended its rules to permit a nondebatable motion for the *Journal*'s approval. Previously, reading the *Journal* was sometimes used as a filbustering device.)

At the start of a new legislative day, following an adjournment, the first two hours of Senate activity is technically called the *morning hour*. (Needless to say, the Senate can order that the morning hour be dispensed with. In fact, recent Senates have not observed the morning hour.) *Morning business* is conducted during this time, including the receipt of messages, reports, and communications from the president, the House, and heads of executive branch departments. Bills and resolutions are introduced and referred to committee, committee reports filed, statements inserted in the *Congressional Record,* and brief speeches delivered. As Senator Byrd summarized:

> "Morning business" and the "morning hour" do not mean the same. The morning hour is the first two hours after the Senate convenes following an adjournment. Morning business is that period within the morning hour during which senators may introduce resolutions, bills, petitions, or memorials; committees may report matters, and certain matters come over from the previous day.[6]

Senators may speak during morning business only by unanimous consent. That is why the party leaders usually ask unanimous consent that there be a period for the transaction of routine morning business and that senators be allowed to speak therein, usually for up to five minutes.

The leadership may restrict or change "morning business" by unanimous consent. (Sometimes there are several morning business periods during a calendar day.) Republican leader Dole once announced, "Mr. President, I ask unanimous consent there now be a period for the transaction of routine morning business not to extend beyond 7:15 p.m."[7] (Dole's request for morning business in the evening illustrates the importance of understanding congressional vocabulary.) A nondebatable motion to proceed to any item on the calendar also is in order during the morning hour. Seldom is such a motion made during this period. However, for an example, see Box 7-4, "A Parliamentary War Erupts Over Defense Bill," pp. 218-219.

It is also during morning business that the leadership may schedule "special orders." Under special orders, members are given permission to speak for a limited time (generally ten to thirty minutes) on any subject. The Senate then proceeds to "unfinished business"—legislation pending from a previous day.

If there is no unfinished business, the majority leader or another senator offers a motion to take up a new measure that the leadership, after consultation with the minority leader and other interested senators, has scheduled for floor action. This may be a critical juncture in the proceedings, for it is at this point that opponents of the bill in question might begin delaying tactics, such as a filibuster to prevent the bill from being considered.

DEBATE IN THE MODERN SENATE

In the early Congresses, the Senate was characterized by protracted debates and great orators: Daniel Webster, John Calhoun, and Stephen Douglas on slavery, and later by Henry Cabot Lodge and others on the League of Nations. Today, senators are so busy, and the legislative agenda so crowded, that extended give-and-take among numerous senators is the exception rather than the rule. "In this United States Senate it is rare indeed to have one-third of the members present to hear debate," observed Sen. Paul Simon, D-Ill. "There is dialogue and debate, but most of it does not take place on the floor under public scrutiny."[8]

To be sure, debate still serves to publicize issues, address constituencies, identify areas of consensus, and influence Senate votes. After one spirited floor session, a senator declared, "I was really undecided on the pending amendment, but [the] Senator so ably presented his case that I will join him" in opposing the amendment.[9] As another example, the first female African-American senator, Carol Moseley-Braun, D-Ill., gave a stirring address when the Senate took up a proposal to extend a patent for a Confederate flag insignia wanted by the United Daughters of the Confederacy. The "subject of her address was nothing less than a discourse on race in America" and it turned the tide against the measure.[10]

On the other hand, as another senator put it, "There almost never is a mind changed by debate on the floor of the Senate because, for the most part, no one is ever listening." Or senators have already committed themselves before debate begins.

There still are "great debates" that capture national attention and mobilize national sentiment on critical issues such as civil rights, amending the Constitution to balance the budget, or Social Security. But debate in the modern Senate often consists of prepared speeches perfunctorily read (or inserted in the *Congressional Record* without having been formally delivered before a largely empty chamber).[11] When intensive debate does occur, it is often among only a handful of senators with special interest in the legislation. To minimize personality clashes, the Senate (like the House) forbids first-person references during debate. "One of the reasons for the rule that a Senator must address another Senator through the Chair and not in the first person," stated Senator Byrd, "is to avoid casting aspersions, and causing acridness in debate and hurt feelings."[12]

Although the Senate is known for its principle of unlimited debate, there are four occasions when debate can be restricted. First, as discussed in Chapter 7, unanimous consent agreements typically limit debate on, for instance, bills, amendments, and various motions. Second, when the Senate invokes cloture (or Rule XXII), debate is limited to a specific number of hours. Cloture will be discussed below. Third, the motion to table is nondebatable and is often used by floor managers to simultaneously stop debate on and to kill floor amendments. Rarely is a motion to table made on the bill itself, because if the motion were agreed to, it would kill the measure. Finally, there are various statutes that have debate-limiting features built into them. The 1974 Budget Act, which was discussed in Chapter 3, is replete with restrictions on debate, such as a two-hour limit on any amendment to the concurrent budget resolution and a ten-hour limit on the budget conference report.

Unlike the House where the Speaker's recognition power is discretionary ("For what purpose does the gentlelady rise?"), the Senate presiding officer (addressed as either "Mr. President" or "Madam President") must recognize the first person seeking to speak unless the majority leader, minority leader, or one of the two floor managers is seeking recognition at the same time. Then Senate precedents stipulate that one of the four in the order mentioned has priority. Once a lawmaker is recognized, however, Senate precedents state that that senator may hold the floor for as long as he or she chooses. When senators yield the floor, others may be recognized to speak. The presiding officer may not put the pending question to a vote if senators are still seeking recognition to speak.

As in the House—even though only a scattering of members are on the floor—a quorum technically is present until a member suggests otherwise. Any senator may suggest the absence of a quorum. When this occurs the presiding officer is obligated to direct the clerk to call the roll of members. In contrast to House practice, the presiding officer may not first count the senators present to determine whether a quorum in fact exists, except during post-cloture proceedings. The calling of the roll is mandatory unless it is dispensed with by unanimous consent.

Quorum calls, however, are commonly employed to give senators time to work out procedural arrangements ("positive" delay, as opposed to "negative" delay), such as a unanimous consent agreement, or to give a member scheduled to speak time to reach the floor. "What I would like to do is suggest the absence of a quorum," said a senator, "so that the parties involved here might sit down in the quiet of some room to see exactly how we can get this particular [amendment] to a point where we can vote up or down."[13] Once this is done, further calling of the roll to establish a quorum is dispensed with by unanimous consent. When Lyndon Johnson was majority leader, he "would ask for a quorum call and wait, sometimes for close to an hour, while the reading clerk droned slowly through the names. Then, when Johnson was ready for the Senate to resume, he would suspend the calling of the roll."[14] Cumulatively, the Senate spends a lot of time on quorum calls. Sen. David Pryor, D-Ark., once calculated that the Senate spends about six weeks of its work year on quorum calls.[15]

Quorum calls to delay proceedings temporarily are to be distinguished from "live" quorums. Here a senator insists that at least a majority of the members come to the chamber and answer to their names. This can be a time-consuming process. Recalling that Sen. Strom Thurmond, R-S.C., once demanded a "live" quorum, a Senate colleague observed, "It took almost one hour to round up fifty-one Senators to respond to their names."[16] The two types of quorum calls are distinguished by the different number of bells that ring in members' offices and Senate committee rooms.

If the Senate officially discovers that it lacks a quorum, it has two options: (1) it must adjourn (recess if there is a previous order to that effect), or (2) it may instruct the sergeant-at-arms to request (compel) the attendance of senators.

TELEVISION AND DEBATE

In 1986, after years of consideration, the Senate authorized gavel-to-gavel coverage of its floor proceedings over C-SPAN (Cable Satellite Public Affairs Network). On February 27, 1986, the Senate adopted a resolution that permitted television coverage on a trial basis (June 2 was the public debut); on July 29, 1986, the Senate voted to make the "electronic gallery" permanent.

Television's impact reveals some change in floor debate or activity. Speeches are more numerous, but they are better organized and livelier than before. Senators "are making better speeches," said Senator Byrd. "They are using more gestures and rhetorical flourishes, and it seems to me that overall, the debate has improved from a substantive point of view."[17]

Staff in senatorial offices regularly monitor floor debate to alert their bosses if issues are being discussed that require their attendance. Senators also watch floor proceedings from their offices, and what they observe may prompt them to go to the floor. "I came here to talk about this amendment," said Sen. Harry Reid, D-Nev., because "I watched with interest from my office," and "I was especially impressed with, and was able to watch, the remarks of my colleague."[18] Senators, too, are using more props, graphs, and charts to illustrate their points. Some senators, to attract local media coverage, wait to offer floor amendments until it is "prime time" back home. The eleven freshman GOP senators in the 104th Congress even formed a "Freshman Focus" to keep the Contract with America and other issues before the chamber. "Each day, one freshman is assigned to speak or engage other members in a debate on Contract items during prime time."[19]

Doubtlessly, television heightens public awareness of issues, of members, and of the Senate as an institution. There are millions of C-SPAN viewers who watch floor proceedings regularly, who listen to the arguments for or against legislation and then communicate (by letter, telephone, faxes, E-mail, or in other ways) their concerns to senators. Senatorial staff alert local television networks about their bosses' floor speeches (so segments might be broadcast back home), and party leaders monitor floor actions to ensure that arguably partisan statements are answered by someone with another viewpoint.

Party leaders may engage in "image politics," as Republicans did in the 104th Congress debate on the constitutional balanced budget proposal. They pitted a youthful junior senator against an elderly senior senator, selecting thirty-seven-year-old freshman Rick Santorum, Pa., to challenge the arguments of seventy-eight-year-old Robert Byrd. "One GOP member said that was an `image decision' by the leadership, designed to maximize the contrast for C-SPAN viewers between the old order and the new."[20] Senators, too, seek to attract national attention by coming up with catchy "sound bites" or dramatic statements that will get them on the nightly news shows. "This game is especially tempting for senators facing reelection campaigns," wrote a journalist, "since appearing on national television makes them look important and their opponents cannot get equal time."[21]

FLOOR MANAGER'S ROLE

Floor managers have the major responsibility for guiding legislation to final passage. "I lean on the manager of the bill and the ranking [committee] members to carry the load" on the floor, Senator Byrd observed.[22] Usually, there are two floor managers (one from each party from the reporting committee) per measure. In the case of multiply referred legislation, there may be several majority and minority floor managers. To avoid having all the managers remain continuously on the floor, the Senate often works out a systematic schedule of senatorial action. Senator Byrd once noted:

> Nine committees have reported components of the overall trade bill. . . . It is hoped that each chairman of each committee that has jurisdiction over a particular title, at a given moment when the Senate reaches that title, will be able to deal with that title so that we could proceed title by title and all nine chairmen [and ranking minority members] will not have to be over here all the time to protect all nine titles.[23]

Senate floor managers, like their House counterparts, have varied responsibilities. They identify favorable times to schedule their legislation;

they negotiate time-limitation agreements; they may offer amendments to strengthen their bills or win more support as well as to counter proposed weakening amendments; they have to respond to any points of order raised against language in the legislation; and they must alert proponents when their support is needed on the floor.

Strategic calculations are a manager's stock in trade. For example, Sen. John C. Culver, D-Iowa (1975-1981), as a floor manager, once was able to persuade Sen. William L. Scott, R-Va. (1973-1979), to offer a troublesome amendment at the most advantageous time from Culver's standpoint.

> The theory behind having Scott bring up the amendment now is that it is better to have such a proposal come up in the morning—a time when many senators are in committee meetings or in their offices and are more distracted than usual from the business that is taking place on the floor. Also, Culver figures that most of his colleagues will assume that at this point, especially after a long day of taking up amendments—and major ones—yesterday, only routine "housekeeping" amendments are being considered, and that they will pay less attention to the issue, be less eager to join the fray, than they might be later on.[24]

By informal custom, floor managers are accorded priority of recognition by the presiding officer. Explained Senator Byrd: "The manager of a bill also is entitled to preferential recognition—not ahead of the [majority leader and minority leader], but following in line, and is accorded that recognition generally by the Chair."[25]

Staff aides often assist floor managers. Senators rely more heavily on staff assistance during floor debate than do House members. Aides draft amendments and arguments and negotiate with aides of other senators to marshal support for legislation being considered.

BILLS CONSIDERED BY UNANIMOUS CONSENT

The importance of unanimous consent agreements to the efficient operation of the legislative process in the Senate has already been cited. A typical example of a unanimous consent agreement, shown in Box 8-1, specifies the bill's number (S 1) and its position on the General Orders Calendar (Order No. 12). It bears repeating, however, that bipartisan trust is essential to its use. Former majority leader George J. Mitchell, D-Maine, underscored this point during floor discussions involving an earlier unanimous consent agreement.

> The [unanimous consent] agreement was reached in good faith, but I am now advised that due to a misunderstanding and an inadvertent error, a Senator's right to make a point of order was not protected and included in the agreement. That was an honest mistake. And since becoming majority leader, I have taken the position that whenever an agreement is reached that includes a provision placing a Senator at a disadvantage as a result of an

A UNANIMOUS CONSENT AGREEMENT
S. 1 (Order No. 12)

Ordered, that at 9:30 a.m. on Friday, Jan. 27, 1995, when the Senate resumes consideration of S. 1, the Unfunded Mandates Bill, the Senator from Michigan (Mr. Levin) be recognized to offer his amendment, No. 175; that no second degree amendments be in order thereto; and that there be 45 minutes for debate prior to a motion to table, with 30 minutes under the control of the Senator from Michigan (Mr. Levin) and 15 minutes under the control of the Senator from Idaho (Mr. Kempthorne).

Ordered further, that following the conclusion or yielding back of time, the Senator from Idaho (Mr. Kempthorne), or his designee, be recognized to make a motion to table, and that the vote be postponed to occur at 11:30 a.m.

Ordered further, That following the debate on the Levin amendment, No. 175, the Senator from Ohio (Mr. Glenn) be recognized to offer his amendment, No. 197; that no second degree amendments be in order; and that there be 45 minutes for debate prior to a motion to table, with 30 minutes under the control of the Senator from Ohio (Mr. Glenn) and 15 minutes under the control of the Senator from Idaho (Mr. Kempthorne).

Ordered further, That following the conclusion or yielding back of time on the Glenn amendment, the Senator from Idaho (Mr. Kempthorne), or his designee, be recognized to make a motion to table, and that the vote occur immediately following the vote on the Levin amendment, No. 175.

Ordered further, That the Senator from Michigan (Mr. Levin) then be recognized to offer his amendment, No. 174; that no second degree amendments be in order; that there be 30 minutes for debate, to be equally divided; that the following debate, the Senate vote on, or in relation to, the Levin amendment, No. 174, following the vote on the Glenn amendment, No. 197. . . .

Ordered further, That following the stacked votes, the Senator from Michigan (Mr. Levin) be recognized to offer his amendment, No. 218 (re: S 993); that no second degree amendments be in order; and that there be 1 hour for debate, prior to a motion to table, with 45 minutes under the control of the Senator from Michigan (Mr. Levin) and 15 minutes under the control of the Senator from Idaho (Mr. Kempthorne).

Ordered further, That following the conclusion or yielding back of time, the Senator from Idaho (Mr. Kempthorne) be recognized to make a motion to table . . .

Ordered further, That following the [disposition] of two [other] amendments, there be 20 minutes for debate under the control of the Senator from Ohio (Mr. Glenn); and following the conclusion of that debate, the bill be read for a third time. *(Jan. 19, 1995.) (Jan. 20, 1995.) (Jan. 23, 1995.)*

BOX 8-1

inadvertent error or mistake, either by a Senator or staff, that the disadvantage should be removed and the agreement modified to reflect the circumstances which should have existed when the agreement was adopted.[26]

Occasionally, hard feelings can be generated over expectations or interpretations associated with unanimous consent agreements. For instance, many senators expected to vote February 28, 1995, on final passage of a constitutional amendment to balance the budget. To the chagrin of opponents, Majority Leader Dole recessed the Senate because he was one vote short of the sixty-seven (or two-thirds) needed to pass a constitutional amendment. "I thought a deal was a deal," complained Minority Leader Tom Daschle, D-S.D.[27]

> The stalling move . . . was technically allowed under the unanimous consent agreement that governed the last several days of the debate. The agreement only promised a final roll call "following the stacked votes" on proposed changes to the amendment on Feb. 28. It did not specify precisely when thereafter the final vote would occur, giving Dole the loophole he needed to claim extra time to search for the 67th vote needed to approve H J Res 1. In addition, a majority leader is traditionally recognized when he calls for the Senate to go into recess.[28]

Dole was unable to find another vote and the Senate later defeated the centerpiece of the Contract with America. (Interestingly, after the outcome was plain, Senator Dole switched his vote from yea to nay to comply with Senate rules requiring members to be on the prevailing side to be eligible to offer the motion to reconsider: giving the Senate another chance to review and revote on the issue at some time in the future. Dole suggested he would call for another vote shortly before the 1996 elections, thus putting electoral "heat" on lawmakers.) Although relations between their parties remained tense for some time, Dole and Daschle of necessity continued to cooperate in crafting unanimous consent agreements.

The complex agreement in Box 8-1, like many others controlling major legislation, reflects standard operating procedure for the Senate. First, the agreement was only one of several on the unfunded mandates bill (see the dates in parentheses at the end of the agreement) and it was focused largely on imposing restrictions on amendments. In addition, no day was specified for final action on the bill; debate on each designated amendment was limited to a specific time, with the time controlled by designated senators; votes on the amendments were to occur in sequence; some amendments were to be subject to a tabling (or killing) motion; and, following disposition of the amendments, the bill was to be read a third time (which generally ends the amending stage and is the last step before the vote on final passage).

Measures governed by unanimous consent agreements are commonly called up by the majority leader or the majority floor manager. Customarily, the presiding officer briefly summarizes the terms of the agreement, then recognizes the bill's floor manager, usually the chairman of the committee or subcommittee that handled the bill, for a short description of the legislation and its intent. The floor manager is followed by the ranking minority committee or subcommittee member, who presents similarly brief opening remarks. The Senate then is ready to debate and consider amendments to the bill.

THE AMENDING PROCESS

Unlike the House, the Senate has no five-minute rule for debating amendments. There are no "closed" rules in the Senate. Any measure is open to virtually an unlimited number of amendments unless a unanimous consent agreement specifies otherwise. (Like the House, Senate amendments are motions that either *strike* language from the measure, *insert* language that is not there, or simultaneously *strike and insert* new language.) On occasion, a floor manager may ask that a measure pass without amendments. Opponents still are likely to offer amendments, but if the floor manager has sufficient support they are likely to be voted down or tabled (killed). For example, in 1987 Agriculture Chairman Patrick J. Leahy, D-Vt., and ranking minority member Richard Lugar, R-Ind. (whose roles became reversed in the GOP-controlled 104th Congress) each put out the word on a farm relief bill they were managing that only technical amendments or amendments that did not add to the cost of the measure would receive their joint support. Otherwise, senators had better be prepared to debate their amendments in great detail, they said, and to answer pointed questions. The Leahy-Lugar strategy worked—the only amendment offered to the bill was rejected. "We really stared them down," said Senator Lugar.[29]

Senators, unlike House members in the Committee of the Whole, can modify their own amendments without the need for unanimous consent or the majority approval of the chamber. A senator, for example, might propose an amendment that the floor manager will support if the language is discretionary rather than mandatory. The senator can make the change on his or her own authority and facilitate the amendment's chances of being adopted by the Senate. These modifications are permissible until the Senate takes some action on the amendment, such as agreeing to take a vote on it or arranging a unanimous consent agreement limiting debate time. Senators sometimes quickly ask for "action" on their amendments because even though they lose the right to modify them they gain the right to offer amendments to their own amendments, should the need arise.

Senators must be recognized by the presiding officer before they can offer amendments. Officially reported committee amendments automatically take precedence over those offered by other members from the floor. Committee amendments, however, are subject to further amendment from the floor.

Senators can propose amendments at any time to any section of a bill. This approach differs from the more orderly routine followed by the House, where the rules specify that each part of a measure be considered in sequential order, usually section by section. Senate custom gives individual senators greater leeway in offering and amending legislation. This flexibility means that a senator can force virtually any issue to the floor through amendments and displace the best-laid agenda of any majority leader. To avoid having senators offer their favorite bill as an amendment to other measures or amendments, a majority leader may promise the lawmaker a specific time when the Senate will consider and vote on the legislation. Amendments must be read by the Senate clerk, but this usually is dispensed with by unanimous consent unless an attempt is being made to delay the bill. (For several House-Senate differences in the amending process, see Table 8-1.)

Principle of "Precedence"

An important concept that shapes the Senate's amending process is *precedence*. While both the House and Senate have a rule specifying that only amendments in the first and second degree are permitted, there are basic differences in how each chamber interprets first- and second-degree amendments. This, in turn, affects the number of amendments that can be pending to a bill at the same time. In the Senate, even third-degree amendments occasionally are made in order by unanimous consent.

The principle of precedence determines which class of amendments (perfecting or substitute) may be offered when others are pending and the order in which those amendments are voted on. A perfecting amendment is one that simply alters language, either to the bill or to a pending amendment, but does not seek to substitute new text for the pending proposal. Perfecting amendments (which are always motions to strike, to insert, or to strike and insert) have precedence over substitutes (always a motion to strike and insert). Thus, if Senator A offers a perfecting amendment to a bill (a first-degree amendment), and Senator B then proposes a second-degree perfecting amendment to it, no other amendments are in order until the second-degree proposal is disposed of. And if the latter is adopted, other second-degree amendments—perfecting or substitute—may be offered until the entire text of the first-degree amendment has been disposed of.

Alternatively, Senator B may offer a second-degree substitute for Senator A's amendment to the bill. Then Senator C, under the Senate's principle of precedence, can introduce a second-degree perfecting amendment to Senator A's amendment, which would be voted upon before the substitute. These steps in the Senate amendment process differ from those followed by the House.

To recapitulate, policy decisions often are affected by the Senate's precedence principle, which determines (1) the number of amendments that may

TABLE 8-1 Selected Bicameral Differences in the Amendment Process

House	Senate
Measures read for amendment section-by-section or title-by-title	Measures open to amendment at any point, unless a unanimous consent agreement states otherwise
Strict germaneness rule	No general germaneness rule
Amendment rights of members are commonly limited by the Rules Committee	Unlimited freedom for senators to offer amendments, unless unanimous consent agreement stipulates otherwise
Third degree amendments are prohibited	Third degree amendments are prohibited, but they can still be offered by unanimous consent
Five-minute rule for discussing amendments	No debate limit for amendments unless imposed by a unanimous consent agreement
Points of order against amendments must be raised after an amendment is read but before debate on it has begun	Points of order against amendments can be raised at any time
Representatives have no right to modify or withdraw amendments on their own authority	Senators have the right to modify or withdraw their amendments unless "action" (such as a call for a vote on the amendment) has been taken on it by the Senate

be pending simultaneously to a bill, and (2) the order of voting on them. For example, when Senator Byrd was majority leader, he used his privilege of being recognized ahead of other senators to offer a nongermane strip mining amendment (first degree, perfecting) to a maritime cargo bill. The GOP leader, who supported Byrd's move, asked for the yeas and nays (a roll-call vote) on Byrd's amendment. Then Byrd offered a second-degree perfecting proposal to his own amendment.

This parliamentary maneuver, which shut off further floor amendments to Byrd's original amendment, angered a senator who opposed the effort to modify the strip mining reclamation law. When you "have access to the floor," he said to Byrd, "and offer a perfecting amendment and then an amendment to that perfecting amendment, you are in a position to foreclose the right of other Members of the Senate to offer their amendments."[30] This senator and another "were ready to introduce 272 amendments to delay debate on the Byrd proposals."[31] Senator Byrd's tactic prevented them from offering their amendments. In the end, the Senate approved the Byrd amendments.

When Byrd headed the Appropriations Committee during the 103d Congress and floor managed President Bill Clinton's $16 billion economic stimulus package, he filled the amendment tree to prevent senators from making any changes in the stimulus plan (see Box 8-2). They could offer their amendments and get votes on them, but the final vote would occur on a Byrd substitute amendment that would wipe out all the others even if they had been adopted.

As Sen. Mark O. Hatfield, R-Ore., noted, "If any one of the senators in this body, on either side of the aisle, wishes to offer an amendment . . . let us say we had 50 amendments that were adopted . . . , [passage of the Byrd substitute amendment] would wipe out all those previous amendments that had been acted upon and perhaps adopted."[32] To confront both Senator Byrd and the Clinton administration, GOP leader Dole sent to the majority leader a letter signed by all forty-three Republican senators pledging to block action on the bill. Unable to break the GOP-led filibuster, Democrats ended up passing a stripped-down version of the bill.

The Senate, unlike the House, commonly employs the motion to recommit with instructions for broad amendment purposes. If troublesome amendments have been agreed to, the majority leader can "move to recommit with instructions to report back with all amendments that have been adopted thus far with the exception" of the troublesome amendments.[33] Because the motion to recommit has precedence under Senate rules over pending amendments, the majority leader can offer this motion and construct an amendment tree (amending the instructions) that forecloses others from offering amendments and produces the first votes on policy alternatives favored by the majority leader.

For instance, Byrd, then the majority leader, offered the motion to recommit with instructions on a bill limiting campaign expenditures for Senate elections. At the time the recommittal motion was offered, two nongermane amendments dealing with controversial foreign policy issues were pending to the campaign bill. Senator Byrd moved "to amend the instructions in such a way that the Senate [had] before it" only issues dealing with campaign finance. "So we have a line of amendments here," said Byrd, "which cannot be amended at the moment until action is taken on the second-degree amendment" that addressed campaign expenditures.[34]

Needless to say, the order of voting on amendments is of strategic importance. Senators may introduce amendments following the precedence principle to obtain an early test vote on their policy alternatives. One purpose

BARKING UP BYRD'S TREE

When Senate Republicans tried to trim President Clinton's economic stimulus proposal, at least 52 Democrats stood in the way. But as far as the GOP was concerned, only one Democrat really mattered: Sen. Robert C. Byrd, D-W.Va.

Byrd, the chairman of the Senate Appropriations Committee, took a hard line on the Senate floor in defense of Clinton's proposal. While Majority Leader George J. Mitchell, D-Maine, tried to negotiate with the bill's opponents, Byrd tried to smother them—playing the bad cop to Mitchell's good cop.

The match that ignited the Republicans' fire was a parliamentary maneuver by Byrd, the Senate's acknowledged master of such tactics. On March 25, Byrd planted a tree of amendments onto the bill that would, if adopted, wipe out all other amendments, giving the president virtually everything he asked for in the stimulus package.

Byrd has done this sort of thing several times before. This time, Republicans howled that Byrd was usurping powers that should be wielded only by the majority leader. Sen. Arlen Specter, R-Penn., said, "Sen. Byrd is not the leader, he's a manager . . . We're just not going to let him do that."

In an interview April 1, Byrd said the Republicans were trying to draw attention away from their own delaying tactics by making him a scapegoat. The tree was his idea, Byrd said, but he told Mitchell of his plans and offered to let him assist in the tree-planting. He briefed Clinton in advance, too, mapping out the procedure on a sheet of paper during a meeting at the White House.

"My basic reason for using the rules to stack the [amendment] tree was to protect the bill against the amendments from my own side, which was divided," he said. "I can't be in a position of facing off Republican amendments . . . as long as my own side is divided."

Republicans tried to play up the notion of a split between Mitchell and Byrd. Byrd scoffed at the idea, although he admitted his move may have prompted "a little dissatisfaction" among Democrats who were less enthusiastic about the stimulus package.

One reason Byrd played hardball with his own party is that Clinton asked him to deliver the stimulus package intact. To Byrd, that meant guarding against every proposed change: "It's a delicately structured program, and if you take out one component of it, it starts to unravel."

Source: Jon Healey, *Congressional Quarterly Weekly Report,* April 3, 1993, 818.

BOX 8-2

would be to identify defecting senators who might be kept in line through personal persuasion. Or members might want their amendment to be voted on last, on the assumption that they have enough support to defeat all damaging amendments and thus can demonstrate to opponents that the choice is between the pending amendment or nothing at all.

STRATEGIC USES OF AMENDMENTS

Timing, strategy, lobbying, patience, and skillful drafting are important parts of the amending process. Party leaders and floor managers often try to get unanimous consent to arrange the order in which senators call up their amendments. On important measures, senators regularly jockey for position in offering amendments. When the 1986 tax overhaul measure reached the floor, senators realized that amendments to the popular package stood a better chance of adoption if proposed early in the debate. Because of the revenue neutral requirement required by budget laws, members who offered amendments to restore tax breaks needed to propose a source of offsetting revenues. "There's only so many ways to raise . . . money," said Finance chairman Bob Packwood, R-Ore. "And if somebody gets an amendment in first and uses up the most attractive way to [raise] the money, that is not available for the next amendment."[35]

In another instance, Majority Leader Mitchell employed second degree amendments (using his priority of recognition) to block GOP attempts to broaden the scope of investigative hearings regarding President Clinton's involvement with the Whitewater Development Corporation when he was governor of Arkansas. Democrats charged that Republicans were trying to embarrass the president; Republicans accused Democrats of unnecessarily limiting the scope of the inquiry. In a bitter partisan struggle, GOP senators began offering amendment after amendment to an airport improvements bill to widen the Whitewater hearings beyond what Democrats wanted. Every time a GOP senator offered a first degree amendment to expand the Banking Committee's Whitewater hearings, the majority leader (or his designee) used his right of first recognition by the presiding officer to offer a second degree amendment that prevented an up or down vote on the GOP proposal. (Second degree amendments are voted on before first degree amendments, and if adopted, they replace or wipe out the first degree proposition.) As Sen. Don Nickles, R-Okla., stated:

> The majority leader . . . has offered the same amendment three or four times as a second-degree amendment to whatever first-degree amendment [that has been offered] from this side of the aisle. . . . [T]he majority leader has offered amendments that strike whatever amendment is offered on this side and inserted new language, and that new language is [the Mitchell plan for Whitewater hearings].[36]

Finally, Senate Republicans ended their opposition to Mitchell's plan in part because the public lacked interest in their efforts. "No one is paying attention," said Sen. William S. Cohen, R-Maine.[37]

Whether an amendment is accepted or rejected sometimes depends on its purpose, and its purpose may not always be to amend the bill under consideration. Two examples that follow will illustrate the point.

DEFEATING LEGISLATION. One strategy of a bill's opponents is to load down the legislation with controversial amendments, possibly sparking a filibuster and jeopardizing Senate passage. "Overweight the plan, sabotage it with an unrealistic amendment," and that will ensure defeat of the legislation, noted Sen. Ernest F. Hollings, D-S.C.[38] Or as Senator Packwood said about a bill he opposed, "If this amendment worsens it a little more, then I'm for it."[39] Floor managers are on the alert for "killer amendments" that can torpedo their measures or treaties.

"MAKE-A-POINT" AMENDMENTS. Senators sometimes offer amendments to make a point or to obtain something they want. For example, Sen. Jesse Helms, R-N.C., offered an amendment to "provide that the Endangered Species Act of 1973 shall not apply with respect to Fort Bragg, N.C." Senator Helms went on to explain that the army was having a problem in protecting several endangered species found on the Fort Bragg grounds, including the red-cockaded woodpecker. The Department of Army, he said, had been required to set aside twelve thousand acres of land and to spend $5 million to protect the woodpecker.

"The last time I checked," said Helms, "the function of the Army is to defend the national security interests of the United States and not birds in trees."[40] Right after Senator Helms offered the amendment, Sen. John H. Chafee, R-R.I., chairman of the Environment and Public Works Committee (which has jurisdiction over the Endangered Species Act), went to the floor and persuaded Helms to withdraw his amendment. Chafee noted that his committee would undertake a major review of the Act and promised Helms a hearing on Fort Bragg's endangered species situation. Your "proposition is fair," stated Senator Helms.[41]

Amendments are also proposed to extract commitments from committees that fail to take action on legislation. For instance, Senator Byrd introduced legislation to require reconfirmation of the president's top officials if they continued in office during the president's second term. The committee of jurisdiction took no action on the measure. "Never do I remember" a situation where a committee refused a colleague's request to hold a hearing on his or her legislation, Byrd remarked. "The only recourse I have," he said, "is to offer the subject matter as an amendment to a vehicle which comes up on the floor." If the committee will not hold a hearing, "then I will let the Senate be the judge, and I will get my hearing on the floor."[42] Of course, Senator

Byrd received quick assurances from the committee chairman that hearings would be held on the reconfirmation proposal.

Voting on Amendments

The Senate has three types of voting: *voice, division* (standing), and *roll call*. Voice and division voting are similar to House procedures, but there is nothing comparable to the electronic voting procedures of the House. The system of buzzers that summons senators to the floor is much like that of the House. During a roll call members respond "yea" or "nay" as their names are called alphabetically.

The Senate establishes the length of time for roll-call votes at the start of each Congress. When the 104th Congress convened on January 4, 1995, the Senate agreed by unanimous consent:

> That for the duration of the 104th Congress, there be a limitation of 15 minutes each upon any roll call vote, with [a] warning signal to be sounded at the midway point, beginning at the last 7-1/2 minutes, and when roll call votes are of 10 minutes duration, the warning signal [is to] be sounded at the beginning of the last 7-1/2 minutes.

When votes are grouped back to back, referred to as "stacking," the second and succeeding votes often occur, by unanimous consent, at ten-minute intervals.

Party leaders and floor managers make every effort to ensure that their supporters are on the floor when needed for a vote. "My experience convinces me," commented Senator Byrd, that voting "is the most critical step in the legislative process. . . . [The leaders and the floor managers must] have the right members at the right place and at the right time."[43]

Party leaders give advance notice of impending votes in whip notices and announcements from the floor. Occasionally, complex unanimous consent agreements specify the exact date and time for votes on final passage of a bill. On the other hand, the times for votes on amendments sometimes are agreed to by unanimous consent without elaborate negotiations during the debate on the bill.

Recorded votes in the Senate usually can be obtained quite easily; only a "sufficient second"—one-fifth of the senators present—is needed, with a minimum of eleven required by the Constitution. If the minimum number is not on the floor at the time the request is made, a senator can summon other colleagues through a quorum call, try to get their support, and then renew the request for a roll-call vote. As Byrd explained: "If any Senator wants a rollcall vote around here, he will ultimately get it. If he does not get it at first, he will put in a quorum and he will not let us call off the quorum. So we have to have a live quorum or give him the yeas and nays."[44] Most roll calls occur on amendments.

Compared with four or five decades ago, there has been a significant jump in the number of roll-call votes. The Senate has gone from fewer than a hundred roll-call votes annually to about four hundred to six hundred annually. Various factors explain the hike, including demonstration of Senate support for a measure that may end up in conference with the House or simply pride of authorship. As he prepared to retire from the Senate at the end of the 103d Congress, Majority Leader Mitchell spotlighted the increase in votes as one of the things wrong with the contemporary Senate. He said:

> I remember John Stennis [D-Miss., who served 1947-1989] telling me that, when he first came to the Senate, there were about 70 roll call votes a year. Now, of course, we have several hundred a year, large numbers of them having no legislative purpose. They are intended to get the other side on record on an issue that's controversial and can be used in a campaign. They are intended for use in fund-raising appeals with direct mass mailings.[45]

Campaign financing will also be invoked as a reason why the majority leader should not schedule floor votes at certain times. As one senator said in explaining why few floor votes are held on Mondays or Fridays, "We have to schedule fundraisers on those evenings and on those days."[46]

"CUE-GIVERS." Senators, like representatives, rely on numerous "cue-givers" for guidance on voting because of the range and complexity of legislation. "When it comes to voting," a senator wrote, "an individual senator will rely heavily not only on the judgment of staff, his own and his committee's, but also on a select number of senators whose knowledge he has come to respect and whose general perspectives he shares."[47] The position of the reporting committee is an important factor to many senators. "A lot of members of the Senate," said another senator, "will arrive on the floor, and there's an amendment up that they really haven't had a chance to look at, and they'll just come up and ask, 'What's the committee position?' "[48]

CASTING PROCEDURAL VOTES. On controversial amendments, members often maneuver for procedural, rather than substantive, votes. A vote to table (kill) amendments or other motions is a classic procedural ploy to avoid being recorded directly on politically sensitive policy issues. Senator Byrd has explained the difference:

> A motion to table is a procedural motion. It obfuscates the issue, and it makes possible an explanation by a Senator to his constituents, if he wishes to do so, that his vote was not on the merits of the issue. He can claim that he might have voted this way or he might have voted that way, if the Senate had voted up or down on the issue itself. But on a procedural motion, he can state he voted to table the amendment, and he can assign any number of reasons therefore, one of which would be that he did so in order that the Senate would get on with its work or about its business.[49]

Therefore, if a procedural vote can be arranged to kill or delay a bill, it is more likely to win the support of senators, who may prefer to duck the substantive issue. Moreover, senators generally support the party leadership on procedural votes. "[B]ecause this is a procedural vote . . . [senators] traditionally stick with the leadership on such votes," declared Senator Packwood.[50]

Part of members' consideration in casting procedural or substantive votes involves their role in political campaigns. Votes are not simply used to make decisions or as trading material; they are used by interest group organizations, who select issues of concern to them, to characterize legislators as "heroes or zeroes," conservatives or liberals, depending on how members voted on the groups' chosen topics.

Like the House, the Senate permits vote "pairing," either "live" or "dead" pairs. In a live pair, one senator is present on the floor during the vote. The practice is for the senator to cast his vote, yea or nay, then withdraw it and announce, "I have a pair with the senator from [naming the state]. If he were present and voting, he would vote [yea or nay]. If I were at liberty to vote, I would vote [yea or nay]." In a dead pair, both senators are absent from the floor. Their positions are published after each roll call in the *Congressional Record*. Live and dead pairs are not tabulated on roll-call votes, but a live pair can affect the outcome of a vote. Explained Senator Byrd:

> The arranging of pairs has been decisive from time to time on very close votes, because it is possible to pair off enough present Senators to affect the outcome of the vote and perhaps make a difference of 1 or 2 votes which, had the Senators present not been paired, would have decided the issue opposite to the outcome that resulted.
>
> However, Senators generally will not agree to give a "live" pair except on the condition that the outcome is not changed by virtue of the pair given.[51]

In 1986 a "live" pair influenced the outcome of a controversial judicial nomination.[52]

FINAL ACTION ON A BILL

"When no Senator seeks recognition," Senator Byrd explained, "the Chair automatically puts the question of adoption of amendments and passage of bills."[53] Thus, once the amending process is completed the Senate proceeds to a vote on final passage, unless a unanimous consent agreement has been made setting a later date and time for the final vote. The floor manager announces that there are no further amendments. He then requests a third, and final, reading of the bill. The presiding officer orders the bill engrossed—put in the precise form in which it emerged from the Senate's amending process—and "read" a third time (the title of the bill only), a procedure that takes only a few seconds.

The final vote is not over until the chair announces the outcome. Senate rules prohibit "any Senator from voting after the Chair has announced the decision," Senator Byrd pointed out. Senate rules provide "that the Chair cannot even entertain a unanimous consent request to suspend this rule."[54] Senators, like House members, may change their vote during the regular fifteen-minute voting period, which in the Senate may be a minimum and not the maximum time allowed. For example, during an unusually lengthy Senate roll call dozens of senators switched their votes and defeated a proposal offered by Sen. Dale Bumpers, D-Ark. "I just want to announce that Dr. Cary's in his office for everyone whose arm is out of socket," exclaimed the senator from Arkansas.[55] (Dr. Freeman Cary was the Senate physician.)

After the result of the final vote on the bill has been announced, there is still one more parliamentary step required before Senate action is complete. This step is available only to the side that prevailed on the final vote. If the bill has been passed, a senator who voted for the bill, or who did not vote, makes a motion to reconsider the vote. (On a voice or standing vote, any senator can offer the motion.) Immediately thereafter, another proponent of the bill moves to table the motion to reconsider. By this procedural device Senate rules protect the bill from further consideration. Rarely does the motion to table fail. This procedure also is used after votes on amendments. The House procedure, described in Chapter 6, is identical.

To summarize, the usual Senate floor procedure for major legislation is as follows: first, a unanimous consent agreement is negotiated; second, the bill is called up by the floor manager after being scheduled by the majority leader, who consults with the minority leader; third, the bill is considered for amendment, with the debate time regulated by the unanimous consent agreement; fourth, there is a final vote (voice vote or roll call) on final passage.

But what happens when a major bill reaches the floor in the absence of a unanimous consent agreement? By and large, the procedural sequence is much the same, but the legislation is much more vulnerable to obstructionist tactics, particularly the filibuster.

BILLS WITHOUT UNANIMOUS CONSENT

Sometimes party leaders are unable to achieve unanimous consent agreements. This may happen for a variety of reasons: intense opposition to the bill by certain senators, a general desire for unrestricted debate and amendment, commitments by some senators to protect the interests of absent colleagues, or simply personal pique of some senators against party leaders. Passage of legislation then becomes a much more difficult task. At the very least, debate will be extensive and amendments will be numerous. Operating under the Senate's rules, this can be extremely time consuming. Moreover, if there is intense opposition to a bill on the part of one or more senators, the well-known device of the filibuster may be threatened (as in the case of holds, this is another version of the "silent filibuster") or actually used.[56] Particularly near scheduled recesses or the end of legislative sessions the threat or use of filibusters is especially effective.

It is sometimes difficult to tell when "extended debate" becomes a filibuster; a senator does not make a motion to filibuster a bill. Extended debate may occur because the issue warrants lengthy discussion. On the other hand, extended debate may occur because senators intend to stall action on measures. How to determine senators' intent during debates is often not an easy task. Senator Byrd once said, "I will be able to perceive one, because I know one when I see it."[57]

The filibuster is often viewed as the last recourse, forcing an almost complete stoppage of normal floor business—a situation most senators try to avoid if at all possible. Filibusters also send signals to the majority leadership that sixty votes (to invoke cloture) may be needed to pass legislation. It is worth underscoring that the Senate, unlike the House, is really a supermajoritarian institution, because sixty votes are commonly required to enact the major and controversial issues of the day. The filibuster (real or threatened) is also a source of bargaining leverage for any senator. "The power to block the other person's bill gives you the power to influence the content," noted Sen. Thad Cochran, R-Miss.[58] Because the filibuster is the most distinctive feature of Senate floor procedures, it deserves thorough discussion.

THE FILIBUSTER

Generally characterized in the public mind as a nonstop speech, a filibuster in the fullest sense employs every parliamentary maneuver and dilatory motion to delay, modify, or defeat legislation. Asked for filibustering pointers by a colleague, one senator said: "If it takes unanimous consent, object. If not, you make a little speech, suggest the absence of a quorum, then . . . use parliamentary procedures . . . motions to adjourn, motions to recess." He added: "You have to have the floor protected 100 percent of the time."[59]

More has been written about "extended debate" in the Senate than about any other congressional procedure. Hollywood even glamorized the filibuster in a 1939 movie, *Mr. Smith Goes to Washington,* starring Jimmy Stewart. Suffice it to say that the filibuster permeates virtually all senatorial decision making. Measures might not be reported from committee or scheduled for floor action because senators are threatening a filibuster. "In many instances, it's the threat of a filibuster that keeps a bill from coming up," observed Senator Byrd.[60]

On the other hand, its threatened use can trigger legislative activity. For example, when Democrats on the Governmental Affairs Committee faced resistance from panel Republicans in holding an extra day of hearings on line-item veto legislation, they threatened to filibuster the bill on the floor. The GOP chairman agreed to another day of hearings.[61] Similarly, forty-two senators wrote to the chairman of the Energy and Natural Resources Committee promising to filibuster a mining reform bill unless some of its provisions were changed to accommodate the concerns of mining companies.[62]

The filibuster has long been part of the Senate, but unrestricted debate aroused little concern during much of the nineteenth century. The number of senators was small, the workload was limited, and lengthy deliberations could be accommodated more easily. Today, the filibuster is a formidable weapon—particularly late in a session when time is running out—that can be used by any senator or group of senators.

Defenders of the filibuster say it is needed to prevent bad bills from becoming law, protect minority rights against majority steamrollers, ensure thorough analysis of legislation, and dramatize issues for the public. As Senator Byrd put it:

> One of the things that makes the United States Senate the unique upper body that it is is the ability to talk at great length. And there have come times when the protection of a minority is highly beneficial to a nation. Many of the great causes in history of the world were at first only supported by a minority. And it's been shown time and again that the minority can be right. So this is one of the things that's so important to the liberties of the people. As long as a people have a forum in which members can speak at length, the people's liberties will be safe.[63]

Majority Leader Bob Dole, R-Kan., concurs with Byrd's viewpoint. "The rights of the minority in the Senate are precious," he said. "[T]hey protect not just the interests of a partisan minority but also the interests of economic and geographic minorities, including individual states."[64]

Opponents argue that the filibuster thwarts majority rule, brings the Senate into disrepute, and permits small minorities to extort unwarranted concessions in bills supported by Senate majorities. Exasperated by the blocking actions of a dozen filibustering senators, then majority leader Mitchell declared in frustration, citing an earlier test vote: "Only in the United States Senate and only in the last few days of a session can 85 Senators vote one way: Yes, for this bill; 12 Senators vote another way: No, against the bill—and the no's prevail."[65] With the close of the session as their ally, the dozen senators were set to launch a series of filibusters against the legislation; Mitchell realized that the lack of time prevented the Senate from proceeding to the measure. He later exclaimed: "What was intended to be minority rights is now a means of minority rule."[66]

These pro and con arguments highlight a dilemma: how to strike a balance between the right to debate and the need to decide. There is no easy answer. What is apparent is that the filibuster is a powerful bargaining device. Even the possibility of its use can force compromises in committee or on the floor. Senators of widely diverse viewpoints have resorted to it from time to time or have threatened to use it in order to influence legislation.

There are numerous examples that can be used to illustrate the impact of the filibuster.

CIVIL RIGHTS FILIBUSTERS. Before the 1970s, filibusters were most often identified with southern Democrats, who used them to defeat or delay civil rights measures. The 1957, 1960, and 1964 Civil Rights Acts were the objects of systematic filibusters by southern senators, each of whom held the floor for several hours, yielding to colleagues for long questions, while others remained in their offices or left Capitol Hill until it was their turn to talk. (Senator Thurmond holds the individual record by talking twenty-four hours and eighteen minutes against the 1957 civil rights bill.) The southerners demanded periodic quorum calls, keeping the pressure on supporters of civil rights legislation, who had to stay near the chamber to prevent the Senate from adjourning rather than recessing.

Adjournment would have played into the hands of the senators conducting the filibusters by requiring a series of routine, but time-consuming, procedures every time the Senate was forced to convene anew. Senators supporting a filibuster certainly would refuse unanimous consent requests to dispense with any of the elements of daily procedure, thereby further delaying action on the bills being filibustered. During an extended filibuster, the Senate sometimes remains in session throughout the night, with filibuster opponents forced to remain near the Senate floor—sometimes sleeping on couches and cots—to be ever ready in the event of quorum calls.

Every bill faces two primary filibusters: the first on the motion to take up the legislation (to expedite the Senate's business, there have been proposals to limit debate on the motion to proceed; see the discussion below) and the second on consideration of the bill itself. The 1964 civil rights filibuster consumed sixteen days on the motion to take up the measure and fifty-seven days on the legislation itself. Those filibusters were unique in that they marked the first time the Senate had ever voted to end an extended debate on a civil rights bill.

WIDER USE OF FILIBUSTERS. Conservative senators traditionally were almost the only users of filibusters, but times changed. Recent decades witnessed an increase in the overal number of filibusters, including those conducted by moderate and liberal senators in each party (see Figure 8-2).

In short, the filibuster is a "parliamentary tool available to liberals and conservatives who wish to dramatize issues in the only forum of our national government that provides for thorough analysis and unhurried consideration of proposed public laws."[67]

In today's Senate, the filibuster (and its threatened use) is employed routinely and with increasing frequency by senators of every ideological stripe against a host of issues, from the Vietnam War to a mid-1990s striker-replacement proposal.

FIGURE 8-2 Average Number of Filibusters per Year, by Decade

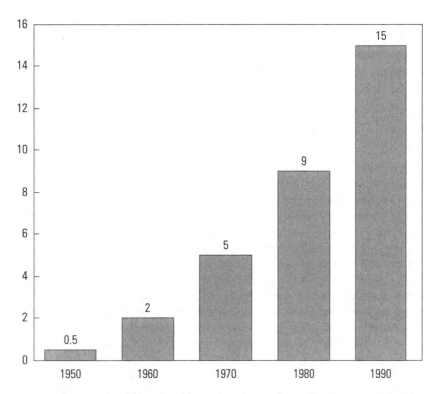

Source: House Democratic Study Group Special Report, "A Look at the Senate Filibuster," June 13, 1994, 7.

Filibusters occur, too, not simply on issues of great national importance and visibility but on a wide range of less momentous topics. Lamented former majority leader Mitchell:

> Not long ago the filibuster or threat of a filibuster was rarely undertaken in the Senate, being reserved for matters of grave national importance. That is no longer the case. . . . The threat of a filibuster is now a regular event in the Senate, weekly at least, sometimes daily. It is invoked by minorities of as few as one or two Senators and for reasons as trivial as a Senator's travel schedule.[68]

Moreover, there is a new-style filibuster that relies less on talking than the exploitation of Senate rules—for instance, offering amendment after amendment or appealing the presiding officer's parliamentary rulings and demanding roll-call votes on them—to frustrate action on measures. The factors that triggered wider use of filibusters will be discussed below in the section on summary observations.

ENDING A FILIBUSTER. There are two interrelated and broad methods of ending a filibuster: by informal compromise or by cloture—a formal Senate procedure used to terminate debate. Frequently, cloture cannot be obtained unless compromises are made. Party leaders sometimes try "shuttle diplomacy" between the two sides, noted Sen. Ted Stevens, R-Alaska, to avoid full-scale filibusters.[69]

Informal Compromise. It is not unusual that the threat of filibusters will encourage policy-making compromises. "In the case of [President Clinton's] motor-voter and national service bills, the threat of a GOP filibuster forced the administration to incorporate some Republican changes before the bills were passed."[70]

During a filibuster, senators may meet in the cloakroom—off the Senate floor—or in the offices of the party leaders to conduct negotiations, which can go on day and night. The process may take several days or even weeks, depending on how controversial the bill may be. If compromise fails, the odds increase that opponents of the legislation may win the battle and thus sidetrack the bill indefinitely. Alternatively, proponents may manage to invoke cloture.

Cloture. After decades of determined resistance by many senators, the Senate in 1917 adopted Rule XXII, which for the first time gave the Senate the formal means (cloture) to end extended debate. Until that time, debate could be terminated only by unanimous consent, an impossibility in the face of a filibuster, or exhaustion. In 1893 Sen. Orville Platt, R-Conn., stated:

> There are just two ways under our rules by which a vote can be obtained. One is by getting unanimous consent—the consent of each Senator—to take a vote at a certain time. Next comes what is sometimes known as the process of "sitting it out," that is for the friends of a bill to remain in continuous session until the opponents of it are so physically exhausted that they can not struggle any longer.[71]

It is fair to say that from the very beginning unanimous consent and exhaustion have been the hardy perennials of Senate procedure.

What finally prompted the Senate to adopt Rule XXII was a filibuster that had killed a bill to arm U.S. merchant ships against attacks by German submarines. President Woodrow Wilson strongly criticized the filibuster and called a special session of the Senate, which adopted the cloture rule on March 8, 1917, five weeks before war was declared.

Under Rule XXII a cloture petition signed by sixteen senators first must be filed with the presiding officer (see Box 8-3). Two days later, and one hour after the Senate convenes, the presiding officer must ascertain whether a quorum is present. That having been established, the presiding officer is obliged

A CLOTURE MOTION

Mr. DOLE. Mr. President, I send a cloture motion to the desk.

The PRESIDING OFFICER. The cloture motion having been presented under rule XXII, the Chair, without objection, directs the clerk to read the motion.

The legislative clerk read as follows:

CLOTURE MOTION

We, the undesigned Senators, in accordance with the provisions of rule XXII of the Standing Rules of the Senate, do hereby move to bring to a close debate on amendment No. 331 to the committee amendment to H.R. 889, the supplemental appropriations bill.

HANK BROWN, NANCY LANDON KASSEBAUM, JOHN ASHCROFT, JON KYL, LAUCH FAIRCLOTH, DON NICKLES, STROM THURMOND, DAN COATS, JUDD GREGG, SLADE GORTON, BOB DOLE, CHUCK GRASSLEY, CRAIG THOMAS, CONRAD BURNS, TRENT LOTT, MIKE DEWINE, PETE DOMENICI.

Source: Congressional Record, March 9, 1995, S3731.

BOX 8-3

to ask, "Is it the sense of the Senate that the debate shall be brought to a close?" A vote immediately is held. If three-fifths of the entire Senate membership (60 of 100 members) vote in favor, cloture is invoked. Thereafter, no senator may speak for more than one hour. Before 1975, when the current three-fifths rule was adopted, a two-thirds majority of those senators present and voting was required to invoke cloture. (The two-thirds requirement still applies to proposals to amend the Senate's rules.)

Once cloture is invoked, only germane amendments may be offered, and the presiding officer on his or her initiative may rule out of order dilatory motions. The cloture rule has helped ease some types of delaying tactics but has not effectively ended all of them, as pointed out in the discussion below of so-called postcloture filibusters.

There is no limit to the number of times cloture can be sought on a single piece of legislation. The record for cloture votes is eight, which occurred during the 100th Congress on a bill (S 2) to limit campaign expenditures for Senate general election races. Majority Leader Byrd had made the spending-limit measure a priority, but Senate action was stymied by a three-month GOP-led filibuster. (On one occasion to make a quorum, Senator Packwood was taken into custody by Capitol police and carried feet-first into the chamber.)

Cloture may be tried immediately when the Senate begins consideration of a bill. For instance, Majority Leader Mitchell was informed by GOP leader Dole that because of the controversial nature of a labor bill, the measure (but not the motion to proceed to it) would be filibustered by a substantial number of senators. This is "an important issue," remarked Senator Dole, "[and] we ought to proceed to the bill and have our debate—I prefer `extended debate' rather than the word `filibuster'—but an extended debate on the bill itself."[72] As a result, Senator Mitchell filed a cloture motion on the bill immediately after the Senate proceeded to consider the bill. "I will now file a cloture motion on the bill," he said, "with the understanding and expectation that any Senator who wishes to do so may, under the rules, file [a germane] amendment to the bill by 1 p.m. tomorrow."[73] (Under Senate Rule XXII, first-degree amendments must be filed by 1 p.m. on the day following the filing of the cloture motion; second-degree amendments also must be filed in a timely manner—until one hour prior to the cloture vote. Only germane amendments that have been filed in a timely manner are eligible for consideration subsequent to a successful cloture vote.)

Cloture, too, may be sought soon after a bill is called up in order to block a threatened filibuster, test sentiment for or against a measure, or expedite action on the legislation. Cloture helps to speed up floor action on a bill because as noted, once cloture is achieved all further amendments must be germane. For example, a senator offered a nongermane amendment (repealing a legislative pay hike) to a homeless-aid measure. "This can very well be a killer amendment," declared Senator Byrd.[74] To prevent a vote on the killer amendment, Byrd filed a cloture petition. Subsequently, the Senate invoked cloture by a 68-29 vote. "Under the precedents of the Senate," said the presiding officer in ruling the amendment out of order, "once cloture is invoked, the Chair is required to rule out of order each nongermane amendment that is pending [or] subsequently called up."[75] In brief, since the 1970s, cloture has commonly been employed multiple times on the same measure and invoked as soon as a bill is called up as a means to prevent nongermane amendments from being offered to legislation.

Recent Congresses have witnessed a marked increase in use of cloture, especially on the motion to proceed ("I move to call up S 1234") to legislation or nominations. A few statistics will illustrate the point. In the "26 Congresses from 1919 through 1970," noted Majority Leader Mitchell, "there were a total of 50 votes on cloture motions; that is an average of less than two cloture motions per Congress. But in the eleven Congresses from 1971 through 1992 there were a total of 295 cloture petition votes. That's an average of almost 27 cloture petitions per Congress." Of even greater significance, he said, "is the growth in the number of cloture motions that have to be filed" on motions to proceed: from two in the 95th Congress (1977-1979) to thirty-five in the 102nd Congress (1991-1993). Table 8-2 presents information on the increased use of cloture in the Senate.

TABLE 8-2 Cloture Motions, Selected Congresses, 1919-1995

Congress	Year	Cloture Motion Votes	Cloture Motions on Motion to Proceed
66th	1919–1921	2	
72d	1931–1933	1	
77th	1941–1943	1	
82d	1951–1953	0	
87th	1961–1963	4	
92d	1971–1973	20	
93d	1973–1975	31	
94th	1975–1977	27	
95th	1977–1979	13	2
96th	1979–1981	21	2
97th	1981–1983	27	3
98th	1983–1985	19	10
99th	1985–1987	23	11
100th	1987–1989	43	11
101st	1989–1991	23	12
102d	1991–1993	48	35
103d	1993–1995	42	9

Source: Compiled and updated by Rick Beth, *Operations of the Congress: Testimony of House and Senate Leaders,* Hearing before the 1993 Joint Committee on the Organization of Congress, January 26, 1993.

Senator Mitchell went on to highlight the obstacle course that legislation must complete if there is strong opposition.

> When a filibuster occurs or is threatened, a cloture motion to terminate debate must be filed. The vote on that motion cannot occur until two days after it is filed. So if a cloture motion were filed today, Tuesday, the vote on it would occur on Thursday. If three-fifths or more vote to invoke cloture, there are still up to thirty hours of debate on the motion, postcloture, or effectively two more days. So right now under Senate rules, cloture could be required up to six separate times on a single bill: on the motion to proceed to the bill, on the committee substitute, on the bill itself, and then . . . three times to get to conference with the House—[on the motions (1) to insist on Senate amendments, or disagree to House amendments, (2) to request a conference with the House, or (3) to authorize the Chair to appoint conferees.][76]

Responding to Mitchell, GOP leader Dole said, "I didn't know we could get six cloture votes. I missed one in there. I am glad I came over."[77]

A particularly compelling dilatory tactic emerged during the 1970s: the *postcloture filibuster.* This innovation in the art of blocking action on legislation led to several changes in the cloture rule. The postcloture battle was joined on a 1977 natural gas bill when Senator Byrd, then the majority leader, devised a method of breaking what he called the "most vicious postcloture filibuster that ever occurred in the history of the Senate."[78]

POSTCLOTURE FILIBUSTER

Filibusters are used to defeat or weaken bills by talking them to death. The postcloture filibuster attempts to do the same thing by employing an array of parliamentary tactics to delay final action. The technique involves extensive use of roll calls, quorum calls, and other delaying tactics, none of which [at that time but not today] counts against the one hour of floor time allotted to each member after cloture is invoked. Before several senators' hour has been used up, weeks may elapse. The postcloture filibuster is particularly effective if opponents of a bill have had the foresight to offer a large number of germane amendments before cloture is achieved. These amendments remain pending after cloture. However, no new amendments are in order after the cloture vote, except by unanimous consent.

For the most part, the postcloture filibuster is a contemporary and innovative dilatory tactic. Senators were long aware of its availability, but they seldom employed it. Members apparently believed that it violated the spirit of fair play. Once the battle had been fought and cloture invoked by a large majority, the informal rules of the game dictated that further delaying actions be ended. The postcloture filibuster, however, was used three times in 1976 and once in 1977. Sen. James B. Allen, D-Ala. (1969-1978), is often credited with discovering this tactic.

In 1977 Democratic senators James G. Abourezk, S.D. (1973-1979), and Howard M. Metzenbaum, Ohio (1974, 1976-1995) prolonged Senate consideration of an intensely controversial natural gas deregulation bill for two weeks after cloture had been invoked. The leadership even held an all-night Senate session, the first in thirteen years, in an attempt to break their postcloture filibuster. The story of the efforts of the two senators and the extraordinary countertactics employed to combat them is a classic example of the use of this form of filibuster and why it provoked changes in Rule XXII.

CLOTURE RULE LOOPHOLES. Under Senate rules, any senator who offers a germane amendment before the vote to invoke cloture occurs is eligible to call it up after cloture is agreed to. Senator Metzenbaum had introduced 212 printed amendments in one day alone. They were a mixture of substance and technicalities. Metzenbaum proposed numerous alternative dates for the various deadlines in the bill, alternative sums of money, redefinitions of terms, and various deletions and additions to the bill. Altogether, 508 amendments were pending when cloture was invoked.

With so many amendments pending, the two senators had plenty of ammunition with which to delay Senate proceedings. Here is how their strategy was carried out:

- Abourezk and Metzenbaum called up numerous amendments and objected to unanimous consent requests to suspend the required reading. In one case, the clerk took fifty-five minutes to read an amendment.
- Occasionally the senators would demand two roll-call votes on a single amendment, one on the proposal itself and another on the routine motion to reconsider. In such instances, the two senators shrewdly voted with the majority to reject the amendments so that they would be eligible to offer the motions to reconsider.
- Although debate on the amendments was minimal under cloture, the two senators demanded roll-call votes on each amendment, a process requiring fifteen minutes. They made repeated quorum calls to ensure that fifty-one senators were present on the floor. Each "live" quorum call could take an hour or more.

These relatively simple steps enabled Abourezk and Metzenbaum to tie the Senate in knots. None of the time consumed for their procedural motions counted against the hour each controlled once cloture was invoked. Frustration and bitterness grew as the postcloture filibuster rolled on. "In the course of the last few days," commented Minority Leader Howard H. Baker, Jr., R-Tenn., "we have gone through a torture that the Senate has seldom encountered, including not just an all-night session, but an all-night session that was unique and different from others, as we painfully knew, because the roll calls and quorum calls came at 15-, 30-, and 45-minute intervals."[79]

Finally, Senator Byrd and several members and staff aides devised a counterstrategy. The aim was to rule out of order the bulk of the Abourezk-Metzenbaum amendments pending at the desk. Byrd enlisted the cooperation of Vice President Walter F. Mondale, the presiding officer of the Senate under the Constitution.

When the Senate convened on October 3, 1977, Mondale recognized Majority Leader Byrd, who made the point of order "that when the Senate is operating under cloture, the Chair is required to rule out of order all amendments which are dilatory or which on their face are out of order." Under previous Senate precedents, the chair had to wait for a point of order to be raised against each amendment before ruling whether it was dilatory.

Mondale sustained Byrd's point of order. Abourezk appealed the decision but lost on a 79-14 vote. The stage then was set for a prearranged plan. Reading from a typed script given him by Byrd, Mondale recognized only the majority leader (recall his priority of recognition), who called up thirty-three of Metzenbaum's amendments. (Technically, a senator can call up any amendment pending at the desk, even if it is not his own.) Each of the senator's amendments was quickly ruled out of order by the presiding officer, who ignored the senators who wanted to appeal the chair's ruling, a customary right of members.

Bedlam broke out on the floor. Cries of "dictatorship" and "steamroller" were heard. "The Senate of the United States has just seen an outrageous act," declared Sen. Gary Hart, D-Colo. Abourezk and Metzenbaum, feeling betrayed by the Carter administration, ended their filibuster. With nine days of debate and 129 roll-call votes behind it, the Senate enacted the natural gas deregulation measure.

1979 REVISION OF RULE XXII. On February 22, 1979, the Senate amended Rule XXII to restrict opportunities for the postcloture filibuster. Once cloture is invoked, under the change, a hundred-hour cap is imposed on all postcloture action, including the time spent reading and voting on amendments, quorum calls, and any other procedural motion. No measure, then, is to be debated beyond a total of one hundred hours following a successful cloture vote. The change also provided "that no Senator shall call up more than two amendments until every other Senator has had the opportunity to call up two amendments."[80] The presiding officer is directed to give priority of recognition to another senator rather than to a member seeking to call up a third amendment.

1986 REVISION

When the Senate took up the proposal to televise floor sessions gavel to gavel, party leaders supported changes to improve senatorial operations and inhibit the spectacle of lengthy filibusters. One of these changes reduced the "time for debate once cloture is invoked from 100 hours to 30 hours."[81] This reduction means that senators during the postcloture period would still be recognized for one hour, but the thirty hours would be allocated on a first come, first served basis. It is common for the full thirty hours to be used, sometimes by a bipartisan agreement to let the clock tick away even during daily Senate adjournments or recesses. There are occasions, too, when the thirty-hour requirement is waived, as agreed in this 1993 exchange between Democratic Whip Wendell H. Ford, Ky., and GOP leader Dole:

> Senator FORD. I wonder if there is a chance we might waive the 30 hours [of debate] and go on and pass this bill.
> Senator DOLE. I have not thought a great deal about it.
> Senator FORD. The senator does not have to think too much. Just say yes.
> Senator DOLE. That is not a requirement in this body. In any event, we will be happy to.[82]

The 1986 revision along with other postcloture rules and precedents, such as dispensing with the reading of amendments and enabling the chair

---

ENDING A SENATE FILIBUSTER

CLOTURE

Day 1   Petition signed by sixteen members.

Day 2   First degree amendments are to be filed by 1 p.m.

Day 3   Second degree amendments are to be filed until one hour before the cloture vote.

Constitutional three-fifths (or sixty) vote is required to invoke cloture in the one hundred-member chamber. A two-thirds vote is required to invoke cloture on proposals to change Senate rules.

POSTCLOTURE

- Thirty-hour debate limit with time counted for votes, quorum calls, and other matters.
- Amendments must be germane.
- One-hour debate per senator.
- Presiding officer can rule out dilatory motions on his own initiative without waiting for a point of order.
- The measure on which cloture has been invoked remains the unfinished business of the Senate to the exclusion of all other business.

BOX 8-4

to rule dilatory amendments and motions out of order, have reduced the inordinate delaying potential of this type of filibuster. "The threat of a [postcloture] filibuster loses some of its sting if only [thirty] postcloture hours are allowed," remarked Senator Bumpers.[83] Another factor dampening use of postcloture filibusters is the senatorial consensus that this type of dilatory tactic is an abuse of the lawmaking process. (For an overview of key cloture and postcloture procedures, see Box 8-4, "Ending a Senate Filibuster.")

REFORM PROPOSALS OF THE 1990s

Growing concern about the use of the filibuster precipitated a variety of reform proposals during the 1990s. Lloyd Cutler, former White House counsel to Presidents Jimmy Carter and Bill Clinton, even argued that Rule XXII is unconstitutional and ought to be overturned by the Supreme Court.

Although Article I of the Constitution grants each chamber the right to determine the rules of its proceedings, Cutler states that this provision cannot be employed to override the implied provisions of the Constitution that mandate a simple majority to enact measures except in those explicit areas (overriding a veto, for instance) where a two-thirds vote is required.[84]

The 1993 Joint Committee on the Organization of Congress recommended a two-hour limit on the motion to proceed, in part to strengthen the capacity of the majority leader to set the Senate's agenda. Congressional scholars proposed a return to all-night, marathon sessions to break talkathons so senators might have to pay a political and physical price if they want to filibuster. They also suggested "a sliding scale for cloture votes: sixty votes required to cut off debate initially; fifty-five votes after a week of debate; and a simple majority two weeks after the initial cloture vote."[85]

When the 104th Congress began, Democratic senators Tom Harkin, Iowa, and Joseph I. Lieberman, Conn., sought to amend Rule XXII with a "decreasing-scale" recommendation: sixty votes on the first try with the vote needed to invoke cloture "reduced by three on each subsequent vote, so that debate would be shut off with 57 votes on the second try, 54 on the third, and 51—a simple majority—on the fourth."[86] Senator Byrd argued strongly against the change, and, in the end, the Senate voted 76 to 19 to kill the Harkin-Lieberman proposal.[87]

SUMMARY OBSERVATIONS

There has been a contemporary surge in filibusters and, relatedly, cloture attempts. Recent decades have witnessed a progression from sparing use of the cloture procedure to its routine use. Where one cloture vote per measure was once the norm, the modern Senate reached a record eight cloture votes on one measure. Cloture, it is worth noting, is also employed by the majority leader as a management or scheduling tool. For example, if cloture can be invoked on the motion to proceed, the majority leader can ensure that his agenda of issues will be subject to Senate consideration. Hence, an increase in cloture votes does not necessarily mean an increase in the number of filibusters.

Nonetheless, there are occasions when dilatory intent is plain. Several factors account for the increase in cloture attempts. One is the influx of new senators (many from the House who have been socialized by the rough partisan politics of that institution) who prefer to push their own agendas even if the Senate's institutional activities grind to a halt. There are occasions, noted Senator Hatfield, when senators are "determined to follow [their] own perspective even to the perversion, the distortion, and the destruction of the [legislative] process."[88] Senate rules permit this behavior. Aggressive senators have an arsenal of devices to advance their objectives in virtually any policy area. (The 1975 amendment to Rule XXII, permitting cloture by a three-fifths vote, also made it easier to invoke this procedure and encouraged the use of postcloture filibusters.)

Among other reasons for wider use of filibusters is their enhanced potency in an institution that is workload-packed and deadline-driven. There is insufficient time to accommodate the manifold claims on the Senate's agenda. In such an environment, senators who even indicate their intention to filibuster can exercise significant policy leverage. The "track system" for scheduling measures, discussed in Chapter 7, may also have made it easier for senators to conduct filibusters.

Gone, too, are internal incentives ("to get along, go along," for instance) that fostered deference to seniority and party leaders. Professor Richard F. Fenno, Jr., the noted congressional scholar, discussed how the 1950s Senate evolved from a "communitarian" institution, where senators were expected to use extended debate sparingly and only for high-stakes national issues, to today's "individualistic" Senate. With "more openness, more media visibility, more candidate-centered elections," more interest groups, more political obligations, and more staff, Senate newcomers are independent entrepreneurs unwilling to submerge their personal political objectives "to the norms of any collectivity."[89] When Lyndon Johnson was majority leader (1955-1960), he exercised tight control over floor proceedings, including use of the filibuster.

> While Johnson went to great lengths to avoid filibusters, once they had begun ... he tended to regard filibusters as a personal challenge to his stewardship. Instead of making an end run around the combatants ... he often preferred to break the filibuster by keeping the Senate in session for long hours, even around the clock, and forcing the minority ultimately to give up in exhaustion.[90]

By contrast, contemporary party leaders may accommodate filibustering senators who have meetings to attend back home.

In brief, filibusters may be terminated through such means as the invocation of cloture, expiration of the thirty-hour cap, compromises between the contending sides, or mistakes that cause filibustering senators to lose the floor, such as violation of the two-speech rule. That rule forbids members from making a third speech on the same question in the same legislative day.[91]

FINAL VOTE ON A BILL

Once cloture is invoked, filibusters by amendment broken, and other delaying tactics ended, the Senate proceeds to a final vote on the bill under consideration. If obstructionist tactics cannot be ended, the leadership may withdraw the bill and proceed to other business.

On legislation not regulated by complex agreements and not the target of deliberate obstructionist tactics, the floor managers and party leaders try to fashion ad hoc agreements under which amendments can be disposed of. But because of the strong commitment in the Senate to giving every member ample opportunity to be heard, this can be a lengthy process. For example, one tax measure, which was not filibustered, consumed twenty-five days of debate. There were 209 amendments and motions on the bill and 129 roll-call votes. The length of debate on this legislation reflected its importance to senators and the country as well as the complexity of its provisions.

Paradoxically, while it is relatively easy to frustrate floor action, Senate rules make it difficult for committees to bottle up legislation and prevent it from reaching the floor. The means by which senators can force bills to be considered by the Senate are discussed in the following section.

PROCEDURES TO CIRCUMVENT COMMITTEES

Bypassing committees, while not an everyday occurrence in the Senate, is easier to accomplish than in the House. In an earlier chapter, it was seen that the House has a number of procedures for bringing to the floor bills that are blocked in committee. These include Calendar Wednesday, the discharge petition, the power of extraction by the Rules Committee, and the suspension of the rules procedure. Except for suspension, which generally is used for relatively noncontroversial bills, these alternative House procedures are seldom employed and rarely successful.

In the Senate, at least four techniques are available: (1) use of nongermane amendments, also known as riders; (2) placing House-passed and Senate-introduced bills immediately on the Calendar of General Orders; (3) suspending Senate rules; and (4) implementing the discharge procedure. The first two are the most effective.

Nongermane Amendments

Unlike the House, the Senate has never had a rule requiring amendments to be germane to pending legislation. This feature probably ranks just below the filibuster as one of the Senate's most distinctive characteristics. "Amendments may be made," Jefferson wrote in the parliamentary manual he prepared during his service as president of the Senate (1797-1801), "so as totally to alter the nature of the proposition."[92] A classic case occurred in 1965 when Sen. Everett McKinley Dirksen, R-Ill. (1951-1969), tried to add a proposal for a constitutional amendment on legislative reapportionment to a joint resolution designating August 6 to September 6 as "National American Legion Baseball Month." Dirksen's amendment had been blocked by the Judiciary Committee. An opponent of the proposal called the senator's attempt a "foul ball."

Periodically, the Senate has considered rules changes that would permit it to impose a germaneness requirement on floor amendments. Proponents argue that such a requirement would improve senatorial efficiency, expedite the workload, enhance relations with the House (which has a strict germaneness requirement), strengthen committees as centers of policy making, and promote predictability in scheduling. Opponents contend that the right of senators to offer nongermane amendments serves as a safeguard against capricious committee actions, permits any senator to raise important issues, and enables the Senate to respond quickly to new developments. "What is at stake [in the ability of senators to offer nongermane amendments] is the right of a minority—even a tiny minority, even one Senator—to raise an issue," declared one senator.[93]

In brief, germaneness sometimes has been a vexing issue for the Senate. On the one hand, the lack of a general prohibition on riders permits senators to raise and debate popular and unpopular issues and lessens the opportunity for arbitrary committee action. On the other hand, some senators complain that the practice wastes the Senate's time by permitting contentious debate on matters unrelated to the fundamental purpose of a pending bill.

SENATE PROHIBITIONS. Although the Senate does not have a general germaneness rule, there are four situations where the chamber requires germane amendments to pending legislation:

1. Unanimous consent agreements as usually drawn up contain a requirement that amendments are to be germane.
2. Amendments to general appropriations bills.
3. When cloture has been invoked.
4. During consideration of concurrent budget resolutions and reconciliation bills.

Interestingly, when the Senate operates under a germaneness requirement, its tests for determining whether amendments are germane are stricter than those in the House. A Senate report noted that "a legislative amendment is germane if, and only if, it proposes to strike out or to change a number or date, or if its effect would be to restrict the scope of the measure or the powers it grants."[94] A presiding officer once noted, if an "amendment expands the effect of the bill or introduces new subject matter it is not germane."[95] Thus, if a farm bill dealt with five items, barley, wheat, rice, cotton, and soybeans, and a senator sought to amend the measure by adding corn to the list, a germaneness point of order could be made against the amendment. Sense of the Senate (or Congress) amendments, which are nonbinding and generally symbolic in intent, and amendments to strike language are considered automatically germane in most circumstances.

It is worth noting that the Senate so narrowed its meaning of what constituted a germane amendment that when the germaneness requirement was in effect it prevented consideration of "policy alternatives that are highly pertinent but nonetheless nongermane because they expand the coverage of the bill or the powers it conveys."[96] The Senate needed a broader term to permit subject-related amendments to be offered to pending measures when they were governed by the germaneness stricture. Starting from the mid to late 1980s, the term that began to be employed was "relevancy." Hence, unanimous consent agreements today often use this term in describing what kinds of amendments are in order. Sometimes a unanimous consent agreement will include the usual (or strict) germaneness standard; sometimes it will use relevancy; and sometimes it will use both terms for different categories of amendments.

PLACING MEASURES ON THE CALENDAR

When measures are either introduced in the Senate or passed by the House and sent to the Senate, they customarily are referred to a committee. As noted earlier, all measures, including House-passed bills, must be read twice on different legislative days before they can be referred to committee. Under Senate Rule XIV, if any senator objects to the second reading the committee stage is bypassed and the House-passed bill, or Senate-introduced bill, is placed directly on the calendar.

This procedure was used by supporters of the 1957 and 1964 Civil Rights Acts (the 1960 Civil Rights Act was introduced as a nongermane amendment). Backers wanted to avoid sending the bills to the Judiciary Committee, which had an unbroken record of never reporting a civil rights bill. Placing a bill on the calendar also gives the leadership the option of calling up either the House-passed measure or, should there be one, the version reported by the Senate committee.

Although effective, Rule XIV is used sparingly because of the general deference to committee prerogatives. It is sometimes used when the proponent of a bill feels intensely enough about it to flout the jurisdiction of a committee that is known to oppose it.[97] In some instances, committee chairmen may even employ the rule to place a bill on the calendar.

More commonly, House-passed measures are held at the clerk's desk by unanimous consent. House-passed measures are also held at the desk when similar Senate bills are already pending on the calendar or are expected shortly to be reported out of committee.

SUSPENSION OF THE RULES

Senate rules can be suspended, provided there is one day's notice in writing and the terms of the suspension motion are published in the *Congressional Record*. The rules are silent on the number of votes needed to suspend Senate rules. Precedents have required two-thirds of those present and voting to approve suspensions. The procedure is rarely used because it represents a challenge to the committee system and is open to dilatory tactics. In effect, three filibusters are possible on suspension motions: first, on the motion to suspend the rules; second, on the motion to take up the bill; and third, on the bill itself.

Suspension motions occasionally are made by senators who want to offer policy amendments to general appropriations measures. Policy amendments (legislative language) to appropriations measures are forbidden by Senate rules but can be made in order in various ways, including the suspension route.

THE DISCHARGE PETITION

Discharging a bill from a committee has taken place only fourteen times in the history of the Senate. It was last employed successfully in 1964. The prevailing sentiment is that the procedure undercuts the committee system and also that the rules governing its use are cumbersome. The discharge motion can be made only during the "morning hour" and must remain at the clerk's desk for one legislative day. Party leaders can forestall discharge motions for days or weeks simply by recessing, thus keeping the Senate in the same legislative day. If debate on the motion is not concluded within the morning hour, the motion is placed on the Calendar where it faces the threat of a series of filibusters. A vote to discharge a committee of a bill requires a simple majority vote unless it is necessary to invoke cloture to stop a filibuster.

There is technically yet another way to bypass a Senate committee: by unanimous consent. The Senate, as has been seen in this chapter, can do almost anything it wants by unanimous consent. However, unanimous consent will not be obtained if a single member—presumably a member of the committee that would be bypassed—objects.

SUMMARY

There are more differences than similarities between Senate and House floor procedures, the result primarily of the smaller size and greater opportunity for informal arrangements in the Senate. Procedures such as unanimous consent agreements, the track system, the filibuster and the cloture rule, nongermane amendments, morning business, and executive sessions have no real counterpart in the House. Conversely, the five-minute rule, rules from the Rules Committee, the Corrections Calendar, and electronic voting cannot be found in the Senate.

The larger, more complex House emphasizes formal rules and precedents. The Senate functions in a largely ad hoc fashion, emphasizing reciprocity and courtesy among senators. House procedure is relatively straightforward, with few detours. The Senate changes its procedures to meet new contingencies, accommodate members, and resolve unforeseen problems. The Senate occasionally observes its formal rules, but more commonly waives them by unanimous consent and modifies its debate arrangements to suit each bill.

Senate rules emphasize the influence of individual members. As Senator Byrd has observed: "The rules of the Senate are made for the convenience of those who wish to delay."[98] As a result, it is often more difficult to create winning coalitions in the Senate than in the House. The discipline imposed by House rules generally aids party leaders in forming and sustaining majorities. These House-Senate procedural differences occasionally produce bicameral dissension even when the same party controls both bodies. Many House Democrats were so frustrated during the 103d Congress (1993-1995) with their majority brethren in the Senate that they encouraged formation of an outside antifilibuster group called "Action, Not Gridlock," to make reform of Rule XXII a national issue. (With Republicans in charge of the 104th Congress, many House Democrats express approval of the Senate's lengthy decision-making processes.)

There also are more opportunities to revise legislation on the Senate floor than in the House. Senators feel freer to offer amendments to legislation coming from committees, other than their own, than do members of the House, who are somewhat more likely to defer to the committees' decisions. And to a far greater degree in the Senate than in the House, members are assured that their party leaders will make every effort to accommodate their scheduling needs.

A crucial legislative arbiter on virtually all important legislation is the conference committee. Composed of groups of legislators from each chamber, this "third house of Congress" reconciles differences between House- and Senate-passed versions of bills. The next chapter examines this important congressional institution and other ways of resolving differences in bills passed by the two houses of Congress.

NOTES

1. *Congressional Record,* April 21, 1987, S5204.
2. *Congressional Record,* May 21, 1980, S5674.
3. On November 17, 1982, for the first time since 1793, the House operated on two legislative days in the same day. It adjourned at 1:19 p.m. (the first legislative day) and then reconvened at 4:00 p.m. that day (the second legislative day). Sharp partisanship stimulated the Democratic leadership to employ this rare scheduling device. On October 29, 1987, the House again adjourned and reconvened.
4. *Congressional Record,* March 28, 1980, S3234.
5. *Senate Procedure, Precedents and Practices,* 97th Cong., 1st sess., S Doc 97–2, 565.
6. *Congressional Record,* March 26, 1987, S3927.
7. *Congressional Record,* September 24, 1986, S13597.
8. *Congressional Record,* April 16, 1985, S4256.

9. *Congressional Record,* June 9, 1977, 18179.
10. *National Journal's CongressDaily/PM,* August 20, 1993, 4. See Mary McGrory, "Freshman Turns Senate Scarlet," *Washington Post,* July 27, 1993, A2.
11. A Senate rule requires three hours of germane discussion at the beginning of each day's debate on a measure. Called the Pastore Rule after its sponsor, Sen. John O. Pastore, D-R.I. (1950–1976), its purpose is to confine debate to pending business.
12. *Congressional Record,* January 21, 1986, S8.
13. *Congressional Record,* May 21, 1987, S6979.
14. Rowland Evans and Robert Novak, *Lyndon B. Johnson: The Exercise of Power* (New York: New American Library, 1966), 115.
15. *Congressional Record,* October 31, 1985, 29990.
16. Joseph S. Clark, *Congress: The Sapless Branch* (New York: Harper & Row, 1964), 247–248.
17. *New York Times,* June 8, 1986, E5.
18. *Congressional Record,* September 27, 1993, S12550.
19. *Washington Times,* March 20, 1995, A8.
20. *CQ's Congressional Monitor,* February 24, 1995, 4.
21. Elizabeth Shogren, "Level of Debate in Senate Hits Comic Low," *Los Angeles Times,* August 25, 1994, A6.
22. *Congressional Record,* October 28, 1977, 5857.
23. *Congressional Record,* June 24, 1987, S8583.
24. Elizabeth Drew, *Senator* (New York: Simon & Schuster, 1979), 173–174.
25. *Congressional Record,* April 18, 1980, S3923. See also Stanley Bach, "Parliamentary Strategy and the Amendment Process: Rules and Case Studies of Congressional Action," *Polity* (Summer 1983): 573–592.
26. *Congressional Record,* February 4, 1992, S872.
27. *Wall Street Journal,* March 2, 1995, A16.
28. *CQ's Congressional Monitor,* March 2, 1995, 5.
29. *New York Times,* May 6, 1987, B10.
30. *Congressional Record,* August 19, 1980, S11212.
31. Kathy Koch, "Senate Votes to Weaken Strip Mining Law," *Congressional Quarterly Weekly Report,* August 23, 1980, 2453.
32. *Congressional Record,* March 25, 1993, S3734.
33. *Congressional Record,* June 30, 1987, S8975.
34. *Congressional Record,* February 17, 1988, S795.
35. *USA Today,* May 19, 1986, 13A.
36. *Congressional Record,* June 15, 1994, S6905.
37. Andrew Taylor, "Whitewater Hearings To Be Held On Democrats' Terms," *Congressional Quarterly Weekly Report,* June 18, 1994, 1588.
38. *Congressional Record,* November 5, 1985, S14793.
39. *Washington Post,* July 24, 1991, A1.
40. *Congressional Record,* March 7, 1995, S3597.
41. Ibid., S3599.
42. *Congressional Record,* June 20, 1985, S8500.
43. *Congressional Record,* January 26, 1973, 2301.
44. *Congressional Record,* December 9, 1987, S17476.
45. *National Journal's CongressDaily/PM,* March 31, 1994, 5.
46. *Congressional Record,* May 18, 1990, S6572.
47. James L. Buckley, *If Men Were Angels* (New York: G. P. Putnam's Sons, 1975), 129.
48. Bernard Asbell, *The Senate Nobody Knows* (Garden City, New York: Doubleday, 1978), 267.
49. *Congressional Record,* September 23, 1975, 29814.

50. *Congressional Record,* June 23, 1987, S8442.
51. *Congressional Record,* April 8, 1981, S3618.
52. Nadine Cohodas, "Decision on Manion Put off after `Roll of Dice' in Senate," *Congressional Quarterly Weekly Report,* June 28, 1986, 1508–1509.
53. *Congressional Record,* July 22, 1983, S10701.
54. *Congressional Record,* October 10, 1985, S13114.
55. *New York Times,* December 21, 1982, D29.
56. The word *filibuster* derives from the Dutch word *Vrijbuiter,* meaning freebooter. Passing into Spanish as *filibustero,* it was used to describe military adventurers from the United States who in the mid-1800s fomented insurrections against various Latin American governments. For an account of William Walker, filibusterer of the 1850s, see *Smithsonian,* June 1981, 117–128. The first legislative use of the word is said to have occurred in the House in 1853, when a representative accused his opponents of "filibustering against the United States." By 1863 the word filibuster had come to mean delaying action on the floor, but the term did not gain wide currency until the 1880s.
57. *Congressional Record,* July 18, 1983, S10216.
58. *Washington Post,* February 20, 1994, A13.
59. *New York Times,* December 12, 1982, 4E.
60. *Washington Times,* November 17, 1987, A6.
61. *CQ's Congressional Monitor,* February 22, 1995, 6.
62. *Washington Times,* June 16, 1994, A4.
63. *National Journal's CongressDaily/AM,* November 10, 1993, 1, 7.
64. *Washington Post,* September 20, 1994, A20. 65. *Congressional Record,* October 5, 1992, S16577.
66. *National Journal's CongressDaily/AM,* March 23, 1994, 8.
67. *Congressional Record,* February 26, 1979, 3232.
68. Operations of Congress: Testimony of House and Senate Leaders, Hearing before the 1993 Joint Committee on the Organization of Congress, January 26, 1993, 50.
69. *Washington Post,* June 11, 1982, A11.
70. *Washington Times,* October 26, 1993, A12.
71. *Congressional Record,* September 21, 1893, 1636.
72. *Congressional Record,* June 9, 1992, S7727.
73. Ibid., S7726.
74. *Congressional Record,* April 9, 1987, S4825.
75. Ibid., S4944.
76. Operations of Congress: Testimony of House and Senate Leaders, Hearing before the Joint Committee on the Organization of Congress, January 26, 1993, 116.
77. Ibid., 53.
78. *Congressional Record,* May 27, 1982, 12218. 79. *Congressional Quarterly Weekly Report,* October 1, 1977, 2070.
80. *Congressional Record,* March 10, 1981, S1934.
81. *Congressional Record,* February 27, 1986, S1752.
82. *National Journal's CongressDaily/PM,* May 12, 1993, 5.
83. *Congressional Record,* February 6, 1986, S1113.
84. See Lloyd Cutler, "On Killing Senate Rule XXII (Cont'd)," *Washington Post,* May 3, 1993, A19.
85. Thomas E. Mann and Norman J. Ornstein, "Renewing Congress: A Progress Report," March 1994, American Enterprise Institute and The Brookings Institution, 15–16.
86. Mary Jacoby, "Harkin, Lieberman Take Up a Lonely Fight To Ban Filibuster—But How to Force Vote?" *Roll Call,* November 28, 1994, 24.

87. *Congressional Record,* January 5, 1995, S438.
88. *Congressional Record,* September 27, 1984, S12137.
89. Richard F. Fenno, Jr., "The Senate Through the Looking Glass: The Debate over Television," *Legislative Studies Quarterly,* August 1989, 316.
90. *Congressional Record,* March 3, 1986, S1915.
91. For a contentious debate on the two-speech rule, see *Congressional Record,* September 25, 1986, S13687–S13710; *Washington Post,* October 1, 1986, A17.
92. *Constitution, Jefferson's Manual and Rules of the House of Representatives,* 102d Cong., 2d sess., H Doc 102-405, 233.
93. *Congressional Record,* February 26, 1986, S1663.
94. *Report on Senate Operations, 1988,* Senate Committee on Rules and Administration, S Print 100–129, September 20, 1988, 55.
95. *Congressional Record,* February 9, 1982, S599.
96. Ibid.
97. For a discussion of the leadership's concern about overuse of Rule XIV, see *Congressional Record,* September 27, 1983, S12971.
98. *Congressional Record,* August 31, 1976, 28607.

CHAPTER 9

Resolving House-Senate Differences

Before legislation can be sent to the president for his consideration, it must be passed by both houses in identical form. House- and Senate-passed versions of the same bill frequently differ, sometimes only slightly but often on critical points. The two versions must be reconciled by mutual agreement. Whenever possible, this is done informally. However, a fair percentage of all bills passed by both chambers require action by a House-Senate conference committee—an ad hoc joint committee composed of members selected by each chamber to resolve differences on a particular bill in disagreement.[1] Of the 465 public laws enacted by the 103d Congress, 13 percent (or 62) went through conference.[2] It is usually major and controversial legislation that requires conference committee action.

OBSCURITY OF THE PROCESS

The conference committee process is older than Congress itself. State legislatures used conference committees before 1789 to reconcile differences between the chambers of their bicameral legislatures. The conference committee system was taken for granted when the first Congress convened, and it has been in use ever since.[3] Nevertheless, for many citizens the conference committee is little known or understood, compared with the other aspects of the legislative process.

The relative obscurity of the conference process is explained by the fact that until the mid-1970s conference committees almost always met in secret sessions with no published record of their proceedings. The conference committees produced a conference committee report that showed the results of the secret negotiations, but the bargaining and deliberations that led to these results were not formally disclosed.

In one of the most significant reforms of congressional procedure, both chambers in 1975 adopted rules requiring open conference committee meetings unless a majority of the conference members (called *conferees* or *managers*) from either chamber voted in public to hold secret sessions. In 1977 the House went a step further, adopting a rule requiring the full House to vote to close a conference. This occurs usually on legislation dealing with national security.

To be sure, conferees still conduct much of their important business in secret. As thirty-eight-year-veteran senator Russell B. Long, D-La. (who voluntarily retired at the end of the 99th Congress), once noted in a statement that holds true today:

> The Senator knows when we started the openness thing we found it more and more difficult to get something agreed to in the conferences, it seemed to take forever. So what did we do? The Senator knows what we did. We would break up into smaller groups and then we would ask our chairman ... to see if he could not find his opposite number on the House side and discuss this matter and come back and tell us what the chances would be of working out various and sundry possibilities.[4]

There are relatively few complaints about closed sessions. No doubt political commentators and others recognize the value of candid exchanges (away from the glare of special interest groups) in closed meetings. Further, reporters are usually kept well informed of the results of closed conferences. In today's open and video politics era, "secret" does not mean what it used to on Capitol Hill.

A CRITICAL JUNCTURE

The conference committee, sometimes called "the third house of Congress," is one of the most critical points in the legislative process. For several reasons, however, members of Congress may try to avoid this stage and resolve House-Senate differences on legislation without recourse to the conference committee process. For one thing, there is pressure to approve the legislation quickly. For another, there may be concern in one house that conferees of the other chamber will try to weaken (or filibuster) the legislation. And third, there always is the possibility that a conference committee will become deadlocked—particularly in the weeks and days before the final adjournment of Congress. Failure of the conferees to reach agreement before the end of a Congress means that the bill dies.

This chapter first discusses how House-Senate differences on a bill are resolved without a conference. It then explores the complexities of the conference committee process. Finally, the chapter examines the last steps of the legislative process—final House and Senate approval of legislation (of the conference compromise for bills sent to conference committees) and presidential approval or veto, with subsequent action by Congress on vetoed bills.

AGREEMENT WITHOUT A CONFERENCE

There are two principal methods of resolving House-Senate differences without a conference. First, there is verbatim adoption of one chamber's ver-

TABLE 9-1 Bicameral Reconciliation of Legislation, 99th (1985–1987) and 103d (1993–1995) Congresses

| | 99th Congress | | 103d Congress | |
Method of Reconciliation	Number	Percent	Number	Percent
Simple adoption by one chamber of the version sent to it by the other	477	(72)	291	(63)
Amendments between the houses	133	(20)	112	(24)
Conference reports	39	(6)	46	(10)
Both conference reports and amendments between the houses	14	(2)	16	(30)
Public laws (total)	663		465	

Source: Ilona Nickels, Government Division, Congressional Research Service, Library of Congress.

sion of a bill by the other. This is a common occurrence and may involve informal consultation before or after passage of the bill by one chamber. Second, the two houses may send measures back and forth several times, amending each other's amendments, before they agree to identical language on all provisions of the legislation. The "back-and-forth" approach may also be employed in combination with conference committee negotiations. Table 9-1 shows how often different procedures for reaching bicameral agreement were used in the 99th and 103d Congresses.

It is usual for House and Senate committee staff to communicate regularly on legislation of mutual interest. (The availability of electronic mail clearly facilitates these exchanges.) Drafts of measures are exchanged for comment and consistency, companion bills are studied, and strategies are devised to facilitate passage in each chamber. Executive branch officials and pressure groups often participate in these informal strategy sessions. This kind of prior consultation frequently helps clear away obstacles to passage— allowing legislation to be approved by both houses in identical form, thus avoiding the need for a conference.

Consultation also may take place after a bill has passed one or both chambers. For example, on the first day of the 104th Congress, the House overwhelmingly passed the Congressional Accountability Act (HR 1), applying federal workplace safety and antidiscrimination laws to the legislative branch. When the legislation went to the Senate, members there wanted to make some changes. After consultations with the House sponsors of the legislation, the Senate passed S 2, its version of the accountability act, and sent that measure to the House. To avoid the need for a conference committee, House Republican leaders decided to take up S 2 under suspension of the rules procedure, where it was passed by more than the two-thirds vote (390 to 0) required under that procedure. The House action cleared the legislation for submission to President Bill Clinton, who signed the measure into law.

LIMITS TO NONCONFERENCE TACTICS

Under the "back-and-forth" approach, two points are worth noting.

First, there is a limit to the number of times measures may be shuffled between the chambers. In brief, the third-degree amendment prohibition, discussed in Chapters 6 and 8, also applies to amendments between the House and Senate. Each chamber gets two shots at amending the amendments of the other body. "In short, after each chamber has passed the same bill for the first time (e.g., the House passes a House bill and the Senate passes the House bill with Senate amendments), each chamber may have one opportunity to amend the amendments of the other chamber."[5] Like many legislative procedures, the "two-shot" principle can be waived, ignored, or overturned. The Consolidated Omnibus Reconciliation Act of 1985, for example, was a record breaker. It was bounced between the chambers a record-setting nine times.

Second, the back-and-forth alternative procedure is employed intentionally to avoid conferences and is feasible only when circumstances warrant its use. For instance, a House chairman may ask the chamber to concur in the Senate amendment to the House amendment to the Senate-passed bill. House approval is "appropriate parliamentary procedure, which allows us to avoid the trouble of a conference when faced with such small [bicameral] differences."[6] The House in this case agreed to the Senate amendment, which cleared the bill for the president. There are also occasions when the lack of time prevents formation of conference committees and necessitates use of the back-and-forth approach.

WHY CONFERENCE COMMITTEES?

It is often clear from the outset that controversial measures will end up in conference. Members plan their floor strategy accordingly. They make floor statements that emphasize their unyielding commitment to their own chamber's positions. In advance of a "House-Senate conference," noted one senator, "it is not unusual for the respective [chambers] to stake out positions for themselves and even to utter statements about their absolute intransigence, that sometimes does not always prevail when the conference convenes."[7]

Members frequently add expendable amendments to use as bargaining chips in conference. Such amendments can be traded away for other provisions considered more important. Use of such tactics has been refined to an art form by some senators. When Senator Long was Finance chairman (1966-1980), he usually came "to conference with a bill loaded up with amendments added on the Senate floor. . . . Long has plenty of things he is willing to jettison to save the goodies."[8] Members who sponsor floor amendments are mindful of the "bargaining chip" ploy. As one senator remarked:

> I have been in this body long enough to beware of the chairman of a committee who says in an enticing voice, "Let me take the amendment to conference," because I think that is frequently the parliamentary equivalent of saying, "Let me take the child into the tower and I will strangle him to death."[9]

On another occasion, a colleague asked Sen. Bob Dole, R-Kan., if certain floor amendments would be dropped in conference. Dole responded, "I have indicated to the Senator from Ohio that we will certainly consider these carefully in conference before they are disposed of."[10]

With conference committees open, or at least subject to public review, it sometimes is necessary for conferees to put up a fight for such amendments before dropping them. Conferees understand, too, that some bargaining chips are more influential than others. Before these amendments are dropped, conferees will consider the implications of offending powerful members.

Another preconference tactic is for one chamber to deliberately keep out of its bill something it knows the other chamber really wants. During a conference, the House conferees, for instance, may give in to the Senate, but only in return for Senate acceptance of something favored by the House. For these reasons it is difficult to identify the winners or losers in conference simply by counting the number of times one house appeared to give in to the other.[11]

House and Senate floor managers also consider whether they want recorded votes on certain amendments when they are debated in their chamber. For example, one senator's strategy on an amendment he opposed was to seek a recorded vote on it "to beat the amendment, and beat it good, burying the issue in the Senate once and for all, and also putting him in a position to tell a Senate-House conference on the bill that the proposal was resoundingly defeated in the Senate."[12] Alternatively, floor managers sometimes prefer not to draw attention to amendments they oppose (or favor)—and thus hope to avoid taking roll-call votes—on the assumption that it then will be easier to drop (or advocate) them in conference.

Finally, members are sensitive to the overall contours of their bill and the margin of support for its passage on the floor. Mindful that many senators, including Republicans, were not strong advocates of the various proposals in the Contract with America pushed by House Speaker Newt Gingrich, R-Ga., one GOP representative said that the "tactics are to [include] the firmest position [in the House tax bill] because we still have to deal with the Senate and the White House."[13] Thus, if the Senate rewrites the House's position, "House leaders vow to fight for the House position in conferences with the Senate."[14] When the Democratic-controlled Congress passed President Clinton's budget reconciliation package in 1993, only Democrats voted for it. The legislation passed by razor-thin margins in each chamber: 219–213 in the House and 50–49 in the Senate, with Vice President Al Gore casting the tie-breaking vote. "With the votes so close in both chambers and Republicans seemingly hardened into adamant opposition to any Democratic [economic] plan," noted one account, "virtually every Democrat has a veto going into the House-Senate conference, and all interests must be accommodated" if a bicameral agreement is to be reached.[15]

CONFERENCE COMMITTEE PROCESS

There are five major steps in the conference committee process: (1) requesting a conference, (2) selecting conferees, (3) bargaining in conference, (4) filing the conference committee report, and (5) taking final House and Senate action on the conference committee version of the bill.

REQUESTING A CONFERENCE

When the House passes a bill, and it then is amended by the Senate and returned, the House has several options. It may (1) refuse to take further action, in which case the measure dies; (2) approve an entirely new version of the bill and send it to the Senate; (3) agree to the Senate's amendments, negating the need for a conference; (4) amend the Senate's amendments and return the measure once again to the Senate; or (5) request a conference.

Occasionally, the Speaker may refer the Senate amendments, especially if they are nongermane to the House-passed measure, to the standing committee having jurisdiction over the subject matter of the amendments. More commonly, though, on major legislation a member will ask and receive unanimous consent for the House to disagree to the Senate's amendments and request a conference with the Senate. The Speaker usually recognizes an appropriate committee member to make the unanimous consent request to go to conference on the bill. ("Mr. Speaker, I ask unanimous consent to take from the Speaker's table the bill HR 1234 with the Senate amendments thereto, disagree to the amendments of the Senate and ask for a conference with the Senate.")

If any representative objects to this request, there are three other ways to get to conference. First, the House can suspend its rules (an action that requires a two-thirds vote) by adopting, for example, the following motion: "Mr. Speaker, I move to suspend the rules and take from the Speaker's table the bill HR 1234 with the Senate amendments thereto, disagree to the amendments of the Senate and ask for a conference with the Senate." If the legislation is controversial, this procedure is unlikely to be employed because of its supermajority requirements.

Second, the Rules Committee can report a rule sending a measure to conference. On occasion, the Rules Committee will report a rule that not only specifies how a House measure will be debated and amended but also provides for an automatic "Senate hookup" following completion of floor action on the bill. A hookup provision permits a companion Senate-passed measure to be immediately called up and the House-passed version inserted after the Senate's bill number. Technically, the House and Senate have passed the same numbered measure (a requirement if a measure is sent to conference). The practical effect is that conference committee negotiations will involve two versions (the House's and Senate's) of the same bill.

Third, representatives can invoke House Rule XX to get a measure to conference. This rule permits legislation to reach conference by majority vote of the House if a member of the committee of jurisdiction, typically the chairman, is authorized by his panel to offer the motion to go to conference. Quite often a chairman will come to the floor armed with such authorization and alert the Speaker of this fact. Then, if a member objects to a unanimous consent request for a conference, the chairman will be immediately recognized by the Speaker to offer the Rule XX motion. (Bills that are multiply referred to several committees require all committees with a primary or initial claim on the legislation, and that have reported the bill, to agree to the Rule XX procedure.)

When the situation is reversed, and a Senate-passed bill is amended by the House and returned to the Senate, it is "held at the desk and almost always subsequently laid before the Senate by the Presiding Officer upon request or motion of a Senator [usually the manager of the bill.]"[16]

The House amendment or amendments may be dealt with in four ways by the Senate: (1) by adopting a motion to refer the amendment(s) to the appropriate standing committee, (2) by further amending the House amendments, (3) by agreeing to the House amendments (thus clearing the bill), or (4) by disagreeing to the House amendments, in which case a conference is requested by motion or unanimous consent.

Typically, the Senate gets to conference with the House by adopting this standard motion: "Mr. President, I move that the Senate insist on its amendments, request a conference with the House on the disagreeing votes thereon, and that the Chair be authorized to appoint conferees." This triple motion rolled into one—to insist (an alternative form is to "disagree to the House amendments" to the Senate-passed bill), to request, and to appoint—is rarely divided into discrete parts and voted upon separately, filibustered, or defeated. The normal routine for the Senate is to agree to the three-part motion by unanimous consent.

On the other hand, there have been a few recent instances where the Senate encountered extraordinary difficulty in proceeding to a conference with the House. Partisan and policy differences precipitated the difficulties. In 1992 the majority leader was forced to invoke cloture, which passed 85 to 6, to get a school-reform bill to conference. As Sen. Edward M. Kennedy, D-Mass., pointed out, the Senate had been trying for a week to go to conference on the bill, but some senators "have refused to give unanimous consent to permit the appointment of conferees."[17] The next year, after a senator objected to the majority leader's unanimous consent request to go to conference, the leader stated "this is the first time this year we have had a filibuster threatened on the naming of conferees after a bill has been passed by the Senate."[18]

Then, in 1994, something precedent-making happened: GOP senators opposed to sending a campaign finance bill to conference during the waning days of the 103d Congress launched filibusters against each part of the triple motion. "In the 210 years in the history of the United States Senate, never—until last week—has there been a series of filibusters on taking a bill to conference," stated Majority Leader George J. Mitchell, D-Maine.[19] With GOP expectations high for recapturing control of the Senate following the November 1994 elections, Republicans wanted to block action on this largely Democratic initiative.

Forcing the majority leader to file cloture motions on each part of the triple motion consumed time—a day to file the motion, another day to allow the petition to "ripen," and then the cloture vote on the third day—during a period when there were only a limited number of days left before the 103d Congress finally ended. The GOP senators opposed to the bill then used all thirty hours of debate provided during the post-cloture period, including talking through the night. As one account noted:

> Overnight, the Republicans worked like tag-team wrestlers. Lauch Faircloth of North Carolina spoke from 2 A.M. to 3 A.M.; Connie Mack of Florida from 3 A.M. to 4 A.M.; Hank Brown of Colorado from 4 A.M. to 5 A.M.; Judd Gregg of New Hampshire from 5 A.M. to 6 A.M., and so forth.[20]

The three-part filibuster prevented the campaign finance conference from ever formally convening, and the bill died with the end of the 103d Congress.

In sum, both chambers vote themselves into a state of disagreement before going to conference. Technically, each chamber goes to conference on one bill—an S- or HR-numbered measure. One house will often take the other's bill, HR 1234, for instance, strike everything after the enacting clause, and then insert its own alternative. The conference meets to resolve differences on one bill, but there are House and Senate versions of the measure.

SELECTING CONFEREES

The selection of conferees is governed in both chambers by rules and precedent. For each occasion on which a bill is sent to conference, the House

Speaker and the presiding officer of the Senate formally appoint the respective conferees. In practice, both chambers usually rely on the chairman and ranking minority member of the committee that originally considered and reported the bill to recommend the selections. Sometimes chairmen will delay in naming conferees to signal displeasure with the other body and to apply "leverage on the other body [and encourage it to] cave in on . . . key issues" even before a conference is formally convened.[21] Other factors, too, may slow the appointment of conferees.

The Speaker and the presiding officer typically appoint conferees from the list given them in advance by the committee leaders, who select members of their own committees. (The Speaker, after the original appointment, also has the authority to remove managers or name additional conferees.) A member of another committee may be appointed when he or she has special knowledge of the subject matter or if the bill is of particular interest to the member's state or district. (Or members may be invited to attend the bicameral meetings without formally being named conferees, because of their specialized knowledge.) When a bill has been referred to several committees (multiple referral), it is common to have conferees from all the committees that handled it. With the new system of "primary" referrals (see Chapter 4) that began with the 104th Congress, most House conferees are selected from the lead committee with other conferees named from the committees of secondary referral.

House and Senate leaders may get directly and aggressively involved in naming conferees on issues of fundamental importance. For example, in a virtually unprecedented decision, Speaker Gingrich named a Democratic member, Gary Condit of California, as a conferee on unfunded mandates legislation. Condit, who ranked tenth in seniority on the committee of jurisdiction (Government Reform and Oversight), supported GOP efforts to inhibit congressional passage of bills that impose financial costs on state governments. However, he could not persuade either the ranking Democrat on the Government Reform panel or Minority Leader Richard A. Gephardt, Mo., to appoint him as a conferee. Speaker Gingrich was amendable to the idea and appointed Condit to one of the designated GOP conferee slots. As a result, the House conference delegation was bipartisan: four Republicans and four Democrats. Condit, it is worth noting, belonged to a conservative Democratic group called "The Coalition," whose support Speaker Gingrich sought to help pass GOP legislation.[22] Gingrich also named another Democrat and Coalition member—Mike Parker of Mississippi—to serve on the concurrent budget resolution conference.

Seniority used to be a dominant criterion in the appointment of conferees. But in the wake of contemporary procedural reforms, junior members, especially those with particular expertise or interest in the legislation going to conference, are now often selected. (Gingrich, for instance, has named freshmen to conference delegations.) Seniority was set aside by the chairmen of

Congress's tax-writing committees when the landmark 1986 tax reform bill went to conference. House Ways and Means Chairman Dan Rostenkowski, D-Ill., bypassed seniority both to get conferees supportive of his views (thus maximizing the chairman's bargaining leverage) and also for partisan purposes. Speaker Thomas P. "Tip" O'Neill, Jr., D-Mass., informed Rostenkowski that he wanted Ways and Means member Gephardt (House minority leader in the 104th Congress) to be a conferee.

> "I want Gephardt on there," O'Neill said. Rep. Gephardt had little seniori-ty on the Ways and Means panel and had not been a major player in draft-ing the tax bill. But O'Neill knew that having Gephardt on the [conference] would highlight the Bradley-Gephardt [tax overhaul] bill and help focus attention on the Democrats' role in reform.[23]

Similarly, then ranking Finance member Russell Long set aside seniority to name Sen. Bill Bradley, D-N.J. (near the bottom in committee seniority on Finance but known as the godfather of tax reform) to the conference. (Party ratios on conference committees generally reflect the party membership in the House and Senate.)

The trend in recent years has been to increase the size of conference delegations. (Before, conference delegations typically ranged from five to twelve conferees from each chamber, but today big conferences are quite common.) Multiple committee consideration of megabills that cross-cut the jurisdiction of several panels is the driving force behind big conferences. Large conference delegations also affect the mechanics of conference decision making; they often divide into smaller groups called "subconferences."

The largest conference in congressional history involved the 1981 omnibus budget reconciliation bill. "Over 250 Senators and Congressmen met in 58 [subconferences] to consider nearly 300 issues" in disagreement, noted Senate Majority Leader Howard H. Baker, Jr., R-Tenn.[24] The use of subconferences enables bicameral negotiators to proceed on several fronts simultaneously and to expedite what is inherently (because of numbers) a more complex process. A Senate chairman described arrangements for the twenty-three House and Senate committees represented on an oversized trade conference.

> Today the chairmen and ranking members of the 23 committees conferring on the trade bill . . . met and established a conference structure designed to finish this massive conference [nearly 200 conferees from both chambers]. We established 17 subconferences and a procedure for coordinating the activities of the subconferences.[25]

To be sure, the nature of the issues in disagreement may account most for the length of conferences on megabills. Large conference delegations invariably require more time to iron out bicameral differences. The diversity of views that need to be harmonized affects the pace of deliberations. The issues in disagreement are likely to be contentious. Having numerous conferees also facilitates access to the negotiations by lawmakers who are not conferees, interest groups, and executive officials. (Many conferences reflect multilateral rather than bilateral negotiations, because scores of outside actors and interests can influence conference outcomes.) If large conferences become unwieldy even if they divide into subconferences, they often break down into smaller and smaller groups. This process was followed during a huge savings and loan conference, which embraced nearly one-quarter of the House including every member of the House Banking Committee. As one House conferee put it:

> One hundred and two conferees were appointed and no progress was made until the four principals [the House and Senate Banking chairmen and ranking minority members] went behind closed doors. And I'm not complaining. If [the House Banking chairman] had not reduced the conference from 102 members to four, we would still be there arguing over this bill. He should get an Oscar for his starring role in, "Honey, I shrunk the conference."[26]

It is worth noting that just as extensive negotiations typically character-ize conference deliberations, many committees and members, especially in the House, make elaborate efforts to be on the conference committee. Recent Speakers, including Thomas S. Foley, D-Wash., and Gingrich, have suggested that it is important to simplify the process of naming conferees. The concept of designating a primary committee when issues overlap several committees is likely to facilitate the simplification process.

The conferees from each house vote as a unit, with a majority vote decid-ing each issue. The House and Senate have, in effect, one vote each. Bargaining and compromises are enhanced by this feature of the conference process.

Rules and precedents require that a majority of conferees must have "generally supported" the bill. In 1960 Sen. Richard B. Russell, D-Ga. (1933–1971), expressed a view that is still strongly held by most members:

> When I go to a conference as a representative of the Senate, I represent the Senate viewpoint as vigorously as possible, even though it may not be in accord with the vote or votes I cast on the floor of the Senate. I conceive that to be the duty of the conferee.[27]

Selecting conferees according to this criterion is not always easy, particularly in the case of highly controversial bills that have passed one or the other chamber by narrow margins.

Usually, a member's vote on final passage is taken as evidence of an overall position on a measure for purposes of selection to a conference com-mittee. Yet a member who votes for the final version may have voted against critical amendments that were adopted during floor debate or for amend-ments intended to cripple the bill. House rules address this knotty issue by directing the Speaker to name no less than a majority of conferees who generally supported the House position "as determined by the Speaker."

In case of a conflict of interest or views, conferees are permitted to resign from conference committees. That step once was taken by Sen. Robert C. Byrd, D-W.Va. He explained:

> I was named as a Senate conferee. I do not feel—after thinking overnight about the matter—that I can conscientiously serve as a conferee on that amendment. Although there is no rule that would bind me to support the Senate position on the amendment, I would not wish to go to the conference and oppose the Senate position, because in so doing I would be putting myself and my will above the Senate and the majority will of the Senate.[28]

Senator Byrd's remarks illustrate another important point about conferees: the House or Senate may adopt motions instructing their conferees to sustain the majority position of the chamber on a particular amendment or provision (see Box 9-1). This places additional political and moral pressure on the conferees and normally hardens their position in conference committee bargaining. "We need to give the House conferees some backbone to stand up to the Senate on this issue," declared a House member in support of a motion to instruct conferees.[29] However, instructions adopted by either chamber are not binding. (The practice is more common in the House than the Senate, in part because it appears unseemly to instruct senators.) Conferees may disregard the instructions, particularly when they feel the need for room to maneuver or compromise. Of course, the full House and Senate still have an opportunity to accept or reject the conference committee report on the bill, and a new conference may be requested if either house feels that its conferees have grossly violated their instructions.

During the early 1990s, when Democrats still controlled the House, Republicans began to use the instruction motion to bring their issues before the chamber. In 1993 it was used eleven times; the following year, more than double that number. Further, instructions can be offered before, during, and even after the conference has reported its compromise product. Only one motion to instruct can be offered prior to the appointment of conferees, and this motion is reserved to the minority. If a conference cannot reach agreement within twenty calendar days, however, House rules permit lawmakers to offer (with one day's notice) an unlimited number of instruction motions. This factor sometimes influences when conferees are appointed.

In 1994 Speaker Foley delayed appointing conferees on a measure because he realized that House and Senate conferees were unlikely to resolve their differences within twenty days. He did not want Democrats to vote on numerous instruction motions addressing issues that could be used against his party colleagues during the November election. During a more-than-twenty-day crime conference, for example, Republicans offered "nine motions to instruct conferees on, among other things, provisions regarding

INSTRUCTION OF CONFEREES

Mr. ARCHER. Mr. Speaker, I ask unanimous consent to take from the Speaker's table the bill (H.R. 831) to amend the Internal Revenue Code of 1986 to permanently extend the deduction for the health insurance costs of self-employed individuals ... and for other purposes, with a Senate amendment thereto, disagree to the Senate amendment and agree to the conference asked by the Senate.

The SPEAKER pro tempore. Is there objection to the request of the gentleman from Texas?

PARLIAMENTARY INQUIRY

Mr. GIBBONS. Reserving the right to object, Mr. Speaker, I only reserve the right to object to propound a parliamentary inquiry.

The SPEAKER pro tempore (Mr. Ewing). The gentleman from Florida will state his parliamentary inquiry.

Mr. GIBBONS. Mr. Speaker, I have a motion to instruct conferees, and will I be recognized, if this unanimous consent request is agreed to, to then present my motion to instruct conferees?

The SPEAKER pro tempore. The gentleman is correct; yes, he will.

Mr. GIBBONS. Mr. Speaker, I do not object, and I withdraw my reservation of objection.

The SPEAKER pro tempore. Is there objection to the request of the gentleman from Texas?

There was no objection.

MOTION TO INSTRUCT OFFERED BY MR. GIBBONS

Mr. GIBBONS. Mr. Speaker, I offer a motion to instruct conferees.

The Clerk read as follows:

Mr. GIBBONS moves that the Managers on the part of the House at the conference on the disagreeing votes of the two Houses on the Senate amendment to the bill H.R. 831 be instructed to agree to the provisions contained in section 5 of the Senate amendment which change the tax treatment of U.S. citizens relinquishing their citizenship.

The SPEAKER pro tempore. Under the rule, the gentleman from Florida [Mr. GIBBONS] will be recognized for 30 minutes, and the gentleman from Texas [Mr. ARCHER] will be recognized for 30 minutes.

The Chair recognizes the gentleman from Florida [Mr. GIBBONS].

Source: Congressional Record, March 28, 1995, H3845. In both chambers, the motion to instruct at this stage is in order immediately after a house agrees to the conference but before it formally names the conferees.

BOX 9-1

`racial justice,' prison construction, and the death penalty."[30] (In the minority, Democrats, too, regularly offer instruction motions to make their substantive and political points.)

The House and Senate rarely reject the list of conferees designated by the Speaker or the presiding officer. The House requires unanimous consent to change the Speaker's choices. The Senate's rules provide several ways to overrule the presiding officer. Senators may offer substitute motions naming conferees other than those appointed by the presiding officer. Senators, as noted earlier, also are free to filibuster or threaten to filibuster the motion to appoint conferees in an effort to change the list. Finally, a senator may challenge the conferees at the time they actually are appointed. These procedures are hardly ever invoked, however.

Challenging the presiding officer's decision is tantamount to questioning the basic prerogative of committee leaders (often in consultation with party leaders) to select the conferees since the presiding officer only *formally* appoints the conference delegation. Challenging conferees is even more difficult in the House, where the Speaker not only endorses the nominees of the committee chairmen but also is the leader of the majority party.

Who gets named a conferee (or who is passed over) sometimes can be critical to conference outcomes. Rep. Bob Wise, D-W.Va., once persuaded the House to delete funding for a dam in his district. The Senate restored the funding and the matter went to conference. Wise was not selected as a conferee. West Virginia's Senator Byrd, a strong proponent of the dam, was a member of the conference. "I'll be a conferee," he said. "I'm not going to take anything lying down."[31] Byrd personally telephoned more than 120 House members to praise the dam. In the end, the two chambers voted to support Byrd's position rather than Representative Wise's. (Of course, there was no guarantee that a majority of the House conferees would have accepted Wise's position on the dam even if he had been named a conferee.)

BARGAINING IN CONFERENCE

Conferees usually convene in the Capitol building itself rather than in one of the Senate or House office buildings. Basically, there are no formal rules, such as quorum or proxy voting requirements, governing internal conference committee bargaining. The only formal stipulation is that the conferences must meet formally at least once in open session (unless they have taken appropriate steps to meet in secret). The lack of rules is deliberate to foster an informal give-and-take environment conducive to reaching bicameral compromises.

A conference chairman is selected in ad hoc fashion, as there are no congressional rules governing the procedure. On recurring measures that go to conference annually, such as appropriations and revenue bills, the chairmanship often rotates between the two houses. Despite the informal nature of the selection process, the chairman plays an important role in the conference process, arranging the time and place of meetings, the agenda of each session, and the order in which the disagreements are negotiated. The chairman sets the pace of conference bargaining, proposes compromises, and recommends tentative agreements.

Staff members, too, play an important role in conference deliberations. They draft compromise amendments, negotiate agreements, provide advice to members, and prepare the conference reports. Aides played a particularly important role during the complex conference on the 1981 omnibus reconciliation bill. According to the executive director of the House Budget Committee:

> The role of the staff has been not only to explore where there may be areas of agreement, but also to make the deal. How else are you going to get hundreds of issues resolved in a couple of weeks unless you give the staff some kind of license?[32]

Conference committee bargaining, like bargaining throughout the legislative process, is subject to outside pressure. Even before the mid-1970s "sunshine" rules that required open conference meetings, conferees were lobbied heavily by special interest groups, executive agency officials, and even the president on occasion. On important measures, the president or presidential aides "write letters to conferees; . . administration personnel show up at conference meetings; and the president freely threatens to use his veto unless conferees compromise."[33] The party leaders of Congress also get directly involved on some occasions—brokering compromises or urging on bicameral negotiations to meet a certain timetable.

BARGAINING OBJECTIVES. Three key, and conflicting, objectives underlie the bargaining and informal give-and-take at conference sessions: first, conferees want to sustain the position of their respective chambers on the bill; second, they want to achieve a result acceptable to a majority of each chamber's conferees; and third, they want to craft a compromise product that is acceptable to a majority of the membership of both chambers. Normally, bargaining and compromise are necessary to achieve the conferees' goals.

The conferees may be able to reach compromises quickly on their differences. For example, it often is relatively painless to split the difference on bills appropriating funds for federal programs. As one senator said, if the Senate bill contains a number, "say it is 200, and the House number is 100, if we cannot get together, we would say `Let's make it 150. Let's split the difference.'"[34] Or logrolling may occur, for instance with House conferees agreeing to certain Senate-passed provisions to gain leverage to win acceptance of House-passed provisions elsewhere in the bill that are strongly supported by members of their own chamber. Offers and counteroffers are part of the often exhausting conference process.

There are scores of other techniques and tactics that conferees employ during the bargaining process. For example, if conferees chair subcommittees they may convene hearings while the conference is under way to generate outside pressures on conference decision making. Senators may say that they cannot accept a House compromise offer, because it would generate a filibuster in the Senate; similarly, House conferees may say that a Senate offer is unacceptable because it violates House rules. One side may fight hard for a position on which it plans to yield, so the conferees can tell their parent chamber that they put up a good battle but the other side would not relent.

There is no question that the bargaining skills of individual conferees can produce favorable results for their chamber's positions. One House staff aide reflected upon the skill of certain conferees during marathon bargaining sessions: "You're talking about a poker game," he said. "There are people with an enormous degree of patience who will just wait and wait and wait until the other side either slips or collapses or falls asleep."[35]

One tactic sometimes used to break a deadlock is for the conferees of one chamber to threaten to break off negotiations and return to their chamber for instructions—thereby reinforcing their position when negotiations resume. A House member once described this ploy as follows:

> Last year there was a difference of about $400 million between the House and Senate versions of the foreign aid appropriations [bill]. The chairman of the House delegation in the conference took a very firm position that we had to end up with slightly less than 50 percent of the difference as a matter of prestige. It was the day we [Congress] were to adjourn. We were in conference until about 10:30 p.m., and the Senate [conferees] wouldn't give in. I think the difference between conferees was only five or ten million dollars. The Senate was fighting for its prestige, and our chairman for his. At 10:30 he started to close his book [staff papers prepared for the conference] and he got up saying he would get instructions from the House. All the rest of our [House] conferees did the same. That prospect was too much for the senators. They capitulated.[36]

This example illustrates a number of factors in conference bargaining: the importance of timing and leadership; the influence of certain members on the negotiations; the impact of threats to convene another series of protracted meetings after one side receives instructions; the role that fatigue can play in resolving hotly contested issues; and the political and professional investment that senators and representatives have in upholding the prestige of their respective chamber and committees.

PROCEDURAL LIMITS ON BARGAINING. During the bargaining process conferees are aware that their completed product may be subject to points of order in either chamber if it violates certain rules and precedents. Conferees may not go beyond the scope of the bills agreed to by the House and Senate. If, for example, the House authorizes $5 million for a program and the Senate authorizes $10 million, precedents state that an agreement must be sought within these high and low figures. Splitting the difference ($7.5 million in this case) is a common compromise device.

Equally important, conferees can consider only the matters in disagreement between the two chambers; they may not reconsider provisions agreed to in identical form by both houses.

Another result of the rule requiring conferees to stick to the specific matters committed to them is that they may not insert in the conference version of the bill provisions on new subjects—such as new programs or amendments to laws not already amended by the bill. This restriction, like many other rules and precedents, sometimes is waived or ignored and new material is in fact incorporated in the conference version.

The congressional budget process places further constraints on conferees. The House and Senate Budget committees monitor the recommendations of all committees, including those of conference committees, to see that they conform to overall budget guidelines.

"AMENDMENT IN THE NATURE OF A SUBSTITUTE." A conference committee has maximum flexibility when, during initial floor action, one of the houses takes a bill from the other and instead of passing it with amendments strikes out everything after the enacting clause and inserts a completely new version of the bill. This is an "amendment in the nature of a substitute." In effect, the House and Senate are dealing with only one amendment in disagreement. In such cases, the conference committee can consider the versions of both houses (in effect, two entirely separate bills) and actually draft a third version of the legislation, provided, of course, that it is a reasonable (that is, germane) modification of either the House or Senate version. The large majority of conferences are of this sort because there are fewer constraints and greater discretion for conferees in negotiating bicameral compromises that meld the two versions into a third.

APPROPRIATIONS CONFERENCES. It is worth noting that appropriations conferences always deal with discrete amendments in disagreement. (Broadly, it is reasonable to say there are two types of conferences: appropriations and all the others). By custom, the House initiates appropriations bills and the Senate adopts separate amendments to the various provisions in appropriations legislation. As a result, appropriations conferees enjoy less latitude in arriving at compromises because it is relatively easy to relate the House provisions to the corresponding Senate amendment (which is numbered for the convenience of everyone); also, the House-passed bill and Senate amendments thereto deal with specific amounts of money that are easy to compare.

On the other hand, an advantage enjoyed by the appropriators is that their conferences, unlike those dealing with one amendment in disagreement, can submit a "partial conference report" to their respective chambers.

Everything they agree upon is included in the partial conference report. Amendments on which they still disagree, either in a technical (they have violated scope, for example) or true (conflicts over policy) sense, are then submitted separately in each chamber without jeopardizing adoption of the partial report. Hence, appropriations conferences reflect the combination approach to resolving bicameral differences on bills: a partial conference report is agreed to first and then the House and Senate send amendments back and forth until they reach agreement.

If the two chambers cannot reconcile their differences on some of the amendments reported in disagreement, another conference may be reconvened. The same conferees are usually reappointed, but they are now limited to resolving the remaining amendments in dispute. They cannot reopen consideration of issues already agreed to by both houses in the partial conference report. Measures cannot be finally enacted by Congress and sent to the White House until both chambers reconcile all their differences, including each of the amendments reported in disagreement.

NONGERMANE SENATE AMENDMENTS. As discussed in Chapter 8, the Senate's practices and flexibility enable it to add amendments that are considered nongermane under House rules. House conferees traditionally opposed amendments of this kind, contending that they undercut the role of House committees and enabled important and controversial issues to be adopted with minimum consideration. House rules permit only one hour of debate on conference reports.

Frequently, the House was faced with a "take-it-or-leave-it" proposition—accept the nongermane Senate amendments or lose the bill in its entirety, including the House-passed provisions, since conference reports are not open to amendment. Members of the House expressed frustration over this recurring dilemma. "I have chafed for years," declared a Rules Committee chairman, "about the other body violating the rules of this House by placing entirely foreign, extraneous, and nongermane matters in House-passed bills."[37] As a result, the House finally acted against the Senate practice in the 1970s by taking several procedural steps including a 1972 rules change permitting separate votes on the nongermane portions of conference reports. The changes were designed to accommodate the Senate's right to offer nongermane amendments while protecting the procedural prerogatives of the House.

Any House member may make a point of order against a conference report when it is called up for final approval on the ground that it contains nongermane material. The member simply says, "Mr. Speaker, I make a point of order under House rule XXVIII that the last section of the conference report contains nongermane material." There are occasions, to be sure, when special rules are obtained from the Rules Committee to protect the conference report against such points of order. Assuming there is no rule, the Speaker sustains the point of order; the representative who raised the objection on the floor then moves to reject the nongermane conference matter. Forty minutes of debate, equally divided between those who support and those who oppose the motion, are permitted under this procedure, after which the House votes on the motion to reject. If it is adopted, the nongermane material is deleted, and the question before the House is disposition of the remaining conference material minus the nongermane portion. Defeat of the motion permits the House to keep the nongermane matter in the conference report.

The effect of these House procedural changes was to cut back somewhat the addition of nongermane Senate amendments to conference reports. House conferees now are able to request that certain Senate nongermane amendments be dropped in conference, as they would otherwise be subject to points of order in the House. And during Senate floor debate, senators sometimes urge their colleagues not to offer nongermane amendments because their adoption might jeopardize enactment of the legislation itself. As one senator emphasized, "We should not add [nongermane] amendments that might prevent . . . bills from getting through the House."[38]

FILING THE CONFERENCE REPORT

When at least a majority of the conferees from each chamber have reached agreement, they instruct committee staff aides to prepare a report explaining their conference decisions (see Figure 9-1 for an example of a conference report). A majority of the conferees from each house must sign the report in order for it to be sent back to the House and Senate.

> When conferences end, the conferees sometimes scatter quickly, forcing staff members clutching official signature pages to track down managers for both Houses in their offices or in elevators, hallways, or restaurants. The Parliamentarians will not accept photocopied signatures or other facsimiles.[39]

After the necessary signatures are obtained, the conference committee has concluded its work.

Conferees who oppose the final conference compromise may refuse to sign the report (unlike reports of standing committees of each chamber, conference committee reports are prohibited by precedent from containing minority or additional viewpoints).

Conference reports must be published in the *Congressional Record* before they are brought before the House or Senate for final action. House rules require a three-day layover for conference reports, which must be available to all members for reading at least two hours prior to floor consideration. Senate rules state that conference reports must be available on each senator's desk before they can be taken up on the floor. In each chamber, these rules can be set aside, usually by a rule from the House Rules Committee and by unanimous consent in the Senate.

104TH CONGRESS ⎱
  1st Session ⎰ HOUSE OF REPRESENTATIVES ⎰ REPORT
                                                 104-92

SELF-EMPLOYED HEALTH INSURANCE ACT

MARCH 29, 1995.—Ordered to be printed

Mr. ARCHER, from the committee of conference,
submitted the following

CONFERENCE REPORT

[To accompany H.R. 831]

The committee of conference on the disagreeing votes of the
two Houses on the amendment of the Senate to the bill (H.R. 831),
to amend the Internal Revenue Code of 1986 to permanently extend the deduction for the health insurance costs of self-employed
individuals, to repeal the provision permitting nonrecognition of
gain on sales and exchanges effectuating policies of the Federal
Communications Commission, and for other purposes, having met,
after full and free conference, have agreed to recommend and do
recommend to their respective Houses as follows:

That the House recede from its disagreement to the amendment of the Senate and agree to the same with an amendment as
follows:

In lieu of the matter proposed to be inserted by the Senate
amendment, insert the following:

***SECTION 1. PERMANENT EXTENSION AND INCREASE OF DEDUCTION
FOR HEALTH INSURANCE COSTS OF SELF-EMPLOYED IN-
DIVIDUALS.***

*(a) PERMANENT EXTENSION.—Subsection (l) of section 162 of the
Internal Revenue Code of 1986 (relating to special rules for health
insurance costs of self-employed individuals) is amended by striking
paragraph (6).*

*(b) INCREASE IN DEDUCTION.—Paragraph (1) of section 162(l) of
the Internal Revenue Code of 1986 is amended by striking "25 percent" and inserting "30 percent".*

(c) EFFECTIVE DATES.—

*(1) EXTENSION.—The amendment made by subsection (a)
shall apply to taxable years beginning after December 31, 1993.*

*(2) INCREASE.—The amendment made by subsection (b)
shall apply to taxable years beginning after December 31, 1994.*

99-006

FIGURE 9-1

In addition, conference reports must be accompanied by a joint explanatory statement that discusses specific changes made by conferees. This statement is prepared jointly by the conferees (and appropriate staff) of both houses so that the explanation of what was decided upon will not be different in the two houses and thus subject to differing interpretations.

Taking Final Floor Action on Conference Reports

Once the conference report is agreed to and filed with the House and Senate, it must be acted upon by both chambers before it is cleared for the president.

Customarily, the chamber that requests a conference acts last on the conference report, but only if the "papers" are in its possession. The papers are the official documents, such as the bill as originally passed by one chamber and the amendments added to it by the other chamber. Normally, the papers are held by the chamber that agreed to go to conference; that house then would be the first to consider the conference report. However, the papers may be transferred to the other chamber by agreement of the conference committee or one house may simply walk out with them.

There are occasions when policy outcomes are influenced by which chamber acts first or last on the conference report. A classic example occurred in 1979. House Government Operations Committee Chairman Jack Brooks, D-Texas, got the House to ask for a conference with the Senate on a measure creating the Department of Education (a target for abolition during the GOP-controlled 104th Congress). He wanted the House to act last on the conference report so that the parliamentary options available to the bill's opponents—who were more numerous in the House—would be limited.

The first chamber to act on a conference report has three options: adopt, reject, or recommit (return it to the conferees for further deliberation). When the first chamber to act adopts the conference report, however, this automatically dissolves the conference committee, and the other chamber is faced with a yes or no vote on the report. Chairman Brooks's strategy worked. After intense lobbying by the White House and various education groups, the House agreed to the conference report establishing the new department.

Conference reports are privileged and may be brought up at almost any time the House and Senate are in session. Typically, this is with the prior approval of the leadership. The senior majority and minority conferees from each house's delegation normally act as the floor managers of the conference version. Both chambers require conference reports to be accepted or rejected in their entirety. It is "take it or leave it" at this stage of the legislative process. In the case of conference reports on appropriations bills, as mentioned earlier, the House and Senate will first agree to a partial conference report and then the "amendments in disagreement" are submitted to each chamber individually and acted upon separately.

CALLING UP A CONFERENCE REPORT

CONFERENCE REPORT ON S. 1, UNFUNDED MANDATES REFORM ACT OF 1995

Mr. CLINGER. Mr. Speaker, I call up the conference report on the Senate bill (S. 1) to curb the practice of imposing unfunded Federal mandates on States and local governments; to strengthen the partnership between the Federal Government and State, local, and tribal governments; to end the imposition, in the absence of full consideration by Congress, of Federal mandates on State, local, and tribal governments without adequate funding, in a manner that may displace other essential governmental priorities; and to ensure that the Federal Government pays the costs incurred by those governments in complying with certain requirements under Federal statutes and regulations; and for other purposes.

The Clerk read the title of the Senate bill.

The SPEAKER pro tempore. Pursuant to the rule, the conference report is considered as having been read.

(For conference report and statement, see proceedings of the House of Monday, March 13, 1995, at page H3053.)

The SPEAKER pro tempore. The gentleman from Pennsylvania [Mr. CLINGER] will be recognized for 30 minutes and the gentleman from New York [Mr. TOWNS] will be recognized for 30 minutes.

The Chair recognizes the gentleman from Pennsylvania [Mr. CLINGER].

Source: Congressional Record, March 16, 1995, H3303.

BOX 9-2

In the Senate, conference reports are usually brought up by unanimous consent at a time agreed to by the party leaders and floor managers. Because conference reports are privileged, if any senator objects to the unanimous consent request the majority leader can offer a nondebatable motion to take up the conference report: "Mr. President, I move to proceed to the conference report to accompany S 1234." The conference report itself, however, can be filibustered. (Commonly, conference reports are debated under a time-limitation agreement.) Furthermore, before the vote actually occurs on the leader's motion to proceed, any senator can request that the entire conference report be read. The reading of reports is typically waived but any senator has the right to force that to be done. Sen. Jesse Helms, R-N.C., for instance, required the clerk to read a 231-page conference report on an education measure because he was unhappy that conferees had removed a school prayer provision. "For more than five hours," noted one report, "clerks took turns reading the dreary rhetoric."[40]

Senators, unlike representatives, can raise points of order against conference reports any time during their consideration on the floor. This seldom happens in large measure because the Senate accords wide latitude to its conferees in reaching agreements with the other body. On one occasion a senator claimed that a conference report was out of order because "it inserted new matter that had been approved at no time by either the Senate or the House." The presiding officer rejected the point of order, saying: "The conferees went to conference with a complete substitute, which gives them the maximum latitude allowable to conferees. The standard [applicable here] is that matter entirely irrelevant to the subject matter is not in order. That standard has not been breached."[41] Needless to say, "entirely relevant" is a standard broad enough to cover virtually any parliamentary transgressions of omission or commission.

In the House, there are three main routes to the floor for conference reports, which because of their privileged character can be called up at almost any time (see Box 9-2). Most conference reports are considered under the one-hour rule, with the time divided equally between the majority and minority floor managers. In 1985 the House changed its rules to permit one-third of the time to be assigned to a member who opposes the conference report if both the GOP and Democratic floor managers support it. Suspension of the rules is sometimes used to bring conference reports to the floor, but this is not a preferred procedure because it involves a severe requirement: a two-thirds rather than majority vote for adoption. Finally, a rule can be obtained from the Rules Committee. Conference managers often do this when they want to seek a waiver of the three-day layover requirement (either to meet deadlines or exploit favorable political circumstances) or to prevent points of order against the conference report for violations of scope or germaneness.

Conference reports are seldom rejected. As one noted congressional attorney explained:

> [The] chief reason conference reports pass is the basic rule that such reports must be adopted or rejected as a whole. No matter how distasteful any particular provision is, or how desirable some amendment would be, generally there is no way to amend a conference report; it can only be accepted or rejected as a whole. Thus, the question for Members is not how they feel about any particular provision, but how they feel about the bill as a whole, and they can always justify a vote for a conference report on the ground that they accepted the distasteful parts only to save the good ones.[42]

Outright rejection of a conference report kills the bill and may require a repetition of the entire legislative process. This becomes particularly significant in the weeks immediately before the final adjournment of a Congress, when members face the choice of (1) accepting the bill as is, (2) recommitting it to a conference committee, in all probability jeopardizing final approval, or (3) killing the bill, knowing there is no time to move a revised bill through Congress.

Once both houses approve the conference report, the papers are delivered to the house that originated the measure. A copy of the bill as finally agreed to by Congress is prepared by an enrolling clerk. The "enrolled bill" is signed by the Speaker and presiding officer of the Senate, or by other authorized officers, and sent to the president.

PRESIDENTIAL APPROVAL OR VETO

Under the Constitution (Article I, section 7), the president has a qualified veto power. The president's options are four. First, the president can sign measures into law. Second, the president can disapprove of legislative acts, subject to the ability of Congress during its two-year life to override the vetoes by a two-thirds vote of the members present and voting in each house. Once an enrolled bill is sent to the White House, the president has ten days, excluding Sundays, to sign or veto it. Third, if no action is taken within the ten-day period, and Congress is in session, the bill automatically becomes law without the president's signature. Fourth, if the final adjournment (called *sine die*) of a Congress takes place before the ten-day period ends preventing the return of a bill, and the president does not sign the measure, the legislation dies as a "pocket veto." Unlike a regular veto, there is no opportunity for Congress to override a pocket veto. Periodically, controversies erupt between Congress and the White House when presidents try to pocket veto measures when Congress is in recess.

Woodrow Wilson wrote that the president, in using the veto power, "acts not as the executive but as a third branch of the legislature."[43] The president can use the veto, or the threat of a veto, to advance legislative and political goals. Often, the threat of a veto is itself enough to persuade Congress to change its legislative course, because it is very difficult to attract the two-thirds vote in each house that is required to override presidential vetoes.

One senator put the matter vividly when he told the Senate why a specific compromise on a measure was agreed to by a conference committee. "There is another fundamental reason we did it—that is because we faced the veto, that great, big monster of a veto."[44]

Presidents veto measures for a variety of reasons: they consider them to be unconstitutional; they believe they encroach on the chief executive's powers and duties; or they hold them to represent ill-advised policies. When President Richard Nixon vetoed the 1973 War Powers Resolution (which Congress subsequently enacted by overriding his veto), he cited all three factors as the basis of his action. Vetoing bills because they cost too much is another favorite rationale of presidents.

Interestingly, President Bill Clinton chose not to exercise the veto during his first two years in office, although he threatened it on a health reform measure (which the 103d Congress never acted upon). Not since 1853, when Millard Fillmore was in the White House, had a president not vetoed "a single bill during an entire Congress."[45] (Clinton used his veto pen for the first time on June 7, 1995, when he rejected an appropriations bill sent to him by the GOP-controlled Congress.) The president, to be sure, receives recommendations from many quarters during the ten-day period allowed under the Constitution to decide whether to sign or veto legislation. He receives advice from the Office of Management and Budget (OMB), appropriate cabinet officers, White House aides, members of Congress, and scores of groups and officials. The OMB, for instance, once prepared a "menu" that contained an "A list" and a "B list." On the A list were provisions that merited a veto; on the B list were items that in some combination could trigger a veto.[46]

Presidents, including Clinton, contemplate how vetoes can be employed to advance their electoral and policy agenda, especially when their party does not control Congress. As national elections approach, for example, presidents will use the veto against an opposition Congress to show how their policies differ from the opposition's and thus highlight their fundamental beliefs to the electorate. This strategy can be called the "politics of differentiation" or "contrast politics." Presidents Richard Nixon and Ronald Reagan even vetoed bills on national television as a way to muster public support for their policies and to prevent an override by Congress. On the other hand, presidents can be foiled by adroit congressional maneuvering. Congress can attempt to force the president to approve unwanted measures by attaching them as "riders" to legislation the president regards as essential.

Speaker Gingrich, for instance, recognized that President Clinton opposed several of the measures associated with the Contract with America. To ward off threatened vetoes, Speaker Gingrich devised a hardball strategy: vetoed bills would be attached to "must-pass" legislation. "He will veto a number of things," said Gingrich, "and we'll put them all on the debt ceiling bill" or other essential measures.[47] If a bill raising the national debt ceiling is not passed, the national government will have no authority to borrow money to pay its fundamental obligations, thus disrupting and even forcing a shutdown of government operations. Faced with this specter, "he'll decide how big a crisis he wants," added the Speaker.

VETO OVERRIDE PROCEDURES

When the president vetoes a measure, the Constitution provides that "he shall return it with his objections to that House in which it shall have originated." Neither chamber is under any obligation to schedule an override attempt. Neither the Constitution nor Congress sets a deadline for overriding a veto. Party leaders may realize they have no chance to override and may

109 STAT. 154   **PUBLIC LAW 104–9—APR. 21, 1995**

Public Law 104–9
104th Congress

An Act

Apr. 21, 1995
[S. 178]

To amend the Commodity Exchange Act to extend the authorization for the
Commodity Futures Trading Commission, and for other purposes.

*Be it enacted by the Senate and House of Representatives of
the United States of America in Congress assembled,*

CFTC
Reauthorization
Act of 1995.
7 USC 1 note.

SECTION 1. SHORT TITLE.

This Act may be cited as the "CFTC Reauthorization Act of
1995"

SEC. 2. AUTHORIZATION OF APPROPRIATIONS.

Section 12(d) of the Commodity Exchange Act (7 U.S.C. 16(d))
is amended to read as follows:

"(d) There are authorized to be appropriated such sums as
are necessary to carry out this Act for each of fiscal years 1995
through 2000.".

Approved April 21, 1995.

LEGISLATIVE HISTORY—S. 178 (H.R. 618):

HOUSE REPORTS: No. 104–104 accompanying H.R. 618 (Comm. on Agriculture).
SENATE REPORTS: No. 104–7 (Comm. on Agriculture, Nutrition, and Forestry).
CONGRESSIONAL RECORD, Vol. 141 (1995):
        Feb. 10, considered and passed Senate.
        Apr. 6, considered and passed House.

○

FIGURE 9-2

not even attempt it. Because of popular support for the president's action, or for other reasons, the political environment may not be conducive to a successful override.

If an override attempt fails in one chamber, the process ends and the bill dies. If it succeeds, the measure is sent to the other chamber, where a second successful override vote makes it law. The Constitution requires roll-call votes on override attempts.

Whether signed by the president or passed over a veto, the bill now becomes a public law and is sent to the National Archives and Records Administration for deposit and publication in *Statutes at Large,* an annual volume that compiles all bills that have been passed by Congress and signed into law, or have become law through a veto override. (Figure 9-2 shows an example of a public law.)

SUMMARY

Both chambers must approve identical versions of a bill before it can be sent to the White House. Usually, House-Senate differences are resolved by informal consultation or by one house's acceptance of the other's bill, without further amendment. Major legislation, however, generally contains controversial provisions on which the House and Senate differ. Resolution of these differences is achieved through the conference committee process. A conference committee is appointed, composed of members selected from the standing committees that handled the legislation.

The conferees are expected to support their chamber's positions on the major issues in the bill regardless of their committees' or their personal views. Sometimes, their bargaining positions are reinforced by instructions from their parent chamber. Conference committee bargaining resembles bargaining elsewhere in the legislative process. It includes the traditional techniques of compromise and logrolling. Important, too, is knowledge by each chamber of what it wants and what the other body wants. There are, however, some restrictions that are unique to the conference process. Conferees are not allowed, for example, to go beyond the scope of the bills agreed to by their respective chambers.

Conference reports generally are accepted by both chambers for three important reasons: (1) members' disinclination to repeat the entire legislative process, (2) the bicameral agreements cannot be amended, and (3) they can be scheduled at times favorable to their passage. To be sure, conferees strive to produce conference agreements that will win approval in both chambers.

The final step of the legislative process is presidential action, but the president's veto power influences the entire legislative process. The extraordinary majority (two-thirds) required to override a veto forces Congress to consider the White House's position from the moment a bill is introduced until it is finally passed in identical form by both houses. Congress occasionally tries to achieve certain objectives by attaching riders opposed by the president to legislation that the administration regards as essential.

Enactment of legislation does not bring the legislative process to a close. Once a bill becomes law, it may set in motion a new federal program, redefine the role of executive branch agencies, or change the responsibilities of federal, state, and local governments in numerous program areas. All these new activities generated by a law become, in time, the subject of renewed congressional scrutiny as Congress endeavors to monitor the implementation and effects of the laws it passes. The next chapter turns to this broad area of congressional activity, usually termed "legislative oversight."

NOTES

1. Ada G. McCown, *The Congressional Conference Committee* (New York: Columbia University Press, 1927), 12. Also see Gilbert Steiner, *The Congressional Conference Committee, Seventieth to Eightieth Congresses* (Urbana: University of Illinois Press, 1951); and David J. Vogler, *The Third House, Conference Committees in the United States Congress* (Evanston, Ill.: Northwestern University Press, 1971); and Lawrence Longley and Walter Oleszek, *Bicameral Politics: Conference Committees in Congress* (New Haven, Conn.: Yale University Press, 1989).
2. Information compiled by Ilona Nickels, Government Division, Congressional Research Service, Library of Congress.
3. Roy Swanstrom, *The United States Senate, 1787–1801*, 87th Cong., 1st sess., S Doc 64 (Washington, D.C.: Government Printing Office, 1962), 232.
4. *Congressional Record*, February 20, 1986, S1463.
5. *Congressional Handbook*, U.S. Senate Edition, 1994. Prepared by the Senate Committee on Rules and Administrtion, III–30.
6. *Congressional Record*, March 21, 1974, 7589. See also the Record for April 10, 1974, 10569.
7. *Congressional Record*, December 20, 1982, S15757.
8. *National Journal*, May 22, 1976, 694.
9. Richard F. Fenno, Jr., *The Power of the Purse* (Boston: Little, Brown, 1966), 610.
10. *Congressional Record*, May 17, 1984, S5969.
11. John Ferejohn, "Who Wins in Conference Committee?" *Journal of Politics* (November 1975): 1033–1046; Walter J. Oleszek, "House-Senate Relationships: Comity and Conflict," *The Annals* (January 1974): 80–81.
12. Elizabeth Drew, *Senator* (New York: Simon & Schuster, 1979), 174.
13. *National Journal's CongressDaily/PM*, March 24, 1995, 4.
14. Andrew Taylor, "House's Magnum Opus Now Subject To Senate's Tender Mercies," *Congressional Quarterly Weekly Report*, April 1, 1995, 914.
15. George Hager and David S. Cloud, "Test For Divided Democrats: Forge a Budget Deal," *Congressional Quarterly Weekly Report*, June 26, 1993, 1633.
16. *Enactment of a Law*, 97th Cong., 2d sess., S Doc 97–20, 24.
17. *Congressional Record*, September 15, 1992, S13438.
18. *Congressional Record*, July 29, 1993, S8954.
19. Ceci Connolly, "Legislation Goes Overboard as Legislators Eye the Exits," *Congressional Quarterly Weekly Report*, October 1, 1994, 2755.
20. *New York Times*, September 24, 1994, 1, 8.
21. *Congressional Record*, July 18, 1985, H5937.

22. *Washington Times,* February 14, 1995, A11.
23. Jeffrey H. Birnbaum and Alan S. Murray, Showdown at Gucci Gulch (New York: Random House, 1987), 257.
24. *Congressional Record,* July 29, 1981, S8711.
25. *Congressional Record,* September 29, 1987, S13055.
26. *Congressional Record,* August 3, 1989, H5003.
27. *Congressional Record,* August 26, 1960, 17831.
28. *Congressional Record,* December 11, 1975, 39864.
29. *Congressional Record,* June 23, 1983, H4435.
30. *CQ's Congressional Monitor,* August 8, 1994, 3.
31. *Washington Post,* June 22, 1983, A2, and July 16, 1983, A23.
32. New York Times, July 23, 1981, A19. Also see Michael J. Malbin, *Unelected Representatives: Congressional Staff and the Future of Representative Government* (New York: Basic Books, 1980), chap. 5.
33. Ted Siff and Alan Weil, *Ruling Congress* (New York: Grossman, 1975), 184.
34. *Congressional Record,* August 1, 1984, S9605.
35. *CQ's Congressional Insight,* October 19, 1990, 1.
36. Quoted in Charles L. Clapp, *The Congressman* (Washington, D.C.: Brookings Institution, 1962), 249.
37. *Congressional Record,* September 15, 1970, 31842.
38. *Congressional Record,* October 1, 1976, 34518.
39. Martin Gold, et. al., *The Book on Congress,* Washington, D.C.: Big Eagle Publishing Co., 1992, 343.
40. *Washington Post,* March 24, 1994, A18.
41. *Congressional Record,* August 19, 1982, S10899.
42. Charles Tiefer, *Congressional Practice and Procedure* (New York: Greenwood Press, 1989), 818.
43. Woodrow Wilson, *Congressional Government* (Boston: Houghton Mifflin, 1885), 52. Later in his book, Wilson wrote that the "president is no greater than his prerogative of veto makes him; he is, in other words, powerful rather as a branch of the legislature than as the titular head of the Executive." 260.
44. *Congressional Record,* December 20, 1982, S15678.
45. *Congressional Quarterly Weekly Report,* December 31, 1994, 3623.
46. *Washington Post,* October 15, 1986, A7.
47. *Washington Times,* April 10, 1995, A13.

CHAPTER 10

Legislative Oversight

"We have a different oversight job than anyone else," Speaker Newt Gingrich, R-Ga., told an audience of House GOP staff aides attending an oversight seminar early in the 104th Congress. "We are trying to reinvent and replace, not just oversee."[1] With Republicans in charge of Congress for the first time in forty years, oversight took on new meaning. Where Democrats, who generally favor an activist national government, often conducted oversight to improve and enhance program efficiency and administration, Republicans appeared ready to use oversight to shrink the size and reach of the federal establishment, overhaul the regulatory process, and devolve power to the states.

There is a difference between making policy and conducting policy. The laws passed by Congress are often general guidelines, and sometimes their wording is deliberately vague. The implementation of legislation involves the drafting of administrative regulations by the executive agencies and day-to-day program management by agency officials. Agency regulations and rules are the subject of *legislative oversight*—the continuing review by Congress of how effectively the executive branch is carrying out congressional mandates. As one senator put it:

> I believe that oversight is one of the Congress's most important constitutional responsibilities. We must do more than write laws and decide policies. It is also our responsibility to perform the oversight necessary to insure that the administration enforces those laws as Congress intended.[2]

Congressional oversight looms large as a legislative activity during this decade of "reinventing," "deinventing," "reengineering," or "rethinking" the federal government's roles, because many Republicans and Democrats are trying to sort out which responsibilities are appropriate to the national government rather than to the states and localities. The Tenth Amendment to the Constitution ("The powers not delegated to the United States by the Constitution, nor prohibited by it to the states, are reserved to the states respectively, or to the people.") is being dusted off as lawmakers move to shift power back to the states and to limit Congress's ability to impose costly national mandates on states and localities. As one national columnist wrote about Speaker Gingrich's Contract with America:

> Whatever you think of it, the contract has triggered the most profound debatfe about government in decades. We are arguing about the worth of many federal programs, about federal-state relations, about the `safety net,' about the limits of regulation and about the fairness of our civil justice system.[3]

Congress, in short, will employ oversight both to take stock of national governmental responsibilities and to ensure that federal administrators carry out the policy intentions of legislators.

Constitutionally, oversight has been part of the principal functions of the legislative branch from the nation's very beginning. Congress's power of the purse, its authority to pass laws that create programs and agencies, and to investigate executive branch activities are among the explicit and implicit oversight functions rooted in the Constitution. The framers, according to historian Arthur M. Schlesinger, Jr., believed it unnecessary to mention the review function specifically in the Constitution. "[I]t was not considered necessary to make an explicit grant of such authority," wrote Schlesinger. "The power to make laws implied the power to see whether they were faithfully executed."[4] Or as Woodrow Wilson put it: "Quite as important as lawmaking is vigilant oversight of administration."[5]

Statutorally, Congress formalized its legislative oversight function in the Legislative Reorganization Act of 1946. That act required congressional committees to exercise "continuous watchfulness" of the agencies under their jurisdictions and implicitly divided oversight functions into three areas:

1. Authorizing committees (such as Agriculture, Banking, and Commerce) were required to review federal programs and agencies under their jurisdictions and propose legislation to remedy deficiencies they uncovered.
2. Fiscal oversight was assigned to the Appropriations committees of each chamber, which were to scrutinize agency spending.
3. Wide-ranging investigative responsibility was assigned to the House Government Reform and Oversight Committee and the Senate Governmental Affairs Committee to probe for inefficiency, waste, and corruption in the federal government. To some degree, all committees perform each type of oversight.

Each of the three overlapping types of oversight—legislative, fiscal, and investigative—aims to fulfill the basic goals or purposes of oversight, such as clarifying statutory intent, evaluating program administration and performance, eliminating waste, fraud, abuse, and red tape, reviewing whether programs have outlived their usefulness, and ensuring that programs and agencies are administered in a cost-effective manner.

FORMALIZING OVERSIGHT

The House and Senate have always had authority to investigate programs and agencies of the executive branch. The first congressional investigation in American history, in 1792, delved into the conduct of the government in the wars against the Indians. One of the broadest investigations was an 1861 inquiry into the conduct of the Civil War. Other notable probes have included investigations into the Crédit Mobilier in 1872-1873, the Money Trust in 1912, the Teapot Dome scandal in 1923, Stock Exchange operations in 1932-1934, and defense spending during World War II. A House and Senate select committee jointly investigated during the mid-1980s, with nationally televised hearings, the Iran-contra affair, which involved covert and deceptive operations by the National Security Council and others. Recently, House and Senate panels have conducted inquiries into the so-called Whitewater affair, which concerns President and Mrs. Clinton's involvement in a real estate venture (called the Whitewater Development Corporation) while he was governor of Arkansas.

The 1946 reorganization act stated Congress's intention to exercise its investigative authority primarily through standing committees rather than by means of specially created investigating committees. (In 1995 the House amended its rules to grant explicit authority to the Speaker to appoint "special ad hoc oversight committees for the purpose of reviewing specific matters within the jurisdiction of two or more standing committees.") The 1946 act provided for continuous review of programs instead of sporadic hearings whenever errors, malfeasance, or injustices surfaced. The "continuous watchfulness" precept of the act implied that Congress henceforth would participate actively in administrative decision making, in line with the observation that "administration of a statute is, properly speaking, an extension of the legislative process."[6]

During the 1970s, both houses amended their rules to grant additional oversight authority to the standing committees. The Legislative Reorganization Act of 1970 rephrased in more explicit language the oversight duties of the committees and required most House and Senate panels to issue biennial reports on their oversight activities. The House Committee Reform Amendments of 1974 assigned "special oversight" responsibilities to several standing committees; the Senate adopted the same approach, called "comprehensive policy oversight," when it adopted the Committee System Reorganization Amendments of 1977. Both special oversight and comprehensive policy oversight are akin to the broad review authority granted the House Government Reform and Oversight Committee and the Senate Governmental Affairs Committee.

Explained Sen. Adlai E. Stevenson III, D-Ill. (1970-1981), floor manager during Senate debate on the 1977 change:

> Standing committees are directed and permitted to undertake investigations and make recommendations in broad policy areas—for example, nutrition, aging, environmental protection, or consumer affairs—even though they lack legislative jurisdiction over some aspects of the subject. Such oversight authority involves subjects that generally cut across the jurisdictions of several committees. Presently, no single committee has a comprehensive overview of these policy areas. [This rule change] corrects that. It assigns certain committees the right to undertake comprehensive review of broad policy issues.[7]

RULES GOVERNING OVERSIGHT

Several other changes in House and Senate rules are worth noting.

- The House directed its committees to create oversight subcommittees, undertake futures research and forecasting, and review the impact of tax expenditures (credits, incentives, and the like) on matters that fall within their respective jurisdictions.[8]
- The Senate required each standing committee to include "regulatory impact statements" in committee reports accompanying the legislation it sends to the floor. One of these statements, for instance, might evaluate the amount of additional paperwork that would result from enactment of a proposed bill.
- Passage of the 1974 Congressional Budget and Impoundment Control Act strengthened Congress's review capabilities by directing the General Accounting Office (GAO)—a legislative support agency of Congress—to assist House and Senate committees in program evaluation and in the development of "methods for assessing and reporting actual program performance."

Most recently, at the start of the 104th Congress, the House adopted a new rule requiring all standing committees to prepare by February 15 of the first session of each Congress a comprehensive oversight plan. The objective was "to ensure that committees make a more concerted, coordinated and conscientious effort to develop meaningful oversight plans at the beginning of each Congress and to follow through on their implementation, with a view to examining the full range of laws under their jurisdiction over a period of five Congresses." [9]

Congress requires these additional oversight devices because it faces an executive establishment of massive size and diffuse direction. Even with the "increasing demand for balanced Federal budgets," wrote a scholar, "we should not deceive ourselves into thinking that the Federal Government of the future will be a shrinking violet, retreating to the modest proportions it had in George Washington's or Grover Cleveland's time."[10] Even in this era where the call for less government and the devolution of national power back to the states is especially strong, it is reasonable to suggest that the federal government will continue to exercise a large role in defense, international policy making, law enforcement, national economic management, environmental protection, health, and in numerous other areas.

Congress, in short, needs a variety of oversight techniques to hold agencies accountable so that if one technique proves to be ineffective, committees and members can employ others singly or in combination.

TECHNIQUES OF OVERSIGHT

The objectives of oversight often vary from committee to committee. The focus may be on promoting administrative efficiency and economy in government; protecting and supporting favored policies and programs; airing an administration's failures or wrongdoing, or its achievements; publicizing a particular member's or a committee's goals; reasserting congressional authority vis-á-vis the executive branch; or assuaging the interests of pressure groups.

The following sections describe several common methods by which Congress exercises its oversight responsibility.

HEARINGS AND INVESTIGATIONS

The traditional method of exercising congressional oversight is through committee hearings and investigations into executive branch operations. Legislators need to know how effectively federal programs are working and how well agency officials are responding to committee directives. And they want to know the scope and intensity of public support for government programs in order to assess the need for legislative changes.

For more than two hundred years, Congress has conducted investigations of varying types with varying results. There have been abuses and excesses, successes and accomplishments. The success or failure of investigating panels hinges on a variety of factors, such as the skill of its committee leaders, the degree of bipartisan cooperation among members, and good preparatory work by competent staff. Surprise and luck are also factors. As Sen. Daniel Inouye, D-Hawaii, the only veteran of both the Watergate and Iran-contra investigating committees, noted:

> I happened to be [at a hearing on Watergate] . . . and the question was asked by one of the Republican staffers [Fred Thompson, minority counsel and now a GOP senator from Tennessee] to one of the lesser witnesses [former Nixon White House aide Alexander P. Butterfield].

Thompson asked, "Mr. Butterfield, are you aware of any listening devices in the Oval Office of the President?" Butterfield responded, "I was aware of listening devices, yes sir."[11]

The rest, said Senator Inouye, was history.

Although excessive use of hearings and investigations can bog down governmental processes, judicious use of such tools helps to maintain a more responsive bureaucracy while supplying Congress with information needed to formulate new legislation.[12] Committee members and committee staffs may conduct oversight hearings around the country (field hearings) to watch public programs in operation and to take testimony from citizens and local officials.

LEGISLATIVE VETO

In 1932 Congress began to include provisions in statutes that, while delegating authority to the executive branch, reserved to Congress the right to approve or disapprove executive actions based on that authority within a specified time period. This power generally is referred to as the "legislative veto." This procedure allows one or both chambers, by majority vote, to veto certain executive branch initiatives, decisions, and regulations. (Sometimes Congress authorizes committees—the "committee veto"—to approve, or disapprove, executive actions. See Box 10-1 for an example.)

The legislative veto was an attractive oversight technique because, even though Congress seldom exercised its veto prerogative to overturn agency decisions, committees and members felt the practice kept federal administrators sensitive and responsive to congressional interests. It was employed in

---

A COMMITTEE VETO

"Funds in the Federal Buildings Fund made available for fiscal year 1995 for Federal Buildings Fund activities may be transferred between such activities only to the extent necesssary to meet program requirements. Any proposed transfers shall be approved in advance by the Committees on Appropriations of the House and Senate." Treasury-Postal Service Appropriations Act for 1995, 108 Stat. 1403, sec. 3 (1994).

Source: Cited in *Congressional Oversight Manual,* Congressional Research Service, February 1995, 71.

BOX 10-1

legislation dealing with both domestic and international issues. The legislative veto also served executive branch purposes by permitting agencies to make binding decisions without going through the lengthy lawmaking process. In short, this device served the interests of both the legislative and executive branches.

On June 23, 1983, however, the Supreme Court declared in a historic decision, *Immigration and Naturalization Service v. Chada*, that the legislative veto was unconstitutional. In a 7-2 vote, the Court majority said the device violated the separation of powers, the principle of bicameralism, and the presentation clause of the Constitution (legislation passed by both chambers must be presented to the president for his signature or veto). The decision, wrote Justice Byron R. White in a dissent, "strikes down in one fell swoop provisions in more laws enacted by Congress than the court has cumulatively invalidated in its entire history."

Despite the *Chadha* ruling, Congress still employs legislative and committee vetoes. As scholar Louis Fisher pointed out:

> In response to the Court's ruling, Congress repealed some legislative vetoes and replaced them with joint resolutions, which satisfy the [Supreme Court's] ruling because joint resolutions must pass both Houses and be presented to the President. However, Congress has also continued to enact legislative vetoes to handle certain situations. From June 23, 1983 to the end of the [.. 103d Congress, more than 200 legislative vetoes] (generally the committee-veto variety) have been enacted into law.[13]

In brief, both Congress and the executive branch have adapted to the post-*Chadha* era largely through informal accommodations and statutory adjustments. On the one hand, executive agencies want discretion and flexibility in running their programs; on the other hand, Congress is generally unwilling to grant open-ended authority to executive entities without strings attached. The legislative and committee vetoes remain important review devices, because both branches recognize their value.

AUTHORIZING PROCESS AS OVERSIGHT

Congress not only has the authority to create or abolish executive agencies and transfer functions between or among them; it also can enact "statutes authorizing the activities of the departments, prescribing their internal organization and regulating their procedures and work methods."[14] The authorization process, as noted in Chapter 3, is an important oversight tool. As a House member observed during debate on a bill to require annual congressional authorization of the Federal Communications Commission (FCC):

> Our subcommittee hearings disclosed that the FCC needs direction, needs guidance, needs legislation, and needs leadership from us in helping to establish program priorities. Regular oversight through the reauthorization

process, as all of us know in Congress, is necessary, and nothing brings everybody's attention to spending more forthrightly than when we go through the reauthorization process.[15]

Congress, too, may pass laws that "deauthorize" previously approved projects, such as the construction of dams.

Other significant issues, too, may be raised during the authorization process. In a political environment where "reining in government" is a popular refrain, lawmakers are asking such questions as: Can we live with a smaller agency? If a program or agency did not exist, would we create it today? Should agencies and cabinet departments be merged or consolidated? What fundamental changes need to be made in how various agencies operate? Can some governmental functions be contracted out to the private sector? In an era of downsizing, what and whose federal jobs should be cut?

APPROPRIATIONS PROCESS AS OVERSIGHT

Congress probably exercises its most effective oversight of agencies and programs through the appropriations process. By cutting off or reducing funds, Congress can abolish agencies or curtail programs. By increasing funds, it can build up neglected program areas. In either case, it has formidable power to shape ongoing public policies. The power is exercised mainly by the House and Senate Appropriations committees, particularly through their powerful subcommittees, whose budgetary recommendations are only infrequently changed by the full committee or by the House and Senate. (Recall that the chairs of the Appropriations subcommittees are called the "College of Cardinals.")[16]

The Appropriations committees define the precise purpose for which money may be spent, they adjust funding levels, and often they attach provisos prohibiting expenditures for certain purposes. In sum, the appropriations process as an oversight technique, notes congressional budget expert Allen Schick, is comparable to a Janus-like weapon: "The stick of spending reductions in case agencies cannot satisfactorily defend their budget requests and past performance, and the carrot of more money if agencies produce convincing success stories or the promise of future results."[17]

In a period of fundamental concern about the size and role of the national government, the appropriations process can be a potent tool for advancing party objectives (attaching riders, for instance, that inhibit implementation of federal regulations) and requiring federal officials to justify the continued existence of their programs and agencies. Appropriators, noted House Appropriations Committee Chairman Robert L. Livingston, R-La., are well positioned to take the lead in making spending cuts.

The unique thing about the appropriations process is that we don't have to go through the Senate and the President. All we have to do at the subcommittee level is put a zero next to a particular item. If the House sustains us, then it doesn't matter what the Senate or the President does. We may not have the power to spend money, but we do have the power to withhold it.[18]

Hard bargaining may be necessary, of course, if the Senate and president want a program or agency funded and the House does not.

INSPECTORS GENERAL

Congress, too, has created statutory offices of inspectors general (IGs) in more than sixty major federal agencies and departments. IGs are located in every cabinet department and major agency, including the Central Intelligence Agency. Granted wide latitude and independence by the Inspectors General Act of 1978, as amended in 1988, these officials conduct investigations and audits of their agencies to improve efficiency, end waste and fraud, and discourage mismanagement. IGs keep Congress fully and currently informed about federal activities, problems, and program performance through the issuance of periodic reports.

Lawmakers like the idea of having an independent office of inspector general located within an agency performing a "watchdog" role for the Congress. The House, in the wake of internal bank and post office scandals, created its own Office of Inspector General in 1992; the position was filled the next year. One function of the House's IG is to conduct periodic audits of the chamber's financial activities. (The House even contracted in 1995 with a major accounting firm—Price Waterhouse—to conduct a comprehensive auditing review of its spending practices.) Members have suggested, too, that the IG concept be extended to other entities, such as Congress's General Accounting Office, the executive office of the president, and the United Nations, and that IGs be granted broader program assessment responsibilities.[19]

NONSTATUTORY, INFORMAL CONTROLS

There are various informal ways in which Congress can influence federal administrators. Executive officials, conscious of Congress's power over the purse strings, are attuned to the nuances of congressional language in hearings, floor debate, committee reports, and conference reports. For example, in committee reports the verbs *expects, urges, recommends, desires,* and *feels* display in roughly descending order how obligatory a committee comment or viewpoint is intended to be.[20] If federal administrators believe congressional directives to be unwise, they are more likely to ask for informal consultation with members and committee staff than to seek new laws or resolutions. In fact, executive officials are in frequent contact with committee members and staff. Analyzing the House Appropriations Committee's relationship with the federal bureaucracy, one scholar wrote:

[There] is a continuing and sometimes almost daily pattern of contacts between the Committee on Appropriations and the executive branch. When Congress is not in session, communication continues by telephone or even, on occasion, by visits to the homes of members of the committee. If the full story were ever known, the record probably would disclose a complex network of relationships between members of the Committee on Appropriations and its staff and officials, particularly budget officers, in the executive branch.[21]

Such informal contacts enable committees to exercise policy influence in areas where statutory methods might be inappropriate or ineffective. Informed methods of program review are probably the most prevalent techniques of oversight.

Members sometimes urge their colleagues, administrative agencies, and the courts to exercise caution in interpreting committee reports, floor debate, and other nonstatutory devices as expressions of the intent of Congress. President Clinton's White House counsel, Abner J. Mikva (a former House member and federal judge), recounted a story about the pitfalls of interpreting a bill's legislative history:

I remember when Mo Udall was managing the strip-mining bill, and there had been all sorts of problems getting it through. They'd put together a very delicate coalition of support. One problem was whether the states or the feds would run the program. One member got up and asked, "Isn't it a fact that under this bill the states will continue to exercise sovereignty over strip mining?" And Mo replied, "You're absolutely right." A little later someone else got up and asked, "Now is it clear that the Federal Government will have the final say on strip mining?" And Mo replied, "You're absolutely right." Later, in the cloakroom, I said, "Mo, they can't both be right." And Mo said, "You're absolutely right."[22]

Interpreting "statutory intent" is a hot issue on the Supreme Court because legal phraseology is often ambiguous. Justice Antonin Scalia advocates rejection of conflicting and unvoted upon committee hearings, reports, or floor debate ("congressional history") in clarifying statutory language. Instead, judges should focus on the exact legal language and the statutory text in which it is embedded (the "plain meaning" principle) rather than picking and choosing among reports (written by unelected staff aides) or floor debate to clarify statutory construction. Justice Stephen G. Breyer, by contrast, recommends use of congressional history in statutory interpretation so judges can better understand the goals and objectives of the legislation signed into law.[23]

GENERAL ACCOUNTING OFFICE AUDITS

The General Accounting Office, created by the Budget and Accounting Act of 1921, conducts audits and investigations of executive agencies and programs at the request of committees and members of Congress to make sure that public funds are properly spent. With a staff of around forty-five hundred, GAO estimates that it has saved the taxpayers more than $107 billion over a five- year-period at the start of the 1990s.[24] The GAO is Congress's premier field investigator. The agency sends Congress more than a thousand reports annually addressing ways to root out waste and fraud in government programs and promote program performance. GAO studies frequently lead to the introduction of legislation, congressional hearings, or cost-saving administrative changes. The head of the GAO, the comptroller general, is appointed for a single fifteen-year term by the president, subject to the advice and consent of the Senate. The GAO works only for Congress.

REPORTING REQUIREMENTS

Numerous laws require executive agencies to submit periodic reports to Congress and its committees. As one scholar explained:

> Reporting requirements are provisions in law requiring the executive branch to submit specified information to Congress or committees of Congress. Their basic purpose is to provide data and analysis Congress needs to oversee the implementation of legislation and foreign policy by the executive branch.[25]

Some reports are of minimal value because they are couched in broad language that reveals little about program implementation; others may be more specific. Some reports address large policy issues and others, the narrow interests of a small number of lawmakers. (One way to resolve problems in the legislative process, such as mobilizing support from lawmakers who are uncertain about the worth of a program or activity, is to ask an agency for a report.) Generally, however, the report requirement encourages self-evaluation by the executive branch and promotes agency accountability to Congress. For example, when Congress became exasperated with Pentagon delays in implementing a major reorganization of defense offices, it directed the secretary of the army "to report every 30 days to Congress on what he is doing to put the legislation into place."[26]

Periodically, Congress and the executive branch recommend the elimination of certain reports (currently, there are more than thirty-five hundred reports submitted to Congress). For example, Sens. William S. Cohen, R-Maine, and Carl Levin, D-Mich., introduced the Federal Reports Elimination and Modification Act to discard more than two hundred unnecessary and obsolete statutory reporting requirements. This bill, said Senator Levin, "is designed to improve the efficiency of agency operations by eliminating unnecessary paperwork and staff time by consolidating the amount of information that flows from the agencies to Congress."[27] Vice President Al Gore's "Reinventing Government" initiative also recommended reductions in the number of congressionally mandated reports.[28]

Sometimes the impulse to eliminate reports reflects legislative and executive concern about "micromanagement" of executive affairs by legislative committees. The ever-present tension (even distrust) that suffuses legislative-executive relations explains to a large degree why Congress gets involved in managerial details and demands reports from federal entities. "We wrote an extraordinary amount of detail into the Clean Air Act," said one House member, "because we didn't trust the Environmental Protection Agency . . . with too much discretion."[29] The concern about reporting requirements involves seeking an appropriate weighing of Congress's need for information to conduct evaluations of agencies and programs against the imposition of burdensome, costly, or irrelevant obligations on executive entities.

AD HOC GROUPS

There are numerous informal groups and caucuses of Senate and House members that focus on specific issues and programs. (When the 104th Congress convened, the House adopted new rules that triggered the elimination, reorganization, privatization, or consolidation of various ad hoc groups.[30]) Examples of ad hoc groups are the "Star Wars" (a missile defense program) and Older Americans caucuses, bipartisan House groups that monitor federal programs and expenditures affecting these areas of concern.

Outside organizations also provide Congress with information on inadequacies in federal programs and other problems with the bureaucracy and exert pressure for more ambitious oversight. For instance, a private group called "Citizens Against Government Waste" annually identifies federal projects which, in their judgment, are a waste of taxpayers' dollars.[31] Many of these groups employ computers "to assist them in research on such subjects as the performance of Governmental agencies."[32] "Think tanks" such as the Brookings Institution and the Heritage Foundation periodically study public policy issues and advise members of Congress and others on how well federal agencies and programs are working.

The conservative-oriented Heritage Foundation, for example, prepared a report that "urged Congress to scuttle nine [of fourteen] Cabinet departments, overhaul Medicare, cut $152 billion in taxes and shift vast federal responsibilities to the states and private sector."[33] In short, Congress receives much free advice from various groups on how to cut back the size of government and, alternatively, how to make federal programs and departments work more effectively as well as which national activities might be candidates for expansion.

SENATE CONFIRMATION PROCESS

High-ranking public officials are chosen by the president "by and with the Advice and Consent of the Senate," in accord with the Constitution. In

THE ADVICE AND CONSENT ROLE OF THE SENATE

The Senate often finds itself in positions where it will draw criticism no matter what it does. If the Senate probes too long or too deeply into a nominee's past, it is accused of denying the president the assistance he needs when he needs it. If the Senate rushes through a nomination without adequate investigation, it is accused of "consent without advice" or "half rubber, half stamp." From years of experience, I would say that we do a president a disservice by rushing any nomination, unless there is a vacancy and a clear record as to the nominee's integrity, his capability, his honesty, his qualifications, and a clear need for speedy action. If damaging information about a nominee's past is to be found, or serious character flaws are to be uncovered, better that it become public knowledge before the individual is confirmed rather than afterwards. That is a hard message to deliver to any president of any party, but it is a lesson that has been learned too frequently to be forgotten. In sum, the Senate must continue to seriously and painstakingly perform its Constitutional responsibility of advising and consent on presidential nominations if we are to maintain the unique system of checks and balances that has brought our democratic form of government to its bicentennial.

Source: Remarks of Sen. Robert C. Byrd, D-W.Va., *Congressional Record,* July 29, 1987, S21504.

BOX 10-2

general, the Senate gives presidents wide latitude in selecting cabinet members (recall, however, that the Senate in 1989 rejected President George Bush's nominee for secretary of defense, former Texas GOP senator John G. Tower), but it closely scrutinizes judicial and diplomatic appointments as well as nominees to regulatory boards and commissions. Increasingly in recent years, Senate committees are probing the qualifications, independence, and policy predilections of presidential nominees, seeking information on everything from physical health to financial assets (see Box 10-2).

Nomination hearings establish a public record of the policy views of nominees, on which appointed officials can be called to account at a later time. "We all ask questions at confirmation hearings, hoping to obtain answers that affect actions," observed Senator Levin.[34] For example, committees try to extract pledges from nominees that they will testify at hearings when requested to do so, with the not-so-subtle threat that otherwise the appointee's name will not be sent to the full Senate for action. In brief, "our constitutional history and tradition," said former Senate Democratic leader and federal jurist George J. Mitchell, Maine, "firmly establish an active role for the Senate in evaluating the fitness of candidates to serve in high executive branch offices."[35]

PROGRAM EVALUATION

Program evaluation is an approach to oversight that uses social science and management methodology, such as surveys, cost-benefit analyses, and efficiency studies, to assess the effectiveness of ongoing programs. It is a special type of oversight that has been specifically provided for in many agency appropriations bills since the late 1960s and in the 1974 Congressional Budget and Impoundment Control Act. The studies often are carried out by the GAO and by the executive agencies themselves.[36] There is little question that the demand for program evaluation has increased in this era of fiscal constraint and antigovernment sentiment.

Despite the multiplicity of methods to evaluate programs, members sometimes disagree about how to measure performance. Several factors frequently account for their divergent perspectives. People may not agree on the objectives of certain programs. Public laws often are the products of conflicts and compromises, and when those compromises are translated into legislative language, ambiguity about program goals may be the result. Many policies have competing objectives or produce unintended results. In addition, there may be no agreement about criteria—quantitative or qualitative—for determining program success or failure. Finally, even if decision makers agree on objectives and criteria, they may interpret the assessments differently. Members and committees who support particular programs are unlikely to view with favor evaluations that recommend repeal or revision of those programs.

CASEWORK

Each senator's and representative's office handles thousands of requests each year from constituents seeking help in dealing with executive agencies. The requests range from inquiries about lost Social Security checks or delayed pension payments to disaster relief assistance and complicated tax appeals to the Internal Revenue Service. "Constituents perceive casework in nonpolitical terms," wrote two scholars. "They *expect* their representatives to provide [this service]."[37] As Rep. Lee H. Hamilton, D-Ind., wrote:

> Last year, one of my constituents, a 63-year old man who requires kidney dialysis, discovered that he would no longer be receiving Medicare because the Social Security Administration thought he was dead. Like residents of

Southern Indiana who have problems dealing with the federal bureaucracy, this man contacted my district office and asked for help. Without difficulty, he convinced my staff that he was indeed alive, and we in turn convinced the Social Security Administration to resume sending him benefits.[38]

Most congressional offices employ specialists, called *case workers,* to process these types of petitions. Depending on the importance or complexity of a case, a member himself may contact federal officials, bring up the matter in committee, or even discuss the case on the floor. Casework has the positive effect of bringing quirks in the administrative machinery to members' attention. And solutions to an individual constituent's problems can suggest legislative remedies on a broader scale.

SUPPORT-AGENCY STUDIES

Congress has three support agencies besides the GAO: the Congressional Research Service (CRS), the Office of Technology Assessment (OTA), and the Congressional Budget Office (CBO). Each prepares, or contracts for, reports or studies to assist committees and members in reviewing federal agency activities, expenditures, and performance. Their analyses frequently spark legislation to correct administrative shortcomings.

RESOLUTIONS OF INQUIRY

On infrequent occasions, a House member will introduce a privileged simple resolution, called a *resolution of inquiry,* which requests the president or the head of an executive department to furnish specific factual information and documentation to the House about the administration of a particular federal program. (A resolution of inquiry enjoys its privileged status only if it asks for facts and not opinion from the executive branch.) When Leon Panetta was a House member (he left to become Clinton's White House chief of staff), he explained some objectives of a resolution of inquiry: "It is a vehicle to provide information to Congress, to foster cooperation between the executive and legislative branches, and to encourage auditing of how taxpayers' dollars are spent."[39] House precedents state that the "effectiveness of such a resolution derives from comity between the branches of government rather than from any element of compulsion."[40]

In the mid-1990s the House considered a resolution of inquiry reported by the Banking Committee. It asked President Clinton, within fourteen legislative days, to provide the House with information on his use of the Exchange Stabilization Fund to shore up the value of Mexico's faltering currency. By a vote of 407 to 21, the House adopted the resolution of inquiry, which requested a large number of specific documents from the president, such as any document containing "a description of the activities of the central

bank of Mexico."[41] Interestingly, a member of the president's own party introduced this resolution of inquiry. Such resolutions "are usually introduced by
partisan opponents of the president, who seek to embarrass him by asking for
potentially damaging details about his actions."[42] The Clinton administration
provided the Banking Committee with, among other items, "more than 3,200
pages of unclassified documents and 475 pages of classified documents."[43]

OVERSIGHT BY INDIVIDUAL MEMBERS

Some members conduct their own personal reviews of agency activities
and develop ways to publicize what they believe to be examples of governmental waste and inefficiency. Former senator William Proxmire, D-Wis.
(1957-1989), periodically bestowed a "Golden Fleece Award" on agencies
that, in his estimation, wastefully spend tax dollars.[44] Former representative
Berkley W. Bedell, D-Iowa (1975-1987), utilized another technique.

> One of the practices I have is to make unannounced visits to the executive
> branch of the Government. I simply select an agency at random, open a
> door, walk in, and start asking questions of the people who work in that
> office.[45]

On occasion, individual members will conduct ad hoc field oversight
hearings of their own. These sessions usually permit constituents to testify
about their problems with federal agencies. They usually garner favorable
publicity for the legislator, too.

OVERSIGHT TRENDS

While some legislators and scholars complain that congressional oversight is irregular and shallow, recent Congresses in the judgment of several
scholars have seen a surge of legislative interest in the process.[46] As one spe-
cialist of the oversight process explained:

> There are no authoritative, comprehensive statistics on the amount of over-
> sight or even the number of specialized investigations throughout the his-
> tory of Congress. This absence is, in part, because scholars have disagreed
> as to what constitutes oversight and, therefore, how it should be measured.
> Nonetheless, some statistics . . . are available. . . . [T]hese data tend to show
> that Congress has increased its oversight activity over history, particularly
> over the past three decades.[47]

Today, there is considerable interest in oversight because a fundamental
topic of our national debate is the appropriate role of the national government. Citizens talk about devolving federal power to the states, but they also
appear to want a government that works more effectively than it does (see

FIGURE 10-1   Attitudes Toward Government

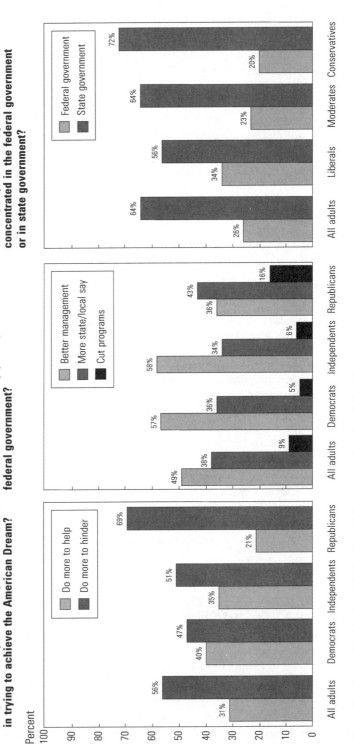

Do government policies help or hinder you in trying to achieve the American Dream?

What should be the top priority for the federal government?

Would you prefer most power to be concentrated in the federal government or in state government?

Source: Hart-Teeter poll for the Council for Excellence in Government, released April 18, 1995.

Figure 10-1). "The public has not really given up on government," noted a pollster. "When you give them a choice, they will tell you that we need better management, not necessarily smaller government or giving all the responsibility to the states."[48]

Among other factors that have contributed to heightened interest in oversight, several are worth noting. They include:

- Public dissatisfaction and concern about governmental waste, fraud, program performance, and escalating expenditures. "It's no accident that every elected president since Lyndon Johnson, with the singular exception of George Bush," wrote journalist Mark Shields, "has won when running against the allegedly rampant stupidity, corruption and/or venality in the federal government he sought to lead."[49]
- Congressional assertiveness and distrust of the executive branch in the wake of the Vietnam War, Watergate, and the Iran-contra affair, and revelations of abuses by agencies such as the CIA, FBI, and IRS.
- The influx of representatives and senators who are skeptical about the national government's ability to resolve public problems.
- The proliferation of federal programs and regulations that touch the lives of practically every citizen; citizens in turn inform their elected officials about problems they encounter with federal agencies.
- The proliferation of interest groups and trade associations that pressure Congress to examine governmental actions that affect their special interests.
- The availability of staff resources and procedural tools, which permits the new breed of aggressive legislators to scrutinize federal activities.
- Aggressive investigative reporting into executive activities by the print and broadcast media.

To be sure, the switch from the "politics of fiscal abundance" to the "politics of fiscal austerity" has compelled members and committees to scrutinize program activities and expenditures. No longer is the debate in the Capitol centered on program initiatives or increases; rather, the debate increasingly addresses whether the national government has the resources to meet new problems, which programs should be cut or kept at the same level, and what can be done to protect valuable programs in the face of competing priorities and limited resources.

"Divided government" (one party in control of the White House and the other, Congress) provides another incentive for oversight. Some opposition lawmakers, for example, may monitor and supervise agency activities and at the same time be on the lookout for ways to politically bash the administration. The Clinton White House complained about the oversight activities of House Republicans. "It seems a pattern has developed where [they] are requesting information not so they can evaluate the effectiveness of the government's performance," stated a White House spokesman, "but so that they can use [requests for information to] thwart those who might be carrying out the laws as they've been properly passed by Congress." In response, a House GOP spokesperson said: "For two years they've gotten nothing from Democratic oversight chairman but postcards from Hawaii saying, `Wish you were here.' "[50]

LACK OF CONSENSUS ON OVERSIGHT

Despite the demonstrable increase in legislative review activities and Congress's augmentation of its staff, budget, and authority for oversight, many members and commentators still fault congressional efforts in this area. Several factors help to explain why doing more in oversight is often perceived as doing less.

First, there is no clear consensus on how to measure oversight, quantitatively or qualitatively. As a result, members' anxiety about Congress's ability to review the massive federal establishment remains high. Quantitatively, no one really knows how much oversight Congress is doing. It is clear, however, that undercounting characterizes statistical analyses of oversight no matter what definition of that activity is employed. Part of the problem is that legislative review is a ubiquitous activity carried out by many entities: committees, members' offices, legislative support agencies, and committee and personal staff aides. Almost any committee hearing, for example, even ones ostensibly devoted to formulating new legislation, might devote considerable attention to reviewing past policy implementation. Qualitatively, there is little agreement among members on the criteria that can be used to evaluate effective oversight.

Second, some legislators hold oversight objectives that appear impossible to meet. They would like to see Congress conduct comprehensive reviews of the entire executive establishment. In brief, they find Congress's selective and unsystematic oversight approach generally unsatisfactory even when there is more of it. Oversight is too often a "guerrilla foray" rather than the continuous watchfulness contemplated by the 1946 Legislative Reorganization Act. Congress performs, two scholars noted, dual types of oversight: "fire-alarm" and "police-patrol." The former occurs when outside events or public interest trigger agency reviews; it is episodic and reactive in character. The latter is proactive and involves deliberate House and Senate decisions to oversee certain federal activities.[51]

Third, some committees and individual members believe they have minimal impact on the bureaucracy. Exclaimed former Speaker Jim Wright, D-Texas:

Fighting the red tape and the overregulation of bureaucratic rulemaking and guideline writing are among the most frustrating things any of us have had to do in Congress—it is almost like trying to fight a pillow. You can hit it—knock it over in the corner—and it just lies there and regroups. You feel sometimes as though you are trying to wrestle an octopus. No sooner do you get a hammerlock on one of his tentacles than the other seven are strangling you.[52]

To many new members of Congress, the best way to handle this problem is to eliminate or downsize agencies or programs.

Fourth, oversight may produce more questions than answers. Congress finds it easier "to highlight what's going wrong and to blame it on someone," declared a senator, "than to try to determine what to do about it."[53] In short, more oversight still can mean that agency problems remain uncorrected.

Fifth, Congress seeks to shape executive actions to its own objectives, not simply to conduct or commission neutral evaluation studies of departmental activities. Oversight is part of the legislative-executive tug-of-war that characterizes our separation of powers system. According to one commentator:

> The key issue for Congress is not administrative performance but its ability to influence agency actions. Congress is interested in performance, but it expresses this interest by seeking dominion over agencies. The distribution of political power between the legislative and executive branches, not simply [or even mainly] the quality of programs, is at stake.[54]

In brief, a fragmented and assertive Congress is sometimes frustrated by its inability to control and coordinate a fragmented and sophisticated bureaucracy. Congress, for instance, confronts the issue of whom to hold accountable for program performance when a contractor work force carries out the bulk of a department's activities with federal employees charged with supervising this "third party" or "shadow" group of employees. The Energy Department has twenty thousand federal employees but a contractor work force of one hundred forty thousand people.[55]

Despite Congress's general interest in oversight, there are other considerations that limit effective performance. Legislators still have too little time to devote to their myriad tasks, including oversight. Huge investments of time, energy, and staff assistance are required to ferret out administrative inadequacies. Some members are reluctant to support massive investigations that may only reveal that a program is working fairly well, not a determination that attracts much constituent attention or media coverage. "Effective oversight is, of necessity, time-consuming and tedious," said a Republican senator. "To do it right, you have to hear an endless stream of witnesses, review numerous records, and at the end of it you may find an agency was doing everything right. It is much more fun to create a new program."[56]

Many members accept the fact, however, that much of their effort in this area is unglamorous. The review process sometimes is inhibited by the alliances that develop between committees, agencies, and clientele groups. Examples of these "subgovernments" or "iron triangles," as the alliances often are called, are the axis of House and Senate Veterans' Affairs commitees, the Department of Veterans Affairs, and veterans' groups, and the combine of congressional Agriculture committees, the Department of Agriculture, and the various farm groups. Each component of such an alliance usually is supportive of the other. In such cases, committees find it harder to review agency programs critically absent a countervailing stimulus.

Finally, there are members and scholars who say that Congress lacks electoral, political, and institutional incentives for oversight. As a result, some legislators are "insufficiently dissatisfied with their oversight behavior to feel a strong enough stimulus to alter existing patterns."[57] On the other hand, given contemporary public support for the concept of governmental "shrinkage," any shortage of oversight incentives is likely to be offset by the public's reassessment of the core responsibilities of the national government.

SUMMARY

To some extent, Congress's interest in oversight has been a cyclical phenomenon. Historically, oversight often has been more intense when the executive and legislative branches of government have been controlled by different parties. Recent changes in rules and procedures, which have strengthened the tools of oversight, may have evened out the cyclical curve somewhat by encouraging regular monitoring of federal programs. In the current climate, these changes, combined with the influx of activist legislators, probably mean that for the next few years at least the legislative branch will actively assert policy and oversight initiatives, regardless of which party occupies the White House.

An important issue is how to balance Congress's oversight responsibilities with the executive's need for reasonable discretion in program administration. Too much congressional interference can wreak havoc with agency routines. On the other hand, for Congress to ignore its oversight role is tantamount to abandoning the implementation of the law—and its interpretation—to the whims of nonelected officials.

NOTES

1. T. R. Goldman, "A New Day Dawns for House Oversight," *Legal Times*, February 20, 1995, 20.
2. *Congressional Record*, June 21, 1983, S8822. For several studies on oversight, see Morris S. Ogul, *Congress Oversees the Bureaucracy* (Pittsburgh: University of Pittsburgh Press, 1976). Professor Ogul's book contains a lengthy bibliography on oversight. Frederick Kaiser, "Congressional Oversight of the Presidency," *The Annals*, September 1988, 75–89; Christopher Foreman, *Signals from the Hill: Congressional Oversight and Social Regulation* (New Haven, Conn.: Yale University Press, 1988); and Joel Aberbach, *Keeping a Watchful Eye: The Politics of Congressional Oversight* (Washington, D.C.: Brookings Institution, 1990).

3. Robert Samuelson, "Deliver Now, Pay Later," *Washington Post*, April 12, 1995, A25.
4. Arthur M. Schlesinger, Jr., and Roger Burns, eds., *Congress Investigates: A Documented History, 1792–1974*, vol. 1 (New York: Chelsea House, 1975), xix.
5. Woodrow Wilson, *Congressional Government*, Boston: Houghton Mifflin, 1885, 297.
6. David B. Truman, *The Governmental Process* (New York: Alfred Knopf, 1953), 439. The continuous-watchfulness provision was retitled legislative "review" in the Legislative Reorganization Act of 1970. That act also directed House and Senate committees to submit biennial reports on their oversight activities.
7. *Congressional Record*, February 1, 1977, 2897.
8. Michael J. Malbin, *Unelected Representatives* (New York: Basic Books, 1979). See Chapter 6 for an analysis of a House oversight subcommittee in action.
9. *Congressional Record*, January 4, 1995, H35.
10. *Workshop on Congressional Oversight and Investigations*, 96th Cong., 1st sess., H Doc 96–217, 198.
11. *Washington Post*, March 17, 1994, A15.
12. Congressional requests for executive agency information may be blocked by executive privilege. See Bernard Schwartz, "Executive Privilege and Congressional Investigatory Power," *California Law Review* (March 1959): 3–50; Raoul Berger, *Executive Privilege: A Constitutional Myth* (Cambridge, Mass.: Harvard University Press, 1974); *U.S. v. Nixon*, 418 U.S. 683 (1974); and "Symposium: United States v. Nixon," UCLA Law Review (October 1974): 1–40.
13. Louis Fisher, Government Division, Congressional Research Service, Library of Congress; information supplied to the author. See Louis Fisher, "The Legislative Veto Invalidation: It Survives," *Law and Contemporary Problems* (Autumn 1993): 273–292.
14. Joseph P. Harris, *Congressional Control of Administration* (Washington, D.C.: Brookings Institution, 1964), 284.
15. Quoted in Louis Fisher, "Annual Authorizations: Durable Roadblocks to Biennial Budgeting," *Public Budgeting and Finance* (Spring 1983): 38.
16. Richard Munson, *The Cardinals of Capitol Hill* (New York: Grove Press, 1993).
17. *Workshop on Congressional Oversight and Investigations*, 199.
18. Jeff Shear, "Pain's the Game," *National Journal*, January 14, 1995, 110.
19. See, for example, Jon Healey, "Taming the Watchdog: A New Role for Inspectors General?" *Congressional Quarterly Weekly Report*, October 23, 1993, 2871–2874; Paul Light, *Monitoring Government: Inspectors General and the Search for Accountability* (Washington, D.C.: Brookings Institution, 1993); *Congressional Record*, September 9, 1993, E2125, September 14, 1994, S12930 and March 30, 1995, S 4929.
20. Michael Kirst, *Government without Passing Laws* (Chapel Hill: University of North Carolina Press, 1969), 37. See also William Rhode, *Committee Clearance of Administrative Decisions* (East Lansing: Michigan State University Press, 1959).
21. Holbert N. Carroll, *The House of Representatives and Foreign Affairs*, rev. ed. (Boston: Little, Brown, 1966), 172. A good example of nonstatutory controls involves the reprogramming of funds within executive accounts. Reprogramming refers to the expenditure of funds for purposes not originally intended when Congress approved the department's budget. Agencies secure approval for reprogramming from the appropriate House and Senate committees.
22. *New York Times*, May 12, 1983, B8. See also *New York Times*, October 22, 1982, A16.
23. See, for example, Robert A. Katzmann, "Justice Breyer: A Rival for Scalia On the Hill's Intent," *Roll Call*, May 30, 1994, 5, 15. Cornell Clayton, "Separate Branches-Separate Politics: Judicial Enforcement of Congressional Intent," *Political Science Quarterly* (Winter 1994–1995), 843–872; Interbranch Relations, Hearings before the Joint Committee on the Organization of Congress, June 29, 1993; and Robert Pear,

"With Rights Act Comes Fight To Clarify Congress's Intent," *New York Times*, November 18, 1991, A1.

24. Robert Pear, "U.S. Watchdog Gets Criticism on Objectivity," *New York Times*, November 17, 1994, A1. See Marcia Gilbert, "Watchdog agency GAO in danger of losing its bit," *The Hill*, February 22, 1995, 1; Frederick C. Mosher, *The GAO: The Quest for Accountability in American Government* (Boulder, Colo.: Westview Press, 1979); and *The Roles, Mission and Operation of the U.S. General Accounting Office*, A report prepared by the National Academy of Public Administration for the Senate Committee on Governmental Affairs, S Print 103–87, 103d Cong., 2d sess., 1994, 106.

25. Ellen C. Collier, "Foreign Policy by Reporting Requirement," *Washington Quarterly* (Winter 1988): 75.

26. *New York Times*, December 31, 1987, A20.

27. *Congressional Record*, March 7, 1995, S3548.

28. *Report of the National Performance Review, From Red Tape to Results: Creating a Government That Works Better and Costs Less*, September 7, 1993, 34.

29. Phillip Davis, "After Losing Pollution Battle, White House Seizes Victory," May 23, 1992, 1440. See Pamela Fessler, "Complaints Are Stacking Up As Hill Piles on Reports," *Congressional Quarterly Weekly Report*, September 7, 1991, 2562–2566.

30. See Kenneth Cooper, "Cut Back, Caucuses Struggle to Go Forward," *Washington Post*, March 23, 1995, A25.

31. *National Journal CongressDaily/AM*, February 16, 1995, 4.

32. *New York Times*, August 26, 1983, A14.

33. Jonathan Peterson, "Think Tank Seeks to Cut Cabinet, Revamp Medicare," *Los Angeles Times*, April 18, 1995, A1.

34. *New York Times*, April 14, 1983, B10.

35. *Congressional Record*, February 4, 1992, S893.

36. See, for example, Robert T. Nakamura and Frank Smallwood, *The Politics of Policy Implementation* (New York: St. Martin's Press, 1980); George C. Edwards III, *Implementing Public Policy* (Washington, D.C.: CQ Press, 1980); and "Program Evaluation: Improving the Flow of Information to the Congress," General Accounting Office Report, GAO/PEMD-95-1, January 1995, 84.

37. John R. Johannes and John C. McAdams, "Entrepreneurs or Agent: Congressmen and the Distribution of Casework, 1977–1978," *Western Political Quarterly* (September 1987): 549.

38. Lee H. Hamilton, "Constituent Service and Representation," *The New Bureaucrat* (Summer 1992): 12.,

39. *Congressional Record*, July 14, 1988, E2397.

40. Richard S. Beth, "Resolutions of Inquiry in the House of Representatives: A Brief Description," Congressional Research Service Rept. 87–365, April 22, 1987, 2.

41. *Congressional Record*, March 1, 1995, H2444–H2458.

42. Benjamin Sheffner, "Rare Parliamentary Tactic Used to Hit Mexico Policy," *Roll Call*, March 2, 1995, 3.

43. Mike Mills, "Treasury Says Congress Given Papers on Mexico," *Washington Post*, April 7, 1995, F1.

44. See *Christian Science Monitor*, August 5, 1982, 1.

45. *Congressional Record*, June 8, 1983, H3737.

46. See especially Aberbach, *Keeping A Watchful Eye*.

47. *History of the United States House of Representatives, 1789–1994*, H Doc 103–324 (Washington, D.C.: Government Printing Office, 1994), 262. (Frederick Kaiser of the Congressional Research Service wrote this study's chapter on oversight.)

48. Guy Gugliotta, "Scaling Down the American Dream," *Washington Post*, April 19, 1995, A21.

49. Mark Shields, "Government Is Us," *Washington Post*, April 23, 1995, C7.
50. Paul Bedard, "White House fumes at probes," Washington Times, April 7, 1995, A1.
51. Matthew D. McCubbins and Thomas Schwartz, "Congressional Oversight Overlooked: Police Patrols versus Fire Alarms," *American Journal of Political Science* (February 1984): 165–179.
52. *Workshop on Congressional Oversight and Investigations*, 5.
53. Ibid., 144.
54. Allen Schick, "Politics through Law: Congressional Limitations on Executive Discretion," in *Both Ends of the Avenue*, ed. Anthony King (Washington, D.C.: American Enterprise Institute for Public Policy Research, 1983), 166.
55. Timothy Noah, "So What Do People at the Energy Department Do All Day Long?" *Wall Street Journal*, December 15, 1994, A8.
56. *Congress Speaks—A Survey of the 100th Congress* (Washington, D.C.: Center for Responsive Politics, 1988), 163.
57. Morris S. Ogul, "Congressional Oversight: Structures and Incentives," in *Congress Reconsidered*, 2d ed., ed. Lawrence C. Dodd and Bruce I. Oppenheimer (Washington, D.C.: CQ Press, 1981), 330.

CHAPTER 11

A Dynamic Process

Anyone who views lawmaking in Congress as a precise, neat process of drafting, debating, and approving legislation overlooks the dynamic forces at work on Capitol Hill. It is not a static institution.

For better or worse, the interests, pressures, perceptions, and prejudices of members of Congress change rather quickly, a result, in part, of the election cycle, but also of other conditions and influences. The demands made by the presidency and the courts, international events, lobbying groups, and media disclosures are some of the ever-present forces that affect lawmaking. Congress, in short, is an institution in which procedures reflect and, in turn, perpetuate the messiness, openness, pragmatism, compromise, and deliberateness so characteristic of much American policy making. As a House chairman said: "Legislation is like a chess game more than anything else. It is a seemingly endless series of moves, until ultimately somebody prevails through exhaustion, or brilliance, or because of overwhelming public sentiment for their side."[1]

Throughout this book, the point has been made that at every stage of the legislative process a new winning coalition must be formed to carry a policy recommendation up the next rung of the legislative ladder; otherwise, its progress is jeopardized. And that coalition is ever changing, as the forces that mold it change. While coalitions are formed to advance legislation, others may form to tear it down. If opponents fail in one session of Congress, they always can come back in the next to try again. In the judgment of Sen. Alan K. Simpson, R-Wyo.:

> In politics there are no right answers, only a continuing flow of compromises between groups resulting in a changing, cloudy, and ambiguous series of public decisions where appetite and ambition compete openly with knowledge and wisdom.[2]

Despite its built-in—and frequently beneficial—inefficiencies, Congress's policy-making role is firmly grounded in the Constitution. It is true that the preeminent place envisioned for Congress by the authors of the Constitution has been modified by the growth of executive power in the twentieth century. But it is equally true that the constitutional separation of powers has preserved for Congress an independent role that distinguishes it from legislative bodies in most other democracies.

Moreover, the power balance between Congress and the president is constantly in flux. During the mid-1990s, unlike earlier periods when presidential initiatives dominated the air waves, the nation's agenda was driven more from Congress than from the White House. This unusual circumstance occurred, said Speaker Newt Gingrich, R-Ga., the architect of this change, because the country wanted to debate the core proposals of the GOP's agenda (a smaller national government, tax cuts, overhaul of the welfare system, and so on) and the Clinton administration, "temporarily at least, lost its sense of authority with the country."[3]

This book has focused on congressional procedures and rules because the mechanics of legislating influence the policy-making process. Procedural details and nuances have a crucial policy impact, and it is impossible to understand why certain policies are adopted and others are not without an appreciation of the rules governing the process. Substance, in short, can be shaped through procedure. The Senate's tradition of lengthy debate is "a wonderful tool to ... expose legislation to more careful consideration," said Minority Leader Tom Daschle, D-S.D. "You hold many of these pieces of legislation up to the light of day and share the concerns you have with the American public, and that exposure is extremely powerful."[4]

Congress's informal procedures and practices are often as important as its formal rules. For instance, neither chamber needed rules changes to permit lawmaking through "packages." Instead, the recent practice of relying on megabills to process much of Congress's annual workload is a product in large measure of legislative-executive conflict and members' need for "political cover." For example, the GOP's Contract with America enabled lawmakers to say to lobbyists, "Gee, I'd like to be with you on that, but I've got to stick with the contract."[5]

Moreover, no rules changes mandated that legislators must play both the "inside" (maneuvering behind the scenes in Congress to pick up support for legislation) and the "outside" game (generating public support) to push controversial legislation through the House and Senate. "Being a good legislator means you have to do both," remarked House Democratic leader Richard A. Gephardt, Mo. "If you are going to pass important legislation, you have to both deal with Members and put together coalitions in the country."[6]

The "rules of the game" are as important in illuminating the outcomes of the legislative process as they are in comprehending who wins at any competition—the presidential nominating system, for example. To use the presidential election analogy, it is difficult to appreciate electoral strategy in the general campaign without understanding the Electoral College or the campaign finance rules. Similarly, one cannot comprehend the behavior of members of Congress as participants in policy formation without a knowledge of the formal and informal rules and procedures under which they operate.

The effect of congressional rules and practices on policy outcomes has been demonstrated repeatedly in these chapters. The requirement for an extraordinary majority of the Senate to invoke cloture gives to a well-organized minority the ability to block passage of legislation desired by a majority. Civil rights legislation, perhaps the classic case, was repeatedly delayed in the 1950s and 1960s by the opponents' use of the filibuster.

On the other hand, the rules themselves may change in response to events or policy goals. Some rules are modified or ignored, while new ones come out of struggles over a particular problem. Cloture was made somewhat easier in 1975 by changing the size of the Senate majority needed to invoke it from two-thirds of those voting to three-fifths of the entire membership. In reaction, a long-ignored procedure was revived: the post-cloture filibuster. That tactic in turn led to two other changes (in 1979 and 1986) to tighten up the cloture rule. The mixed results and unanticipated consequences that attend some procedural revisions can even disgruntle members who originally supported rules changes. It is no easy task, for instance, to simplify the complexities of the budget process when 535 lawmakers want a say in how and what fiscal decisions are made.

This book also has cited cases where an ostensibly procedural decision can be used to mask a policy objective. When members vote to table a bill, procedurally it appears as if they are merely postponing consideration of it. Nevertheless, such a procedure usually sidetracks the legislation permanently, while allowing members to say they did not take a position on the measure.

Important, too, are the differences in the way the two chambers operate. Each chamber functions under rules and procedures that reflect its basic constitutional design. A close examination of the differences as well as the similarities between the two bodies is indispensable to an accurate understanding of how Congress functions. Unlike those of the House, said Sen. Robert C. Byrd, D-W.Va., the rules in the Senate favor the minority: "They were meant to favor the minority to prevent the majority from running over the minority. That is why there is a Senate. That is why this Senate ought to remain a Senate and not become a second House of Representatives."[7]

The most significant and enduring feature of the rules is that they usually require bills to pass through a labyrinth of decision points before they can become law. It is generally more difficult to pass legislation than to defeat it. These multiple decision points make necessary a constant cycle of coalition building—by means of the various bargaining techniques—to move legislation past each potential roadblock. The shifting coalitions, as noted earlier, combine, dissolve, and recombine in response to the widely varying issues and needs of members. Unlike in the past, when a few "barons" dominated legislative policy making, today's Congress operates in an environment where scores of members have some—and often significant—bargaining power.

Coalition building is possible primarily for two reasons. First, members of Congress, who represent diverse constituencies, are not equally concerned about every item on the legislative agenda. Second, members pursue many objectives other than the enactment of legislation. They may seek reelection, election to higher office, appointment to prestigious committees, or simply personal conveniences such as additional staff or office space. These conditions create numerous opportunities for coalition building through the three types of bargaining discussed—logrolling, compromise, and the distribution of nonlegislative favors (primarily by the congressional leadership).

Another factor determining whether a series of majority coalitions can be built is the extent to which members are in general agreement that a law is required or inevitable on a particular subject. Members may have widely divergent views on the solution to the problem, but they usually will work to compromise their differences when dealing with "must" legislation.

Time influences the entire congressional process. As the two-year cycle of a Congress runs its course, every procedural device that can be employed has a policy consequence—either delaying or speeding up the processing of legislation. Frequently, as the countdown to final adjournment occurs, the bargaining process shifts into high gear. Bills that have been deadlocked for months are moved along swiftly as logrolling and compromises "save" bills in which members have a vested interest. Deadlines and threatened or actual procedural and policy crises frequently activate the lawmaking process. The "end game," in brief, is often played in the legislative process.

> [T]he sharpness of the ideological, political, and partisan divisions [in contemporary Congresses] means that most controversial areas come down to end games; every major player is willing to wait, believing that he, she, or they will have maximum leverage at the end of the tunnel.[8]

Stalled legislation dies if not enacted before Congress's final adjournment.

Congressional Procedures and the Policy Process has been revised during a period when Congress has undergone significant transformations. Some of the changes resulted from the GOP takeover of Congress after Republicans had been the "permanent" House minority for forty years; other changes have been under way for a number of years. Together, they have influenced the character of Congress's procedural and policy politics. Brief mention of five important developments discussed at various places earlier in this book will highlight some significant legislative trends.

CENTRALIZATION OF AUTHORITY IN THE SPEAKERSHIP. Recent Speakers of the House, such as Jim Wright, D-Texas (1987-1989) and Thomas S. Foley, D-Wash. (1989-1995), had an impressive array of formal and informal powers that strengthened their hand in the lawmaking process. None, however, compares with Speaker Newt Gingrich's exercise of authority in the House and in the larger political system. Strongly supported by party colleagues, especially junior Republicans, Gingrich took command of the House as few leaders before him. Not only did he set the nation's agenda when he assumed the speakership, functioning as the House's chief executive officer and relying on Majority Leader Dick Armey of Texas to be the chief operating officer on the House floor, he bypassed the custom of seniority to handpick loyalists to chair committees crucial to the success of the Republican agenda. As one congressional journalist put it:

> The notion of a House that's balkanized into legislative fiefdoms ... has become antiquated. Instead, the House is driven by a Speaker who wields extraordinary power and by rank-and-file Members who are intent on proving to a skeptical public that they can change how Washington works.[9]

In an unprecedented event and path-breaking expansion of the "bully-pulpit" role long associated with presidents, Speaker Gingrich even requested and received free, prime-viewing television time to address the nation following House action on the Contract with America.[10] (Congressional history, it is worth noting, demonstrates that centralized authority is not a permanent condition in either chamber; rather, the forces of centralization versus decentralization are constantly in play, and they regularly adjust and reconfigure in response to new conditions and circumstances.)

PROCEDURAL-POLICY CHOREOGRAPHY. Both congressional parties in each chamber regularly employ a mix of political strategies to win outside support for their fundamental procedural and policy priorities. They have "theme teams," "message boards," and scores of party sessions to coordinate and transmit a clear and coherent message to the public. A key objective is to frame the national debate in a way that mobilizes public support behind their congressional objectives and that rebuts attacks by opponents. Republicans, for instance, employed field hearings, polls, radio, television, publications, and focus groups to identify how they can advance their goal of cutting back on government without losing political support and credibility.

> The Republicans hope to employ all elements of the party, from congressional and state party officials to allied organizations at the grass roots, along with all the communications technology they can muster, to prevent President Clinton and the Democrats from taking control of the debate and successfully portraying Republicans as heartless opponents of worthy social programs.[11]

In short, making major policy innovations today usually requires combining various external campaigning techniques with internal procedural coordination (for example, who should offer amendments, when, how, and should they be agreed to, modified, or killed). The hoped-for-objective of these efforts: building extra political pressure to pass significant legislation.

CONGRESS AND THE INFORMATION AGE. Congress is fast becoming "wired" to a high-tech world that enables members, party leaders, and constituents to communicate politically to shape the legislative process. As Speaker Gingrich, a strong advocate for making Congress "state of the art" in communications technology, stated:

> We will change the rules of the House to require that all documents and conference reports and all committee reports be filed electronically as well as in writing and that they cannot be filed until they are available to any citizen who wants to pull them up simultaneously so that information is available to every citizen in the country at the same moment that it is available to the highest paid Washington lobbyist.[12]

Internally, communications technology can be employed, for example, to facilitate committee and floor scheduling, transmit messages over E-mail, or tap into various data bases available on the Internet. Externally, advances in electronic technology have added a plebiscitary quality to congressional policy making. Today, many citizens can engage in electronic advocacy and almost instantaneously make their preferences known to lawmakers. Talk radio, faxes, teleconferencing, interactive opinion polls, and computerized bulletin boards are examples of the techniques employed to advance or derail legislation. An important issue for Congress and constituents is how to achieve an effective balance between representative government (where policy often proceeds slowly) with participatory politics (where contradictory sentiments are often expressed by the electorate and fast action is an oft-cited objective).[13]

UNCONVENTIONAL LAWMAKING. Today, unconventional lawmaking is a growth industry on Capitol Hill. The textbook discussion of lawmaking—introduction, referral to committee, hearings and markup, floor deliberation and conference action, and presidential consideration—remains valid for much legislation. However, for many priority measures, unconventional lawmaking is the name of the game. Members find new uses for old rules, employ innovative devices, or bypass traditional procedures and processes altogether to achieve their political and policy objectives. In an era where it is hard to separate functions or concerns into categories such as national and state, public and private, or domestic and international, it should come as no surprise that new circumstances and conditions add unusual features to discussions of "normal" versus unconventional lawmaking.

A good example is the development of legislation by partisan or bipartisan task forces rather than by the committees. Speaker Gingrich, for instance, relies heavily on task forces, in part because it dilutes the power of committee chairmen and it gives him greater control over the legislative process. A top leadership aide noted that these Speaker-appointed task forces are an important "device for finessing some institutional obstacles to decisionmaking."[14] House Democrats, too, employ task forces to craft policy alternatives to legislation advocated by the majority Republicans. For example, a group within the Democratic Caucus—and not Ways and Means Democrats—drafted a comprehensive welfare substitute for the plan offered by House Republicans. Task forces are only one example of procedural innovation. Others include such techniques as budget summits, the use of reconciliation to initiate new programs, the creation of outside commissions to develop policy options, the preparation of party leadership substitutes for committee-reported recommendations, or using megabills as major policy-making instrumentalities.

RESURGENCE OF PARTISANSHIP. Parties have always been important in the modern Congress. Among other things, they organize the House and Senate and advocate subtantive agendas. Recent Congresses, as mentioned in Chapter 2, have witnessed heightened political rancor between the parties. Various scholars have highlighted the reasons for this development.[15] Although bitter partisanship has been more evident in the House (in part because of GOP members' frustration with their long minority status, ended by the November 1994 election) than the Senate, it surfaces in that chamber, too, even with its reputation for greater reciprocity among its smaller membership. "When I came to the Senate in 1959," said Senator Byrd, "there was partisanship. Everett Dirksen was a partisan. Mike Mansfield was a partisan. But they were not bitter partisans. We didn't have the negativism, the bitter partisanship that we have seen rule the Senate the last two years—and it is getting worse."[16]

Today, both parties employ public relations strategies and parliamentary techniques, and even use ethics as a political weapon, to frustrate lawmaking, vilify lawmakers, and embarrass the other party. Suffice it to say that when procedural rules are used solely for dilatory purposes, sometimes blocking legislation to affect election outcomes, it becomes that much harder for Congress to forge consensus on legislation.

And so the dynamic interplay between policy making and the rules continues. Precedents and practices are revised or abandoned and new ones established, often with great difficulty, in response to changing needs and pressures. "We always learn in this organization, even though we may think the rules are fixed and firm," observed Sen. Bob Packwood, R-Ore., "how the fertility of the minds of the Members manages to find ways to expand those rules."[17]

Congress's dynamism is ensured by the regular infusion of new members, changing events and conditions, and the fluctuating expectations of citizens. If Congress reduces or increases its lawmaking activity, it usually is not by accident but as a reaction to members' perceptions of what their constituents and the country want. For its part, the nation expects Congress to use its considerable powers and policy-making procedures to help resolve, or at least allay, the pressing issues facing the country as it approaches the fast-arriving twenty-first century.

NOTES

1. *Washington Post,* June 26, 1983, A14.
2. *Congressional Record,,* May 20, 1987, S6798.
3. David S. Cloud, "Speaker Wants His Platform To Rival the Presidency," *Congressional Quarterly Weekly Report,* February 4, 1995, 331.
4. *New York Times,* April 9, 1995, 18.
5. *Newsweek,* January 16, 1995, 18.
6. Richard Cohen, "Taking Advantage of Tax Reform Means Different Strokes for Different Folks," *National Journal,* June 22, 1985, 1459.
7. *Congressional Record,* February 23, 1988, S1124.
8. Norman Ornstein, "Let the End Games Begin," *Roll Call,* September 12, 1994, A–23.
9. Richard Cohen, "The Transformers," *National Journal,* March 4, 1995, 528–529.
10. *New York Times,* April 8, 1995, 1.
11. *Washington Post,* April 30, 1995, A19.
12. Albert Eisele, "The new electronic populism," *The Hill,* January 4, 1995, 20.
13. See, for example, Graeme Browning, "Zapping the Capitol," *National Journal,* October 22, 1994, 2446–2450, and Graeme Browning, "Return to Sender," *National Journal,* April 1, 1995, 794–798.
14. Deborah Kalb, "Government by task force: The Gingrich model," *The Hill,* February 22, 1995, 3.
15. See, for example, David W. Rohde, *Parties and Leaders in the Postreform House,* Chicago: University of Chicago Press, 1991.
16. *Los Angeles Times,* January 30, 1995, A12.
17. *Congressional Record,* February 26, 1988, S1521.

Glossary of Congressional Terms

ACT. The term for legislation once it has passed both houses of Congress and has been signed by the president or passed over his veto, thus becoming law. Also used in parliamentary terminology for a bill that has been passed by one house and engrossed. (See LAW, ENGROSSED BILL.)

ADJOURNMENT SINE DIE. Adjournment without definitely fixing a day for reconvening; literally "adjournment without a day." Usually used to connote the final adjournment of a session of Congress. A session can continue until noon, January 3, of the following year, when, under the Twentieth Amendment to the Constitution, it automatically terminates. Both houses must agree to a concurrent resolution for either house to adjourn for more than three days.

ADJOURNMENT TO A DAY CERTAIN. Adjournment under a motion or resolution that fixes the next time of meeting. Under the Constitution, neither house can adjourn for more than three days without the concurrence of the other. A session of Congress is not ended by adjournment to a day certain.

AMENDMENT. A proposal of a member of Congress to alter the language, provisions, or stipulations in a bill or in another amendment. An amendment usually is printed, debated, and voted upon in the same manner as a bill.

AMENDMENT IN THE NATURE OF A SUBSTITUTE. Usually an amendment that seeks to replace the entire text of a bill. Passage of this type of amendment strikes out everything after the enacting clause and inserts a new version of the bill. An amendment in the nature of a substitute also can refer to an amendment that replaces a large portion of the text of a bill.

APPEAL. A member's challenge of a ruling or decision made by the presiding officer of the chamber. In the Senate, the senator appeals to members of the chamber to override the decision. If carried by a majority vote, the appeal nullifies the chair's ruling. In the House, the decision of the Speaker traditionally has been final; seldom are there appeals to the members to reverse the Speaker's stand. To appeal a ruling is considered an attack on the Speaker.

APPROPRIATIONS BILL. A bill that gives legal authority to spend or obligate money from the Treasury. The Constitution disallows money to be drawn from the Treasury "but in Consequence of Appropriations made by Law."

An appropriations bill usually provides the actual monies approved by authorization bills, but not necessarily the full amount permissible under the authorization measures. By congressional custom, an appropriations bill originates in the House, and it is not supposed to be considered by the full House or Senate until the related authorization measure is enacted. In addition to general appropriations bills, there are two specialized types. (See CONTINUING RESOLUTION, SUPPLEMENTAL APPROPRIATIONS BILL.)

AUTHORIZATION BILL. Basic, substantive legislation that establishes or continues the legal operation of a federal program or agency, either indefinitely or for a specific period of time, or which sanctions a particular type of obligation or expenditure. An authorization normally is a prerequisite for an appropriation or other kind of budget authority. Under the rules of both the House and Senate, the appropriation for a program or agency may not be considered until its authorization has been considered. An authorization also may limit the amount of budget authority to be provided or may authorize the appropriation of "such sums as may be necessary."

BILLS. Most legislative proposals before Congress are in the form of bills and are designated by HR in the House of Representatives or S in the Senate, according to the house in which they originate, and by a number assigned in the order in which they are introduced during the two-year period of a congressional term. "Public bills" deal with general questions and become public laws if approved by Congress and signed by the president. "Private bills" deal with individual matters such as claims against the government, immigration and naturalization cases, land titles, etc., and become private laws if approved and signed. (See also CONCURRENT RESOLUTION, JOINT RESOLUTION, RESOLUTION.)

BILLS INTRODUCED. In both the House and the Senate, any number of members may join in introducing a single bill or resolution. The first member listed is the sponsor of the bill, and all members' names following the sponsor's are the bill's cosponsors. Many bills are committee bills and are introduced under the name of the chairman of the committee or subcommittee. All appropriations bills fall into this category. A committee frequently holds hearings on a number of related bills and may agree to one of them or to an entirely new bill. When introduced, a bill is referred to the committee or committees that have jurisdiction over the subject with which the bill is concerned. Under the standing rules of the House and Senate, bills are referred by the Speaker in the House and by the presiding officer in the Senate. In practice, the House and Senate parliamentarians act for these officials and refer the vast majority of bills. (See also CLEAN BILL, REPORT.)

BUDGET AUTHORITY. Authority to enter into obligations that will result in immediate or future outlays involving federal funds. The basic forms of budget authority are appropriations, contract authority, and borrowing authority. Budget authority may be classified by (1) the period of availability (one-year, multiple-year, or without a time limitation), (2) the timing of congressional action (current or permanent), or (3) the manner of determining the amount available (definite or indefinite).

CALENDAR. An agenda or list of business awaiting possible action by each chamber. The House uses five legislative calendars. (See CORRECTIONS, DISCHARGE, HOUSE, PRIVATE, AND UNION CALENDARS.)

In the Senate, all legislative matters reported from committee go on one calendar. They are listed there in the order in which committees report them, or the Senate places them on the calendar, but may be called up out of order by the majority leader, either by obtaining unanimous consent of the Senate or by a motion to call up a bill. The Senate uses one nonlegislative calendar; this is used for treaties and nominations. (See EXECUTIVE CALENDAR.)

CALENDAR WEDNESDAY. In the House, committees, on Wednesdays, may be called in the order in which they appear in Rule X of the House, for the purpose of bringing up any bills from either the House or the Union Calendar, except bills that are privileged. General debate is limited to two hours. Bills called up from the Union Calendar are considered in Committee of the Whole. Calendar Wednesday is not observed during the last two weeks of a session and may be dispensed with at other times by a two-thirds vote. This procedure is rarely used and routinely is dispensed with by unanimous consent.

CALL OF THE CALENDAR. Senate bills that are not brought up for debate by a motion, unanimous consent, or a unanimous consent agreement are brought before the Senate for action when the calendar listing them is "called." Bills must be called in the order listed. Measures considered by this method usually are noncontroversial, and debate is limited to a total of five minutes for each senator on the bill and any amendments proposed to it.

CLEAN BILL. Frequently after a committee has finished a major revision of a bill, one of the committee members, usually the chairman, will assemble the changes and what is left of the original bill into a new measure and introduce it as a "clean bill." The revised measure, which is given a new number, then is referred back to the committee, which reports it to the floor for consideration. This often is a timesaver, as committee-recommended changes in a clean bill do not have to be considered and voted on by the chamber. Reporting a clean bill also protects committee amendments that might be subject to points of order concerning germaneness.

CLOTURE. The process by which a filibuster can be ended in the Senate other than by unanimous consent. A motion for cloture can apply to any measure before the Senate, including a proposal to change the chamber's rules. A cloture motion requires the signatures of sixteen senators to be introduced, and to end a filibuster the cloture motion must obtain the votes of three-fifths of the entire Senate membership (sixty if there are no vacancies), except that to end a filibuster against a proposal to amend the standing rules of the Senate a two-thirds vote of senators present and voting is required. The cloture request is put to a roll-call vote one hour after the Senate meets on the second day following introduction of the motion. If approved, cloture limits each senator to one hour of debate. The bill or amendment in question comes to a final vote after thirty hours of consideration (including debate time and the time it takes to conduct roll calls, quorum calls, and other procedural motions). (See FILIBUSTER.)

COMMITTEE. A division of the House or Senate that prepares legislation for action by the parent chamber or makes investigations as directed by the parent chamber. Most standing committees are divided into subcommittees, which study legislation, hold hearings, and report bills, with or without amendments, to the full committee. Only the full committee can report legislation to the House or Senate.

COMMITTEE OF THE WHOLE. The working title of what is formally "The Committee of the Whole House [of Representatives] on the State of the Union." The membership is comprised of all House members sitting as a committee. Any one hundred members who are present on the floor of the chamber comprise a quorum of the committee. Any legislation, however, must first have passed through the regular legislative committee or the Appropriations Committee and have been placed on the calendar before it can be heard by the Committee of the Whole. Technically, the Committee of the Whole considers only bills directly or indirectly appropriating money, authorizing appropriations, or involving taxes or charges on the public. Because the Committee of the Whole need number only one hundred representatives, a quorum is more readily attained, and legislative business is expedited. Before 1971, members' positions were not individually recorded on votes taken in Committee of the Whole.

When the full House resolves itself into the Committee of the Whole, it supplants the Speaker with a "chairman." A measure is debated and amendments may be proposed, with votes on amendments as needed. When the committee completes its work on the measure, it dissolves itself by "rising." The Speaker returns, and the chairman of the Committee of the Whole reports to the House that the committee's work has been completed. At this time members may demand a roll-call vote on any amendment adopted in the Committee of the Whole. The final vote is on passage of the legislation.

CONCURRENT RESOLUTION. A concurrent resolution, designated H Con Res or S Con Res, must be adopted by both houses, but it is not sent to the president for his signature and therefore does not have the force of law. A concurrent resolution, for example, is used to fix the time for adjournment of a Congress. It also is used as the vehicle for expressing the sense of Congress on various foreign policy and domestic issues, and it serves as the vehicle for coordinated decisions on the federal budget under the 1974 Congressional Budget and Impoundment Control Act. (See also BILLS, JOINT RESOLUTION, RESOLUTION.)

CONFERENCE. A meeting between representatives of the House and the Senate to reconcile differences when each chamber passes dissimilar versions of the same bill. Members of the conference committee are appointed formally by the Speaker and the presiding officer of the Senate and are called "managers" for their respective chambers.

A majority of the managers for each house must reach agreement on the provisions of the bill (usually a compromise between the versions of the two chambers) before it can be considered by either chamber in the form of a "conference report." When the conference report goes to the floor, it cannot be amended, and, if it is not approved by both chambers, the bill may go back to conference or a new conference may be convened. Informal practices largely govern the conduct of conference committees.

Bills that are passed by both houses with only minor differences need not be sent to conference. Either chamber may "concur" in the other's amendments, completing action on the legislation. Sometimes leaders of the committees of jurisdiction work out an informal compromise instead of having a formal conference.

CONTINUING RESOLUTION. A joint resolution drafted by Congress that continues appropriations for specific ongoing activities of a government department or departments when a fiscal year begins and Congress has not yet enacted all of the regular appropriations bills for that year. The continuing resolution usually specifies a maximum rate at which the agency may incur obligations. This usually is based on the rate for the previous year, the president's budget request, or an appropriation bill for that year passed by either or both houses of Congress, but not cleared.

CORRECTIONS CALENDAR. A House Calendar, established in 1995, to which relatively noncontroversial legislation is assigned. To be eligible for placement on the Corrections Calendar, measures must have been favorably reported from committees and assigned to either the House or Union calendars. The Corrections Calendar is in order, at the Speaker's discretion, on the second and fourth Tuesdays ("Correction Days") of each month. Debate on bills correcting overly burdensome, arbitrary, or costly laws and regulations is limited to one hour. Further, no amendments are permitted (unless offered by the chairman of the primary committee of jurisdiction) and a three-fifths vote is required to pass correction bills.

DILATORY MOTION. A motion made for the purpose of killing time and preventing action on a bill or amendment. House rules outlaw dilatory motions, but enforcement is largely within the discretion of the Speaker or chairman of the Committee of the Whole. The Senate does not have a rule banning dilatory motions, except under cloture.

DISCHARGE A COMMITTEE. Occasionally, attempts are made to relieve a committee from jurisdiction over a measure before it. This is attempted more often in the House than in the Senate, and the procedure rarely is successful.

In the House, if a committee does not report a bill within thirty days after the measure is referred to it, any member may file a discharge motion. Once offered the motion is treated as a petition needing the signatures of 218 members (a majority of the House). After the required signatures have been obtained, there is a delay of seven days. Thereafter, on the second and fourth Mondays of each month, except during the last six days of a session, any member who has signed the petition must be recognized, if he so desires, to move that the committee be discharged. Debate on the motion to discharge is limited to twenty minutes, and, if the motion is carried, consideration of the bill becomes a matter of high privilege.

If a resolution to consider a bill is held up in the Rules Committee for more than seven legislative days, any member may enter a motion to discharge the committee. The motion is handled like any other discharge petition in the House. (Senate Procedure, see DISCHARGE RESOLUTION.)

DISCHARGE CALENDAR. The House calendar to which motions to discharge committees are referred when they have the required number of signatures (218) and are awaiting floor action.

DISCHARGE PETITION. (See DISCHARGE A COMMITTEE.)

DISCHARGE RESOLUTION. In the Senate, a special motion that any senator may introduce to relieve a committee from consideration of a bill before it. The resolution can be called up for Senate approval or disapproval in the same manner as any other Senate business. (House Procedure, see DISCHARGE A COMMITTEE.)

DIVISION VOTE. (See STANDING VOTE.)

ENACTING CLAUSE. Key phrase in bills beginning, "Be it enacted by the Senate and House of Representatives. . . ." A successful motion to strike it from legislation kills the measure.

ENGROSSED BILL. The final copy of a bill as passed by one chamber, with the text as amended by floor action and certified by the clerk of the House or the secretary of the Senate.

ENROLLED BILL. The final copy of a bill that has been passed in identical form by both chambers. It is certified by an officer of the house of origin (clerk of the House or secretary of the Senate) and then sent on for the signatures of the House Speaker, the Senate president pro tempore, and the president of the United States. An enrolled bill is printed on parchment.

EXECUTIVE CALENDAR. This is a nonlegislative calendar in the Senate on which presidential documents such as treaties and nominations are listed.

EXECUTIVE SESSION. A meeting of a Senate or House committee (or occasionally of either chamber) that only its members may attend. Witnesses regularly appear at committee meetings in executive session—for example, Defense Department officials during presentations of classified defense information. The public and press are not allowed to attend.

FILIBUSTER. A time-delaying tactic associated with the Senate and used by a minority in an effort to prevent a vote on a bill or amendment that probably would pass if voted upon directly. The most common method is to take advantage of the Senate's rules permitting unlimited debate, but other forms of parliamentary maneuvering may be used. The stricter rules used by the House make filibusters more difficult, but delaying tactics are employed occasionally through various procedural devices allowed by House rules. (See CLOTURE.)

FIVE-MINUTE RULE. A debate-limiting rule of the House that is invoked when the House sits as the Committee of the Whole. Under the rule, a member offering an amendment is allowed to speak five minutes in its favor, and an opponent of the amendment is allowed to speak five minutes in opposition. Debate is then closed. In practice, amendments regularly are debated more than ten minutes, with members gaining the floor by offering pro forma amendments or obtaining unanimous consent to speak longer than five minutes. (See STRIKE OUT THE LAST WORD.)

GERMANE. Pertaining to the subject matter of the legislation at hand. House amendments must be germane to the bill being considered. The Senate requires that amendments be germane when they are proposed to general appropriation bills, bills being considered once cloture has been adopted, or, frequently, when proceeding under a unanimous consent agreement placing a time limit on consideration of a bill. The 1974 budget act also requires that amendments to concurrent budget resolutions be germane. In the House, floor debate must be germane, and the first three hours of debate each day in the Senate must be germane to the pending business.

HOUSE CALENDAR. A listing for action by the House of public bills that do not directly or indirectly appropriate money or raise revenue.

JOINT RESOLUTION. A joint resolution, designated H J Res or S J Res, requires the approval of both houses and the signature of the president, just as a bill does, and has the force of law if approved. There is no practical difference between a bill and a joint resolution.

A joint resolution generally is used to deal with a limited matter such as a single appropriation. Joint resolutions also are used to propose amendments to the Constitution in Congress. They do not require a presidential signature but become a part of the Constitution when three-fourths of the states have ratified them.

LAW. An act of Congress that has been signed by the president or passed over his veto by Congress. Public bills, when signed, become public laws, and are cited by the letters PL and a hyphenated number. The two digits before the number correspond to the Congress, and the one or more digits after the hyphen refer to the numerical sequence in which the bills were signed by the president during that Congress. Private bills, when signed, become private laws.

LEGISLATIVE DAY. The "day" extending from the time either house meets after an adjournment until the time it next adjourns. Because the House normally adjourns from day to day, legislative days and calendar days usually coincide. But in the Senate, a legislative day may, and frequently does, extend over several calendar days. (See RECESS.)

LEGISLATIVE VETO. A procedure permitting either the House or Senate, or both chambers, to review proposed executive branch regulations or actions and to block or modify those with which they disagree. The specifics of the procedure may vary, but Congress generally provides for a legislative veto by including in a bill a provision that administrative rules or action taken to implement the law are to go into effect at the end of a designated period of time unless blocked by either or both houses (even committees) of Congress. Another version of the veto provides for congressional reconsideration and rejection of regulations already in effect. The Supreme Court on June 23, 1983, restricted the form and use of the legislative veto, ruling that it is an unconstitutional violation of the lawmaking procedure provided in the Constitution.

MAJORITY LEADER. The majority leader is elected by members of the majority party. In the Senate, in consultation with the minority leader and other senators, the majority leader directs the legislative schedule and serves as party spokesperson and chief strategist. In the House, the majority leader is second to the Speaker in the majority party's leadership and serves as the party's legislative strategist.

MAJORITY WHIP. In effect, the assistant majority leader in either the House or Senate. The majority whip helps marshal majority forces in support of party strategy and legislation.

MARKING UP A BILL. Going through the contents of a piece of legislation in committee or subcommittee, considering its provisions in large and small portions, acting on amendments to provisions and proposed revisions to the language, inserting new sections and phraseology, etc. If the bill is extensively amended, the committee's version may be introduced as a separate bill, with a new number, before being considered by the full House or Senate. (See CLEAN BILL.)

MINORITY LEADER. Floor leader for the minority party in each chamber.

MINORITY WHIP. Performs duties of whip for the minority party.

MOTION. In the House or Senate chamber, a request by a member to institute any one of a wide array of parliamentary actions. A member "moves" for a certain procedure, the consideration of a measure, etc. The precedence of motions, and whether they are debatable, is set forth in the House and Senate manuals.

ONE-MINUTE SPEECHES. Addresses by House members at the beginning of a legislative day. The speeches may cover any subject but are limited to one minute's duration.

OVERRIDE A VETO. If the president disapproves a bill and sends it back to Congress with his objections, Congress may try to override his veto and enact the bill into law. Neither house is required to attempt to override a veto. The override of a veto requires a recorded vote with a two-thirds majority in each chamber. The question put to each house is: "Shall the bill pass, the objections of the president to the contrary notwithstanding?" (See also POCKET VETO, VETO.)

PAIR. A voluntary arrangement between two lawmakers, usually on opposite sides of an issue. If passage of the measure requires a two-thirds majority vote, a pair would require two members favoring the action to one opposed to it. The names of lawmakers pairing on a given vote and their stands, if known, are printed in the *Congressional Record.*

PAYGO (Pay-As-You-Go). A procedure established in the Budget Enforcement Act of 1990 requiring that mandatory spending or revenue legislation which increases the deficit must be offset to avoid a sequester of certain financial accounts. (See SEQUESTRATION.)

POCKET VETO. The act of the president in withholding approval of a bill after Congress has adjourned. When Congress is in session, a bill becomes law without the president's signature if the president does not act upon it within ten days, excluding Sundays, of receiving it. But if Congress adjourns *sine die* within that ten-day period, the bill will die even if the president does not formally veto it. (See also VETO.)

POINT OF ORDER. An objection raised by a member that the chamber is departing from rules governing its conduct of business. The objector cites the rule violated, and the chair sustains the objection if correctly made. Order is restored by the chair's suspending proceedings of the chamber until it conforms to the prescribed order of business.

PRESIDENT OF THE SENATE. Under the Constitution, the vice president of the United States presides over the Senate. In the vice president's absence, the president pro tempore, or a senator designated by the president pro tempore, presides over the chamber.

PRESIDENT PRO TEMPORE. The chief officer of the Senate in the absence of the vice president; literally, but loosely, the president for a time. The president pro tempore is elected by the full membership of the Senate, and the recent practice has been to choose the senator of the majority party with the longest period of continuous service.

PREVIOUS QUESTION. A motion for the previous question, when carried, has the effect of cutting off all debate, preventing the offering of further amendments, and forcing a vote on the pending matter. In the House, the previous question is not permitted in the Committee of the Whole. The motion for the previous question is a debate-limiting device and is not in order in the Senate.

PRIVATE CALENDAR. In the House, private bills dealing with individual matters such as claims against the government, immigration, land titles, etc., are put on this calendar. The private calendar must be called on the first Tuesday of each month, and the Speaker may call it on the third Tuesday of each month as well.

When a private bill is before the chamber, two members may block its consideration, which recommits the bill to committee. Backers of a recommitted private bill have recourse.

The measure can be put into an omnibus claims bill—several private bills rolled into one. As with any bill, no part of an omnibus claims bill may be deleted without a vote.

PRIVILEGE. Privilege relates to the rights of members of Congress and to the relative priority of the motions and actions they may make in their respective chambers. The two are distinct. "Privileged questions" deal with legislative business. "Questions of privilege" concern members themselves.

PRIVILEGED QUESTIONS. The order in which bills, motions, and other legislative measures are considered by Congress is governed by strict priorities. A motion to table, for instance, is more privileged than a motion to recommit. Thus, a motion to recommit can be superseded by a motion to table, and a vote would be forced on the latter motion only. A motion to adjourn, however, takes precedence over a tabling motion and thus is considered of the "highest privilege." (See also QUESTIONS OF PRIVILEGE.)

PRO FORMA AMENDMENT. (See STRIKE OUT THE LAST WORD.)

QUESTIONS OF PRIVILEGE. These are matters affecting members of Congress individually or collectively. Matters affecting the rights, safety, dignity, and integrity of proceedings of the House or Senate as a whole are questions of privilege in both chambers.

Questions involving individual members are called questions of "personal privilege." A member rising to ask a question of personal privilege is given precedence over almost all other proceedings. An annotation in the House rules points out that the privilege is derived chiefly from the Constitution, which gives a member a conditional immunity from arrest and an unconditional freedom to speak in the House. (See also PRIVILEGED QUESTIONS.)

QUORUM. The number of members whose presence is necessary for the transaction of business. In the Senate and House, it is a majority of the membership. A quorum is one hundred in the Committee of the Whole

House. If a point of order is made that a quorum is not present, the only business that is in order is either a motion to adjourn or a motion to direct the sergeant-at-arms to request the attendance of absentees.

READINGS OF BILLS. Traditional parliamentary procedure required bills to be read three times before they were passed. This custom is of little modern significance. Normally a bill is considered to have its first reading when it is introduced and printed, by title, in the *Congressional Record*. In the House, its second reading comes when floor consideration begins. (This is the most likely point at which there is an actual reading of the bill, if there is any.) The second reading in the Senate is supposed to occur on the legislative day after the measure is introduced, but before it is referred to committee. The third reading (again, usually by title) takes place when floor action has been completed on amendments.

RECESS. Distinguished from adjournment in that a recess does not end a legislative day and therefore does not interrupt unfinished business. The rules in each house set forth certain matters to be taken up and disposed of at the beginning of each legislative day. The House usually adjourns from day to day. The Senate often recesses, thus meeting on the same legislative day for several calendar days or even weeks at a time. (See ADJOURNMENT.)

RECOGNITION. The power of recognition of a member is lodged in the Speaker of the House and the presiding officer of the Senate. The presiding officer names the member who will speak first when two or more members simultaneously request recognition.

RECOMMIT TO COMMITTEE. A motion, made on the floor after a bill has been debated, to return it to the committee that reported it. If approved, recommittal usually is considered a death blow to the bill. In the House, a motion to recommit can be made only by a member opposed to the bill, and, in recognizing a member to make the motion, the Speaker gives preference to members of the minority party over majority party members.

A motion to recommit may include instructions to the committee to report the bill again with specific amendments or by a certain date. Or, the instructions may direct that a particular study be made, with no definite deadline for further action. If the recommittal motion includes instructions to "report the bill back forthwith" and the motion is adopted, floor action on the bill continues; the committee does not actually reconsider the legislation.

RECONSIDER A VOTE. A motion to reconsider the vote by which an action was taken has, until it is disposed of, the effect of putting the action in abeyance. In the Senate, the motion can be made only by a member who voted on the prevailing side of the original question or by a member who did not vote at all. In the House, it can be made only by a member on the prevailing side.

A common practice in the Senate after close votes on an issue is a motion to reconsider, followed by a motion to table the motion to reconsider. On this motion to table, senators usually vote as they voted on the original question, which allows the motion to table to prevail, assuming there are no switches. The matter then is finally closed and further motions to reconsider are not entertained. In the House, as a routine precaution, a motion to reconsider usually is made every time a measure is passed. Such a motion almost always is tabled immediately, thus shutting off the possibility of future reconsideration, except by unanimous consent. Motions to reconsider must be entered in the Senate within the next two days of actual session after the original vote has been taken. In the House they must be entered either on the same day or on the next succeeding day the House is in session.

RECORDED VOTE. A vote upon which each member's stand is individually made known. In the Senate, this is accomplished through a roll call of the entire membership, to which each senator on the floor must answer "yea," "nay" or, if he does not wish to vote, "present." Since January 1973, the House has used an electronic voting system for recorded votes, including yea-and-nay votes formerly taken by roll calls. When not required by the Constitution, a recorded vote can be obtained on questions in the House on the demand of one-fifth (forty-four members) of a quorum or one-fourth (twenty-five members) of a quorum in the Committee of the Whole. (See YEAS AND NAYS.)

REPORT. Both a verb and a noun as a congressional term. A committee that has been examining a bill referred to it by the parent chamber "reports" its findings and recommendations to the chamber when it completes consideration and returns the measure. The process is called "reporting" a bill.

A "report" is the document setting forth the committee's explanation of its action. Senate and House reports are numbered separately and are designated S Rept or H Rept. When a committee report is not unanimous, the dissenting committee members may file a statement of their views, called minority views and referred to as a minority report. Members in disagreement with some provisions of a bill may file additional or supplementary views. Sometimes a bill is reported without a committee recommendation. Adverse reports occasionally are submitted by legislative committees. When a committee is opposed to a bill, it usually fails to report the measure at all. Some laws require that committee reports, favorable or adverse, be made.

RESOLUTION. A "simple" resolution, designated H Res or S Res, deals with matters entirely within the prerogatives of one house or the other. It requires neither passage by the other chamber nor approval by the president, and it does not have the force of law. Most resolutions deal with the rules or procedures of one house. They also are used to express the sentiments of a single house, such as condolences to the family of a deceased member, or to comment on foreign policy or executive business. A simple resolution is the vehicle for a "rule" from the House Rules Committee. (See also CONCURRENT RESOLUTION, JOINT RESOLUTION, RULES.)

RIDER. An amendment, usually not germane, which its sponsor hopes to get through more easily by including it in other legislation. Riders become law if the bills embodying them are enacted. Amendments providing legislative directives in appropriations bills are outstanding examples of riders, though technically legislation is banned from appropriations bills. The House, unlike the Senate, has a strict germaneness rule; thus, riders usually are Senate devices to get legislation enacted quickly or to bypass lengthy House consideration and, possibly, opposition.

RULES. The term has two specific congressional meanings. A rule may be a standing order governing the conduct of House or Senate business and listed among the permanent rules of either chamber. The rules deal with such matters as the duties of officers, the order of business, admission to the floor, parliamentary procedures on handling amendments and voting, and jurisdictions of committees.

In the House, a rule also may be a resolution reported by the Rules Committee to govern the handling of a particular bill on the floor. The committee may report a "rule," also called a "special order," in the form of a simple resolution. If the resolution is adopted by the House, the temporary rule becomes as valid as any standing rule and lapses only after action has been completed on the measure to which it pertains. A rule sets the time limit on general debate. It also may waive points of order against provisions of the bill in question, such as nongermane language, or against certain amendments intended to be proposed to the bill from the floor. It may even forbid all amendments or all amendments except those proposed by the legislative committee that handled the bill. In this instance, it is known as a "closed" or "gag" rule as opposed to an "open" rule, which puts no limitation on floor amendments, thus leaving the bill completely open to alteration by the adoption of germane amendments.

SENATORIAL COURTESY. Sometimes referred to as "the courtesy of the Senate," it is a general practice—with no written rule—applied to consideration of executive nominations. Generally, it means that nominations from a state are not to be confirmed unless they have been approved by the senators of the president's party of that state, with other senators following their colleagues' lead in the attitude they take toward consideration of such nominations.

SEQUESTRATION. The cancellation (or withholding) of budgetary resources pursuant to the Gramm-Rudman-Hollings Act. Once canceled, sequestered funds are no longer available for obligation or expenditure.

SPEAKER. The presiding officer of the House of Representatives and the overall leader of the majority party in the chamber. The Speaker is selected by the caucus of the majority party's members and formally elected by the full House at the beginning of each new congress.

STANDING COMMITTEES. (See COMMITTEE.)

STANDING VOTE. A nonrecorded vote used in both the House and the Senate. (A standing vote also is called a division vote.) Members in favor of a proposal stand and are counted by the presiding officer. Then members opposed stand and are counted. There is no record of how individual members voted.

STRIKE OUT THE LAST WORD. A motion whereby a House member is entitled to speak for five minutes on an amendment then being debated by the chamber. A member gains recognition from the chair by moving to "strike out the last word" of the amendment or section of the bill under consideration. The motion is pro forma, requires no vote and does not change the amendment being debated.

SUBSTITUTE. A motion, amendment, or entire bill introduced in place of the pending legislative business. Passage of a substitute measure kills the original measure by supplanting it. The substitute also may be amended. (See also AMENDMENT IN THE NATURE OF A SUBSTITUTE.)

SUPPLEMENTAL APPROPRIATIONS BILL. Legislation appropriating funds after the regular annual appropriations bill for a federal department or agency has been enacted. A supplemental appropriation provides additional budget authority beyond original estimates for programs or activities, including new programs authorized after the enactment of the regular appropriations act. (See also APPROPRIATIONS BILL.)

SUSPEND THE RULES. Often a time-saving procedure for passing bills in the House. The wording of the motion, which may be made by any member recognized by the Speaker, is: "I move to suspend the rules and pass the bill. . . ." A favorable vote by two-thirds of those present is required for passage. Debate is limited to forty minutes and no amendments from the floor are permitted. If a two-thirds favorable vote is not attained, the bill may be considered later under regular procedures. The suspension procedure is in order every Monday and Tuesday and is intended to be reserved for noncontroversial bills.

TABLE A BILL. A motion to "lay on the table" is not debatable in either house, and usually it is a method of making a final, adverse disposition of a matter. In the Senate, however, different language sometimes is used. The motion may be worded to let a bill "lie on the table," perhaps for subsequent "picking up." This motion is more flexible, keeping the bill pending for later action, if desired. Tabling motions on amendments are effective debate-ending devices in the Senate.

TREATIES. Executive proposals—in the form of resolutions of ratification—that must be submitted to the Senate for approval by two-thirds of the senators present. Treaties are normally sent to the Foreign Relations Committee for scrutiny before the Senate takes action. Foreign Relations has jurisdiction over all treaties, regardless of the subject matter. Treaties are read three times and debated on the floor in much the same manner as legislative proposals. After approval by the Senate, treaties are formally ratified by the president. Unlike legislative documents, however, treaties do not die at the end of a Congress but remain "live" proposals until acted on by the Senate or withdrawn by the president.

UNANIMOUS CONSENT. Proceedings of the House or Senate and action on legislation often take place upon the unanimous consent of the chamber, whether or not a rule of the chamber is being violated. Unanimous consent is used to expedite floor action and frequently is used in a routine fashion, for example, when a senator requests the unanimous consent of the Senate to have specified members of his staff present on the floor during debate on an amendment.

UNANIMOUS CONSENT AGREEMENT. A device used in the Senate to expedite legislation. Much of the Senate's legislative business, dealing with both minor and controversial issues, is conducted through unanimous consent or unanimous consent agreements. On major legislation, such agreements usually are printed and transmitted to all senators in advance of floor debate. Once agreed to, they are binding on all members unless the Senate, by unanimous consent, agrees to modify them. An agreement may list the order in which various bills are to be considered, specify the length of time bills and contested amendments are to be debated and when they are to be voted upon, and, frequently, require that all amendments introduced be germane to the bill under consideration. In this regard, unanimous consent agreements are similar to the rules issued by the House Rules Committee for bills pending in the House. (See RULES.)

UNION CALENDAR. Bills that directly or indirectly appropriate money or raise revenue are placed on this House calendar according to the date they are reported from committee.

VETO. Disapproval by the president of a bill or joint resolution (other than one proposing an amendment to the Constitution). When Congress is in session, the president must veto a bill within ten days, excluding Sundays, of receiving it; otherwise, the bill becomes law without the president's signature. When the president vetoes a bill, it must be returned to the house of origin with a message stating the president's objections. (See also OVERRIDE A VETO, POCKET VETO.)

VOICE VOTE. In either the House or Senate, members answer "aye" or "no" in chorus, and the presiding officer decides the result. The term also is used loosely to indicate action by unanimous consent or without objection.

YEAS AND NAYS. The Constitution requires that yea-and-nay votes be taken and recorded when requested by one-fifth of the members present. In the House, the Speaker determines whether one-fifth of the members present requested a vote. In the Senate, practice requires only eleven members. The Constitution requires the yeas and nays on a veto override attempt. (See RECORDED VOTE.)

YIELDING. When a member has been recognized to speak, no other member may speak without permission from the member recognized. This permission is called yielding and usually is requested in the form, "Will the gentleman yield to me?" While this activity occasionally is seen in the Senate, the Senate has no rule or practice to parcel out time, other than in unanimous consent agreements.

Selected Bibliography

CHAPTER 1. CONGRESS AND LAWMAKING

Bacon, Donald C., Roger H. Davidson, and Morton Keller, eds. *The Encyclopedia of the United States Congress.* 4 vols. New York: Simon & Schuster, 1995.

Burnham, James. *Congress and the American Tradition.* Chicago: Henry Regnery, 1959.

Davidson, Roger H., and Walter J. Oleszek. *Congress and Its Members.* 4th ed. Washington, D.C.: CQ Press, 1994.

Goehlert, Robert U., and Fenton S. Martin. *The United States Congress: An Annotated Bibliography, 1980-1993.* Washington, D.C.: Congressional Quarterly, 1995.

Gross, Bertram M. *The Legislative Struggle.* New York: McGraw-Hill, 1953.

Luce, Robert. *Legislative Procedures.* Boston: Houghton Mifflin, 1922.

___. *Legislative Assemblies.* Boston: Houghton Mifflin, 1924.

___. *Legislative Principles.* Boston: Houghton Mifflin, 1930.

___. *Legislative Problems.* Boston: Houghton Mifflin, 1935.

Rieselbach, Leroy N. *Congressional Politics,* 2d ed. Boulder, Colo.: Westview Press, 1995.

Schneier, Edward V., and Bertram Gross. *Legislative Strategy: Shaping Public Policy.* New York: St. Martin's Press, 1993.

Silbey, Joel H., ed. *Encyclopedia of the American Legislative System,* 3 vols. New York: Charles Scribner's Sons, 1994.

Tiefer, Charles. *Congressional Practice and Procedure: A Reference, Research, and Legislative Guide.* New York: Greenwood Press, 1989.

Wise, Charles R. *The Dynamics of Legislation: Leadership and Policy Change in the Congressional Process.* San Francisco: Jossey-Bass, 1991.

CHAPTER 2. THE CONGRESSIONAL ENVIRONMENT

Arnold, R. Douglas. *The Logic of Congressional Action.* New Haven, Conn.: Yale University Press, 1990.

Baker, Ross K. *House and Senate,* 2d ed. New York: W.W. Norton, 1995.

Bolling, Richard. *House Out of Order.* New York: E.P. Dutton, 1965.

___. *Power in the House.* New York: E.P. Dutton, 1968.

Chamberlain, Lawrence H. *The President, Congress and Legislation.* New York: Columbia University Press, 1946.

Cooper, Joseph, and G. Calvin Mackenzie, eds. *The House at Work.* Austin: University of Texas Press, 1981.

Cox, Gary W., and Mathew D. McCubbins. *Legislative Leviathan: Party Government in the House.* Berkeley: University of California Press, 1993.

Dodd, Lawrence C., and Bruce I. Oppenheimer, eds. *Congress Reconsidered.* 5th ed. Washington, D.C.: CQ Press, 1995.

Fenno, Richard F., Jr. *Home Style: House Members in Their Districts.* Boston: Little, Brown, 1978.

Hasbrouck, Paul. *Party Government in the House of Representatives.* New York: Macmillan, 1927.

Heinz, John P., et. al. *The Hollow Core: Private Interests in National Policy Making.* Cambridge: Harvard University Press, 1993.

Hibbing, John R. *Congressional Careers.* Chapel Hill: University of North Carolina Press, 1991.

Jones, Charles O. *The Presidency in a Separated System.* Washington, D.C.: Brookings Institution, 1994.

Loomis, Burdett. *The New American Politician.* New York: Basic Books, 1988.

Mann, Thomas E., and Norman J. Ornstein, eds. *Congress, the Press, and the Public.* Washington, D.C.: American Enterprise Institute for Public Policy Research and Brookings Institution, 1994.

Mayhew, David R. *Divided We Govern.* New Haven: Yale University Press, 1991.

Price, David E. *The Congressional Experience: A View from the Hill.* Boulder, Colo.: Westview Press, 1992.

Rohde, David W. *Parties and Leaders in the Postreform House.* Chicago: University of Chicago Press, 1991.

Sorauf, Frank J. *Inside Campaign Finance.* New Haven, Conn.: Yale University Press, 1992.

Thomas, Sue. *How Women Legislate.* New York: Oxford University Press, 1994.

Wayne, Stephen. *The Legislative Presidency.* New York: Harper & Row, 1978.

CHAPTER 3. THE CONGRESSIONAL BUDGET PROCESS

Fenno, Richard F., Jr. *The Power of the Purse.* Boston: Little, Brown, 1966.

Fisher, Louis. "Annual Authorizations: Durable Roadblocks to Biennial Budgeting." *Public Budgeting and Finance,* Spring 1983, 23-40.

___. "The Authorization-Appropriation Process in Congress: Formal Rules and Informal Practices." *Catholic University Law Review,* Fall 1979, 51-105.

Franklin, Daniel P. *Making Ends Meet: Congressional Budgeting in the Age of Deficits.* Washington, D.C.: CQ Press, 1993.

Munson, Richard. *The Cardinals of Capitol Hill.* New York: Grove Press, 1993.

Schick, Allen. *Congress and Money.* Washington, D.C.: Urban Institute Press, 1980.

___. *The Capacity to Budget.* Washington, D.C.: Urban Institute Press, 1990.

___. *The Federal Budget: Politics, Policy, Process.* Washington, D.C.: Brookings Institution, 1995.

Stockman, David. *The Triumph of Politics.* New York: Harper & Row, 1986.

Strahan, Randall. *New Ways and Means: Reform and Change in a Congressional Committee.* Chapel Hill: University of North Carolina Press, 1990.

White, Joseph, and Aaron Wildavsky. *The Deficit and the Public Interest.* Berkeley: University of California Press, 1989.

Wildavsky, Aaron. *The Politics of the Budgetary Process.* 4th ed. Boston: Little, Brown, 1984.

Wilmerding, Lucius. *The Spending Power.* New Haven, Conn.: Yale University Press, 1943.

CHAPTER 4. PRELIMINARY LEGISLATIVE ACTION

Bisnow, Mark. *In the Shadow of the Dome: Chronicles of a Capitol Hill Aide.* New York: William Morrow, 1990.

Cooper, Joseph. *The Origins of the Standing Committees and the Development of the Modern House.* Rice University Monograph in Political Science, vol. 56, no. 3, Summer 1970.

Davidson, Roger H., and Walter J. Oleszek. *Congress against Itself.* Bloomington: Indiana University Press, 1977.

Davidson, Roger H., Walter J. Oleszek, and Thomas Kephart. "One Bill, Many Committees: Multiple Referrals in the U.S. House of Representatives." *Legislative Studies Quarterly,* February 1988, 3-28.

Deering, Christopher J., and Steven S. Smith. *Committees in Congress.* 2d ed. Washington, D.C.: CQ Press, 1990.

Elving, Ronald D. *Conflict and Compromise: How Congress Makes the Law.* New York: Simon & Schuster, 1995.

Evans, C. Lawrence. *Leadership in Committee.* Ann Arbor: University of Michigan Press, 1991.

Fenno, Richard F., Jr. *Congressmen in Committees.* Boston: Little, Brown, 1973.

Kravitz, Walter. "Evolution of the Senate's Committee System." *The Annals,* January 1974, 27-38.

Light, Paul C. *Forging Legislation.* New York: W.W. Norton, 1992.

Malbin, Michael J. *Unelected Representatives: Congressional Staff and the Future of Representative Government.* New York: Basic Books, 1979.

"Private Bills in Congress." *Harvard Law Review,* vol. 79, 1966, 1684-1706.

Wilson, Woodrow. *Congressional Government.* Gloucester, Mass.: Peter Smith, 1885.

CHAPTER 5. SCHEDULING LEGISLATION IN THE HOUSE

Albert, Carl. *The Office and Duties of the Speaker of the House of Representatives.* H Doc 94-582, 94th Cong., 2d sess., 1976.

Connelly, William F., Jr., and John J. Pitney, Jr. *Congress' Permanent Minority?* Lanham, Md.: Littlefield Adams, 1994.

Cooper, Joseph, and David W. Brady. "Institutional Context and Leadership Style: The House From Cannon to Rayburn." *American Political Science Review,* June 1981, 411-425.

Hardeman, D. B., and Donald C. Bacon. *Rayburn.* Austin: Texas Monthly Press, 1987.

"A History of the Committee on Rules." Committee Print, 97th Cong., 2d sess. Washington, D.C.: Government Printing Office, 1983.

Kornacki, John J., ed. *Leading Congress.* Washington, D.C.: CQ Press, 1990.

Mackaman, Frank H., ed. *Understanding Congressional Leadership.* Washington, D.C.: CQ Press, 1981.

Peters, Ronald M., Jr. *The American Speakership.* Baltimore, Md.: Johns Hopkins University Press, 1990.

Young, Garry, and Joseph Cooper. "Multiple Referral and the Transformation of House Decision Making," in *Congress Reconsidered,* eds. Lawrence C. Dodd and Bruce I. Oppenheimer. 5th ed. Washington, D.C.: CQ Press, 1993.

CHAPTER 6. HOUSE FLOOR PROCEDURE

Alexander, DeAlva Stanwood. *History and Procedure of the House of Representatives.* Boston: Houghton Mifflin, 1916.

Bach, Stanley, and Steven S. Smith. *Managing Uncertainty in the House of Representatives: Adaptation and Innovation in Special Rules.* Washington, D.C.: Brookings Institution, 1988.

Damon, Richard E. *The Standing Rules of the U.S. House of Representatives.* Ph.D. diss., Columbia University, 1971.

Froman, Lewis A. *The Congressional Process: Strategies, Rules and Procedures.* Boston: Little, Brown, 1967.

Harlow, Ralph V. *The History of Legislative Methods in the Period Before 1825.* New Haven, Conn.: Yale University Press, 1917.

MacNeil, Neil. *Forge of Democracy: The House of Representatives.* New York: David McKay, 1963.

Polsby, Nelson W. "The Institutionalization of the House of Representatives." *American Political Science Review,* March 1968, 144-168.

Sinclair, Barbara. *Legislators, Leaders, and Lawmaking: The U.S. House of Representatives in the Postreform Era.* Baltimore, Md.: Johns Hopkins University Press, 1995.

Smith, Steven S. *Call To Order: Floor Politics in the House and Senate.* Washington, D.C.: Brookings Institution, 1989.

CHAPTER 7. SCHEDULING LEGISLATION IN THE SENATE

Clark, Joseph S. *The Senate Establishment.* New York: Hill & Wang, 1963.

Ehrenhalt, Alan. "Special Report: The Individualist Senate." *Congressional Quarterly Weekly Report,* September 4, 1982, 2175-2182.

Fenno, Richard F., Jr. *Learning to Legislate: The Senate Education of Arlen Specter.* Washington, D.C.: CQ Press, 1991.

Harris, Fred R. *Deadlock or Decision: The U.S. Senate and the Rise of National Politics.* New York: Oxford University Press, 1993.

Hibbing, John R., ed. *The Changing World of the U.S. Senate.* Berkeley, Calif.: IGS Press, 1990.

Riddick, Floyd M. *Majority and Minority Leaders of the Senate.* S Doc 97-12, 97th Cong., 1st sess. Washington, D.C.: Government Printing Office, 1981.

CHAPTER 8. SENATE FLOOR PROCEDURE

Burdette, Franklin L. *Filibustering in the Senate.* Princeton, N.J.: Princeton University Press, 1940.

Denardis, Lawrence J. *The New Senate Filibuster: An Analysis of Filbustering and Gridlock in the U.S. Senate, 1977-1986.* Ph.D. diss., New York University, 1989.

Drew, Elizabeth. *Senator.* New York: Simon & Schuster, 1979.

Evans, Rowland, and Robert Novak. *Lyndon B. Johnson: The Exercise of Power.* New York: New American Library, 1966.

Harris, Joseph P. *The Advice and Consent of the Senate.* Berkeley: University of California Press, 1953.

Matthews, Donald. *U.S. Senators and Their World.* Chapel Hill: University of North Carolina Press, 1960.

Shuman, Howard E. "Senate Rules and the Civil Rights Bill: A Case Study." *American Political Science Review,* December 1957, 955-975.

Sinclair, Barbara. *The Transformation of the U.S. Senate.* Baltimore, Md.: Johns Hopkins University Press, 1989.

CHAPTER 9. RESOLVING HOUSE-SENATE DIFFERENCES

Bach, Stanley, "Germaneness Rules and Bicameral Relations in the U.S. Congress." *Legislative Studies Quarterly,* August 1982, 341-357.

Fenno, Richard F., Jr. *The United States Senate: A Bicameral Perspective.* Washington, D.C.: American Enterprise Institute for Public Policy Research, 1982.

Longley, Lawrence D., and Walter J. Oleszek. *Bicameral Politics: Conference Committees in Congress.* New Haven, Conn.: Yale University Press, 1989.

McCown, Ada C. *The Congressional Conference Committee.* New York: Columbia University Press, 1927.

Pressman, Jeffrey L. *House vs. Senate: Conflict in the Appropriations Process.* New Haven, Conn.: Yale University Press, 1966.

Steiner, Gilbert. *The Congressional Conference Committee, Seventieth to Eightieth Congresses.* Urbana: University of Illinois Press, 1951.

Vogler, David J. *The Third House: Conference Committees in the U.S. Congress.* Evanston, Ill.: Northwestern University Press, 1971.

CHAPTER 10. LEGISLATIVE OVERSIGHT

Aberbach, Joel D. *Keeping a Watchful Eye: The Politics of Congressional Oversight.* Washington, D.C.: Brookings Institution, 1990.

Art, Robert J. "Congress and the Defense Budget: Enhancing Policy Oversight." *Political Science Quarterly,* Summer 1985, 227-248.

Dodd, Lawrence C., and Richard L. Schott. *Congress and the Administrative State.* New York: John Wiley & Sons, 1979.

Fisher, Louis. *The Politics of Shared Power: Congress and the Executive.* 2d ed. Washington, D.C.: CQ Press, 1987.

Foreman, Christopher H. *Signals From the Hill: Congressional Oversight and the Challenge of Social Regulation.* New Haven, Conn.: Yale University Press, 1988.

Freeman, J. Leiper. *The Political Process: Executive Bureau-Legislative Committee Relations.* rev. ed. Garden City, N.Y.: Doubleday, 1965.

Gilmour, Robert S., and Alexis A. Halley, eds. *Who Makes Public Policy: The Struggle for Control Between Congress and the Executive.* Chatham, N.J.: Chatham House, 1994.

Harris, Joseph P. *Congressional Control of Administration.* Washington, D.C.: Brookings Institution, 1964.

Light, Paul C. *Monitoring Government: Inspectors General and the Search for Accountability.* Washington, D.C.: Brookings Institution, 1993.

Ogul, Morris S. *Congress Oversees the Bureaucracy.* Pittsburgh: University of Pittsburgh Press, 1976.

Ripley, Randall B., and Grace A. Franklin. *Congress, the Bureaucracy, and Public Policy,* 5th ed. Pacific Grove, Calif.: Brooks/Cole Publishing, 1991.

Taylor, Telford. *Grand Inquest: The Story of Congressional Investigations.* New York: Simon & Schuster, 1955.

Tiefer, Charles. *The Semi-Sovereign Presidency: The Bush Administration's Strategy for Governing Without Congress.* Boulder, Colo.: Westview Press, 1994.

CHAPTER 11. A DYNAMIC PROCESS

Bailey, Stephen K. *Congress Makes a Law.* New York: Columbia University Press, 1950.

Baumgartner, Frank R., and Bryan D. Jones. *Agendas and Instability in American Politics.* Chicago: University of Chicago Press. 1993.

Birnbaum, Jeffrey H., and Alan S. Murray. *Showdown at Gucci Gulch*. New York: Random House, 1987.

Davidson, Roger H., ed. *The Postreform Congress*. New York: St. Martin's Press, 1992.

Harris, Fred R. *In Defense of Congress*. New York: St. Martin's Press, 1995.

Jones, Bryan D., ed. *The New American Politics*. Boulder, Colo.: Westview Press, 1995.

Jones, Charles O. "A Way of Life and Law." *American Political Science Review*, March 1995, 1-9.

King, Anthony, ed. *The New American Political System, Second Version*. Washington, D.C.: AEI Press, 1990.

Redman, Eric. *The Dance of Legislation*. New York: Simon & Schuster, 1973.

Rieselbach, Leroy N. *Congressional Reform*. 2d ed. Washington, D.C.: CQ Press, 1994.

Sheppard, Burton D. *Rethinking Congressional Reform*. Cambridge, Mass.: Schenkman Books, 1985.

Sundquist, James L. *The Decline and Resurgence of Congress*. Washington, D.C.: Brookings Institution, 1981.

Index